Practical RDF

Other XML resources from O'Reilly

Related titles
XML in a Nutshell	Programming Web Services
Learning XML	with XML-RPC
XML Pocket Reference	XPath and XPointer
XSLT	XSL-FO
XSLT Cookbook	Perl & XML
XML Schema	Python & XML
Web Services Essentials	Java & XML
SVG Essentials	Java & XML Data Binding
Programming Web Services	Java & XSLT
with SOAP	

XML Books Resource Center

xml.oreilly.com is a complete catalog of O'Reilly's books on XML and related technologies, including sample chapters and code examples.

XML.com helps you discover XML and learn how this Internet technology can solve real-world problems in information management and electronic commerce.

Conferences

O'Reilly & Associates brings diverse innovators together to nurture the ideas that spark revolutionary industries. We specialize in documenting the latest tools and systems, translating the innovator's knowledge into useful skills for those in the trenches. Visit *conferences.oreilly.com* for our upcoming events.

Safari Bookshelf (*safari.oreilly.com*) is the premier online reference library for programmers and IT professionals. Conduct searches across more than 1,000 books. Subscribers can zero in on answers to time-critical questions in a matter of seconds. Read the books on your Bookshelf from cover to cover or simply flip to the page you need. Try it today with a free trial.

Practical RDF

Shelley Powers

O'REILLY®

Beijing · Cambridge · Farnham · Köln · Paris · Sebastopol · Taipei · Tokyo

Practical RDF
by Shelley Powers

Published by O'Reilly & Associates, Inc., 1005 Gravenstein Highway North, Sebastopol, CA 95472.

O'Reilly & Associates books may be purchased for educational, business, or sales promotional use. Online editions are also available for most titles (*safari.oreilly.com*). For more information, contact our corporate/institutional sales department: (800) 998-9938 or *corporate@oreilly.com*.

Editor:	Simon St.Laurent
Production Editor:	Mary Brady
Cover Designer:	Ellie Volckhausen
Interior Designer:	David Futato

Printing History:

July 2003:	First Edition.

ISBN: 0-596-00263-7
[C]

Table of Contents

Preface

The Resource Description Framework (RDF) offers developers a powerful toolkit for making statements and connecting those statements to derive meaning. The World Wide Web Consortium (W3C) has been developing RDF as a key component of its vision for a *Semantic Web*, but RDF's capabilities fit well in many different computing contexts. RDF offers a different, and in some ways more powerful, framework for data representation than XML or relational databases, while remaining far more generic than object structures.

RDF's foundations are built on a very simple model, but the basic logic can support large-scale information management and processing in a variety of different contexts. The assertions in different RDF files can be combined, providing far more information together than they contain separately. RDF supports flexible and powerful query structures, and developers have created a wide variety of tools for working with RDF.

While RDF is commonly described as an arcane tool for working with an enormous volume of complex information, organized with ontologies and other formal models, it also has tremendous value for smaller, more informal projects. I learned about RDF, specifically RDF/XML, when I started working with Mozilla back in the early days of development for this project. At the time, the Mozilla team was using RDF as a way of defining the XML used to provide the data for dynamic tables of contents (TOC) in the application framework. This included providing the data for the favorites, the sidebar, and so on.

I created a tutorial about developing applications using the Mozilla components as part of a presentation I was giving at an XML-related conference. Unfortunately, every time a new release of Mozilla was issued, my tutorial would break. The primary reason was the RDF/XML supported by the application; it kept changing to keep up with the changes currently underway with the RDF specification itself. At that point I went to the RDF specifications, managed to read my way through the first specification document (the RDF Model and Syntax Specification), and have been following along with the changes related to RDF ever since.

One main reason I was so interested in RDF and the associated RDF/XML is that, ever since I started working with XML in its earliest days, I've longed for a meta-model to define vocabularies in XML that could then be merged with other vocabularies, all of which can be manipulated by the same APIs (Application Programming Interfaces) and tools. I found this with RDF and RDF/XML.

Because my introduction to RDF and RDF/XML had such pragmatic beginnings, my interest in the specification has always focused on how it can be used in business applications today, rather than in some Semantic Web someday. When I approached O'Reilly & Associates about the possibility of writing a book on RDF, I suggested a practical introduction to RDF, and the title and focus of the book was born.

This book attempts to present all the different viewpoints of RDF in such a way that we begin to see a complete picture of RDF from all of its various components. I say "attempt" because I'm finding that just when I think I have my arms around all the different aspects of the RDF specification, someone comes along with a new and interesting twist on a previously familiar concept. However, rather than weaken RDF's overall utility, these new variations actually demonstrate the richness of the specification.

It is only fair to give you a warning ahead of time that I'm a practical person. When faced with a new technology, rather than ooh and aah and think to myself, "New toy!", my first response tends to be, "Well, that's great. But, what can I do with it?" I am, by nature, an engineer, and this book reflects that bias. Much of RDF is associated with some relatively esoteric efforts, including its use within the implementation of the so-called Semantic Web. However, rather than get heavily into the more theoretical aspects of RDF, in this book I focus more on the practical aspects of the RDF specification and the associated technologies.

This isn't to say I won't cover theory—all engineers have to have a good understanding of the concepts underlying any technology they use. However, the theory is presented as a basis for understanding, rather than as the primary focus. In other words, the intent of *Practical RDF* is on using RDF and the associated RDF/XML in our day-to-day technology efforts in order to meet our needs as programming, data, and markup technologists, in addition to the needs of the businesses we support.

This book provides comprehensive coverage of the current RDF specifications, as well as the use of RDF for Semantic Web activities such as the ontology efforts underway at the W3C. However, the focus of this book is on the use of RDF to manage data that may, or may not, be formatted in XML to manage data, often XML data.

Audience

If you want to know how to apply RDF to information processing, this book is for you. Whether your interests lie in large-scale information aggregation and analysis or in smaller-scale projects like weblog syndication, this book will provide you with a solid foundation for working with RDF. If you are looking for a theoretical explanation of intelligent web bots, tutorials on how to create knowledge systems, or an in-depth look at topic maps and ontologies, you should probably look elsewhere. Also, a basic understanding of XML and web technologies is helpful for reading this book, so you may want to start with those first if you don't have any background in them.

Structure of This Book

The first section of this book (Chapters 1 through 6) focuses on the RDF specifications. Chapter 1 focuses on introducing RDF, but more than that, it also looks at some of the historical events leading up to the current RDF effort. In addition, this chapter also looks at issues of when you would, and would not, use RDF/XML as compared to "standard" XML.

Following the introductory chapter, the rest of the first section covers the RDF specification documents themselves. This includes coverage of the RDF Semantics and Concepts and Abstract Model specifications (covered in Chapter 2); the basic XML syntax (covered in Chapter 3); coverage of some of the more unusual RDF constructs—containers, collections, and reification (covered in Chapter 4); and the RDF Schema (covered in Chapter 5). As a way of pulling all of the coverage together, Chapter 6 then uses all we've learned about RDF to that point to create a relatively complex vocabulary, which is then used for demonstration purposes throughout the rest of the book.

The second section of the book focuses on programming language support, as well as the tools and utilities that allow a person to review, edit, parse, and generally work with RDF/XML. Chapter 7 focuses on various RDF editors, including those with graphical support for creating RDF models. In addition, the chapter also covers an RDF/XML browser, as well as a couple of the more popular RDF/XML parsers.

To be useful, any specification related to data requires tools to work with the data, and RDF is no exception. Chapter 8 provides an overview and examples of accessing and generating RDF/XML using Jena, a Java-based RDF API. Chapter 9, which covers APIs that are based in PHP, Perl, and Python—the three Ps—follows this.

After the programming language grounding, the book refocuses on RDF's data roots with a chapter that examines some of the RDF query languages used to query RDF model data, in a database or as persisted to RDF/XML documents. Chapter 10 also has the code for the RDF Query-O-Matic, a utility that processes RDQL (RDF Query Language) queries.

The last chapter in the second section finishes the review of programming and framework support for RDF by looking at some other programming language support, as well as some of the frameworks, such as Redland and Redfoot.

The last section of the book then focuses on the use of RDF and RDF/XML, beginning with an overview of the W3C's ontology language effort, OWL. If RDF is analogous to the relational data model, and RDF/XML is analogous to relational database systems, then OWL is equivalent to applications such as SAP and PeopleSoft, which implement a business domain model on top of the relational store.

The next chapter focuses on RSS, the implementation of RDF/XML most widely used, which supports syndication and aggregation of news sources. RSS is used to syndicate news sources as diverse as *salon.com* and Wired, as well as online personal journals known as weblogs, a web technology gaining popularity.

A specification is only as good as the applications that use it, and RDF is used in a surprising number of sophisticated commercial and noncommercial applications. I say "surprising" primarily because RDF is not a well-known specification. However, it is one of the older specifications. RDF's maturity, combined with the specification's data manipulation and organizational capabilities, makes it easy to see why the growing interest in RDF is arising.

 The RDF Validator–generated graphs have been replaced with illustrations in order to fit the examples within the constraints imposed by the page width.

Conventions Used in This Book

The following font conventions are used in this book:

Italic is used for:

- Pathnames, filenames, and program names
- Internet addresses, such as domain names and URLs
- New items where they are defined

`Constant width` is used for:

- Command lines and options that should be typed verbatim
- Names and keywords in programs, including method names, variable names, and class names
- XML element tags
- URIs used as identifiers by RDF

`Constant-width bold` is used for emphasis in program code lines.

`Constant-width italic` is used for replaceable arguments within program code.

This icon indicates a tip, suggestion, or general note.

 This icon indicates a warning or caution.

How to Contact Us

We have tested and verified the information in this book to the best of our ability, but you may find that features have changed (or even that we have made a few mistakes!). Please let us know about any errors you find, as well as your suggestions for future editions, by writing to:

O'Reilly & Associates, Inc.
1005 Gravenstein Highway North
Sebastopol, CA 95471
1-800-998-9938 (in the U.S. or Canada)
1-707-829-0515 (international/local)
1-707-829-0104 (fax)

You can also send us messages electronically. To be put on the mailing list or request a catalog, send email to:

info@oreilly.com

To ask technical questions or comment on the book, send email to:

bookquestions@oreilly.com

We have a web site for the book, where we'll list examples, errata, and any plans for future editions. You can access this page at:

http://www.oreilly.com/catalog/pracrdf/

For more information abut this book and others, see the O'Reilly web site:

http://www.oreilly.com/

Acknowledgments

First among the people I want to acknowledge is the RDF Working Group, the folks who have worked the last two-plus years to get the updated RDF specifications out on the street and into action. The listing of people is quite extensive, but I want to specifically mention a few who were particularly helpful to me while I worked on the book: Brian McBride, Pat Hayes, Dave Beckett, and Frank Manola.

This book would never have hit the streets if it weren't for the patience and good humor of the lead editor, Simon St.Laurent. During the almost year and a half this book was in development, Simon never once lost patience, though other editors might have given up on RDF as a topic.

In addition to Simon, I want to extend my appreciation to the technical editors on the book including Dorothea Salo, Dave Beckett, Uche Ogbuji, and Andy Seaborne. Less formally, I want to also extend my appreciation to those from the RDF community who were so kind as to review one or more chapters in the book for completeness and accuracy:

- Danny Ayers
- Chris Parnell
- Chris Dolin
- Emmanual Pietriga
- Ken MacLeod
- York Sure
- Ben Hammersley
- David Allsop
- Barry Sheward
- Kevin Marks
- Aaron Swartz
- David Jacobs
- Bill Simoni
- Seth Ladd
- Bill Kerney
- Jens Jacob Andersen
- Resty Cena
- Tingley Chase

My apologies if I have inadvertently left someone off this list.

Finally, I want to extend my thanks and appreciation to the organizations and people responsible for the software and technologies covered in this book. These include:

- Jena—Hewlett-Packard and Brian McBride, Janet Bruten, Jeremy Carroll, Steve Cayzer, Ian Dickinson, Chris Dollin, Martin Merry, Dave Reynolds, Andy Seaborne, Paul Shabajee, and Stuart Williams
- Brownsauce—Hewlett-Packard and Damien Steer
- IsaViz—Emmanual Pietriga
- The RDF Validator—Art Barstow and Emmanual Pietriga
- Intellidimension's RDF Gateway and Geoff Chappell
- AmphetaDesk and Morbus Iff
- Ginger Alliance PerlRDF and Petr Cimprich
- RDFLib and Redfoot from Daniel "elkeon" Krech
- RDFStore and Alberto Reggiori
- SMORE and Aditya Kalyanpur
- RDF API for PHP and Chris Bizer
- Redland and Dave Beckett
- C# Drive and Rahul Singh

- Wilbur from Ora Lassila and Nokia
- Plugged In Software's Tucana Knowledge Store and David Wood
- Sidrean Software's Seamark Server and Bradley Allan
- Adobe's XMP
- Sesame's Arjohn Kampan
- Meerkat—O'Reilly and Rael Dornfest
- Ranchero Software's NetNewsWire and Brent Simmons
- The Mozilla development team members
- Stanford University's Knowledge Modeling Group and Protégé
- The Dublin Core effort
- FOAF, FOAFbot, and FOAF-O-Matic by Leigh Dobbs, Edd Dumbill, Dan Brickley, Libby Miller, rdfweb-dev, and friends
- The web sites from several weblogging friends including Allan Moult, Chris Kovacs, Jonathon Delacour, Loren Webster, and Dorothea Salo

Books don't get written in a vacuum and this book is no exception. I'd like to thank some special friends for their support and encouragement during the long, long period this book was in development. This includes my best friend, Robert Porter, as well as AKM and Margaret Adam, Jonathon Delacour, Simon St.Laurent, Allan Moult, Chris Kovacks, Loren Webster, Jeneane Sessum, Chris Locke, Dorothea Salo, and others whom I met in the threaded void known as the Internet. Thanks, friends. It's finally done.

## CHAPTER 1

RDF: An Introduction

The Resource Description Framework (RDF) is an extremely flexible technology, capable of addressing a wide variety of problems. Because of its enormous breadth, people often come to RDF thinking that it's one thing and find later that it's much more. One of my favorite parables is about the blind people and the elephant. If you haven't heard it, the story goes that six blind people were asked to identify what an elephant looked like from touch. One felt the tusk and thought the elephant was like a spear; another felt the trunk and thought the elephant was like a snake; another felt a leg and thought the elephant was like a tree; and so on, each basing his definition of an elephant on his own unique experiences.

RDF is very much like that elephant, and we're very much like the blind people, each grabbing at a different aspect of the specification, with our own interpretations of what it is and what it's good for. And we're discovering what the blind people discovered: not all interpretations of RDF are the same. Therein lies both the challenge of RDF as well as the value.

 The main RDF specification web site is at *http://www.w3.org/RDF/*. You can access the core working group's efforts at *http://www.w3.org/2001/sw/RDFCore/*. In addition, there's an RDF Interest Group forum that you can monitor or join at *http://www.w3.org/RDF/Interest/*.

The Semantic Web and RDF: A Brief History

RDF is based within the Semantic Web effort. According to the W3C (World Wide Web Consortium) Semantic Web Activity Statement:

> The Resource Description Framework (RDF) is a language designed to support the Semantic Web, in much the same way that HTML is the language that helped initiate the original Web. RDF is a framework for supporting resource description, or metadata (data about data), for the Web. RDF provides common structures that can be used for interoperable XML data exchange.

Though not as well known as other specifications from the W3C, RDF is actually one of the older specifications, with the first working draft produced in 1997. The earliest editors, Ora Lassila and Ralph Swick, established the foundation on which RDF rested—a mechanism for working with metadata that promotes the interchange of data between automated processes. Regardless of the transformations RDF has undergone and its continuing maturing process, this statement forms its immutable purpose and focal point.

In 1999, the first recommended RDF specification, the RDF Model and Syntax Specification (usually abbreviated as RDF M&S), again coauthored by Ora Lassila and Ralph Swick, was released. A candidate recommendation for the RDF Schema Specification, coedited by Dan Brickley and R.V. Guha, followed in 2000. In order to open up a previously closed specification process, the W3C also created the RDF Interest Group, providing a view into the RDF specification process for interested people who were not a part of the RDF Core Working Group.

As efforts proceeded on the RDF specification, discussions continued about the concepts behind the Semantic Web. At the time, the main difference between the existing Web and the newer, smarter Web is that rather than a large amount of disorganized and not easily accessible data, something such as RDF would allow organization of data into knowledge statements—assertions about resources accessible on the Web. From a *Scientific American* article published May 2001, Tim Berners-Lee wrote:

> The Semantic Web will bring structure to the meaningful content of Web pages, creating an environment where software agents roaming from page to page can readily carry out sophisticated tasks for users. Such an agent coming to the clinic's Web page will know not just that the page has keywords such as "treatment, medicine, physical, therapy" (as might be encoded today) but also that Dr. Hartman works at this clinic on Mondays, Wednesdays and Fridays and that the script takes a date range in *yyyy-mm-dd* format and returns appointment times.

As complex as the Semantic Web sounds, this statement of Berners-Lee provides the key to understanding the Web of the future. With the Semantic Web, not only can we find data about a subject, we can also infer additional material not available through straight keyword search. For instance, RDF gives us the ability to discover that there is an article about the Giant Squid at one of my web sites, and that the article was written on a certain date by a certain person, that it is associated with three other articles in a series, and that the general theme associated with the article is the Giant Squid's earliest roots in mythology. Additional material that can be derived is that the article is still "relevant" (meaning that the data contained in the article hasn't become dated) and still active (still accessible from the Web). All of this information is easily produced and consumed through the benefits of RDF without having to rely on any extraordinary computational power.

However, for all of its possibilities, it wasn't long after the release of the RDF specifications that concerns arose about ambiguity with certain constructs within the document. For instance, there was considerable discussion in the RDF Internet Group about containers—are separate semantic and syntactic constructs really needed?—as well as other elements within RDF/XML. To meet this growing number of concerns, an RDF Issue Tracking document was started in 2000 to monitor issues with RDF. This was followed in 2001 with the creation of a new RDF Core Working Group, chartered to complete the RDF Schema (RDFS) recommendation as well as address the issues with the first specifications.

The RDF Core Working Group's scope has grown a bit since its beginnings. According to the Working Group's charter, they must now:

- Update and maintain the RDF Issue Tracking document
- Publish a set of machine-processable test cases corresponding to technical issues addressed by the WG
- Update the errata and status pages for the RDF specifications
- Update the RDF Model and Syntax Specification (as one, two, or more documents) clarifying the model and fixing issues with the syntax
- Complete work on the RDF Schema 1.0 Specification
- Provide an account of the relationship between RDF and the XML family of technologies
- Maintain backward compatibility with existing implementations of RDF/XML

The WG was originally scheduled to close down early in 2002, but, as with all larger projects, the work slid until later in 2002. This book finished just as the WG issued the W3C Last Call drafts for all six of the RDF specification documents, early in 2003.

The Specifications

As stated earlier, the RDF specification was originally released as one document, the RDF Model and Syntax, or RDF M&S. However, it soon became apparent that this document was attempting to cover too much material in one document, and leaving too much confusion and too many questions in its wake. Thus, a new effort was started to address the issues about the original specification and, hopefully, eliminate the confusion. This work resulted in an updated specification and the release of six new documents: RDF Concepts and Abstract Syntax, RDF Semantics, RDF/XML Syntax Specification (revised), RDF Vocabulary Description Language 1.0: RDF Schema, the RDF Primer, and the RDF Test Cases.

The RDF Concepts and Abstract Syntax and the RDF Semantics documents provide the fundamental framework behind RDF: the underlying assumptions and structures that makes RDF unique from other metadata models (such as the relational data model). These documents provide both validity and consistency to RDF—a way of verifying that data structured in a certain way will always be compatible with other data using the same structures. The RDF model exists independently of any representation of RDF, including RDF/XML.

The RDF/XML syntax, described in the RDF/XML Syntax Specification (revised), is the recommended serialization technique for RDF. Though several tools and APIs can also work with N-Triples (described in Chapter 2) or N3 notation (described in Chapter 3), most implementation of and discussion about RDF, including this book, focus on RDF/XML

The RDF Vocabulary Description Language defines and constrains an RDF/XML vocabulary. It isn't a replacement for XML Schema or the use of DTDs; rather, it's used to define specific RDF vocabularies; to specify how the elements of the vocabulary relate to each other. An RDF Schema isn't required for valid RDF (neither is a W3C XML Schema or an XML 1.0 Document Type Definition—DTD), but it does help prevent confusion when people want to share a vocabulary.

A good additional resource to learn more about RDF and RDF/XML is the RDF Primer. In addition to examples and accessible descriptions of the concepts of RDF and RDFS, the primer also, looks at some uses of RDF. I won't be covering the RDF Primer in this book because its use is somewhat self-explanatory. However, the primer is an excellent complement to this book, and I recommend that you spend time with it either while you're reading this book or afterward if you want another viewpoint on the topics covered.

The final RDF specification document, RDF Test Cases, contains a list of issues arising from the original RDF specification release, their resolutions, and the test cases devised for use by RDF implementers to test their implementations against these resolved issues. The primary purpose of the RDF Test Cases is to provide examples for testing specific RDF issues as the Working Group resolved them. Unless you're writing an RDF/XML parser or something similar, you probably won't need to spend much time with that document, and I won't be covering it in the book.

When to Use and Not Use RDF

RDF is a wonderful technology, and I'll be at the front in its parade of fans. However, I don't consider it a replacement for other technologies, and I don't consider its use appropriate in all circumstances. Just because data is on the Web, or accessed via the Web, doesn't mean it has to be organized with RDF. Forcing RDF into uses that don't realize its potential will only result in a general push back against RDF in its entirety—including push back in uses in which RDF positively shines.

This, then, begs the question: when should we, and when should we not, use RDF? More specifically, since much of RDF focuses on its serialization to RDF/XML, when should we use RDF/XML and when should we use non-RDF XML?

As the final edits for this book were in progress, a company called Semaview published a graphic depicting the differences between XML and RDF/XML (found at *http://www.semaview.com/c/RDFvsXML.html*). Among those listed was one about the tree-structured nature of XML, as compared to RDF's much flatter triple-based pattern. XML is hierarchical, which means that all related elements must be nested within the elements they're related to. RDF does not require this nested structure.

To demonstrate this difference, consider a web resource, which has a history of movement on the Web. Each element in that history has an associated URL, representing the location of the web resource after the movement has occurred. In addition, there's an associated reason why the resource was moved, resulting in this particular event. Recording these relationships in non-RDF XML results in an XML hierarchy four layers deep:

```
<?xml version="1.0"?>
<resource>
  <uri>http://burningbird.net/articles/monsters3.htm</uri>
  <history>
    <movement>
        <link>http://www.yasd.com/dynaearth/monsters3.htm</link>
        <reason>New Article</reason>
    </movement>
  </history>
</resource>
```

In RDF/XML, you can associate two separate XML structures with each other through a Uniform Resource Identifier (URI, discussed in Chapter 2). With the URI, you can link one XML structure to another without having to embed the second structure directly within the first:

```
<?xml version="1.0"?>
<rdf:RDF
    xmlns:rdf="http://www.w3.org/1999/02/22-rdf-syntax-ns#"
    xmlns:pstcn="http://burningbird.net/postcon/elements/1.0/"
    xml:base="http://burningbird.net/articles/">

    <pstcn:Resource rdf:about="monsters3.htm">

<!--resource movements-->
        <pstcn:history>
          <rdf:Seq>
          <rdf:_3 rdf:resource="http://www.yasd.com/dynaearth/monsters3.htm" />
          </rdf:Seq>
        </pstcn:history>

    </pstcn:Resource>

    <pstcn:Movement rdf:about="http://www.yasd.com/dynaearth/monsters3.htm">
        <pstcn:movementType>Add</pstcn:movementType>
        <pstcn:reason>New Article</pstcn:reason>
    </pstcn:Movement>

</rdf:RDF>
```

Ignore for the moment some of the other characteristics of RDF/XML, such the use of namespaces, which we'll get into later in the book, and focus instead on the structure. The RDF/XML is still well-formed XML—a requirement of RDF/XML—but the use of the URI (in this case, the URL `"http://www.yasd.com/dynaearth/monsters3.htm"`) breaks us out of the forced hierarchy of standard XML, but still allows us to record the relationship between the resource's history and the particular movement.

However, this difference in structure can make it more difficult for people to read the RDF/XML document and actually see the relationships between the data, one of the more common complaints about RDF/XML. With non-RDF XML, you can, at a glance, see that the history element is directly related to this specific resource element and so on. In addition, even this small example demonstrates that RDF adds a layer of complexity on the XML that can be off-putting when working with it manually. Within an automated process, though, the RDF/XML structure is actually an advantage.

When processing XML, an element isn't actually complete until you reach its end tag. If an application is parsing an XML document into elements in memory before transferring them into another persisted form of data, this means that the elements that contain other elements must be retained in memory until their internal data members are processed. This can result in some fairly significant strain on memory use, particularly with larger XML documents.

RDF/XML, on the other hand, would allow you to process the first element quickly because its "contained" data is actually stored in another element somewhere else in the document. As long as the relationship between the two elements can be established through the URI, we'll always be able to reconstruct the original data regardless of how it's been transformed.

Another advantage to the RDF/XML approach is when querying the data. Again, in XML, if you're looking for a specific piece of data, you basically have to provide the entire structure of all the elements preceding the piece of data in order to ensure you have the proper value. As you'll see in RDF/XML, all you have to do is remember the triple nature of the specification, and look for a triple with a pattern matching a specific resource URI, such as a property URI, and you'll find the specific value. Returning to the RDF/XML shown earlier, you can find the reason for the specific movement just by looking for the following pattern:

```
<http://www.yasd.com/dynaearth/monsters3.htm> pstcn:reason ?
```

The entire document does not have to be traversed to answer this query, nor do you have to specify the entire element path to find the value.

 If you've worked with database systems before, you'll recognize that many of the differences between RDF/XML and XML are similar to the differences between relational and hierarchical databases. Hierarchical databases also have a physical location dependency that requires related data to be bilocated, while relational databases depend on the use of identifiers to relate data.

Another reason you would use RDF/XML over non-RDF XML is the ability to join data from two disparate vocabularies easily, without having to negotiate structural differences between the two. Since the XML from both data sets is based on the same model (RDF) and since both make use of namespaces (which prevent element name collision—the same element name appearing in both vocabularies), combining data from both vocabularies can occur immediately, and with no preliminary work. This is essential for the Semantic Web, the basis for the work on RDF and RDF/XML. However, this is also essential in any business that may need to combine data from two different companies, such as a supplier of raw goods and a manufacturer that uses these raw goods. (Read more on this in the sidebar "Data Handshaking Through the Ages").

As excellent as these two reasons (less strain on memory and joining vocabularies) are for utilizing RDF as a model for data and RDF/XML as a format, for certain instances of data stored on the Web, RDF is clearly not a replacement. As an example, RDF is not a replacement for XHTML for defining web pages that are displayed in a browser. RDF is also not a replacement for CSS, which is used to control how that data is displayed. Both CSS and XHTML are optimized for their particular uses, organizing and displaying data in a web browser. RDF's purpose differs—it's used to capture specific statements about a resource, statements that help form a more complete picture of the resource. RDF isn't concerned about either page organization or display.

Now, there might be pieces of information in the XHTML and the CSS that could be reconstructed into statements about a resource, but there's nothing in either technology that specifically says "this is a statement, an assertion if you will, about this resource" in such a way that a machine can easily pick this information out. That's where RDF enters the picture. It lays all assertions out—bang, bang, bang—so that even the most amoeba-like RDF parser can find each individual statement without having to pick around among the presentational and organizational constructs of specifications such as XHTML and CSS.

Additionally, RDF/XML isn't necessarily well suited as a replacement for other uses of XML, such as within SOAP or XML-RPC. The main reason is, again, the level of complexity that RDF/XML adds to the process. A SOAP processor is basically sending a request for a service across the Internet and then processing the results of that request when it's answered. There's a mechanism that supports this process, but the basic structure of SOAP is request service, get answer, process answer. In the case of SOAP, the request and the answer are formatted in XML.

Though a SOAP service call and results are typically formatted in XML, there really isn't the need to persist these outside of this particular invocation, so there really is little drive to format the XML in such a way that it can be combined with other vocabularies at a later time, something that RDF/XML facilitates. Additionally, one hopes that we keep the SOAP request and return as small, lightweight, and uncomplicated answers as possible, and RDF/XML does add to the overhead of the XML.

Though bandwidth is not the issue it used to be years ago, it is still enough of an issue to not waste it unnecessarily.

Ultimately, the decision about using RDF/XML in place of XML is based on whether there's a good reason to do so—a business rather than a technical need to use the model and related XML structure. If the data isn't processed automatically, if it isn't persisted and combined with data from other vocabularies, and if you don't need RDF's optimized querying capability, then you should use non-RDF XML. However, if you do need these things, consider the use of RDF/XML.

Some Uses of RDF/XML

The first time I saw RDF/XML was when it was used to define the table of contents (TOC) structures within Mozilla, when Mozilla was first being implemented. Since then, I've been both surprised and pleased at how many implementations of RDF and RDF/XML exist.

One of the primary users of RDF/XML is the W3C itself, in its effort to define a Web Ontology Language based on RDF/XML. Being primarily a data person and not a specialist in markup, I wasn't familiar with some of the concepts associated with RDF when I first started exploring its use and meaning. For instance, there were references to *ontology* again and again, and since my previous exposure to this word had to do with biology, I was a bit baffled. However, *ontology* in the sense of RDF and the Semantic Web is, according to *dictionary.com*, "An explicit formal specification of how to represent the objects, concepts and other entities that are assumed to exist in some area of interest and the relationships that hold among them."

As mentioned previously, RDF provides a structure that allows us to make assertions using XML (and other serialization techniques). However, there is an interest in taking this further and expanding on it, by creating just such an ontology based on the RDF model, in the interest of supporting more advanced agent-based technologies. An early effort toward this is the DARPA Agent Markup Language program, or DAML. The first implementation of DAML, DAML+OIL, is tightly integrated with RDF.

A new effort at the W3C, the Web Ontology Working Group, is working on creating a Web Ontology Language (OWL) derived from DAML+OIL and based in RDF/XML. The following quote from the OWL Use Cases and Requirements document, one of many the Ontology Working Group is creating, defines the relationship between XML, RDF/XML, and OWL:

> The Semantic Web will build on XML's ability to define customized tagging schemes and RDF's flexible approach to representing data. The next element required for the Semantic Web is a Web ontology language which can formally describe the semantics of classes and properties used in web documents. In order for machines to perform useful reasoning tasks on these documents, the language must go beyond the basic semantics of RDF Schema.

Data Handshaking Through the Ages

I started working with data and data interchange at Boeing in the late 1980s. At that time, there was a data definition effort named Product Data Exchange Specification (PDES) underway between several manufacturing companies to define one consistent data model that could be used by all of them. With this model, the companies hoped to establish the ability to interchange data among themselves without having to renegotiate data structures every time a new connection was made between the companies, such as adding a new supplier or customer. (This effort is still underway and you can read more about it at *http://pdesinc.com*.)

PDES was just one effort on the part of specific industries to define common business models that would allow them to interoperate. From Boeing, I went to Sierra Geophysics, a company in Seattle that created software for the oil industry. Sierra Geophysics and its parent company, Halliburton, Inc., were hard at work on POSC, an effort similar to PDES but geared to the oil and gas industries. (You can read more about POSC at *http://posc.org*; be sure to check out POSC's use of XML, specifically, at *http://posc.org/ebiz/xmlLive.shtml*.)

One would think this wouldn't be that complex, but it is almost virtually impossible to get two companies to agree on what "data" means. Because of this difficulty, to this day, there's never been complete agreement as to data interchange formats, though with the advent of XML, there was hope that this specification would provide a syntax that most of the companies could agree to use. One reason XML was hailed as a potential savior is that it represented a neutral element in the discussions—no one could claim either the syntax or the syntactic rules.

Would something like RDF/XML work for both of these organizations and their efforts? Yes and no. If the interest in XML is primarily for network protocol uses, I wouldn't necessarily recommend the use of RDF/XML for the same reasons I wouldn't recommend its use with SOAP and XML/RPC—RDF/XML adds a layer of complexity and overhead that can be counterproductive when you're primarily doing nothing more than just sending messages to and from services. However, RDF/XML would fit the needs of POSC and PDES if the interest were on merging data between organizations for more effective supply chain management—in effect, establishing a closer relationship between the supplier of raw goods on one hand and a manufacturer of finished goods on the other. In particular, with an established ontology built on RDF/XML (ontologies are discussed in Chapter 12) defining the business data, it should be a simple matter to add new companies into an existing supply chain.

When one considers that much of the cost of a manufactured item resides in the management of the supply chain and within the manufacturing process, not in the raw material used to manufacture the item, I would expect to see considerable progress from industry efforts such as POSC and PDES in RDF/XML.

Drawing analogies from other existing data schemes, if RDF and the relational data model were comparable, then RDF/XML is also comparable to the existing relational databases, and OWL would be comparable to the business domain applications such as PeopleSoft and SAP. Both PeopleSoft and SAP make use of existing data storage mechanisms to store the data and the relational data model to ensure that the data is stored and managed consistently and validly; the products then add an extra level of business logic based on patterns that occur and reoccur within traditional business processes. This added business logic could be plugged into a company's existing infrastructure without the company having to build its own functionality to implement the logic directly.

OWL does something similar except that it builds in the ability to define commonly reoccurring inferential rules that facilitate how data is queried within an RDF/XML document or store. Based on this added capability, and returning to the RDF/XML example in the last section, instead of being limited to queries about a specific movement based on a specific resource, we could query on movements that occurred because the document was moved to a new domain, rather than because the document was just moved about within a specific domain. Additional information can then allow us to determine that the document was moved because it was transferred to a different owner, allowing us to infer information about a transaction between two organizations even if this "transactional" information isn't stored directly within elements.

In other words, the rules help us discover new information that isn't necessarily stored directly within the RDF/XML.

 Chapter 12 covers ontologies, OWL, and its association with RDF/XML. Read more about the W3C's ontology efforts at *http://www.w3.org/2001/sw/WebOnt/*. The Use Cases and Requirements document can be found at *http://www.w3.org/TR/webont-req/*.

Another very common use of RDF/XML is in a version of RSS called RSS 1.0 or RDF/RSS. The meaning of the RSS abbreviation has changed over the years, but the basic premise behind it is to provide an XML-formatted feed consisting of an abstract of content and a link to a document containing the full content. When Netscape originally created the first implementation of an RSS specification, RSS stood for RDF Site Summary, and the plan was to use RDF/XML. When the company released, instead, a non-RDF XML version of the specification, RSS stood for Rich Site Summary. Recently, there has been increased activity with RSS, and two paths are emerging: one considers RSS to stand for Really Simple Syndication, a simple XML solution (promoted as RSS 2.0 by Dave Winer at Userland), and one returns RSS to its original roots of RDF Site Summary (RSS 1.0 by the RSS 1.0 Development group).

RSS *feeds*, as they are called, are small, brief introductions to recently released news articles or weblog postings (weblogs are frequently updated journals that may include links to other stories, comments, and so on). These feeds are picked up by *aggregators*, which format the feeds into human consumable forms (e.g., as web pages or audio notices). RSS files normally contain only the most recent feeds, newer items replacing older ones.

Given the transitory nature of RSS feeds as I just described them, it is difficult to justify the use of RDF for RSS. If RDF's purpose is to record assertions about resources that can be discovered and possibly merged with other assertions to form a more complete picture of the resource, then that implies some form of permanence to this data, that the data hangs around long enough to be discovered. If the data has a life span of only a minute, hour, or day, its use within a larger overall "semantic web" tends to be dubious, at best.

However, the data contained in the RSS feeds—article title, author, date, subject, excerpt, and so on—is a very rich source of information about the resource, be it article or weblog posting, information that isn't easily scraped from the web page or pulled in from the HTML meta tags. Additionally, though the purpose of the RSS feed is transitory in nature, there's no reason tools can't access this data and store it in a more permanent form for mergence with other data. For instance, I've long been amazed that search tools don't use RSS feeds rather than the HTML pages themselves for discovering information.

Based on these latter views of RSS, there is, indeed, a strong justification for building RSS within an RDF framework—to enhance the discovery of the assertions contained within the XML. The original purpose of RSS might be transitory, but there's nothing to stop others from pulling the data into more permanent storage if they so choose or to use the data for other purposes.

I'll cover the issue of RSS in more detail in Chapter 13, but for now the point to focus on is that when to use RDF isn't always obvious. The key to knowing when to make extra effort necessary to overlay an RDF model on the data isn't necessarily based on the original purpose for the data or even the transitory nature of the data— but on the data itself. If the data is of interest, descriptive, and not easily discovered by any other means, little RDF alarms should be ringing in our minds.

As stated earlier, if RDF isn't a replacement for some technologies, it is an opportunity for new ones. In particular, Mozilla, my favorite open source browser, uses RDF extensively within its architecture, for such things as managing table of contents structures. RDF's natural ability to organize XML data into easily accessible data statements made it a natural choice for the Mozilla architects. Chapter 14 explores how RDF/XML is used within the Mozilla architecture, in addition to its use in other open source and noncommercial applications such as MIT's DSpace, a tool and technology to track intellectual property, and FOAF, a toolkit for describing the connections between people.

Chapter 15 follows with a closer look at the commercial use of RDF, taking a look at OSA's Chandler, Plugged In Software's Tucana Knowledge Store, Siderean Software's Seamark, the Intellidimension RDF Gateway, and how Adobe is incorporating RDF data into its products.

Related Technologies

Several complementary technologies are associated with RDF. As previously discussed, the most common technique to serialize RDF data is via RDF/XML, so influences on XML are likewise influences on RDF. However, other specifications and technologies also impact on, and are impacted by, the ongoing RDF efforts.

Though not a requirement for RDF/XML, you can use XML Schemas and DTDs to formalize the XML structure used within a specific instance of RDF/XML. There's also been considerable effort to map XML Schema data types to RDF, as you'll see in the next several chapters.

One issue that arises again and again with RDF is where to include the XML. For instance, if you create an RDF document to describe an HTML page resource, should the RDF be in a separate file or contained within the HTML document? I've seen RDF embedded in HTML and XML using a variety of tricks, but the consensus seems to be heading toward defining the RDF in a separate file and then linking it within the HTML or XHTML document. Chapter 3 takes a closer look at issues related to merging RDF with other formats.

A plethora of tools and utilities work with RDF/XML. Chapter 7 covers some of these. In addition, several different APIs in a variety of languages, such as Perl, Java, Python, C, C++, and so on, can parse, query, and generate RDF/XML. The remainder of the second section of the book explores some of the more stable or representative of these, including a look at Jena, a Java-based API, RAP (RDF API for PHP), Redland's multilanguage RDF API, Perl and Python APIs and tools, and so on.

Going Forward

The RDF Core Working Group spent considerable time ensuring that the RDF specifications answered as many questions as possible. There is no such thing as a perfect specification, but the group did its best under the constraints of maintaining connectivity with its charter and existing uses of RDF/XML.

RDF/XML has been used enough in so many different applications that I consider it to be at a release level with the publication of the current RDF specification documents. In fact, I think you'll find that the RDF specification will be quite stable in its current form after the documents are released—it's important that the RDF specification be stabilized so that we can begin to build on it. Based on this hoped-for stability, you can use the specification, including the RDF/XML, in your applications and be comfortable about future compatibility.

We're also seeing more and more interest in and use of RDF and its associated RDF/XML serialization in the world. I've seen APIs in all major programming languages, including Java, Perl, PHP, Python, C#, C++, C, and so on. Not only that, but there's a host of fun and useful tools to help you edit, parse, read, or write your RDF/XML

---

documents. And most of these tools, utilities, APIs, and so on are free for you to download and incorporate into your current work.

With the release of the RDF specification documents, RDF's time has come, and I'm not just saying that because I wrote this book. I wrote this book because I believe that RDF is now ready for prime time.

Now, time to get started.

CHAPTER 2

RDF: Heart and Soul

RDF's purpose is fairly straightforward: it provides a means of recording data in a machine-understandable format, allowing for more efficient and sophisticated data interchange, searching, cataloging, navigation, classification, and so on. It forms the cornerstone of the W3C effort to create the Semantic Web, but its use isn't restricted to this specific effort.

Perhaps because RDF is a description for a data model rather than a description of a specific data vocabulary, or perhaps because it has a foothold in English, logic, and even in human reasoning, RDF has a strong esoteric element to it that can be intimidating to a person wanting to know a little more about it. However, RDF is based on a well-defined set of rules and constraints that governs its format, validity, and use. Approaching RDF through the specifications is a way of grounding RDF, putting boundaries around the more theoretical concepts.

The chapter takes a look at two RDF specification documents that exist at opposite ends of the semantic spectrum: the RDF Concepts and Abstract Model and the RDF Semantics documents. In these documents we're introduced to the concepts and underlying strategy that form the basis of the RDF/XML that we'll focus on in the rest of the book. In addition, specifically within the Semantics document, we'll be exposed to the underlying meaning behind each RDF construct. Though not critical to most people's use of RDF, especially RDF/XML, the Semantics document ensures that all RDF consumers work from the same basic understanding; therefore, some time spent on this document, primarily in overview, is essential.

Both documents can be accessed directly online, so I'm not going to duplicate the information contained in them in this chapter. Instead, we'll take a look at some of the key elements and unique concepts associated with RDF.

 The RDF Concepts and Abstract Syntax document can be found at *http://www.w3.org/TR/rdf-concepts/*. The RDF Semantics document can be found at *http://www.w3.org/TR/rdf-mt/*.

The Search for Knowledge

Occasionally, I like to write articles about non-Internet-related topics, such as marine biology or astronomy. One of my more popular articles is on *Architeuthis Dux*—the giant squid. The article is currently located at *http://burningbird.net/articles/ monsters1.htm*.

According to the web profile statistics for this article, it receives a lot of visitors based on searches performed in Google, a popular search engine. When I go to the Google site, though, to search for the article based on the term *giant squid*, I find that I get a surprising number of links back. The article was listed on page 13 of the search results (with 10 links to a page). First, though, were several links about a production company, the Jules Verne novel *10,000 Leagues Under the Sea*, something to do with a comic book character called the Giant Squid, as well as various other assorted and sundry references such as a recipe for cooking giant squid steaks (as an aside, giant squids are ammonia based and inedible).

For the most part, each link does reference the giant squid as a marine animal; however, the context doesn't match my current area of interest: finding an article that explores the giant squid's roots in mythology.

I can refine my search, specifying separate keywords such as *giant*, *squid*, and *mythology* to make my article appear on page 6 of the list of links—along with links to a Mexican seafood seller offering giant squid meat slabs and a listing of books that discuss a monster called the Giant Squid that oozes green slime.

The reason we get so many links back when searching for specific resources is that most search engines use keyword-based search engine functionality, rather than searching for a resource *within the context of a specific interest*. The search engines' data is based on the use of automated agents or robots and web spiders that traverse the Web via in-page links, pulling keywords from either HTML `meta` tags or directly from the page contents themselves.

A better approach for classifying resources such as the giant squid article would be to somehow attach information about the context of the resource. For instance, the article is part of a series comparing two legendary creatures: the giant squid and the Loch Ness Monster. It explores what makes a creature legendary, as well as current and past efforts to find living representatives of either creature. All of this information forms a description of the resource, a *picture* that's richer and more complex than a one-dimensional keyword-based categorization.

What's missing in today's keyword-based classification of web resources is the ability to record statements about a resource. Statements such as:

- The article's title is "*Architeuthis Dux*."
- The article's author is Shelley Powers.
- The article is part of a series.

- A related article is ...
- The article is about the giant squid and its place in the legends.

General keyword scanning doesn't return this type of specific information, at least, not in such a way that a machine can easily find and process these statements without heroic computations.

RDF provides a mechanism for recording statements about resources so that machines can easily interpret the statements. Not only that, but RDF is based on a domain-neutral model that allows one set of statements to be merged with another set of statements, even though the information contained in each set of statements may differ dramatically.

One application's interest in the resource might focus on finding new articles posted on the Web and providing an encapsulated view of the articles for news aggregators. Another application's interest might be on the article's long-term relevancy and the author of the article, while a third application may focus specifically on the topics covered in the article, and so on. Rather than generating one XML file in a specific XML vocabulary for all of these different applications' needs, one RDF file can contain all of this information, and each application can pick and choose what it needs. Better yet, new applications will find that everything they need is already being provided, as the information we record about each resource gets richer and more comprehensive.

And the basis of all this richness is a simple little thing called the RDF triple.

I use the word *context* in this chapter and throughout the book. However, the folks involved with RDF, including Tim Berners-Lee, director of the W3C, are hesitant about using the term *context* in association with RDF. The main reason is there's a lot of confusion about what *context* actually means. Does it mean the world of all possible conditions at any one point? Does it mean a specific area of interest?

To prevent confusion when I use *context* in the book, I use the term to refer to a certain aspect of a subject at a given time. For instance, when I look for references for a subject, I'm searching for information related to one specific aspect of the subject—such as the giant squid's relevance to mythology—but only for that specific instance in time. The next time I search for information related to the giant squid, I might be searching for information based on a different aspect of giant squids, such as cooking giant squid steaks.

The RDF Triple

Three is a magical number. For instance, three legs are all you need to create a stable stool, and a transmitter and two receivers are all you need to triangulate a specific transmission point. You can create a perfect sphere with infinitely small triangles. (Triangles are a very useful geometric shape, also used to find the heights of mountains and the distances between stars.)

RDF is likewise based on the principle that three is a magic number—in this case, that three pieces of information are all that's needed in order to fully define a single bit of knowledge. Within the RDF specification, an RDF *triple* documents these three pieces of information in a consistent manner that ideally allows both human and machine consumption of the same data. The RDF triple is what allows human understanding and meaning to be interpreted consistently and mechanically.

Of the three pieces of information, the first is the *subject*. A property such as *name* can belong to a dog, cat, book, plant, person, car, nation, or insect. To make finite such an infinite universe, you must set boundaries, and that's what subject does for RDF. The second piece of information is the *property type* or just plain *property*. There are many facts about any individual subject; for instance, I have a gender, a height, a hair color, an eye color, a college degree, relationships, and so on. To define which aspect of me we're interested in, we need to specifically focus on one property.

If you look at the intersection of subject and property, you'll find the final bit of information quietly waiting to be discovered—the *value* associated with the property. X marks the spot. I (subject) have a name (property), which is Shelley Powers (property value). I (subject) have a height (property), which is five feet eleven inches (property value). I (subject) also have a location (property), which is St. Louis (property value). Each of these assertions adds to a picture that is *me*; the more statements defined, the better the picture. Stripping away the linguistic filler, each of these statements can be written as an RDF triple.

With consideration of the differing linguistics based on different languages, simple facts can almost always be defined given three specific pieces of information: the subject of the fact, the property of the subject that is currently being defined, and its associated value. This correlates to what we understand to be a complete thought, regardless of differing syntaxes based on language.

A basic rule of English grammar is that a complete sentence (or statement) contains both a *subject* and a *predicate*: the subject is the *who* or *what* of the sentence and the predicate provides information about the subject. A sentence about the giant squid article mentioned in the last section could be:

```
The title of the article is "Architeuthis Dux."
```

This is a complete statement about the article. The subject is *the article*, and the predicate is *title*, with a matching value of "*Architeuthis Dux.*" Combined, the three separate pieces of information triangulate a specific, completely unique piece of knowledge.

In RDF, this English statement translates to an RDF *triple*. In RDF, the *subject* is the thing being described—in RDF terms, a *resource* identified by a URI (more fully explained in a later section with the same title)—and the *predicate* is a property type of the resource, such as an attribute, a relationship, or a characteristic. In addition to the subject and predicate, the specification also introduces a third component, the *object*. Within RDF, the object is equivalent to the value of the resource property type for the specific subject.

Working with the example sentence earlier, "The title of the article is '*Architeuthis Dux*,'" the generic reference to *article* is replaced by the article's URI, forming a new and more precise sentence:

```
The title of the article at http://burningbird.net/articles/monsters3.htm is
"Architeuthis Dux."
```

With this change, there is no confusion about which article titled "Architeuthis Dux" we're discussing—we're talking about the one with the URI at `http://burningbird.net/articles/monsters3.htm`. Providing a URI is equivalent to giving a person a unique identifier within a personnel system. The individual components of the statement we're interested in can be further highlighted, with each of the three components specifically broken out into the following format:

```
<subject> HAS <predicate> <object>
```

Don't let the angle brackets fool you within this syntax—this isn't XML; this is a representation of a statement whereby three components of the statement can be replaced by instances of the components to generate a specific statement. The example statement is converted to this format as follows:

```
http://burningbird.net/articles/monsters3.htm has a title of
"Architeuthis Dux."
```

In RDF, this new statement, redefined as an RDF triple, can be considered a complete RDF graph because it consists of a complete fact that can be recorded using RDF methodology, and that can then be documented using several different techniques. For instance, one shorthand technique is to use the following to represent a triple:

```
{subject, predicate, object}
```

If you're familiar with set theory, you might recognize this shorthand as a 3-tuple representation. The giant squid example then becomes:

```
{http://burningbird.net/articles/monsters3.htm, title, "Architeuthis Dux"}
```

This representation of the RDF triple is just one of many ways of serializing RDF data. The formal way is the directed graph, discussed in the next section. Popular choices to serialize the data are N-Triples, a subset of N3 notation (both of which are briefly discussed in this chapter), and RDF/XML, which forms the basis of the remainder of this book.

Regardless of the manner in which an RDF triple is documented, four facts are immutable about each:

- Each RDF triple is made up of subject, predicate, and object.
- Each RDF triple is a complete and unique fact.
- An (RDF) triple is a 3-tuple, which is made up of a subject, predicate and object—which are respectively a uriref or bnode; a uriref; and a uriref, bnode or literal (This is from a comment made by Pat Hayes in *http://lists.w3.org/Archives/Public/w3c-rdfcore-wg/2003Feb/0152.html*)
- Each RDF triple can be joined with other RDF triples, but it still retains its own unique meaning, regardless of the complexity of the model in which it is included.

That last item is particularly important to realize about RDF triples—regardless of how complex an RDF graph, it still consists of only a grouping of unique, simple RDF triples, and each is made up of a subject, predicate, and object.

N3 notation does have some major fans as an approach to serializing RDF graphs, including Tim Berners-Lee. However, the W3C has officially sanctioned RDF/XML as the method to use for serializing RDF. One overwhelming advantage of RDF/XML is the wide acceptance of and technical support for XML. Though N3 notation is not covered in detail in this book, you can read a primer on N3 and RDF at *http://www.w3.org/2000/10/swap/Primer*.

The Basic RDF Data Model and the RDF Graph

The RDF Core Working Group decided on the RDF graph—a directed labeled graph—as the default method for describing RDF data models for two reasons. First, as you'll see in the examples, the graphs are extremely easy to read. There is no confusion about what is a subject and what are the subject's property and this property's value. Additionally, there can be no confusion about the statements being made, even within a complex RDF data model.

The second reason the Working Group settled on RDF graphs as the default description technique is that there are RDF data models that can be represented in RDF graphs, but not in RDF/XML.

The addition of `rdf:nodeIDs`, discussed in Chapter 3, provided some of the necessary syntactic elements that allow RDF/XML to record all RDF graphs. However, RDF/XML still can't encode graphs whose properties (predicates) cannot be recorded as namespace-qualified XML names, or *QNames*. For more on QNames, see *XML in a Nutshell*, Second Edition (O'Reilly).

The RDF directed graph consists of a set of nodes connected by arcs, forming a pattern of *node-arc-node*. Additionally, the nodes come in three varieties: *uriref*, *blank nodes*, and *literals*.

A uriref node consists of a Uniform Resource Identifier (URI) reference that provides a specific identifier unique to the node. There's been discussion that a uriref must point to something that's accessible on the Web (i.e., provide a location of something that when accessed on the Internet returns something). However, there is no formal requirement that urirefs have a direct connectivity with actual web resources. In fact, if RDF is to become a generic means of recording data, it can't restrict urirefs to being "real" data sources.

Blank nodes are nodes that don't have a URI. When identifying a resource is meaningful, or the resource is identified within the specific graph, a URI is given for that resource. However, when identification of the resource doesn't exist within the specific graph at the time the graph was recorded, or it isn't meaningful, the resource is diagrammed as a blank node.

Within a directed graph, resource nodes identified as urirefs are drawn with an ellipse around them, and the URI is shown within the circle; blank nodes are shown as an empty circle. Specific implementations of the graph, such as those generated by the RDF Validator, draw a circle containing a generated identifier, used to distinguish blank nodes from each other within the single instance of the graph.

The literals consist of three parts—a character string and an optional language tag and data type. Literal values represent RDF objects only, never subjects or predicates. RDF literals are drawn with rectangles around them.

The arcs are directional and labeled with the RDF predicates. They are drawn starting from the resource and terminating at the object, with arrows documenting the direction from resource to object (in all instances of RDF graphs I've seen, this is from right to left).

Figure 2-1 shows a directed graph of the example statement discussed in the previous section. In the figure, the subject is contained within the oval to the left, the object literal is within the box, and the predicate is used to label the arrowed line drawn from the subject to the object.

Figure 2-1. RDF directed graph of giant squid article statement

As you can see in the figure, the direction of the arrow is from the subject to the object. In addition, the predicate is given a uriref equal to the schema for the RDF vocabulary elements and the element that serves as predicate itself. Every arc, without exception, must be labeled within the graph.

Blank nodes are valid RDF, but most RDF parsers and building tools generate a unique identifier for each blank node. For example, Figure 2-2 shows an RDF graph generated by the W3C RDF Validator, complete with generated identifier in place of the blank node, in the format of:

```
genid(unique identifier)
```

The identifier shown in the figure is genid:158, the number being the next number available for labeling a blank node and having no significance by itself. The use of genid isn't required, but the recommended format for blank node identifiers is some form similar to that used by the validator.

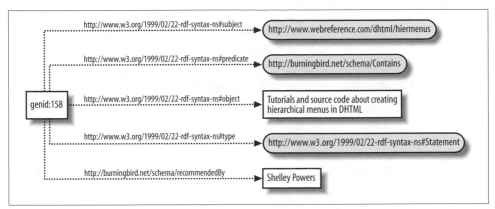

Figure 2-2. Example of autogenerated identifier representing blank node

Blank nodes (sometimes referred to as bnodes or, previously, anonymous nodes) can be problematic within automated processes because the identifier that's generated for each will change from one application run to the next. Because of this, you can't depend on the identifier remaining the same. However, since blank nodes represent placeholder nodes rather than more meaningful nodes, this shouldn't be a problem. Still, you'll want to be aware of the nonpersistent names given to blank nodes by RDF parsers.

 The figures shown in this chapter were transformed from graphics generated by the RDF Validator, an online resource operated by the W3C for validation of RDF syntax (found at *http://www.w3.org/RDF/ Validator/*). This tool will be used extensively throughout this book, and its use is detailed in Chapter 7.

The components of the RDF graph—the uriref, bnode, literal, and arc—are the only components used to document a specific instance of an RDF data model. This small number of components isn't surprising when you consider that, as demonstrated earlier, an RDF triple is a fact comprised of subject-predicate-object. Only when we start recording more complicated assertions and start merging several triples together do the RDF graph and the resulting RDF/XML begin to appear more complex.

URIs

Since an understanding of urirefs is central to working with RDF, we'll take a moment to look at what makes a valid URI—the identifiers contained within a uriref and used to identify specific predicates.

Resources can be accessed with different protocols and using different syntaxes, such as using `http://` to access a resource as a web page and `ftp://` to access another resource using FTP. However, one thing each approach shares is the need to access a specific object given a unique name or identifier. URIs provide a common syntax for naming a resource regardless of the protocol used to access the resource. Best of all, the syntax can be extended to meet new needs and include new protocols.

URIs are related to URLs (Uniform Resource Locators) in that a URL is a specific instance of a URI scheme based on a known protocol, commonly the Hypertext Transfer Protocol (HTTP). URIs, and URLs for that matter, can include either a complete location or path to a resource or a partial or relative path. The URI can optionally include a fragment identifier, separated from the URI by a pound sign (#). In the following example, `http://burningbird.net/articles/monsters3.htm` is the URI and `introduction` is the fragment:

```
http://burningbird.net/articles/monsters3.htm#introduction
```

A URI is only an identifier. A specific protocol doesn't need to be specified, nor must the object identified physically exist on the Web—you don't have to specify a resolvable protocol such as `http://` or `ftp://`, though you can if you like. Instead, you could use something as different as a UUID (Universally Unique Identifier) referencing a COM or other technology component that exists locally on the same machine or within a network of machines. In fact, a fundamental difference between a URL and a URI is that a URL is a location of an object, while a URI can function as a name or a location. URIs also differ from URNs (Uniform Resource Name) because URIs can refer to a location as well as a name, while URNs refer to globally unique names.

The RDF specification constrains all urirefs to be absolute or partial URIs. An absolute URI would be equivalent to the URL:

```
http://burningbird.net/articles/monsters3.htm
```

A relative URI is just as it sounds—relative to an absolute path. A relative reference to the Monsters article could be:

```
Monsters3.htm
```

If a reference to the base location of the relative URI is not given, it's assumed to be base to the URI of the containing document. The use of URIs and the concepts of namespaces and QNames are discussed in more detail in Chapter 3.

RDF Serialization: N3 and N-Triples

Though RDF/XML is the serialization technique used in the rest of this book, another serialization technique supported by many RDF applications and tools is N-Triples. This format breaks an RDF graph into its separate triples, one on each line. Regardless of the shorthand technique used within RDF/XML, N-Triples generated from the same RDF graph always come out the same, making it an effective way of validating the processing of an RDF/XML document. For instance, the test cases in the RDF Test Cases document, part of the RDF specification, are given in both the RDF/XML format and the N-Triples format to ensure that the RDF/XML (and the underlying RDF concepts) are consistently interpreted.

> Though other techniques for serialization exist, as has been previously discussed, the only serialization technique officially adopted by the RDF specifications is RDF/XML.

N-Triples itself is based on another notation, called N3.

A Brief Look at N3

RDF/XML is the official serialization technique for RDF data, but another notation is also used frequently, which is known as N3 or Notation3. It's important you know how to read it; however, since this book is focusing on RDF/XML, we'll look only briefly at N3 notation.

> N3 exists independent of RDF and can extend RDF in such a way as to violate the semantics of the underlying RDF graph. Some prefer N3 to RDF/XML; I am not one of them, primarily because I believe RDF/XML is a more comfortable format for people more used to markup (such as XML or HTML).

The basic structure of an N3 triple is:

```
subject predicate object .
```

In this syntax, the subject, predicate, and object are separated by spaces, and the triple is terminated with a period (.). An actual example of N3 would be:

```
<http://weblog.burningbird.net/fires/000805.htm>
                          <http://purl.org/dc/elements/1.1/creator> Shelley .
```

In this example, the absolute URIs are surrounded by angle brackets. To simplify this even further, namespace-qualified XML names (QNames) can be used instead of the full namespace, as long as the namespaces are declared somewhere within the document. If QNames are used, the angle brackets are omitted for the predicates:

```
<bbd:000805.htm> dc:creator Shelley.
```

To represent multiple triples, with related resources, just list out the triples. Converting the RDF/XML in Example 3-9 into N3 we have:

```
<bbd:monsters1.htm> pstcn:bio <#monster1> .
<#monster1> pstcn.title "Tale of Two Monsters: Legends .
<#monster1> pstcn.description Part 1 of four-part series on cryptozoology, legends,
Nessie the Loch Ness Monster and the giant squid" .
<#monster1> pstcn:creator "Shelley" Powers .
<#monster1> pstcn:created "1999-08-01T00:00:00-06:00" .
```

To represent bnodes or blank nodes, use whatever designation you would prefer to identify the bnode identifier. An example from the RDF Primer is:

```
exstaff:85740  exterms:address  _:johnaddress .
_:johnaddress  exterms:street   "1501 Grant Avenue" .
```

```
_:johnaddress    exterms:city       "Bedford" .
_:johnaddress    exterms:state      "Massachusetts" .
_:johnaddress    exterms:Zip        "01730" .
```

Though brief, these notes should enable you to read N3 notation all through the RDF specification documents. However, since the focus of this book is RDF/XML, N3 notation won't be used again.

N-Triples

Since N-Triples is a subset of N3, it supports the same format for RDF triples:

```
subject predicate object .
```

According to the Extended Backus-Naur Form (EBNF) for N-Triples, a space or a tab separates the three elements from each other, and a space or a tab can precede the elements. In addition, each triple is ended with a period (.) followed by a line-feed or carriage-return/line-feed. An N-Triples file can also contain comments in the following format:

```
# comment
```

Each line in an N-Triples file consists of either a triple or a comment, but not both.

As for the triple elements themselves, the subject can consist of either a uriref or a blank node identifier The latter is a value generated for blank nodes within N-Triples syntax, as there can be no blank subjects within legal N-Triples-formatted output. The blank node identifier format is:

```
_:name
```

where *name* is a string. The predicate is always a uriref, and the object can be a uriref, a blank node, or a literal.

Given an RDF graph as shown in Figure 2-3, N-Triples would be returned representing both the title triple and the author triple. Adding in a comment, the output in Example 2-1 is valid N-Triples output for the same RDF graph.

Figure 2-3. RDF graph with two RDF triples and one subject

Example 2-1. N-Triples output

```
# Chapter 2 Example1
<http://burningbird.net/articles/monsters3.htm> . <http://burningbird.net/postcon/
elements/1.0/author> "Shelley Powers" .
<http://www.burningbird.net/articles/monsters3.htm> <http://burningbird.net/postcon/
elements/1.0/title> "Architeuthis Dux" .
```

Note that angle brackets are used in N-Triples notation only when the object enclosed is a complete, absolute URI. QNames are not enclosed in angle brackets.

A slightly more complex example of N-Triples can be seen in Example 2-2. In this example, four triples are given for one subject, which in this case happens to be a blank node. Since nodes without labels are not allowed in N-Triples format, the RDF parser (NTriple, included with the ARP parser discussed in Chapter 7) generated an identifier to represent the subject in each triple.

Example 2-2. N-Triples output with generated blank node identifier

```
_:j0 <http://www.w3.org/1999/02/22-rdf-syntax-ns#subject> <http://www.webreference.com/
dhtml/hiermenus> .

_:j0 <http://www.w3.org/1999/02/22-rdf-syntax-ns#predicate> <http://burningbird.net/
schema/Contains> .

_:j0 <http://www.w3.org/1999/02/22-rdf-syntax-ns#object>
"Tutorials and source code about creating hierarchical menus in DHTML" .

_:j0 <http://www.w3.org/1999/02/22-rdf-syntax-ns#type>
<http://www.w3.org/1999/02/22-rdf-syntax-ns#Statement> .

_:j0 <http://burningbird.net/schema/recommendedBy> "Shelley Powers" .
```

Talking RDF: Lingo and Vocabulary

Right at this moment, you have enough understanding of the RDF graph to progress into the RDF/XML syntax in the next chapter. However, if you follow any of the conversations related to RDF, some terms and concepts might cause confusion. Before ending this chapter on the RDF graph, I thought I would spend some time on these potentially confusing concepts.

Graphs and Subgraphs

In any RDF graph, a *subgraph* of the graph would be a subset of the triples contained in the graph. As I said earlier, each triple is uniquely its own RDF graph, in its own right, and can actually be modeled within a separate directed graph. In Figure 2-3, the triple represented by the following is a subgraph of the entire set of N-Triples representing the entire graph:

```
<http://burningbird.net/articles/monsters3.htm> <http://burningbird.net/postcon/
elements/1.0/title> "Architeuthis Dux"
```

Taking this concept further, a union of two or more RDF graphs is a new graph, which the Model document calls a *merge* of the graphs. For instance, Figure 2-4 shows one graph containing exactly one RDF triple (one statement).

Figure 2-4. RDF graph with exactly one triple

Adding the following triple results in a new merged graph, as shown previously in Figure 2-3. Since both triples share the same subject, as determined by the URI, the mergence of the two attaches the two different triples to the same subject:

```
<http://burningbird.net/articles/monsters3.htm> <http://burningbird.net/postcon/
elements/1.0/author> "Shelley Powers"
```

Now, if the subjects differed, the merged graph would still be valid—there is no rule or regulation within the RDF graph that insists that all nodes be somehow connected with one another. All the RDF graph insists on is that the triples are valid and that the RDF used with each is valid. Figure 2-5 shows an RDF graph of two merged graphs that have disconnected nodes.

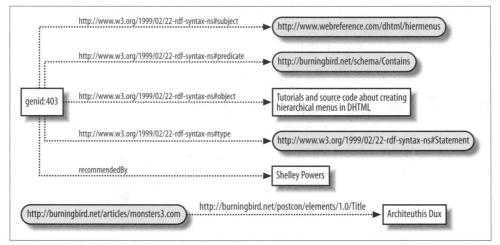

Figure 2-5. Merged RDF graph with disconnected nodes

Blank nodes are never merged in a graph because there is no way of determining whether two nodes are the same—one can't assume similarity because of artificially generated identifiers. The only components that are merged are urirefs and literals (because two literals that are syntactically the same can be assumed to be the same). In fact, when tools are given two graphs to merge and each graph contains blank nodes, each blank node is given a unique identifier in order to separate it from the others before the mergence.

Ground and Not Graph

An RDF graph is considered *grounded* if there are no blank nodes. Figure 2-4 is an example of a grounded RDF graph, while Figure 2-5 is not because of the blank node (labeled *genid:403*). Additionally, an *instance* of an RDF graph is a graph in which each blank node has been replaced by an identifier, becoming a named node. In Figure 2-5, a named node replaced the blank node; if I were to run the RDF Validator against the RDF/XML that generated this example I would get a second instance, and the names used for the blank nodes would differ. Semantically the two graphs would represent the same RDF graph but are considered separate instances of the graph.

Finally, an RDF *vocabulary* is the collection of all urirefs from a specific RDF graph. Much discussion is made of the Dublin Core vocabulary or the RSS vocabulary and so on (discussed more in Chapter 6). However, a true RDF vocabulary can differ from an official implementation of it by the very fact that the urirefs may differ between the two.

Since this is a bit confusing, for the rest of the book when I refer to an RDF vocabulary, I'm referring to a schema of a particular vocabulary, rather than any one particular implementation or document derived from it.

Entailment

Within the RDF Semantics document, *entailment* describes two graphs, which are equal in all aspects. By this I mean that every assertion made about one RDF graph can be made with equal truth about the other graph. For instance, statements made in one graph are implicitly made in the other; if you believe the statement in the first, you must, through entailment, believe the same statement in the other.

As examples of entailment, the formal term *subgraph lemma* states that a graph entails all of its subgraphs, because whatever assertions can be made about the whole graph can also be made against the subgraphs, aside from differences associated with the subgraphing process (e.g., the original graph had two statements, while the subgraph had only one). Another lemma, *instance lemma*, states that all instances of a graph are entailed by the graph—*instance* in this case an implementation of a graph in which all blank nodes have been replaced by a literal or a uriref.

Earlier I talked about merging graphs. The *merging lemma* states that the merged graph entails all the graphs that form its final construction. Another lemma, *monotonicity lemma*, states that if a subgraph of a graph entails another graph, then the original graph also entails that second graph.

 Within web specifications, one hopes not to run into terms such as *lemma*, which means "subsidiary proposition assumed to be valid and used to demonstrate a principal proposition," according to the dictionary. However, I know that the main purpose of the Semantics document within the RDF specification is to provide fairly concrete interpretations of the RDF graph theory so that implementers of the technology can provide consistent implementations. For those who primarily use RDF/XML technology rather than create parsers or RDF databases, an understanding of the pure RDF semantics isn't essential—but it is helpful, which is why I'm covering it, however lightly.

The *interpolation lemma* actually goes more into the true nature of entailment than the others, and so I'll cover it in more detail.

The interpolation lemma states:

```
S entails a graph E if and only if a subgraph of the merge of S is an instance of E.
```

This lemma basically states that you can tell whether one set of graphs entails another if you take a subgraph of the mergence of the graphs, replace the named nodes with blank nodes, and, if the result is an instance of the second set of graphs, the first set is said to entail them. From an editor's draft:

> "To tell whether a set of RDF graphs entails another, check that there is some instance of the entailed graph which is a subset of the merge of the original set of graphs."

Oversimplification aside, what's important to realize about entailment is that it's not the same thing as equality. Equality is basically two graphs that are identical, even down to the same named nodes. Entailment implies something a little more sophisticated—that the semantics of an RDF construct as shown in a specific implementation of a graph map to that which is defined within the formal semantics of the model theoretic viewpoint of the abstract RDF graph. The information in the entailed graph is the same as the information in the other but may have a different physical representation. It is entailment that allows us to construct a graph using a node-edge-node pattern and know that this instance of the RDF graph is a valid one, and that whatever semantic constraints exist within the model theoretic viewpoint of RDF also exist within this real-world instance of RDF. Additionally, entailment allows different manipulations of the data in the graphs, as long as the original information is preserved.

## CHAPTER 3

The Basic Elements Within the RDF/XML Syntax

The usability of RDF is heavily dependent on the portability of the data defined in the RDF models and its ability to be interchanged with other data. Unfortunately, recording the RDF data in a graph—the default RDF documentation format—is not the most efficient means of storing or retrieving this data. Instead, transporting RDF data, a process known as *serialization*, usually occurs with RDF/XML.

Originally, the RDF model and the RDF/XML syntax were incorporated into one document, the Resource Description Framework (RDF) Model and Syntax Specification. However, when the document was updated, the RDF model was separated from the document detailing the RDF/XML syntax. Chapter 2 covered the RDF abstract model, graph, and semantics; this chapter provides a general introduction to the RDF/XML model and syntax (RDF M&S).

The original RDF M&S Specification can be found at *http://www.w3. org/TR/REC-rdf-syntax/*. The updated RDF/XML Syntax Specification (revised) can be found at *http://www.w3.org/TR/rdf-syntax-grammar/*.

Some RDF-specific aspects of RDF/XML at first make it seem overly complex when compared to non-RDF XML. However, keep in mind that RDF/XML is nothing more than well-formed XML, with an overlay of additional constraints that allow for easier interchange, collection, and mergence of data from multiple models. In most implementations, RDF/XML is parsable with straight XML technology and can be manipulated manually if you so choose. It's only when the interchangeability of the data is important and the data can be represented only by more complex data structures and relationships that the more formalized elements of RDF become necessary. And in those circumstances, you'll be glad that you have the extra capability.

All examples listed in the chapter are validated using the W3C's RDF Validator, located at *http://www.w3.org/RDF/Validator/*.

Serializing RDF to XML

Serialization converts an object into a persistent form. The RDF/XML syntax provides a means of documenting an RDF model in a text-based format, literally *serializing* the model using XML. This means that the content must both meet all requirements for well-formed XML and the additional constraints of RDF. However, before showing you some of these constraints, let's walk through an example of using RDF/XML.

 RDF doesn't require XML-style validity, just well-formedness. RDF/XML parsers and validators do not use DTDs or XML Schemas to ensure that the XML used is valid. Norman Walsh wrote a short article for *xml.com* on what it means for an XML document to be well formed and/or valid; it explains the two concepts in more detail. See it at *http://www.xml.com/pub/a/98/10/guide3.html*.

In Chapter 2, I discussed an article I wrote on the giant squid. Now, consider attaching context to it. Among the information that could be exposed about the article is that it explores the idea of the giant squid as a legendary creature from myths and lore; it discusses the current search efforts for the giant squid; and it provides physical characteristics of the creature. Putting this information into a paragraph results in the following:

```
The article on giant squids, titled "Architeuthis Dux," at
http://burningbird.net/articles/monsters3.htm, written by Shelley Powers, explores
the giant's squid's mythological representation as the legendary Kraken as well
as describing current efforts to capture images of a live specimen. In addition,
the article also provides descriptions of a giant squid's physical
characteristics. It is part of a four-part series, described at
http://burningbird.net/articles/monsters.htm and entitled "A Tale of Two
Monsters."
```

Reinterpreting this information into a set of statements, each with a specific predicate (property or fact) and its associated value, I come up with the following list:

- The article is uniquely identified by its URI, `http://burningbird.net/articles/monsters3.htm`.
- The article was written by Shelley Powers—predicate is *written by*, value is *Shelley Powers*.
- The article's title is "Architeuthis Dux"—predicate is *title*, value is *Architeuthis Dux*.
- The article is one of a four-part series—predicate is *series member*, value is *http://burningbird.net/articles/monsters.htm*.
- The series is titled "A Tale of Two Monsters"—series predicate is *title*, value is *A Tale of Two Monsters*.

- The article associates the giant squid with the legendary Kraken—predicate is *associates*, value is *Kraken and giant squid.*

- The article provides physical descriptions of the giant squid—predicate is *provides*, value is *physical description of giant squid.*

 You'll notice in this chapter and elsewhere in the book that I tend to use *RDF statement* and *RDF triple* seemingly interchangeably. However, I primarily use *RDF statement* when referring to the particular fact being asserted by an RDF triple and use *RDF triple* when referring to the actual, physical instantiation of the statement in RDF triple format.

Starting small, we'll take a look at mapping the article and the author and title, only, into RDF. Example 3-1 shows this RDF mapping, wrapped completely within an XML document.

Example 3-1. Preliminary RDF of giant squid article

```
<?xml version="1.0"?>
<rdf:RDF
  xmlns:rdf="http://www.w3.org/1999/02/22-rdf-syntax-ns#"
  xmlns:pstcn="http://burningbird.net/postcon/elements/1.0/">
  <rdf:Description rdf:about="http://burningbird.net/articles/monsters3.htm">
    <pstcn:author>Shelley Powers</pstcn:author>
    <pstcn:title>Architeuthis Dux</pstcn:title>
  </rdf:Description>
</rdf:RDF>
```

Tracing the XML from the top, the first line is the traditional XML declaration line. Following it is the RDF element, rdf:RDF, used to enclose the RDF-based content.

 If the fact that the content is RDF can be determined from the context of the XML, the containing RDF element isn't necessary and can be omitted. In addition, the RDF content can be embedded within another document, such as an XML or HTML document, as will be discussed later in the section titled "RDF/XML: Separate Documents or Embedded Blocks."

Contained as attributes within the RDF element is a listing of the namespaces that identify the vocabulary for each RDF element. The first, with an rdf prefix, is the namespace for the RDF syntax; the second, with a prefix of pstcn, identifies elements I've created for the example RDF in this book. The namespace references an existing schema definition (see more on RDF Schemas in Chapter 5), but the schema itself doesn't have to exist on the Web, because it's not used for validation. However, as you will see in Chapter 5, there is good reason to physically create the RDF Schema document in the location given in the namespace URI.

In the example, after the enclosing `rdf:RDF` element is the RDF *Description*. An RDF Description begins with the opening RDF Description tag, `rdf:Description`, which in this case includes an attribute (`rdf:about`) used to identify the resource (the subject). The resource used within the specific element could be an identifier to a resource defined elsewhere in the document or the URI for the subject itself. In the example, the resource identifier is the URI for the giant squid article page.

The RDF Description wraps one or more resource predicate/object pairs. The predicate objects (the values) can be either literals or references to another resource. Regardless of object type, each RDF statement is a complete triple consisting of subject-predicate-object. Figure 3-1 shows the relationship between the RDF syntax and the RDF trio from the example.

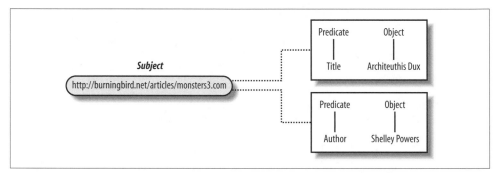

Figure 3-1. An example of two RDF statements, each with the same subject (resource), as well as a mapping between statement elements and values

As you can see, a complete RDF statement consists of the resource, a predicate, and its value. In addition, as the figure shows, resources can be described by more than one property (in RDF parlance, the subject can participate in more than one RDF statement within the document).

Running Example 3-1 through the RDF Validator results in a listing of N-Triples in the form of subject, predicate, and object:

```
<http://dynamicearth.com/articles/monsters3.htm>
            <http://burningbird.net/postcon/elements/1.0/author> "Shelley Powers"
    .
<http://dynamicearth.com/articles/monsters3.htm>
            <http://burningbird.net/postcon/elements/1.0/title> "Architeuthis Dux"
    .
```

The N-Triples representation of each RDF statement shows the formal identification of each predicate, as it would be identified within the namespace schema.

The validator also provides a graphic representation of the statement as shown in Figure 3-2. As you can see, the representation matches that shown in Figure 3-1— offering validation that the model syntax used does provide a correct representation of the statements being modeled.

Figure 3-2. RDF Validator–generated directed graph of Example 3-1

In Example 3-1, the objects are literal values. However, there is another resource described in the original paragraph in addition to the article itself: the series the article is a part of, represented with the URI `http://burningbird.net/articles/monsters.htm`. The series then becomes a new resource in the model but is still referenced as a property within the original article description.

To demonstrate this, in Example 3-2 the RDF has been expanded to include the information about the series, as well as to include the additional article predicate/object pairs. The modifications to the original RDF/XML are boldfaced.

Example 3-2. Expanded version of the giant squid RDF

```
<?xml version="1.0"?>
<rdf:RDF
  xmlns:rdf="http://www.w3.org/1999/02/22-rdf-syntax-ns#"
  xmlns:pstcn="http://burningbird.net/postcon/elements/1.0/">

<rdf:Description rdf:about="http://burningbird.net/articles/monsters3.htm">
    <pstcn:author>Shelley Powers</pstcn:author>
    <pstcn:title>Architeuthis Dux</pstcn:title>
    <pstcn:series rdf:resource="http://burningbird.net/articles/monsters.htm" />
    <pstcn:contains>Physical description of giant squids</pstcn:contains>
    <pstcn:alsoContains>Tale of the Legendary Kraken</pstcn:alsoContains>
</rdf:Description>

<rdf:Description rdf:about="http://burningbird.net/articles/monsters.htm">
    <pstcn:seriesTitle>A Tale of Two Monsters</pstcn:seriesTitle>
</rdf:Description>
</rdf:RDF>
```

The `rdf:resource` attribute within the `pstcn:series` predicate references a resource object, in this case one that's defined later in the document and which has a predicate of its own, `pstcn:seriesTitle`. Though the statements for the linked resource are separate from the enclosed statements in the original resource within the RDF/XML, the RDF graph that's generated in Figure 3-3 shows the linkage between the two.

The linked resource could be nested directly within the original resource by enclosing it within the original resource's `rdf:Description` element, in effect nesting it within the original resource description. Example 3-3 shows the syntax for the example after this modification has been applied. As you can see with this XML, the second resource being referenced within the original is more apparent using this approach, though the two result in equivalent RDF models.

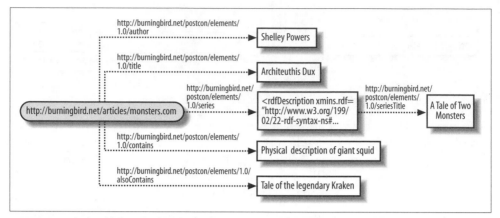

Figure 3-3. Using rdf:resource to set an object to another resource

Example 3-3. Expanded RDF modified to use nested resources

```
<?xml version="1.0"?>
<rdf:RDF
  xmlns:rdf="http://www.w3.org/1999/02/22-rdf-syntax-ns#"
  xmlns:pstcn="http://burningbird.net/postcon/elements/1.0/">
  <rdf:Description rdf:about="http://burningbird.net/articles/monsters3.htm">
    <pstcn:author>Shelley Powers</pstcn:author>
    <pstcn:title>Architeuthis Dux</pstcn:title>
    <pstcn:series>
      <rdf:Description rdf:about=
                    "http://burningbird.net/articles/monsters.htm">
        <pstcn:SeriesTitle>A Tale of Two Monsters</pstcn:SeriesTitle>
      </rdf:Description>
    </pstcn:series>
    <pstcn:contains>Physical description of giant squids</pstcn:contains>
    <pstcn:alsoContains>Tale of the Legendary Kraken</pstcn:alsoContains>
  </rdf:Description>
</rdf:RDF>
```

Though nesting one resource description in another shows the connection between the two more clearly, I prefer keeping them apart—it allows for cleaner RDF documents in my opinion. If nesting becomes fairly extreme—a resource is an object of another resource, which is an object of another resource, and so on—trying to represent all of the resources in a nested manner soon becomes unreadable (though automated processes have no problems with it).

Example 3-3 demonstrates a fundamental behavior with RDF/XML: subjects and predicates occur in layers, with subjects separated from other subjects by predicates and predicates separated from other predicates by subjects. Subjects are never nested directly within subjects, and predicates are never nested directly within predicates. This RDF/XML *striping* is discussed next.

Striped Syntax

In a document titled "RDF: Understanding the Striped RDF/XML Syntax" (found at *http://www.w3.org/2001/10/stripes/*), the author, Dan Brickley, talks about a specific pattern of node-edge-node that forms a striping pattern within RDF/XML. This concept has been included in the newer Syntax document as a method of making RDF/XML a little easier to read and understand.

If you look at Figure 3-3, you can see this in the thread that extends from the subject (`http://burningbird.net/articles/monsters3.htm`) to the predicate (`pstcn:series`) to the object, which is also a resource (`http://burningbird.net/articles/monsters.htm`) to another predicate (`pstcn:seriesTitle`) to another object, a literal in this case (`A Tale of Two Monsters`). In this thread, no two predicates are nested directly within each other. Additionally, all nodes (subject or object) are separated by an arc—a predicate—providing a node-arc-node-arc-node... pattern.

Within RDF/XML this becomes particularly apparent when you highlight the predicates and their associated objects within the XML. Example 3-3 is replicated in Example 3-4, except this time the predicate/objects are boldfaced to make them stand out.

Example 3-4. Expanded RDF modified to use nested resources, predicates bolded to make them stand out

```
<?xml version="1.0"?>
<rdf:RDF
  xmlns:rdf="http://www.w3.org/1999/02/22-rdf-syntax-ns#"
  xmlns:pstcn="http://burningbird.net/postcon/elements/1.0/">

  <rdf:Description rdf:about="http://burningbird.net/articles/monsters3.htm">
    <pstcn:author>Shelley Powers</pstcn:author>
    <pstcn:title>Architeuthis Dux</pstcn:title>
    <pstcn:series>
      <rdf:Description rdf:about=
                    "http://dynamicearth.com/articles/monsters.htm">
        <pstcn:seriesTitle>A Tale of Two Monsters</pstcn:seriesTitle>
      </rdf:Description>
    </pstcn:series>
    <pstcn:contains>Physical description of giant squids</pstcn:contains>
    <pstcn:alsoContains>Tale of the Legendary Kraken</pstcn:alsoContains>
  </rdf:Description>

</rdf:RDF>
```

Viewed in this manner, you can see the striping effect, whereby each predicate is separated by a resource, each resource by a predicate. This maps to the node-arc-node pattern established in the abstract RDF model based on directed graphs. This visualization clue can help you read RDF/XML more easily and allow you to differentiate between predicates and resources.

Another convention, though it isn't a requirement within the RDF specifications, is that all predicates (properties) start with lowercase (such as title, author, and alsoContains), and all classes start with an uppercase. However, in the examples just shown, other than the classes defined within the RDF Schema (such as Description), there is no implementation-specific class. Most of the XML elements present are RDF/XML properties. Later we'll see how to formally specify the PostCon classes within the RDF/XML.

Predicates

As you've seen in the examples, a predicate value (object) can be either a resource or a literal. If the object is a resource, an oval is drawn around it; otherwise, a rectangle is drawn. RDF parsers (and the RDF Validator) know which is which by the context of the object itself. However, there is a way that you can specifically mark the type of property—using the rdf:parseType attribute.

By default, all literals are plain literals and can be strings, integers, and so on. Their format would be the string value plus an optional xml:language. However, you can also embed XML within an RDF document by using the rdf:parseType attribute set to a value of "Literal". For instance, Example 3-5 shows the RDF/XML from Example 3-4, but in this case the pstcn:alsoContains predicate has an XML-formatted value.

Example 3-5. RDF/XML demonstrating use of rdf:parseType

```
<?xml version="1.0"?>
<rdf:RDF
  xmlns:rdf="http://www.w3.org/1999/02/22-rdf-syntax-ns#"
  xmlns:pstcn="http://burningbird.net/postcon/elements/1.0/">

  <rdf:Description rdf:about="http://burningbird.net/articles/monsters3.htm">
    <pstcn:author>Shelley Powers</pstcn:author>
    <pstcn:title>Architeuthis Dux</pstcn:title>
    <pstcn:series>
      <rdf:Description rdf:about=
                       "http://dynamicearth.com/articles/monsters.htm">
        <pstcn:seriesTitle>A Tale of Two Monsters</pstcn:seriesTitle>
      </rdf:Description>
    </pstcn:series>
    <pstcn:contains>Physical description of giant squids</pstcn:contains>
    <pstcn:alsoContains rdf:parseType="Literal">
                        <h1>Tale of the Legendary Kraken
                        </h1></pstcn:alsoContains>
  </rdf:Description>

</rdf:RDF>
```

Without the `rdf:parseType="Literal"` attribute, the RDF/XML wouldn't be valid. Running the text through the RDF Validator results in the following error:

```
Error: {E202} Expected whitespace found: &apos;Tale of the Legendary Kraken&apos;.
[Line = 17, Column = 69
```

Specifically, `rdf:parseType="Literal"` is a way of embedding XML directly into an RDF/XML document. When used, RDF processors won't try to parse the element for additional RDF/XML when it sees the XML tags. If you used `rdf:parseType="Literal"` with `series`, itself, the RDF parser would place the literal value of the `rdf:Description` block within a rectangle, rather than parse it out. You'd get a model similar to that shown in Figure 3-4

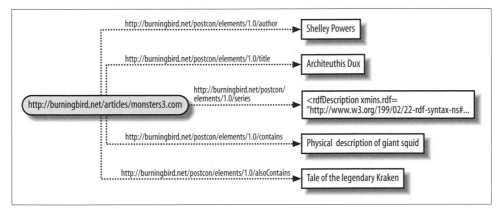

Figure 3-4. Using rdf:parseType of "Literal" for a property surrounding an RDF:Description block

Another `rdf:parseType` option, `"Resource"`, identifies the element as a resource without having to use `rdf:about` or `rdf:ID`. In other words, the surrounding `rdf:Description` tags would not be necessary:

```
<rdf:Description rdf:about="http://burningbird.net/articles/monsters3.htm">
    <pstcn:series rdf:parseType="Resource">
        <pstcn:seriesTitle>A Tale of Two Monsters</pstcn:seriesTitle>
    </pstcn:series>
...
</rdf:Description>
```

The RDF/XML validates, and the RDF Validator creates an oval for the property. However, it would add a generated identifier in the oval, because the resource is a blank node. There is no place to add a URI for the object in the bubble, because there is no resource identifier for the series property. You can list the `seriesTitle` directly within the series property, and the property would be attached to it in the RDF graph. But there would be no way to attach a URI to the resource—it would remain as a blank node.

The `rdf:parseType` property can be used to mark a property as `"Resource"`, even if there is no property value given yet. For instance, in Example 3-6, the property is marked as `"Resource"`, but no value is given.

Example 3-6. RDF/XML demonstrating use of rdf:parseType

```
<?xml version="1.0"?>
<rdf:RDF
  xmlns:rdf="http://www.w3.org/1999/02/22-rdf-syntax-ns#"
  xmlns:pstcn="http://burningbird.net/postcon/elements/1.0/">
  <rdf:Description rdf:about="http://burningbird.net/articles/monsters3.htm">
    <pstcn:author rdf:parseType="Resource" />
  </rdf:Description>

</rdf:RDF>
```

This approach can be used to signify that the object value isn't known but is none-theless a valid property. Within the RDF directed graph resulting from this RDF/XML, an oval with a generated identifier is drawn to represent the object, as shown in Figure 3-5.

Figure 3-5. RDF directed graph of model containing "Resource" object with no value provided

Namespaces and QNames

An important goal of RDF is to record knowledge in machine-understandable for-mat and then provide mechanisms to facilitate the combination of the data. By allowing combinations of multiple models, additions can be incorporated without necessarily impacting an existing RDF Schema. To ensure that RDF/XML data from different documents and different specifications can be successfully merged, namespace support has been added to the specification to prevent element collision. (Element collision occurs when an element with the same name is identified in two different schemas used within the same document.)

 Read more on XML namespaces in the document "Namespaces in XML" at *http://www.w3.org/TR/1999/REC-xml-names-19990114/*. You may also want to explore the commentary provided in "XML Namespace Myths Exploded," available at *http://www.xml.com/pub/a/2000/03/08/namespaces/index.html*.

To add namespace support to an RDF/XML document, a namespace attribute can be added anywhere in the document; it is usually added to the RDF tag itself, if one is used. An example of this would be:

```
<rdf:RDF
  xmlns:rdf="http://www.w3.org/1999/02/22-rdf-syntax-ns#"
  xmlns:pstcn="http://burningbird.net/postcon/elements/1.0/">
```

In this XML, two namespaces are declared—the RDF/XML syntax namespace (a requirement) and the namespace for the PostCon vocabulary. The format of namespace declarations in RDF/XML usually uses the following format:

```
xmlns:name="URI of schema"
```

The name doesn't have to be provided if the namespace is assumed to be the default (no prefix is used) within the document:

```
xmlns="URI of schema"
```

The namespace declaration for RDF vocabularies usually points to the URI of the RDF Schema document for the vocabulary. Though there is no formalized checking of this document involved in RDF/XML—it's not a DTD—the document should exist as documentation for the schema. In particular, as we'll see in later chapters, this schema is accessed directly by tools and utilities used to explore and view RDF/XML documents.

An element that has been known to generate a great deal of conversation within the RDF/XML and XML community is the *QName*—a namespace prefix followed by a colon (:) followed by an XML local name. In the examples shown so far, all element and attribute names have been identified using the QName, a requirement within RDF/XML. An example use of a QName is:

```
<rdf:Description rdf:about="http://burningbird.net/articles/monsters3.htm">
  <pstcn:author rdf:parseType="Literal" />
</rdf:Description>
```

In this example, the QName for the RDF Description class and the about and rdf: parseType attributes is rdf, a prefix for the RDF syntax URI, given earlier. The QName for the author element is pstcn, the PostCon URI prefix.

The actual prefix used, such as rdf and pstcn, can vary between documents, primarily because automated processes replace the prefix with the full namespace URI when processing the RDF data. However, by convention, the creators of a vocabulary usually set the particular prefix used, and users of the vocabulary are encouraged to use the same prefix for consistency. This makes the RDF/XML documents easier for humans to read.

In particular, the prefix for the RDF Syntax Schema is usually given as rdf, the RDF Schema is given as rdfs, and the Dublin Core schema (described in Chapter 6) is usually abbreviated as dc. And of course, PostCon is given as pstcn.

Earlier I mentioned that the QName is controversial. The reason is twofold:

First, the RDF specification requires that all element and attribute types in RDF/XML must be QNames. Though the reason for this is straightforward—allowing multiple schemas in the same document—the rule was not established with the very first releases of RDF/XML, and there is RDF/XML in use today, such as in Mozilla, (described in Chapter 14), in which attributes such as about are not decorated with the namespace prefix.

In order to ensure that these pre-existing applications don't break, the RDF Working Group has allowed some attributes to be non-namespace annotated. These attributes are:

- `ID`
- `bagID` (removed from the specification based on last call comments)
- `about`
- `resource`
- `parseType`
- `type`

When encountered, RDF/XML processors are required to expand these attributes by concatenating the RDF namespace to the attribute. Though these nonannotated attributes are allowed for backward compatibility, the WG (and yours truly) strongly recommend that you use QNames with your attributes. In fact, RDF/XML parsers may give a warning (but not an error) when these are used in a document. The only reason I include these nonannotated attributes in the book is so that you'll understand why these still validate when you come upon them in older uses of RDF/XML.

Another controversy surrounding QNames is their use as attribute values: specifically, using them as values for `rdf:about` or `rdf:type`. Example 3-7 shows an earlier version of the RDF/XML vocabulary used for demonstrations throughout the book and uses a QName for a attribute value. QName formatting is boldfaced in the example.

Example 3-7. Demonstrations of QName attribute values

```
<?xml version="1.0"?>
<rdf:RDF
  xmlns:rdf="http://www.w3.org/1999/02/22-rdf-syntax-ns#"
  xmlns:bbd="http://www.burningbird.net/schema#">
  <rdf:Description rdf:about="http://www.burningbird.net/identifier/tutorials/xul.htm">
    <bbd:bio rdf:resource="bbd:bio"/>
    <bbd:relevancy rdf:resource="bbd:relevancy" />
  </rdf:Description>

  <rdf:Description rdf:about="bbd:bio">
    <bbd:Title>YASD Does Mozilla/Navigator 6.0</bbd:Title>
    <bbd:Description>Demonstrations of using XUL for interface development
    </bbd:Description>
    <bbd:CreationDate>May 2000</bbd:CreationDate>
    <bbd:ContentAuthor>Shelley Powers</bbd:ContentAuthor>
    <bbd:ContentOwner>Shelley Powers</bbd:ContentOwner>
    <bbd:CurrentLocation>N/A</bbd:CurrentLocation>
  </rdf:Description>

  <rdf:Description rdf:about="bbd:relevancy">
    <bbd:CurrentStatus>Inactive</bbd:CurrentStatus>
    <bbd:RelevancyExpiration>N/A</bbd:RelevancyExpiration>
```

Example 3-7. Demonstrations of QName attribute values (continued)

```
    <bbd:Dependencies>None</bbd:Dependencies>
  </rdf:Description>

</rdf:RDF>
```

Running this example through the RDF Validator results in a perfectly good RDF graph and no errors or warnings. Many tools also have no problems with the odd use of QName. Apply this practice in your RDF/XML vocabulary, though, and you'll receive howls from the RDF community—this is a bad use of QNames, though not necessarily a specifically stated *invalid* use of them. The relationship between QNames and URIs is still not completely certain.

RDF Blank Nodes

It would be easy to extrapolate a lot of meaning about blank nodes but, bottom line, a blank node represents a resource that isn't currently identified. As with the infamous null value from the relational data model, there could be two reasons why the identifying URI is absent: either the value will never exist (isn't meaningful) or the value could exist but doesn't at the moment (currently missing).

Most commonly, a blank node—known as a *bnode*, or occasionally *anonymous node*—is used when a resource URI isn't meaningful. An example of this could be a representation of a specific individual (since most of us don't think of humans with URIs).

In RDF/XML, a blank node is represented by an oval (it is a resource), with either no value in the oval or a computer-generated identifier. The RDF/XML Validator generates an identifier, which it uses within the blank node to distinguish it from other blank nodes within the graph. Most tools generate an identifier for blank nodes to differentiate them.

In Example 3-8, bio attributes are grouped within an enclosing PostCon bio resource. Since the bio doesn't have its own URI, a blank node represents it within the model.

Example 3-8. Blank node within RDF model

```
<?xml version="1.0"?>
<rdf:RDF
  xmlns:rdf="http://www.w3.org/1999/02/22-rdf-syntax-ns#"
  xmlns:pstcn="http://burningbird.net/postcon/elements/1.0/"
  xml:base="http://burningbird.net/articles/">

  <rdf:Description rdf:about="monsters1.htm">
    <pstcn:bio>
      <rdf:Description>
        <pstcn:title>Tale of Two Monsters: Legends</pstcn:title>
```

Example 3-8. Blank node within RDF model (continued)

```
            <pstcn:description>
                Part 1 of four-part series on cryptozoology, legends,
                Nessie the Loch Ness Monster and the giant squid.
            </pstcn:description>
        <pstcn:created>1999-08-01T00:00:00-06:00</pstcn:created>
        <pstcn:creator>Shelley Powers</pstcn:creator>
    </rdf:Description>
    </pstcn:bio>
  </rdf:Description>
</rdf:RDF>
```

Running this example through the RDF Validator gives the directed graph shown in Figure 3-6 (modified to fit within the page).

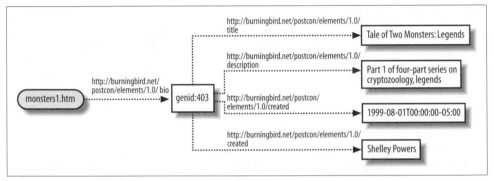

Figure 3-6. Directed graph demonstrating blank node

As you can see in the graph, the RDF Validator has generated a node identifier for the blank node, `genid:403`. This identifier has no meaning other than being a way to differentiate this blank node from other blank nodes, within the graph and within the generated N-Triples.

> Example 3-8 also uses `xml:base` to establish a base URI for the other URIs in the document, avoiding a lot of repetition. This technique is described in more detail in the next section titled "URI References."

Instead of letting the tools provide a blank node identifier, you can provide one yourself. This is particularly useful if you want to reference a resource that's not nested within the outlying element but occurs elsewhere in the page as a separate RDF/XML triple. The `rdf:nodeID` is used to provide a specific identifier, as demonstrated in Example 3-9, when the embedded `bio` is pulled out into a separate triple. The `rdf:nodeID` attribute is used within the predicate of the original triple, as well as within the description of the newly created triple, as noted in bold type.

Example 3-9. Using rdf:nodeID to identify a unique blank node

```
<?xml version="1.0"?>
<rdf:RDF
  xmlns:rdf="http://www.w3.org/1999/02/22-rdf-syntax-ns#"
  xmlns:pstcn="http://burningbird.net/postcon/elements/1.0/"
  xml:base="http://burningbird.net/articles/">

  <rdf:Description rdf:about="monsters1.htm">
    <pstcn:bio rdf:nodeID="monsters1">
    </pstcn:bio>
  </rdf:Description>

  <rdf:Description rdf:nodeID="monsters1">
    <pstcn:title>Tale of Two Monsters: Legends</pstcn:title>
    <pstcn:description>
        Part 1 of four-part series on cryptozoology, legends,
        Nessie the Loch Ness Monster and the giant squid.
    </pstcn:description>
    <pstcn:created>1999-08-01T00:00:00-06:00</pstcn:created>
    <pstcn:creator>Shelley Powers</pstcn:creator>
  </rdf:Description>
</rdf:RDF>
```

The `rdf:nodeID` is unique to the document but not necessarily to all RDF/XML documents. When multiple RDF models are combined, the tools used could redefine the identifier in order to ensure that it is unique. The `rdf:nodeID` is *not* a way to provide a global identifier for a resource in order to process it mechanically when multiple models are combined. If you need this type of functionality, you're going to want to give the resource a formal URI, even if it is only a placeholder URI until a proper one can be defined.

As noted in the RDF Syntax Specification document, nodeID is unique to RDF/XML only, and does not have any representation within the RDF abstract model. It's a tool to help people work with RDF/XML; not part of the RDF model.

URI References

All predicates within RDF/XML are given as URIs, and most resources—other than those that are treated as blank nodes—are also given URIs. A basic grounding of URIs was given in Chapter 2, but this section takes a look at how URIs are used within the RDF/XML syntax.

Resolving Relative URIs and xml:base

Not all URI references in a document are full URIs. It's not uncommon for relative URI references to be given, which then need to be resolved to a base URI location. In the previous examples, the full resource URI is given within the `rdf:about` attribute.

Instead of using the full URI, the example could be a relative URI reference, which resolves to the base document concatenated with the relative URI reference. In the following, the relative URI reference "#somevalue.htm":

```
<rdf:Description rdf:about="#somevalue">
```

then becomes http://burningbird.net/articles/somedoc.htm#somevalue if the containing document is http://burningbird.net/articles/somedoc.htm. To resolve correctly, the relative URI reference must be given with the format of pound sign (#) followed by the reference ("#somevalue").

Normally, when a full URI is not provided for a specific resource, the owning document's URL is considered the base document for forming full URIs given relative URI references. So if the document is http://burningbird.net/somedoc.htm, the URI base is considered to be this document, and changes of the document name or URL change the URI for the resource.

With xml:base, you can specify a base document that's used to generate full URIs when given relative URI references, regardless of the URL of the owning document. This means that your URIs can be consistent regardless of document renaming and movement.

The xml:base attribute is added to the RDF/XML document, usually in the same element tag where you list your namespaces (though it can be placed anywhere). Redefining Example 3-6 with xml:base and using a relative URI reference would give you the RDF/XML shown in Example 3-10.

Example 3-10. Using xml:base to define the base document for relative URI references

```
<?xml version="1.0"?>
<rdf:RDF
  xmlns:rdf="http://www.w3.org/1999/02/22-rdf-syntax-ns#"
  xmlns:pstcn="http://burningbird.net/postcon/elements/1.0/
  xml:base="http://burningbird.net/articles/">
  <rdf:Description rdf:about="monsters3.htm">
    <pstcn:author rdf:parseType="Literal" />
  </rdf:Description>
</rdf:RDF>
```

The URI for the article, given as relative "monsters3.htm", is correctly expanded to the proper full URI of http://burningbird.net/articles/monsters3.htm.

Resolving References with rdf:ID

In the previous example, the rdf:about attribute was used to provide the URI reference. Other ways of providing a URI for a resource are to use the rdf:resource, rdf:ID, or rdf:bagID attributes. The rdf:bagID attribute is discussed in the next chapter, but we'll take a quick look at rdf:ID and rdf:resource.

Unlike the `rdf:about` attribute, which refers to an existing resource, `rdf:ID` generates a URI by concatenating the URI of the enclosing document (or the one provided by `xml:base`) to the identifier given, preceded by the relative URI # symbol. Rewriting Example 3-5 to use `rdf:ID` for the second resource results in the RDF/XML shown in Example 3-11.

Example 3-11. Using rdf:ID to provide identifier for resource

```
<?xml version="1.0"?>
<rdf:RDF
  xmlns:rdf="http://www.w3.org/1999/02/22-rdf-syntax-ns#"
  xmlns:pstcn="http://burningbird.net/postcon/elements/1.0/">

  <rdf:Description rdf:ID="monsters3.htm">
    <pstcn:author>Shelley Powers</pstcn:author>
    <pstcn:title>Architeuthis Dux</pstcn:title>
    <pstcn:series>
      <rdf:Description rdf:ID="monsters.htm">
        <pstcn:seriesTitle>A Tale of Two Monsters
               </pstcn:seriesTitle>
      </rdf:Description>
    </pstcn:series>
    <pstcn:contains>Physical description of giant squids</pstcn:contains>
    <pstcn:alsoContains>Tale of the Legendary Kraken
               </pstcn:alsoContains>
  </rdf:Description>

</rdf:RDF>
```

The generated RDF graph would show a resource giving the URI of the enclosing document, a pound sign (#), and the ID. In this case, if the enclosing document was at *http://burningbird.net/index.htm*, it would show a URI of `http://burningbird.net/index.htm#monsters3.htm`. This same effect can be given with the `rdf:about` by using a URI of `"#monsters"`.

As you can see, the URI of the resolved relative URI reference doesn't match that given previously: `http://burningbird.net/index.htm#monsters3.htm` does not match `http://burningbird.net/articles/monsters3.htm`. Based on this, I never use `rdf:ID` for actual resources; I tend to use it when I'm defining a resource that usually wouldn't have an actual URI but would have one primarily to support the required node-arc-node-arc-node nature of RDF/XML.

For example, the `pstcn:series` attribute given to the `http://burningbird.net/articles/monsters.htm` URI really doesn't exist—it's a way of showing a relationship between the article and a particular series, which has properties in its own right though it does not actually exist as a single object. Instead of using the full URI, what I could have done is use ID, as shown in Example 3-12.

Example 3-12. Using xml:base to identify the base document for all relative URI references

```
<?xml version="1.0"?>
<rdf:RDF
  xmlns:rdf="http://www.w3.org/1999/02/22-rdf-syntax-ns#"
  xmlns:pstcn="http://burningbird.net/postcon/elements/1.0/"
  xml:base="http://burningbird.net/articles/">
  <rdf:Description rdf:about="monsters3.htm">
    <pstcn:author>Shelley Powers</pstcn:author>
    <pstcn:title>Architeuthis Dux</pstcn:title>
    <pstcn:series>
      <rdf:Description rdf:ID="monsters">
        <pstcn:seriesTitle>A Tale of Two Monsters
                </pstcn:seriesTitle>
      </rdf:Description>
    </pstcn:series>
    <pstcn:contains>Physical description of giant squids</pstcn:contains>
    <pstcn:alsoContains>Tale of the Legendary Kraken
                </pstcn:alsoContains>
  </rdf:Description>
</rdf:RDF>
```

The relative URI then resolves to http://burningbird.net/articles/#monsters, forming a representation of the URI as an identifier rather than an actual URL (a misunderstanding that can occur with URI references, since not all URIs are URLs). The rdf:ID is considered to have reified the statement (i.e., formally identified the statement within the model). The discussion about reification is continued in Chapter 4.

Representing Structured Data with rdf:value

Not all data relations in RDF represent straight binary connections between resource and object value. Some data values, such as measurement, have both a value and additional information that determines how you treat that value. In the following RDF/XML:

```
<pstcn:lastEdited>18</pstcn:lastEdited>
```

the statement is ambiguous because we don't know exactly what 18 means. Is it 18 days? Months? Hours? Did a person identified by the number 18 edit it?

To represent more structured data, you can include the additional information directly in the value:

```
<pstcn:lastEdited>18 days</pstcn:lastEdit>
```

However, this type of intelligent data then requires that systems know enough to split the value from its qualifier, and this goes beyond what should be required of RDF parsers and processors. Instead, you could define a second vocabulary element to capture the qualifier, such as:

```
<pstcn:lastEdited>18</pstcn:lastEdited>
<pstcn:lastEditedUnit>day</pstcn:lastEditedUnit>
```

This works, but unfortunately, there is a disconnect between the value and the unit because the two are only indirectly related based on their relationship with the resource. So the syntax is then refined, which is where `rdf:value` enters the picture. When dealing with structured data, the `rdf:value` predicate includes the actual value of the structure—it provides a signal to the processor that the data itself is included in this field, and all other members of the structure are qualifiers and additional information about the structure.

Redefining the data would then result in:

```
<pstcn:lastEdited rdf:parseType="Resource">
    <rdf:value>18</rdf:value>
    <pstcn:lastEditedUnit>day</pstcn:lastEditedUnit>
</pstcn:lastEdited>
```

Now, not only do we know that we're dealing with structured data, we know what the actual value, the kernel of the data so to speak, is by the use of `rdf:value`. You could use your own predicate, but `rdf:value` is global in scope—it crosses all RDF vocabularies—making its use much more attractive if you're concerned about combining your vocabulary data with other data.

The rdf:type Property

One general piece of information that is consistent about an RDF resource—outside of the URI to uniquely identify it—is the resource or class type. In the examples shown thus far, this value could implicitly be `"Web Resource"` to refer to all of the resources, or could be explicitly set to `"article"` for articles. All these would be correct, depending on how generically you want to define the resource and the other properties associated with the resource. To explicitly define the resource type, you would use the RDF `rdf:type` property.

Usually the `rdf:type` property is associated at the same level of granularity as the other properties. As the resources defined using RDF in this chapter all have properties associated more specifically with an article than a web resource, the RDF type property would be `"article"` or something similar.

In the next section, covering RDF containers, we will learn that the resource type for an RDF container would be the type of container rather than the type of the contained property or resource. Again, the type is equivalent to the granularity of the resource being described, and with containers, the resource is a canister (or group) of resources or properties rather than a specific resource or property.

The value of the RDF `rdf:type` property is a URI identifying an `rdfs:Class`-typed resource (`rdfs:Class` is described in detail in Chapter 5). To demonstrate how to attach an explicit type to a resource, Example 3-13 shows the resource defined in the RDF/XML for Example 3-1, but this time explicitly defining an RDF Schema element for the resource.

Example 3-13. Demonstrating the explicit resource property type

```
<?xml version="1.0"?>
<rdf:RDF
  xmlns:rdf="http://www.w3.org/1999/02/22-rdf-syntax-ns#"
  xmlns:pstcn="http://burningbird.net/postcon/elements/1.0/">
  <rdf:Description rdf:about="http://burningbird.net/articles/monsters3.htm">
    <pstcn:Author>Shelley Powers</pstcn:Author>
    <pstcn:Title>Architeuthis Dux</pstcn:Title>
    <rdf:type rdf:resource="http://burningbird.net/postcon/elements/1.0/Article" />
  </rdf:Description>
</rdf:RDF>
```

The type property includes a resource reference for the schema element, in this case for the Article class.

Rather than formally list out an `rdf:Description` and then attach the `rdf:type` predicate to it, you can cut through all of that using an RDF/XML shortcut. Incorporating the formal syntax of the type property directly into XML, as before, the type property is treated as an embedded element of the outer resource.

Within the shortcut, the type property is created directly as the element type rather than as a generic RDF Description element. This new syntax, demonstrated in Example 3-14, leads to correct interpretation of the RDF within an XML parser.

Example 3-14. Abbreviated syntax version of type property

```
<?xml version="1.0"?>
<rdf:RDF
  xmlns:rdf="http://www.w3.org/1999/02/22-rdf-syntax-ns#"
  xmlns:pstcn="http://burningbird.net/postcon/elements/1.0/">
  <pstcn:Article rdf:about="http://burningbird.net/articles/monsters3.htm">
    <pstcn:Author>Shelley Powers</pstcn:Author>
    <pstcn:Title>Architeuthis Dux</pstcn:Title>
  </pstcn:Article>
</rdf:RDF>
```

Notice the capitalization of the first letter for Article. This provides a hint that the element is a resource, rather than a predicate type.

This shortcut approach is particularly effective in ensuring that there is no doubt as to the nature of the resource being described, especially since formally listing an `rdf:type` predicate isn't a requirement of the RDF/XML. As you'll see later, in Chapter 6, the PostCon vocabulary uses this shortcut technique to identify the major resource as a web document.

Other RDF/XML shortcuts that can help cut through some of the rather stylized RDF/XML formalisms and make the underlying model a little more opaque are described in the next section.

An RDF resource can have more than one `rdf:type` associated with it.

RDF/XML Shortcuts

An RDF/XML shortcut is just what it sounds like—an abbreviated technique you can use to record one specific characteristic of an RDF model within RDF/XML. In the last section, we looked at using a shortcut to embed a resource's type with the resource definition. Other RDF/XML shortcuts you can use include:

- Separate predicates can be enclosed within the same resource block.
- Nonrepeating properties can be created as resource attributes.
- Empty resource properties do not have to be formally defined with description blocks.

The first shortcut or abbreviated syntax—enclosing all predicates (properties) for the same subject within that subject block—is so common that it's unlikely you'll find RDF/XML files that repeat the resource for each property. However, the RDF/XML in Example 3-13 is equivalent to that shown in Example 3-15.

Example 3-15. Fully separating each RDF statement into separate XML block

```
<?xml version="1.0"?>
<rdf:RDF
  xmlns:rdf="http://www.w3.org/1999/02/22-rdf-syntax-ns#"
  xmlns:pstcn="http://burningbird.net/postcon/elements/1.0/">
  <rdf:Description rdf:about="http://dynamicearth.com/articles/monsters3.htm">
    <pstcn:author>Shelley Powers</pstcn:author>
  </rdf:Description>
  <rdf:Description rdf:about="http://burningbird.net/articles/monsters3.htm">
    <pstcn:title>Architeuthis Dux</pstcn:title>
  </rdf:Description>
</rdf:RDF>
```

If you try this RDF/XML within the RDF Validator, you'll get exactly the same model as you would with the RDF/XML from Example 3-1.

 The RDF/XML from Examples 3-1 and 3-13 also demonstrates that you can generate an RDF graph from RDF/XML, but when you then convert it back into RDF/XML from the graph, you won't always get the same RDF/XML that you started with. In this example, the graph for both RDF/XML documents would most likely reconvert back to the document shown in Example 3-1, rather than the one shown in Example 3-13.

For the second instance of abbreviated syntax, we'll again return to RDF/XML in Example 3-1. Within this document, each of the resource properties is listed within a separate XML element. However, using the second abbreviated syntax—nonrepeating properties can be created as resource attributes—properties that don't repeat and are literals can be listed directly in the resource element, rather than listed out as separate formal predicate statements.

Rewriting Example 3-1 as Example 3-16, you'll quickly see the difference with this syntactic shortcut.

Example 3-16. Original RDF/XML document rewritten using an abbreviated (shortcut) syntax

```
<?xml version="1.0"?>
<rdf:RDF
 xmlns:rdf="http://www.w3.org/1999/02/22-rdf-syntax-ns#"
 xmlns:pstcn="http://burningbird.net/postcon/elements/1.0/">
  <rdf:Description rdf:about="http://burningbird.net/articles/monsters3.htm"
    pstcn:author="Shelley Powers"
    pstcn:title="Architeuthis Dux" />
</rdf:RDF>
```

As you can see, this greatly simplifies the RDF/XML. RDF parsers interpret the XML in Examples 3-1 and 3-14 as equivalent, as you can see if you run this newer example through the RDF Validator.

There are actually two different representations of the third abbreviation type, having to do with formalizing predicate objects that are resources. In the examples, RDF resources have been identified within the <rdf:Description>...</rdf:Description> tags, using a formal striped XML syntax format, even if the resource is an object of the statement rather than the subject. However, the rdf:Description block doesn't have to be provided if the resource objects match one of two constraints.

The first constraint is that the resource object must have a URI but must not itself have predicates. It is an empty element. For instance, to record information about documents that are related to the document being described, you could use a related predicate with an rdf:resource value giving the document's URI, as shown in Example 3-17.

Example 3-17. Using rdf:resource to identify an empty resource object

```
<?xml version="1.0"?>
<rdf:RDF
  xmlns:rdf="http://www.w3.org/1999/02/22-rdf-syntax-ns#"
  xmlns:pstcn="http://burningbird.net/postcon/elements/1.0/">
  <rdf:Description rdf:about="http://burningbird.net/articles/monsters3.htm">
    <pstcn:Author>Shelley Powers</pstcn:Author>
    <pstcn:Title>Architeuthis Dux</pstcn:Title>
    <pstcn:related rdf:resource="http://burningbird.net/articles/monsters1.htm" />
  </rdf:Description>
</rdf:RDF>
```

You can also use the `rdf:resource` attribute to designate a resource that's described later in the document. This is an especially useful technique if a resource object is identified early on, but you didn't know if the object had properties itself. If you discover properties for the object at a later time, a separate `rdf:Description` can be defined for the resource object, and the properties added to it.

In Example 3-17, the related resource object is shown without properties itself. In Example 3-18, properties for this resource have been given, in this case a reason that the resource object is related to the original resource.

Example 3-18. Using rdf:resource to identify a resource that's defined later in the document

```
<?xml version="1.0"?>
<rdf:RDF
  xmlns:rdf="http://www.w3.org/1999/02/22-rdf-syntax-ns#"
  xmlns:pstcn="http://burningbird.net/postcon/elements/1.0/">
  <rdf:Description rdf:about="http://burningbird.net/articles/monsters3.htm">
    <pstcn:Author>Shelley Powers</pstcn:Author>
    <pstcn:Title>Architeuthis Dux</pstcn:Title>
    <pstcn:related rdf:resource="http://burningbird.net/articles/monsters1.htm" />
  </rdf:Description>

  <rdf:Description rdf:about="http://burningbird.net/articles/monsters1.htm">
    <pstcn:reason>First in the series</pstcn:reason>
  </rdf:Description>
</rdf:RDF>
```

Of course, this wouldn't be RDF if there weren't options in how models are serialized with RDF/XML. Another variation on using `rdf:resource` for an object resource is to identify the property object as a resource and then use the shortcut technique shown earlier—adding predicates as attributes directly. With this, you wouldn't need to define a separate `rdf:Description` block just to add the related property's reason. In fact, Example 3-19 shows all of the shortcut techniques combined to simplify one RDF/XML document.

Example 3-19. RDF/XML document demonstrating all RDF/XML shortcuts

```
<?xml version="1.0"?>
<rdf:RDF
  xmlns:rdf="http://www.w3.org/1999/02/22-rdf-syntax-ns#"
  xmlns:pstcn="http://burningbird.net/postcon/elements/1.0/">
  <pstcn:Article
    pstcn:author="Shelley Powers"
    pstcn:title="Architeuthis Dux"
    rdf:about="http://dynamicearth.com/articles/monsters3.htm" >
    <pstcn:related rdf:resource="http://burningbird.net/articles/monsters1.htm"
        pstcn:reason="First in the series" />
  </pstcn:Article>

</rdf:RDF>
```

Again, running this example through the validator results in a graph that's identical to that given if more formalized RDF/XML were used, as shown in Figure 3-7.

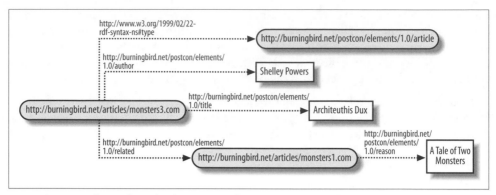

Figure 3-7. RDF directed graph of RDF/XML document created using shortcut techniques shown in Example 3-19

Which syntax should you use, formal or shortcut? According to the W3C Syntax Specification (revised), applications that can generate, query, or consume RDF are expected to support both the formal syntax and the abbreviated syntax, so you should be able to use both, either separately or together. The abbreviated syntax is less verbose, and the RDF model documented within the RDF is more clearly apparent. In fact, according to the specification, a benefit of using the abbreviated syntax is that the RDF model can be interpreted directly from the XML (with the help of some carefully designed DTDs).

What do I mean by that last statement? As an example, within the formal syntax, RDF properties are included as separate tagged elements contained within the outer RDF Description element. Opening an XML file such as this using an XML parser, such as in a browser, the properties would display as separate elements—connected to the description, true, but still showing, visibly, as separate elements.

Using the second form of the abbreviated syntax, the properties are included as attributes within the description tag and therefore don't show as separate elements. Instead, they show as descriptive attributes of the element being described, the resource. With rules and constraints enforced through a DTD, the attributes can be interpreted, directly and appropriately, within an XML document using an XML parser (not a specialized RDF parser) as a resource with given attributes (properties)— not an element with embedded, nested elements contained within an outer element.

This same concept of direct interpretation of the RDF model applies to nested resources. Using the formal syntax, a property that's also a resource is listed within a separate Description element and associated to the original resource through an identifier. An XML parser would interpret the two resources as separate elements without any visible association between the two. Using the abbreviated syntax, the resource property would be nested within the original resource's description; an XML parser would show that the resource property is a separate element, but associated with the primary resource by being embedded within the opening and closing tags of this resource.

More on RDF Data Types

RDF data types were discussed in Chapter 2, but their impact extends beyond just the RDF abstract model and concepts. RDF data types have their own XML constructs within the RDF/XML specification.

For instance, you can use the `xml:lang` attribute to specify a language for each RDF/XML element. In the examples in this English-language book, the value would be "en", and would be included within an element as follows:

```
<pstcn:reason xml:lang="en">First in the series</pstcn:reason>
```

You can find out more about `xml:lang` at *http://www.w3.org/TR/REC-xml#sec-lang-tag*.

You can also specify a general type for a predicate object with `rdf:parseType`. We've seen `rdf:parseType` of "Resource", but you can also use `rdf:parseType` of "Literal":

```
<pstcn:reason xml:lang="en" rdf:parseType="Literal"><h1>Reason</h1></pstcn:reason>
```

By using `rdf:parseType="Literal"`, you are telling the RDF/XML parser to treat the contents of a predicate as a literal value rather than parse it out for new RDF/XML elements. This allows you to embed XML into an element that is not parsed.

 Some implementations of RDF/XML specifically recommend using `rdf:parseType="Literal"` as a way of including unparsed XML within a document, to bypass having to formalize the XML into an RDF/XML valid syntax. This attribute was never intended to bypass best practices. If the data contained in the attribute is recurring, best practice would be to formalize the XML into RDF/XML and incorporate it into the vocabulary or create a new vocabulary.

RDF also allows for typed literals, which contain a reference to the data type of the literal compatible with the XML Schema data types. In the N3 notation, the typed literal would look similar to the following, as pulled from the RDF Primer:

```
ex:index.html  exterms:creation-date  "1999-08-16"^^xsd:date .
```

The format of the literal string is value (1999-08-16), data type URI (^^ in this example), and XML Schema data type (`xsd:date`).

As interesting as this format is, one could see how this approach lacks some popularity, primarily because of the intelligence built directly into the string, which can be missed depending on the XML parser that forms the basis of the RDF/XML parser. Luckily, within RDF/XML, the data type is specified as an attribute of the element, using the `rdf:datatype` attribute, as demonstrated in Example 3-20, which is a copy of Example 3-1, but with data typing added.

Example 3-20. Demonstration of typed literal in RDF/XML

```
<?xml version="1.0"?>
<rdf:RDF
```

Example 3-20. Demonstration of typed literal in RDF/XML (continued)

```
  xmlns:rdf="http://www.w3.org/1999/02/22-rdf-syntax-ns#"
  xmlns:pstcn="http://burningbird.net/postcon/elements/1.0/">
  <rdf:Description rdf:about="http://burningbird.net/articles/monsters3.htm">
    <pstcn:author rdf:datatype="http://www.w3.org/2001/XMLSchema#string">
                                            Shelley Powers</pstcn:author>
    <pstcn:title rdf:datatype="http://www.w3.org/2001/XMLSchema#string">
                                            Architeuthis Dux</pstcn:title>
  </rdf:Description>
</rdf:RDF>
```

There is no requirement to use data types with literals—it is up to not only the vocabulary designer but also those who generate instances of the vocabulary to decide if they wish to use typed literals. No implicit semantics are attached to typed literals, by which I mean toolmakers are not obliged to double-check the validity of a particular literal against its type. Additionally, there's no requirement that toolmakers even have to differentiate between the types or ensure that typed literals used in an instance map to the same typed literals for the RDF Schema of the vocabulary. Typed literals are more of a way to communicate data types between vocabulary users than between vocabulary-automated processes.

 You can read more about XML Schema built-in data types at *http://www.w3.org/TR/xmlschema-2/*. *XML.com* also has a number of articles covering XML Schema and data typing in general.

RDF/XML: Separate Documents or Embedded Blocks

By convention, RDF/XML files are stored as separate documents and given the extension of *.rdf* (just *rdf* for Mac systems). The associated MIME type for an RDF/XML document is: *application/rdf+xml*.

There's been considerable discussion about embedding RDF within other documents, such as within non-RDF XML and HTML. I've used RDF embedded within HTML pages, and I know other applications that have done the same.

The problem with embedding, particularly within HTML documents, is that it's not a simple matter to separate the RDF/XML from the rest of the content. If the RDF/XML used consists of a resource and its associated properties listed as attributes of the resource, this isn't a problem. An example of this would be:

```
  <rdf:RDF xmlns:rdf="http://www.w3.org/1999/02/22-rdf-syntax-ns#"
           xmlns:dc="http://purl.org/dc/elements/1.1/">
  <rdf:Description
      about="http://burningbird.net/cgi-bin/mt-tb.cgi?tb_id=121"
      dc:title="Good RSS"
      dc:identifier="http://weblog.burningbird.net/archives/000619.php"
```

```
        dc:subject="Technology"
        dc:description="Mark Pilgrim and Sam Ruby created an RSS Validator for us to use
    to validate our RSS feeds, and Bill Kearney was kind enough to host it. Many
    appreciations, folks. I ran the Validator against my RSS feeds (both Userland..."
        dc:creator="shelley"
        dc:date="2002-10-2209:46:26-06:00" />
    </rdf:RDF>
```

This is RDF/XML that's generated by a weblogging tool called Movable Type (found at *http://moveabletype.org*). It's used for the tool's trackback feature, which allows webloggers to notify each other when they reference each other's posts in their own.

All of the data is contained in RDF/XML element attributes. Including all of the properties as attributes means that there is no visible XML content contained within any element and therefore parsed by the HTML parser and displayed in the page—all of the data is contained in RDF/XML element attributes.

This is pretty handy, but not all RDF/XML can use the abbreviated syntax that allows us to convert RDF properties to XML attributes. In those cases, the approach I use to embed RDF within an HTML document is to include it within script tags, as demonstrated in Example 3-21.

Example 3-21. Embedding RDF in HTML script elements

```
<script type="application/rdf+xml">
<rdf:RDF xmlns:rdf="http://www.w3.org/1999/02/22-rdf-syntax-ns#"
        xmlns:trackback="http://madskills.com/public/xml/rss/module/trackback/"
        xmlns:dc="http://purl.org/dc/elements/1.1/">
<rdf:Description
    rdf:about="http://weblog.burningbird.net/fires/000805.htm"
    trackback:ping="http://burningbird.net/cgi-bin/mt-tb.cgi/304"
    dc:title="Apple&apos;s Open Core"
    dc:identifier="http://weblog.burningbird.net/fires/000805.htm"
    dc:subject="technology"
    dc:description="As happened last year with the Macworld conference, you
might as well bag writing about anything else because this week will be
Apple, Apple, Apple. Two big stories - a newer, longer TiBook and Safari,
Apple&apos;s entry into the browsing market. I liked some features of the
new TiBook such as the backlit keyboard, which I think is one of the best
ideas I&apos;ve heard with a laptop; I know I wish I had this with my
TiBook. However, I&apos;m less impressed with the length of the TiBook -
17 inches. My 15 inch works nicely, I drag it about the house and everywhere
I go with no effort. All that extra length with the new TiBook does is make
it too long for most computer carry bags. Heck, it&apos;s too long for most
laps. What Apple needs to do is incorporate all the other goodies into its
15 inch model. Including the airport, Bluetooth, the graphics card, and that
nifty backlit feature. That would be a tasty morsel, and I&apos;d be putting
up a PayPal donation button to have you all buy it for me. And the Titanium
PowerBooks are still the sexiest computer on earth. An even bigger..."
    dc:creator="yasd"
    dc:date="2003-01-08T09:34:36-06:00" />
```

Example 3-21. Embedding RDF in HTML script elements (continued)

```
</rdf:RDF>
</script>
```

The HTML parser ignores the script contents, assuming that the text/rdf content will be processed by some application geared to this data type. This approach works rather well except for one thing: it doesn't allow an HTML page to validate as XHTML. And many organizations insist that web pages validate as XHTML.

To allow the page with the embedded RDF to validate, you can then surround the contents with HTML comments:

```
<!--
RDF/XML
-->
```

Unfortunately, HTML comments are also XML comments, and any content within them tends to be ignored by most XML parsers, including RDF/XML parsers.

Until XML can be embedded into an XHTML document in such a way that allows the page to be validated, the only approach you can take for the RDF data is to include it in an external RDF document and then link the document into the XHTML page using the link element:

```
<link rel="meta" type="application/rdf+xml" title="RSS"
href="http://burningbird.net/index.rdf" />
```

Another approach is to embed the RDF/XML into the XHTML using comments but to pull this data out and feed it directly to an RDF/XML parser. It's a bit cumbersome, but doable, especially since most screen-scraping technologies such as Perl's LWP provide for finding specific blocks of data and grabbing them directly.

## CHAPTER 4

Specialized RDF Relationships: Reification, Containers, and Collections

Reification, collections, and containers deserve separate coverage from the rest of the RDF/XML syntax, primarily because these constructs have caused the most controversy and confusion. And most of this has to do with meaning.

It isn't precisely clear what is happening, for instance, when I use reification syntax within an RDF/XML document. Am I making a statement about a statement? Am I claiming a special truth for the statement? Or how about the use of a collection or container—is there an interpretation of the relationship of the items within the groups that extends beyond the fact that the items are grouped?

During the process of revamping the RDF specification, the RDF Working Group at one time actually pushed for the removal of containers because the semantics associated with them could be easily emulated using rdf:type. There was also less than general approbation for the concept of reification, which no one seemed to be quite happy with. However, the group kept containers and reification, as well as adding in collections, but with a caveat: no additional semantics are attached to these constructs other than those that carefully delimited within the RDF documentation. Any additional interpretation would then be between the RDF toolmaker and the people who built the RDF vocabularies and used the tools. However, even within this, there is common acceptance of additional semantics, particularly as semantics relate to containers; of that, one can almost be guaranteed.

In this chapter, we'll not only look more closely at the physical aspects of reification, collections, and containers, we'll also look at what they "mean," intended or otherwise.

Containers

As I was writing this book, the RDF Working Group issued a document titled "Refactoring RDF/XML Syntax" detailing modifications to the RDF Model and Syntax Specification. One of the major changes to the specification was a modification related to RDF containers, the subject of this section. However, since the recommended modifications were fairly extensive, they couldn't be covered within a note.

I rewrote this section of the book only to have the Working Group somewhat reverse itself as to the legitimacy of containers—containers would be included in the RDF/XML syntax, but their meaning would be constrained.

To ensure a proper perspective of containers, the next section contains an overview of containers as they were modeled in the original specification; a section detailing the changes from the refactoring follows. Finally, at the end I summarize containers as they are understood in the newest release of the RDF Syntax Specification.

Containers as Covered Within the Initial Specification Release

Resource properties can occur singly or in groups. To this point, we've looked at recording only individual properties, but RDF needs to record multiply occurring properties.

The creators of the RDF syntax were aware of this and created the concept of RDF Containers specifically for handling multiple resources or for handling multiple literals (properties). Each of the several types of RDF Containers has different behaviors and constraints.

 This section covers containers as implemented in the first release of the RDF Model and Syntax Specification. It's included for historical perspective and as an aid in understanding previous implementations of containers.

The first container we'll look at is `rdf:Bag`, containing unordered lists of resources or literals, with duplicate data allowed. An example of a Bag could be an inventory of photographs, whereby the sequence that the photos are listed in isn't relevant. Example 4-1 demonstrates an RDF document using a Bag.

Example 4-1. Group of photo resources contained within an RDF Bag

```
<?xml version="1.0"?>
<rdf:RDF
  xmlns:rdf="http://www.w3.org/1999/02/22-rdf-syntax-ns#"
  xmlns:pstcn="http://burningbird.net/postcon/elements/1.0/">

<rdf:Description rdf:about="http://burningbird.net/earthstars/contest.htm">
 <pstcn:photos>
  <rdf:Bag>
   <rdf:li rdf:resource="http://burningbird.net/earthstars/capo.jpg" />
   <rdf:li rdf:resource="http://burningbird.net/earthstars/baritea.jpg" />
   <rdf:li rdf:resource="http://burningbird.net/earthstars/cfluorite.jpg" />
   <rdf:li rdf:resource="http://burningbird.net/earthstars/ccinnibar.jpg" />
   <rdf:li rdf:resource="http://burningbird.net/earthstars/baryto.jpg" />
   <rdf:li rdf:resource="http://burningbird.net/earthstars/cbarite2a.jpg" />
  </rdf:Bag>
```

```
  </pstcn:photos>
</rdf:Description>

</rdf:RDF>
```

Figure 4-1 shows the RDF graph for this RDF/XML.

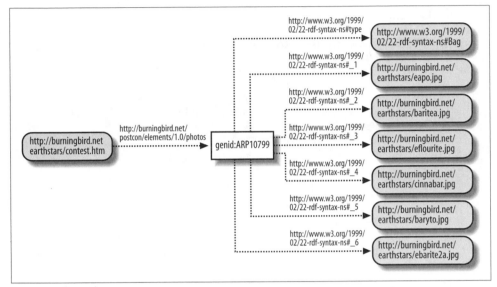

Figure 4-1. RDF graph of RDF Bag Container

Within the RDF Validator, the elements of the Bag are also given labels of _1, _2, and so on; automated processes identify each individual element in the container with an automatically generated number, preceded by an underscore (_). In addition, the validator also provides a unique identifier for the resource bubble representing the Bag of the format genid:*number*, where *number* is, again, an automatically generated number representing the resource.

In the example, the listed items within the RDF container are identified with an RDF rdf:li or list item tag, similar in semantics to the HTML li tag. Each resource is identified with a resource attribute. If the container contained literals instead of resources as items, then the format used for each item would be similar to the following:

```
<rdf:li>Barite Photo</rdf:li>
```

A second type of container is the sequence, or rdf:Seq. An rdf:Seq groups resources or literals, just as a Bag does, but unlike with rdf:Bag, the ordering of the contained elements is considered significant and is indicated by the ordering of the rdf:_n membership properties. As with rdf:Bag, duplicate resources or literals are allowed.

If you're grouping web pages within a menu on your main web page, you'll most likely want to group the pages in RDF in such a way that the order of the grouping is maintained. Using `rdf:Seq`, automated procedures can pick up the pages and add them to your menu as new resources are added. An example of the RDF file to support this is shown in Example 4-2.

Example 4-2. Group of menu resources contained within an RDF Sequence

```
<?xml version="1.0"?>
<rdf:RDF
  xmlns:rdf="http://www.w3.org/1999/02/22-rdf-syntax-ns#"
  xmlns:pstcn="http://burningbird.net/postcon/elements/1.0/">
  <rdf:Description rdf:about="http://burningbird.net/earthstars/contest.htm">
   <pstcn:menu>
     <rdf:Seq>
      <rdf:li rdf:resource="http://burningbird.net/articles.htm" />
      <rdf:li rdf:resource="http://burningbird.net/dynatech.htm" />
      <rdf:li rdf:resource="http://burningbird.net/interact.htm" />
     </rdf:Seq>
   </pstcn:menu>
  </rdf:Description>

</rdf:RDF>
```

The last container type is the Alternative container, `rdf:Alt`. This container variation provides alternatives for a specific value. An excellent use for it is a listing of expressions written in different languages, such as a greeting or label for a user interface item. The application that processes the RDF would then pick the alternative based on a locale setting for the environment in which the application is running.

The `rdf:Alt` syntax does not differ from that of the `rdf:Bag` and `rdf:Seq`, except for the element name. However, there must be at least one item within an `rdf:Alt` container, to act as the default value for the resource—the first member listed.

Earlier I mentioned that a resource identifier could be a URI or an identifier to a URI given elsewhere in the RDF document. The latter is particularly helpful when using RDF Containers, providing a way to associate information with the group of items. Example 4-3 demonstrates how this would work with the RDF shown in Example 4-2.

Example 4-3. Grouping an RDF Description and identifier to attach information to a container

```
<?xml version="1.0"?>
<rdf:RDF
  xmlns:rdf="http://www.w3.org/1999/02/22-rdf-syntax-ns#"
  xmlns:pstcn="http://burningbird.net/postcon/elements/1.0/">

  <rdf:Description rdf:about="http://burningbird.net/earthstars/contest.htm">
    <pstcn:menu>
       <rdf:Description rdf:about="#menuitems">
         <pstcn:menu>Links to additional resources</pstcn:menu>
```

```
      </rdf:Description>
    </pstcn:menu>
  </rdf:Description>

  <rdf:Seq rdf:ID="menuitems">
   <rdf:li rdf:resource="http://burningbird.net/articles.htm" />
   <rdf:li rdf:resource="http://burningbird.net/dynatech.htm" />
   <rdf:li rdf:resource="http://burningbird.net/interact.htm" />
  </rdf:Seq>

</rdf:RDF>
```

In the original container specification, the document refers to the individual container items as *referents*. To specifically associate a statement with each referent rather than with the container as a whole, the `rdf:aboutEach` attribute was to be used with the RDF Description, rather than `rdf:about`:

```
<rdf:Description aboutEach="#menuitems">
```

When this type of statement is applied to container elements, they're then referred to as *distributive referents*. Though not restricted specifically to the Bag container within the RDF syntax, the `aboutEach` attribute is usually associated with the Bag due to the unordered nature of the Bag's items.

Another RDF attribute for Bag elements is `rdf:aboutEachPrefix`. This is used to associate information about each resource within a specific directory or web location. If used with Example 4-3, it would look like this:

```
<rdf:Decription aboutEachPrefix="http://burningbird.net">
    <pstcn:phototype>JPEG</pstcn:phototype>
</rdf:Description>
```

Instead of using an RDF Container for groups of properties, you can repeat the property (the predicate), modifying the value assigned to the property (the object) with each:

```
<rdf:Description rdf:about="http://burningbird.net/articles/monsters3.htm">
    <pstcn:Contains>Physical description of giant squids</pstcn:Contains>
    <pstcn:Contains>Tale of the Legendary Kraken</pstcn:Contains>
</rdf:Description>
```

Which you use depends on whether you want to refer to the collection of items as a singular unit or not. If you do, you would use the Container; otherwise, you would most likely use the repeated property, as the syntax is simpler.

This section contained a description of containers as implemented in the original RDF Model and Syntax document. This description changed dramatically during the re-examination of the RDF specification, as detailed next.

Containers as Typed Nodes

The RDF Working Group states the following:

> On 29th June 2001, the WG decided that containers will match the typed node production in the grammar (production 6.13) and that the container-specific productions (productions 6.25 to 6.31) and any references to them be removed from the grammar. rdf:li elements will be translated to rdf:_nnn elements when they are found matching either a propertyElt (production 6.12) or a typedNode (production 6.13).

The RDF Working Group and people implementing RDF solutions had two concerns about containers: first, that the functionality represented with containers can be expressed with the typed node production, leading to confusion about which representation should be used to express a specific statement; second, that RDF applications have to have *special knowledge* of containers in order to interpret the rdf:li elements—unlike other RDF elements, rdf:li elements get translated into numbered elements with the format of _1, _2, and so on.

To deal with both of these issues, the group released a document, "Refactoring RDF/XML Syntax" (at *http://www.w3.org/TR/2001/WD-rdf-syntax-grammar-20010906/*) that recommended the removal of all special container constructs; container-like behavior will be implemented with typed node productions instead.

At first glance, this looked to be a significant change, and I was concerned about its impact on my own RDF implementations as well as this book. However, the Working Group assured us that these changes are to the specification and not necessarily changes to the syntax represented by the specification.

As contradictory as this first sounds, closer examination of the changes does reflect that, though the specification is modified, the actual syntax remains the same. This can be proven by taking a closer look at containers and reinterpreting them as typed nodes: how would something such as the container RDF in Example 4-1 fit within this newly modified syntax?

In the original specification, rdf:li elements are translated into sequentially numbered elements of the format rdf:_n—rdf:_1, rdf:_2, and so on. Within the newly modified specification, rdf:li elements are still translated into numbered elements; however, you can also specify the numbered elements directly yourself or mix elements, though the results of such mixing may be unexpected. Example 4-4 shows a modification of the RDF/XML shown in Example 4-2 that fits within the newly modified specification.

Example 4-4. Container as typed node

```
<?xml version="1.0"?>
<rdf:RDF
  xmlns:rdf="http://www.w3.org/1999/02/22-rdf-syntax-ns#"
  xmlns:pstcn="http://burningbird.net/postcon/elements/1.0/">
  <rdf:Description rdf:about="http://burningbird.net/earthstars/contest.htm">
   <pstcn:menu>
```

Example 4-4. Container as typed node (continued)

```
    <rdf:Seq>
      <rdf:_1 rdf:resource="http://burningbird.net/articles.htm" />
      <rdf:li rdf:resource="http://burningbird.net/dynatech.htm" />
      <rdf:li rdf:resource="http://burningbird.net/interact.htm" />
    </rdf:Seq>
  </pstcn:menu>
</rdf:Description>

</rdf:RDF>
```

The use of the Seq container type is still allowed; however, rather than representing a specific container construct, it now represents a typed node. The following would provide the same results:

```
<pstcn:MyBag>
   <rdf:_1 rdf:resource="http://burningbird.net/articles.htm" />
   <rdf:li rdf:resource="http://burningbird.net/dynatech.htm" />
   <rdf:li rdf:resource="http://burningbird.net/interact.htm" />
</pstcn:MyBag>
```

Implicit with both the `rdf:Seq` and the custom element is a type statement associated with the node automatically when the type attribute isn't provided.

When the RDF Validator parses Example 4-4, you might expect that the numbering of the `rdf:li` nodes would begin with `rdf_2`, following from the value set for the first contained element, `rdf:_1`. This isn't the result and won't be the result from the RDF triples associated with the test cases; numbering begins with `rdf:_1` for each grouping and isn't impacted by manual settings of the other contained and grouped elements.

How does this fit the typed node syntax? Remembering that associated with an element such as `rdf:Seq` is a type=*URI* property assignment, the following steps map the EBNF of the typed node production directly to the instance diagrammed in Example 4-4:

```
<rdf:Seq> is derived directly from '<' typeName  propAttr* '>'
      where  typeName = QName and
          QName = rdf:Seq
      where propAttr is the implicit type=URI for Seq
<rdf:_1> is derived directly from propertyElt
      where propertyElt = '<' propName idRefAttr '/>'
      where propName = QName
          QName = rdf:_1
    where   idRefAttr = resourceAttr
          resourceAttr = ' resource="' URI-Reference '"'
```

And so on for the other properties.

As you can see, the container instance does map directly to the typed node production, and there is no loss of functionality based on dropping the container-specific syntax. However, just when I was starting to become comfortable with replacing the

Container with a typed node, the Working Group reversed itself and included support for Containers—with modifications and a whole lot of annotations about "meaning."

Containers Today

Containers are included within the RDF/XML Syntax Specification, but without some of the supporting attributes, such as `rdf:aboutEach` and `rdf:aboutEachPrefix`, which have been removed from the syntax. The key to the current status of Containers is this sentence within the specification (as it existed in its Last Call state):

> RDF has a set of container membership properties and corresponding property elements that are mostly used with instances of the `rdf:Seq`, `rdf:Bag` and `rdf:Alt` classes which may be written as typed node elements.

The Container classes of `rdf:Seq`, `rdf:Bag`, and `rdf:Alt` are still in the documentation, with an understanding that these may be replaced with typed node productions. And this does impose an implication constraint on the container classes—as typed node productions, no additional semantics as to the application of containers can exist outside of what could be implied with typed nodes.

From an application perspective, containers are a grouping of related items, each of which can be given a unique list property, represented by `rdf:li` within RDF/XML, or more properly, `rdf:_n`, with the value of n representing the ordering within the container (if ordering is implied by the container, such as `rdf:Seq`). Example 4-5 is a valid use of containers, in this case an `rdf:Seq` with its intended semantic assumptions of ordering of the members of the container.

Example 4-5. "Container" implemented using custom container-like class

```
<?xml version="1.0"?>
<rdf:RDF
  xmlns:rdf="http://www.w3.org/1999/02/22-rdf-syntax-ns#"
  xmlns:pstcn="http://burningbird.net/postcon/elements/1.0/">
  <rdf:Description rdf:about="http://burningbird.net/earthstars/contest.htm">
   <pstcn:menu>
     <rdf:Seq>
      <rdf:_1 rdf:resource="http://burningbird.net/articles.htm" />
      <rdf:_2 rdf:resource="http://burningbird.net/dynatech.htm" />
      <rdf:_3 rdf:resource="http://burningbird.net/interact.htm" />
     </rdf:Seq>
   </pstcn:menu>
  </rdf:Description>

</rdf:RDF>
```

The RDF/XML in Example 4-4 could be replaced with the RDF/XML in Example 4-5, and the meaning associated with the construction would be the same; the resulting RDF graph replaces all `rdf:li` items with `rdf:_n` items based on the position of the item within the container, as shown in Figure 4-2. The `rdf:li` property is a construct of the RDF/XML syntax only and not a part of the RDF graph (or associated RDF data model).

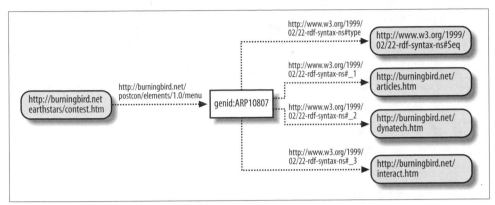

Figure 4-2. Graph of custom typed node production emulating RDF Container class

 Though `rdf:li` is used and still documented within the RDF specifications, its use is discouraged within RDF/XML documents.

There are intended but not formally described semantics associated with `rdf:Seq`—that the contained items are ordered and that the number of items in `rdf:Bag` is finite and unordered and duplicates are allowed. There are also intended but not formally described semantics with `rdf:Alt` that each item is an option, with the first item being the default if no other is specified. However, there is nothing within the RDF specification that formally requires applications heed these intended semantics, other than general consensus. In fact, the documented semantics surrounding containers are quite vague, which, in my opinion, makes the use of containers suspect. Because of this, I recommend caution when using containers.

Collections

Unlike a container, a collection is considered to be a finite grouping of items, with a given terminator. Within RDF/XML, a collection is defined through the use of `rdf:parseType="Collection"` and through listing the collected resources within the other collection block.

The use of Collection within RDF/XML is fairly straightforward and uncomplicated. Example 4-6 demonstrates how easy it is to gather together like items into one collection, just through the use of the Collection `rdf:parseType`.

On Containers and Semantics

The RDF Primer states the following about Containers:

> it is important to understand that while these types of containers are described using pre-defined RDF types and properties, any special meanings associated with these containers, e.g., that the members of an Alt container are alternative values, are only *intended* meanings. These specific container types, and their definitions, are provided with the aim of establishing a shared convention among those who need to describe groups of things. All RDF does is provide the types and properties that can be used to construct the RDF graphs to describe each type of container. RDF has no more built-in understanding of what a resource of type rdf:Bag is than it has of what a resource of type ex:Tent...

This concept of promoting intended semantics without formalization—because there is no formal entailment associated with the semantics of containers—will most likely continue to generate some confusion in the future about exactly what is meant when one uses a specific container.

Example 4-6. RDF/XML Document containing Collection with three items

```
<?xml version="1.0"?>
<rdf:RDF
  xmlns:rdf="http://www.w3.org/1999/02/22-rdf-syntax-ns#"
  xmlns:pstcn="http://burningbird.net/postcon/elements/1.0/">
  <rdf:Description rdf:about="http://dynamicearth.com/earthstars/contest.htm">
    <pstcn:menu rdf:parseType="Collection">
      <rdf:Description rdf:about="http://burningbird.net/articles.htm" />
      <rdf:Description rdf:about="http://burningbird.net/dynatech.htm" />
      <rdf:Description rdf:about="http://burningbird.net/interact.htm" />
    </pstcn:menu>
  </rdf:Description>

</rdf:RDF>
```

The extraordinary thing about Collection is the resulting RDF directed graph. One could be amazed at how the simple little addition of an rdf:parseType="Collection" could result in the rather complex model that's generated. Figure 4-3 shows what would result from this type of RDF/XML construct.

As the graph demonstrates, a collection is a list (with rdf:type of rdf:List), and each node on the list has an associated predicate of type (List) as well as the first value in the list, given by the predicate rdf:first. Additionally, there is a relationship between the nodes, with an associated rdf:predicate of rdf:rest. The list is then terminated with a node, whose value is rdf:nil.

Traversing a collection becomes a matter of finding the start and then accessing the rdf:next predicate for that node and finding the associated resource attached to it, which then points to the value associated with it, and so on.

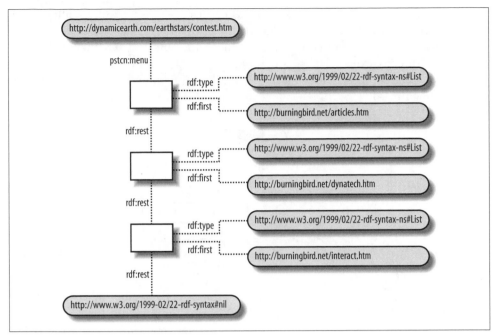

Figure 4-3. Generated RDF directed graph of a collection

As complex as this structure is, though, there are still loopholes in the semantics associated with it. For instance, one could have multiple instances of `rdf:first` within a document; however, it would require a deliberate act to create this condition, which is unlikely to happen. Again, the RDF specification enforces only some basic understanding about lists, such as (as previously mentioned) each consists of a finite number of items with a terminator (though the terminator itself could be left off). Based on this, my recommendation is that you use the RDF collection as sparingly as you would use the RDF Container—use only when no other construct matches your specific needs, and use it specifically as the specification intended it to be used. If you're unsure about the intent, then don't use it.

Now that we've had a chance to look at the various grouping constructs of RDF—and to understand the associated dangers associated with them—it's time to look at another RDF construct that's caused even more controversy and confusion: reification.

Reification: The RDF Big Ugly

In our legal system, a statement about a statement is considered hearsay and isn't admissible in a court of law. Within the Resource Description Framework (RDF), this is also true—the implied statement is considered hearsay and can't be accepted as an assertion by itself. However, the outer statement is treated as an assertion.

In a sentence such as "Jonathon says those cherries are sweet," we're really reading two statements. The first, inner statement is "Those cherries are sweet." Since we haven't tried the cherries directly, we can't judge for ourselves whether this is true. But we do directly experience the outer statement, "Jonathon says...," and we can judge this to be an assertion of fact. Graphically, this would look like the picture shown in Figure 4-4.

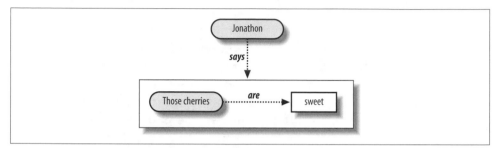

Figure 4-4. An example of a statement about a statement

Now depending on our trust in Jonathon—that he tells the truth, that his interpretation of *sweet* is the same as ours—we can infer a trust for the inner statement, "those cherries are sweet," based on our trust of the outer statement. If I run into Jonathon at a market and he says "Those cherries are sweet," and I trust Jonathon and his judgment, I might be moved to purchase some of the cherries.

This same process of validating an inner statement based on trust of the outer— validation of hearsay—formed the basis of much of the earlier communication about the RDF construct called *reification*. And it is the implied trust that has created much of the push back against it, when there is no true implied trust with reification. With reification, a statement is modeled as a resource referenced by another statement. No more, no less.

Within the RDF semantics, a statement such as the following (from the specification), is easily documented with the RDF syntax provided in Chapter 3:

```
Ora Lassila is the creator of the resource http://www.w3.org/Home/Lassila.
```

In this statement, the RDF components of subject, predicate, and object are clearly understood: the subject (resource) is `http://www.w3.org/Home/Lassila`, predicate is creator, and object is Ora Lassila.

However, attach this statement as a statement being asserted by another person:

```
Ralph Swick says that Ora Lassila is the creator of the resource
http://www.w3.org/Home/Lassila.
```

The syntax used in the examples in Chapter 3 doesn't provide a mechanism to capture this type of assertion—this statement about another statement. However, capturing this type of information is exactly what's needed when trying to assert that a statement about another statement is the fact being defined.

Statements such as "Ralph Swick says..." or "Jonathon says..." are termed metastatements; reification is a method of formally modeling a statement in such a way that it can actually be attached as a property to the new statement.

We'll take a look at how reification is handled currently within the RDF specification. Later in the chapter, we'll look at some of the discussions about reification, as well as uses of the concept.

 A difficulty associated with reification and the current RDF specification documents is that nowhere in the documents, other than the grammar productions, is the RDF/XML associated with formal reification demonstrated.

Reified Statements

Occasionally I receive emails asking me to recommend web pages that contain tutorials, technical articles, and other helpful information. Instead of answering individual emails, my preference is to post a web page with links to resources that might be of interest to folks. For instance, I'm frequently asked about creating drop-down menus in Dynamic HTML (DHTML), and I'll recommend the DHTML menu tutorials at *WebReference.com*, a very popular web site for the web developer:

```
http://www.webreference.com/dhtml/hiermenus
is a source containing tutorials and source code about
creating hierarchical menus in DHTML.
```

Mapping this recommendation into RDF/XML, I would have something similar to the following:

```
<rdf:Description rdf:about="http://www.webreference.com/dhtml/hiermenus/">
  <pstcn:Contains>Tutorials and source code about creating hierarchical
             menus in DHTML</pstcn:Contains>
</rdf:Description>
```

Now, this description is sufficient if all I want to do is describe the resource (the web page) and the context (provides tutorials and source code on creating DHTML hierarchical menus). But it's missing one thing: an assertion about who is making the recommendation (me). Remove this RDF content from my web site, and you've lost the original context of the recommendation—the person making the recommendation. Within the RDF lexicon, we're missing the statement about the statement.

To fill this gap, we need to associate the original statement to the new statement—the recommendation of the resource. To do this, we model the original statement so that it can be referenced as the subject of the newer statement. This forms the basis of reification in RDF. You can do this in a couple of different ways—using the long form or the short form of reification.

The long form of reification formally defines types—rdf:subject, rdf:predicate, and rdf:object—and makes use of a fourth, rdf:type, with a predefined value of rdf:Statement. The three new predicates capture the information about the inner statement, the statement being reified if you will. rdf:type specifies that the resource is a statement.

 As discussed in Chapter 3, rdf:type isn't limited to use within reification.

At its simplest, the outer statement is attached as a statement directly to the reified statement. Example 4-7 contains an example of this type of reification.

Example 4-7. Formal reification of a statement

```
<?xml version="1.0"?>
<rdf:RDF
  xmlns:rdf="http://www.w3.org/1999/02/22-rdf-syntax-ns#"
  xmlns:pstcn="http://burningbird.net/postcon/elements/1.0/">
  <rdf:Description rdf:about="http://burningbird.net/recommendation.htm">
    <rdf:subject rdf:resource="http://www.webreference.com/dhtml/hiermenus" />
    <rdf:predicate rdf:resource="http://burningbird.net/schema/Contains" />
    <rdf:object>Tutorials and source code about creating hierarchical menus in DHTML</rdf:object>
    <rdf:type rdf:resource="http://www.w3.org/1999/02/22-rdf-syntax-ns#Statement" />
    <pstcn:recommendedBy>Shelley Powers</pstcn:recommendedBy>
  </rdf:Description>
</rdf:RDF>
```

In this document, graphically demonstrated in Figure 4-5, a statement is being made about a resource: the resource at http://www.webreference.com/dhtml/hiermenus contains tutorials and source code about creating hierarchical menus in DHTML. Who made the statement is given in the value of the pstcn:recommendedBy predicate: Shelley Powers. However, what we're saying is that this statement about the statement, the "Shelley Powers recommends…" itself, is the assertion; we can't determine the truthfulness of the actual recommendation until we visit the site or we take my statement as truth based on the trust placed in me.

Though this is valid RDF, it isn't my preferred way of demonstrating a clear-cut separation between the reified statement and the assertion attached to that statement (demonstrating the inner and outer statements). My preferred approach for reification is to formally define a separate RDF resource for the outer statement and then attach it to the reified statement. Example 4-8 demonstrates this. The use of rdf:resource in the outer statement connects the two statements.

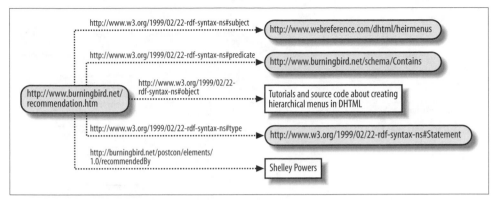

Figure 4-5. Graph showing simple example of RDF reification

Example 4-8. Providing a statement about a statement within RDF

```
<?xml version="1.0"?>
<rdf:RDF
  xmlns:rdf="http://www.w3.org/1999/02/22-rdf-syntax-ns#"
  xmlns:pstcn="http://burningbird.net/postcon/elements/1.0/"
  xml:base="http://burningbird.net/">
  <rdf:Description rdf:about="#s1">
    <rdf:subject rdf:resource="http://www.webreference.com/dhtml/hiermenus" />
    <rdf:predicate rdf:resource="http://burningbird.net/schema/Contains" />
    <rdf:object>Tutorials and source code about creating hierarchical menus
              in DHTML</rdf:object>
    <rdf:type rdf:resource="http://www.w3.org/1999/02/22-rdf-syntax-ns#Statement" />
  </rdf:Description>

  <rdf:Description rdf:about="http://burningbird.net/person/001">
    <pstcn:recommends rdf:resource="#s1" />
  </rdf:Description>
</rdf:RDF>
```

In the example, the assertion about the reified statement is formally separated out. The RDF Validator–generated graphic of the RDF is shown in Figure 4-6.

In my opinion, this RDF results in a clearer and cleaner interpretation of the "statement about a statement."

 Some RDF Validators that incorporate RDF Schema validation would likely generate warnings for the RDF graph in Figure 4-6.

Having to repeat the subject, predicate, and object statements in every instance of reification is cumbersome, so there's a short form you can use to achieve exactly the same RDF graph. And if the graphs agree, the RDF statements are guaranteed to agree.

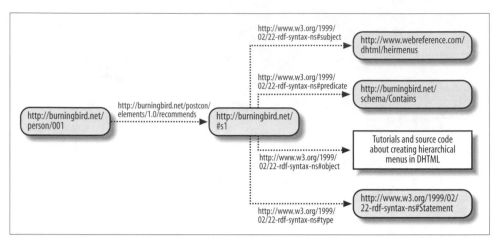

Figure 4-6. RDF Validator–generated graph of reification example

The subject, predicate, and object of the reified statement are the familiar RDF trio, but the context of their use differs with reification. With reified statements, the subject, predicate, and object attributes are formal RDF elements that, combined, also happen to be a statement. These new components are used to model the statement.

A more detailed description of these new RDF elements is:

subject
> Contains the identifier for the resource referenced within the statement

predicate
> Contains the property that forms the original context of the resource (the property)

object
> Contains the value of the property that forms the original context of the resource (the value)

type
> Contains the type of the resource—in the example, the type of RDF statement

The formal representation of reification is based on N-Triples syntax. The reification from Examples 4-1 and 4-2 could be represented as:

```
{[X], type, [RDF:Statement]}
{[X], predicate, [contains]}
{[X], subject, [http://www.webreference.com/dhtml/hiermenus]}
{[X], object, "Tutorial..."}
```

This representation strips the statement to its essential components sans XML syntax.

It's interesting that within the RDF Syntax Specification, the quad or 4-tuple representing a reified statement (subject, predicate, object, and type) is really a formalized model of our old friend, the RDF Description.

Consider for a moment that an RDF Description with at least one property is an RDF statement, containing subject, object, and predicate. This is represented by:

```
<rdf:Description rdf:about="http://www.webreference.com/dhtml/hiermenus/">
  <pstcn:Contains>Tutorials and source code about creating hierarchichal
                  menus in DHTML</pstcn:Contains>
</rdf:Description>
```

However, let's look at identifying this in "straight" XML as follows, using a custom XML vocabulary called myrdf:

```
<myrdf:element>
  <myrdf:subject>http://www.webreference.com/dhtml/hiermenus/"</myrdf:subject>
  <myrdf:predicate>Contains</myrdf:predicate>
  <myrdf:object>Tutorials and source code about
                creating hierarchical menus in DHTML</myrdf:object>
</myrdf:element>
```

As you can see, this formal modeling of RDF Description is equivalent to the syntax used to model the reified statement given earlier. Following from this, then, you could say that all asserted statements within RDF (all statements given within RDF Description elements) are reified statements, and you would be correct—sort of.

The key to understanding reification within RDF is that a reified statement isn't the statement itself, but the model of the statement. Reification isn't the process of making a statement about another statement; it's the process of formally modeling the statement.

From this example, you might be wondering why reification is necessary. After all, for this particular example, the recommendation could be attached directly as another statement about the web resource.

The Necessity of Reification and Metastatements

Why is reification necessary? One could model the example shown in Example 4-1 in serialized RDF syntax and not lose the information about who recommends the resource, as shown in Example 4-9.

Example 4-9. Using RDF/XML to model a recommendation

```
<?xml version="1.0"?>
<rdf:RDF
  xmlns:rdf="http://www.w3.org/1999/02/22-rdf-syntax-ns#"
  xmlns:pstcn="http://burningbird.net/postcon/elements/1.0/"
  <rdf:Description rdf:about="http://www.webreference.com/dhtml/hiermenus/">
    <pstcn:Contains>Tutorials and source code about creating hierarchichal
                    menus in DHTML</pstcn:Contains>
    <pstcn:recommendedBy>Shelley Powers</pstcn:recommendedBy>
  </rdf:Description>
</rdf:RDF>
```

In this document, information about the person making the recommendation is attached as an additional statement about the original subject. At first glance, the new version of the RDF syntax used to describe the recommendation seems acceptable. However, using this interpretation, key information is lost—the statement about the resource is being treated as the fact, not the recommendation itself. With something such as the following:

```
Shelley Powers recommends http://www.webreference.com/dhtml/hiermenus
as a source of tutorials and source code for hierarchical menus created in DHTML.
```

the fact being described in the RDF document is "Shelley Powers recommends...," not the actual web resource. The web resource is actually an ancillary component of the recommendation.

By being able to model the statement about the web resource, you can treat it as a property of another statement, and be able to distinguish without confusion and without ambiguity what "fact" you're describing in an RDF statement. The importance of the distinction between the thing described (the web site) and the object making the description (the person making a recommendation of the web site) is both the key and the confusion of reification.

As handy as reification is, it is a bit wordy. The next section discusses a shorthand technique that can be used to reify several statements at a time.

A Shorthand Reification Syntax

Specifying the full predicate, subject, object, and type for each reified statement isn't difficult, but it does get cumbersome after a while. Fortunately, there is a shorthand technique that you can use in place of the more formal syntax.

In Example 4-10, rather than specifying each subject, predicate, object, and type, the reified statement is identified through the rdf:ID property, and the RDF parser automatically annotates the subject, predicate, object, and type.

Example 4-10. Shorthand technique for RDF reification

```
<?xml version="1.0"?>
<rdf:RDF
  xmlns:rdf="http://www.w3.org/1999/02/22-rdf-syntax-ns#"
  xmlns:pstcn="http://burningbird.net/postcon/elements/1.0/">

  <!--The statement-->
  <rdf:Description rdf:about="http://www.webreference.com/dhtml/hiermenus">
    <pstcn:Contains rdf:ID='s1'>
    Tutorials and source code about creating hierarchical menus in DHTML</pstcn:Contains>
  </rdf:Description>

  <!--The statement about the statement-->
  <rdf:Description rdf:about="http://burningbird.net/person/001">
```

Example 4-10. Shorthand technique for RDF reification (continued)

```
  <pstcn:recommendedBy rdf:resource="#s1" />
  </rdf:Description>
```

```
</rdf:RDF>
```

This approach is cleaner to read and follow manually, and the graph is the same—almost. From an entailment point of view, though, these are the same, even though the model differs. Still, be forewarned on the use of this shortcut.

This shorthand technique is particularly helpful in circumstances other than just wanting a cleaner syntax. When you describe something, you usually don't make just one statement about the thing you're describing. For instance, if you're recommending an article, you'll usually give a description of the article, the name of the article, how to find a copy of the article, and so on.

In the recommendation example earlier, this original statement could be extended to provide the author of the web resource as well as the content:

```
Shelley Powers recommends http://www.webreference.com/dhtml/hiermenus,
written by Peter Belesis, as a source of tutorials and source code
for hierarchical menus created in DHTML.
```

In this sentence, I'm recommending a web site that contains defined material *and* is authored by a specific individual.

The formal syntactic method of modeling this statement using the 4-tuple reification syntax doesn't fit this particular data instance very well, because there's confusion about exactly what I'm recommending—the web site or the author? There is no clean way to add in the additional statements.

To demonstrate my point, I modified the RDF/XML from Example 4-7 to add the additional statement related to the author. In this example, shown in Example 4-11, I interpreted the statement to break down into a couple of different assertions:

- Shelley Powers recommends *http://www.webreference.com/dhtml/hiermenus* as a source of tutorials and source code for hierarchical menus created in DHTML.

- Shelley Powers recommends *http://www.webreference.com/dhtml/hiermenus*, which is written by Peter Belesis.

I then modified the RDF/XML to reify both statements from the same subject.

Example 4-11. An attempt at diagramming a statement about multiple statements with the same subject

```
<?xml version="1.0"?>
<rdf:RDF
  xmlns:rdf="http://www.w3.org/1999/02/22-rdf-syntax-ns#"
  xmlns:pstcn="http://burningbird.net/postcon/elements/1.0/">
```

Example 4-11. An attempt at diagramming a statement about multiple statements with the same subject (continued)

```
  <rdf:Description>
    <rdf:subject rdf:resource="http://www.webreference.com/dhtml/hiermenus" />

    <rdf:predicate rdf:resource="http://burningbird.net/schema/Contains" />
    <rdf:object>Tutorials and source code about creating hierarchical menus
               in DHTML</rdf:object>

    <rdf:predicate rdf:resource="http://burningbird.net/schema/WrittenBy" />
    <rdf:object>Peter Belesis</rdf:object>
    <rdf:type rdf:resource="http://www.w3.org/1999/02/22-rdf-syntax-ns#Statement" />

    <pstcn:recommendedBy>Shelley Powers</pstcn:recommendedBy>
  </rdf:Description>
</rdf:RDF>
```

This RDF/XML in this document validates with the RDF Validator (at least, when this book was written), and the resultant graph shown in Figure 4-7 does represent what we want to say, in a way. However, our reaction to both the RDF/XML and the graph is "ugh." I was surprised this would validate because there is an assumption, though not specifically mentioned in the RDF Syntax Specification, that a predicate, object, and type for a reified statement are attached to one subject, and one subject has only one predicate and object.

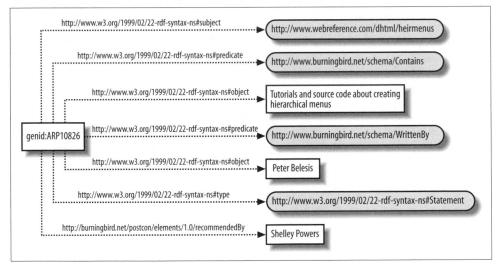

Figure 4-7. Graph of two reified statements sharing one subject—ugh

Happily, there's a better approach to modeling this type of statement.

In RDF, statements about a specific subject can be included within the same description through the use of multiple predicates and objects associated with the subject.

With the web resource example, the site contents and author are both facts about the resource and can be modeled as:

```
<rdf:Description rdf:about="http://www.webreference.com/dhtml/hiermenus/">
  <pstn:Contains>Tutorials and source code about creating hierarchichal
            menus in DHTML</pstn:Contains>
  <pstcn:writtenBy>Peter Belesis</pstcn:writtenBy>
</rdf:Description>
```

Several statements can be included within one RDF Description because there's an implicit grouping associated with this element, an `rdf:Bag` that acts as a container for all statements about a specific resource. The concept of an implicit description container also works with reified statements through the introduction of a new RDF attribute, `rdf:bagID`. The `rdf:bagID` attribute is used to identify the implicit Bag defined with the RDF Description element that groups multiple statements about a specific subject.

 During Last Call, the RDF Working Group decided that `bagID` was leading to confusion in tool makers about the type of triples to generate. Since it's use has been limited, the WG removed `rdf:bagID` from the current RDF specification. It's inclusion in this book is for historical perspective.

With the example about the web content, the `rdf:bagId` is used to wrap both statements about the web site being recommended:

```
<rdf:Description rdf:about="http://www.webreference.com/dhtml/hiermenus"
                                              rdf:bagID="R01">
  <pstcn:Contains> Tutorials and source code about creating hierarchical menus
            in DHTML</pstcn:Contains>
  <pstcn:Author>Peter Belesis</pstcn:Author>
</rdf:Description>
```

In this XML example, both statements being made—what the content of the resource is and who authored it—are contained within an RDF Description identified by the given `rdf:bagID`. With this approach, there is no confusion that we have two statements being made about one resource and that the higher-order recommendation is being made against the resource, rather than any one individual statement about the resource.

To complete the RDF document, all that's left is to attach the higher-order statement. A complete XML document containing the new RDF is shown in Example 4-12.

Example 4-12. Syntactic shorthand demonstrating higher-order and reified RDF statements

```
<?xml version="1.0"?>
<rdf:RDF
  xmlns:rdf="http://www.w3.org/1999/02/22-rdf-syntax-ns#"
  xmlns:pstcn="http://burningbird.net/postcon/elements/1.0/">
 <rdf:Description rdf:about="http://www.webreference.com/dhtml/hiermenus"
              rdf:bagID="R01">
```

```
   <pstcn:contains> Tutorials and source code about creating hierarchical menus
              in DHTML</pstcn:contains>
   <pstcn:author>Peter Belesis</pstcn:author>
 </rdf:Description>

 <rdf:Description rdf:about="http://burningbird.net/person/001">
   <pstcn:recommendeds rdf:resource="#R01" />
 </rdf:Description>
</rdf:RDF>
```

The complete example, converted to a directed graph, is shown in Figure 4-8.

What Reification Solves

As we've seen in the examples earlier in the chapter, RDF reification is the only technique within RDF to model statements so that they can be grouped or attached as properties to another statement. In the examples, reified statements were used to capture information about a statement (a recommendation) made about another statement (a web resource).

In real-world situations, how would reification be used? What would it solve? Well, the key component of reification is the ability to make a statement and have the statement be treated as fact, without any implication that the contents of the statement are themselves facts. This has particular interest when it comes to trust.

Implying trust

In the earlier examples, we looked at modeling a recommendation for a web site using RDF and reification. The recommendation didn't specifically address any level of trust—just the nature of the contents of the site and who wrote it. However, reification can be used to establish a level of trust.

As an example, 10 years ago if someone asked where you shopped for books, you might recommend a local neighborhood bookstore and say something along the lines of "they have a good selection," or "Joe will let you browse all day without hassling you," or even "the store cat's a real sweetie." You would then follow this person's recommendation based on your own belief in that person's judgment and honesty.

(During direct verification of the facts represented in the recommendation, if your hand gets shredded by the "sweet cat" when you try to pet it, you might modify your level of trust in the person's judgment when it comes to animals.)

Nowadays when the "neighborhood" is several million kilometers of wire, providing recommendations to your neighbors is a bit more complicated. You can create web pages with reviews and attach links to stores, but this won't provide useful information to automated agents that are out to do more than randomly collect links to stores. No, instead of just specifying a link to a store, you want to attach your views, your opinions, to the store.

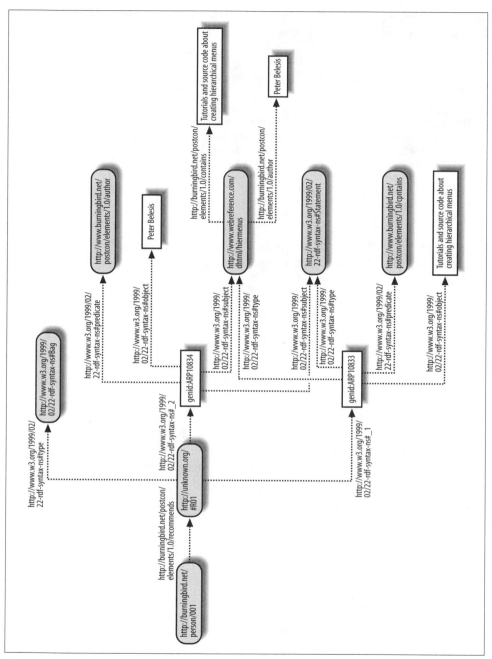

Figure 4-8. Reification when more than one inner statement is being made

Let's say you shop at a bookstore called Some Bookstore. You like and trust this store so you provide a link to it at your web site. In addition, you also provide an

RDF Description of the store, given in Example 4-13, for any RDF consumable agents that are looking for stores that can be trusted.

Example 4-13. RDF Description of a bookstore

```
<?xml version="1.0"?>
<rdf:RDF
  xmlns:rdf="http://www.w3.org/1999/02/22-rdf-syntax-ns#"
  xmlns:pstcn="http://burningbird.net/postcon/elements/1.0/">
  <rdf:Description rdf:about="http://www.somebookstore.com/">
    <pstcn:webPurpose>online store</pstcn:webPurpose>
    <pstcn:name>Some Bookstore</pstcn:name>
    <pstcn:storeType>bookstore</pstcn:storeType>
    <pstcn:trustLevel>High</pstcn:trustLevel>
  </rdf:Description>
</rdf:RDF>
```

An agent would be able to not only collect the link for the store, it would also collect information about the store (the link belongs to an online bookstore that can be trusted—i.e., the trust level is high).

The agent would store the information about the link in its online storage, which is then used by a person searching for an online bookstore that can be trusted. The results of the search would display the following:

```
Some Bookstore, found at http://www.somebookstore.com/, is an online bookstore.
Trust in this store is high.
```

This is great, just what the person wanted—or is it?

Some of the information collected by the agent and supplied in the Example 4-8 RDF/XML can be easily verified just by going out to the store web site. However, the issue of trust implied in the search results can't be verified because the context of that trust—the originator of the statement about trust—is gone.

The RDF supplied in Example 4-13 is modified to use a higher-order statement supplying information about the originator of the trust specification. The modified RDF is shown in Example 4-14.

Example 4-14. Using reification to attach the originator of trust

```
<?xml version="1.0"?>
<rdf:RDF
  xmlns:rdf="http://www.w3.org/1999/02/22-rdf-syntax-ns#"
  xmlns:pstcn="http://burningbird.net/postcon/elements/1.0/">
 <rdf:Description rdf:about="http://www.somebookstore.com" rdf:bagID="s1">
   <pstcn:name>Some Bookstore</pstcn:name>
   <pstcn:storeType>bookstore</pstcn:storeType>
   <pstcn:trustLevel>High</pstcn:trustLevel>
 </rdf:Description>

<!--The statement about the statement-->
  <rdf:Description rdf:about="http://burningbird.net/schema/ShelleyPowers">
```

Example 4-14. Using reification to attach the originator of trust (continued)

```
  <pstcn:recommendedBy rdf:resource="#s1" />
  </rdf:Description>

</rdf:RDF>
```

With this modification, the search engine results would be:

```
Some Bookstore, found at http://www.somebookstore.com/, is an online bookstore.
Trust in this store is high. The assertion about the type of store and the trust
in the store is provided by Shelley Powers.
```

Now the person shopping for an online bookstore has the information necessary to verify the source of the level of trust. Of course, the person would then have to determine if the source of the information is someone who can *also* be trusted. (Trust me. I can be trusted.)

Metadata about statements

Another use of reification is to record metadata information about a specific statement. For instance, if the statement about the resource (not the resource itself) is valid only after a specific date or only within a specific area or use, this type of information can be recorded using reification. Reification should be used because statement properties would associate the information directly to the resource, rather than to the statement.

One of the problems with the web today is that so many links to sites are obsolete, primarily because the original resource has been removed or moved to a new location. Web pages can have an expiration date attached to them, but that's not going to help when adding a link to the web resource among your own pages. It's the link or reference that needs to age gracefully, not the original resource.

To solve this, valid date information can be attached to the reference to the web resource, rather than being attached directly to the resource itself.

In Example 4-15, very simple RDF is used to describe a resource, an article, containing vacation and travel spot information. Attached to this recommendation is a constraint that the reference to this article is valid only for the year 2002.

Example 4-15. Providing a valid date for an article

```
<?xml version="1.0"?>
<rdf:RDF
  xmlns:rdf="http://www.w3.org/1999/02/22-rdf-syntax-ns#"
  xmlns:pstcn="http://burningbird.net/postcon/elements/1.0/">
  <rdf:Description>
    <rdf:subject rdf:resource="http://burningbird.net/somearticle.htm" />
    <rdf:predicate rdf:resource=
                        "http://burningbird.net/schema/Recommendations" />
    <rdf:object>Vacation and Travel Spots</rdf:object>
    <rdf:type rdf:resource="http://www.w3.org/1999/02/22-rdf-syntax-ns#Statement" />
```

Example 4-15. Providing a valid date for an article (continued)

```
    <pstcn:validFor>2002</pstcn:validFor>
  </rdf:Description>
</rdf:RDF>
```

By using reification, we've attached a valid date range to the *reference* to the article rather than directly to the article. We're saying that this reference (link) is valid only in the year 2002, rather than implying that the article the link is referencing is valid only in the year 2002.

## CHAPTER 5

Important Concepts from the W3C RDF Vocabulary/Schema

When discussing the Resource Description Framework (RDF) specification, we're really talking about two different specifications—a Syntax Specification and a Schema Specification. As described in Chapters 3 and 4, the Syntax Specification shows how RDF constructs relate to each other and how they can be diagrammed in XML. For instance, elements such as rdf:type and pstcn:bio are used to describe a specific resource, providing information such as the resource's type and the author of the resource. The different namespace prefixes associated with each element (such as rdf: and pstcn:) represent the schema that particular element is defined within.

In the context of RDF/XML, a vocabulary or schema is a rules-based dictionary that defines the elements of importance to a domain and then describes how these elements relate to one another. It provides a type system that can then be used by domain owners to create RDF/XML vocabularies for their particular domains. For example, the pstcn:bio element is from a custom vocabulary created for use with this book while the rdf:type element is from the RDF vocabulary. These are different vocabularies and have different vocabulary owners, but both follow rules defined within the RDF Vocabulary Description Language 1.0: RDF Schema.

However, before getting into the details of the RDF Schema, consider the following: if RDF is a way of describing data, then the RDF Schema can be considered a domain-neutral way of describing the metadata that can then be used to describe the data for a domain-specific vocabulary.

If all this seems convoluted, then you'll appreciate reading more about the concept of metadata, its importance to existing applications, and how RDF fits into the concept, all discussed in the next section.

 The material in this chapter references the RDF Vocabulary Description Language 1.0: RDF Schema. The most recent version of the document can be found at *http://www.w3.org/TR/rdf-schema/*.

RDF Vocabulary: Describing the Data

The last few chapters have emphasized that the RDF specification is about metadata—data about data. This is a key RDF concept; by creating a domain-neutral specification to describe resources, the same specification can then be used with many different domains but still be processed by the same RDF agents or parsed by the same RDF parsers.

Because of the importance of understanding metadata's role within RDF, we'll start by taking a closer look at the concept of metadata, particularly as it's used in applications today.

Metadata's Role in Existing Applications

If you've worked with any kind of relational database such as Oracle, Sybase, MySQL, or Microsoft's SQL Server, you've used metadata. The way that these database management systems can be used for many different applications, and to store many different types of data, is by using metadata structures.

For instance, an application database might have three database tables such as CUSTOMER, ORDER, and CUSTOMER_ORDER, with both the CUSTOMER and ORDER tables related to the third CUSTOMER_ORDER table through primary/foreign key relationships, as diagrammed in Figure 5-1.

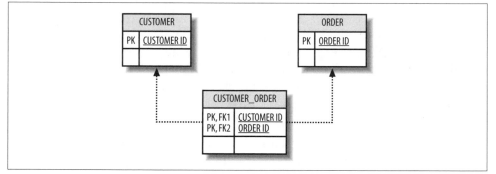

Figure 5-1. Three related database tables

The ORDER table could have other fields associated with it such as ORDER_DATE and TOTAL_COST, each containing values describing the order date and cost, respectively. Additional information could be stored about the fields, such as the ORDER_DATE is a timestamp and a required value, while the total cost field is a currency value that can be null.

To create storage specifically designed to store CUSTOMER, ORDER, and CUSTOMER_ORDER might be effective for one application but won't be useful for another application that needs to store information about objects such as STUDENT and CLASS (for an academic setting). In other words, change the domain and the domain-specific storage constructs become pretty useless.

To facilitate multiple uses of the same storage mechanism for different domains, the relational database schema defines elements such as database tables, primary and foreign keys, and columns that provide a domain-neutral description of the information about the different aspects of the CUSTOMER, ORDER, and CUSTOMER_ORDER objects. In SQL Server, the information would be stored in constructs such as TABLES, COLUMNS, and KEY_COLUMN_USAGE. COLUMNS contain a row for each element within the domain being described. Therefore, TABLES would contain one row for each of the application data objects CUSTOMER, CUSTOMER_ORDER, and ORDER; the COLUMNS table would contain one row for each table column; and so on. More complex information such as column constraints and foreign key relationships are also stored, individually, as rows within some metadata table.

 Within any tablelike structure, you can think of metadata as column headers converted to rows. The describer then becomes the described.

At runtime, the database management system hides the higher-level nature of the data storage by allowing applications to access objects such as CUSTOMER, CUSTOMER_ORDER, and ORDER, directly, as if they were actual objects rather than mappings between domain elements and a generic relational database schema. This process works so well that there are few companies in the world that don't have at least one relational database, and many have several.

The concept of runtime metadata can be extended to applications other than just relational databases. Large multiuse applications such as PeopleSoft, SAP, and Oracle Financials also make use of the concept of real-time metadata. Even without viewing each of these application's actual data stores, one can assume that the applications allow extensions to their systems by the expedient of recording metadata as records rather than as columns within a table. With this, the applications can create a generic application that follows a well-defined business model—such as a Customer Resource Management (CRM) system—that can then be extended and used within many different types of businesses.

RDF acts in a manner similar to a relational database system or these large, multiple-purpose application frameworks. Within RDF, instead of creating a custom XML vocabulary to describe resources, you use a predefined syntax and schema that allow you to store information about the resource domain, but in such a way that automated RDF processes can access and process the data regardless of the domain.

Based on this domain-neutral approach, you don't store information about a web resource in a domain-specific XML element called WEB_PAGE; instead, you store it in an `rdf:Description` element and use RDF to define the properties for this new resource. This same syntax can then be used to describe online books, photos, or even an article on giant squids (as demonstrated in Chapter 2). Most importantly, the same automated processes can manipulate the information regardless of either the resource or the domain.

Within relational database systems, the metadata process works because the schema used to capture the business information follows specific rules and makes use of a common set of system objects, such as tables and columns. The same applies to RDF: for all this to work, the RDF Schema also has to be described, and that's where the concept of metadata about metadata enters the picture. It is at this point that the RDF Schema enters the RDF specification universe.

RDF Schema: Metadata Repository

In the last section, you had a chance to see that relational databases can provide storage for a multitude of domains through the use of a set of objects that store information about every aspect of the domain, but in a neutral manner. These objects form what is known as the database system's system objects or metadata schema objects.

Within SQL Server, the objects can be queried through a custom view called the INFORMATION_SCHEMA, which contains references to elements such as the aforementioned TABLES and COLUMNS, though the actual internal tables are hidden to allow the SQL Server architects to make changes if necessary without impacting the exposed view.

The basic elements underlying the INFORMATION_SCHEMA view, such as TABLES and COLUMNS, aren't specific to any one relational database vendor; they're based on the relational database schema, defined within an industry standard. All of these elements are then governed by well-understood (and mathematically proven) rules and procedures. Because of this, you can use different relational database systems and be assured that for certain basic objects and functionality, the exposed behavior is the same regardless of the type of system. Within an Oracle database, you can have at most one primary key for a table; this same rule applies to a table within Microsoft's SQL Server and a table within Sybase.

In other words, the relational database schema, its objects, rules, and regulations are the metadata used to define and describe the metadata (TABLES, COLUMNS) that are then used to describe and manage domain-specific data (CUSTOMER, ORDER, CUSTOMER_ORDER).

 A key characteristic of the relational data model is that data is viewed logically rather than physically. Data is viewed within the context of its use rather than its physical storage method. For more on the relational model, see the classic article on the subject, "A Relational Model of Data for Large Shared Data Banks" from E. F. Codd, found at *http://www.acm.org/classics/nov95/toc.html*. Read more about the association between relational data and RDF in Chapter 10.

The RDF Schema provides the same functionality as the relational database schema. It provides the resources necessary to describe the objects and properties of a domain-specific schema—a vocabulary used to describe objects and their attributes and relationships within a specific area of interest.

The best way to fully understand how the RDF Schema works is by looking at the elements that make up the schema.

Core RDF Schema Elements

The RDF Schema elements are marked by a specific namespace, identified within a document with the following namespace declaration:

```
xmlns:rdfs="http://www.w3.org/2000/01/rdf-schema#"
```

Within the Schema Specification, there is a core group of classes and properties used to describe domain-specific RDF elements. These, combined with a specific set of constraints (described later in the section "Refining RDF Vocabularies with Constraints"), form the foundation of the schema.

 RDF Schema elements are defined in the RDFMS as well as within the RDF Schema. RDFMS elements are identified with the rdf namespace:

```
xmlns:rdf="http://www.w3.org/1999/02/22-rdf-syntax-ns#"
```

Overview of the RDF Classes

There are surprisingly few RDF Schema classes:

rdfs:Resource
> All resources within RDF are implicitly members of this class.

rdfs:Class
> Type or category of resource.

rdfs:Literal
> Literals within RDF documents, such as text strings.

rdfs:XMLLiteral
> Literals with RDF documents that use XML syntax.

rdfs:Container
> Superclass of all container classes.

rdfs:ContainerMembershipProperty
> Members of containers.

rdfs:Datatype
> Data typing information.

Taking a closer look at each of these classes, the rdfs:Resource element is used to describe a basic resource within the RDF. It is the set of these elements that literally forms both the reason and focus of the entire RDF specification.

Example 5-1 demonstrates a very simple RDF/XML document that contains a description of an article, including the article's title and author.

Example 5-1. Demonstrating the explicit resource property type

```
<?xml version="1.0"?>
<rdf:RDF
  xmlns:rdf="http://www.w3.org/1999/02/22-rdf-syntax-ns#"
  xmlns:pstcn="http://burningbird.net/postcon/elements/1.0/">
  <rdf:Description rdf:about="http://burningbird.net/articles/monsters3.htm">
    <pstcn:author>Shelley Powers</pstcn:author>
    <pstcn:title>Architeuthis Dux</pstcn:title>
  </rdf:Description>
</rdf:RDF>
```

Every resource within an RDF document, such as the article shown in Example 5-1, has a common ancestor class: `rdfs:Resource`. Because of this commonality, you generally won't see an explicit use of `rdfs:Resource` within an RDF vocabulary document. However, if you did, you would see it used in a manner similar to the following schema representation of the article resource from Example 5-1:

```
<rdfs:Class rdf:ID="Article">
<rdfs:subClassOf rdf:resource="http://www.w3.org/2000/01/rdf-schema#Resource" />
</rdfs:Class>
```

The RDF fragment also uses `rdfs:Class`. All new resource types are identified by an `rdfs:Class` statement, including the `rdfs:Resource` element itself. The `Class` element is very similar to its same-name counterpart in object-oriented development—a unique object that can be described and can have associated behaviors.

 In the RDF Schema Specification, the `rdf:Description` element is also used to identify a particular class.

Within the RDF Schema, RDF properties (discussed in the next section) have a given range of allowable values, such as `rdfs:Class`, `rdfs:Property`, or `rdfs:Literal`. The last is used to describe what the Schema Specification terms *self-denoting nodes*, which are nodes that can contain literals such as strings. An example of one such property *is* `rdfs:Comment`, used as follows:

```
<rdfs:Comment>This is a comment within the RDF Schema</rdfs:Comment>
```

The comment's value is a text string, a literal, parsed out in its entirety without additional processing.

`rdfs:Container` is the superclass of all RDF container elements: `rdf:Bag`, `rdf:Seq`, and `rdf:Alt`. The `rdfs:ContainerMembershipProperty` class consists of the Container elements themselves (usually denoted by _1, _2, _3, and so on). It also contains `rdfs:member`.

The `rdfs:Datatype` class is the class of all data types and is, itself, a subclass of `rdfs:Literal`. The data type values follow the constraints defined for RDF data types, covered in Chapters 2 and 3, which means that there is a mapping of both the value as well as the data type.

 Actual instances of data types are recorded using `rdf:datatype` within each instance, basically associating each field with a specific data type. However, you can specify a data type within the schema, also, but there's nothing associated with RDF Schemas that would enforce data types between the schema and each instance. This disconnect can potentially lead to some problems, as detailed in Chapter 6.

`rdfs:XMLLiteral` is a subclass of `rdfs:Literal` and an instance of `rdfs:Datatype`, and is the class of all XML literals. This is somewhat equivalent to CDATA within XML and HTML, and allows one to embed XML into the RDF/XML document that is not processed as RDF/XML. Associated with the XML is an arbitrary but fixed pattern:

```
"<rdf-wrapper xml:lang='"
lang
"'>"
str
"</rdf-wrapper>"
```

According to the document, `rdf-wrapper` is arbitrary but fixed. This means that the format remains the same, but the actual element names can differ. This makes sense—whatever is contained within the field designated as `XMLLiteral` would, we assume, follow standard XML formatting.

In addition to the RDF Schema classes, a few RDF classes cross the boundary between the metalanguage and instances of the same. These are:

`rdf:Statement`
    Class of all RDF statements

`rdf:Bag`, `rdf:Seq`, *and* `rdf:Alt`
    Container classes

`rdf:List`
    Class of all RDF lists

`rdf:Property`
    Resources that are RDF properties

The `rdf:Statement` class includes as members all reified RDF statements within a vocabulary (all resources that have an `rdf:type` of `rdf:Statement`).

The container classes—`rdf:Bag`, `rdf:Seq`, and `rdf:Alt`—are used to group members, positioning within the grouping dependent on the type of container class (Chapter 4 goes into detail on the container classes).

The `rdf:List` class has as members all RDF lists within a vocabulary, as `rdfs:Container` is a superclass of all RDF container elements.

The `rdf:Property` class is used to define the attributes that, in turn, describe the resource. In Example 5-1, the attributes for `Article` are `author` and `title`. The minimum RDF Schema definition that could describe the RDF/XML used in this example resource are shown in Example 5-2.

Example 5-2. RDF Schema for Article

```
<?xml version="1.0"?>
<rdf:RDF
  xmlns:rdf="http://www.w3.org/1999/02/22-rdf-syntax-ns#"
  xmlns:rdfs="http://www.w3.org/2000/01/rdf-schema#"
  xmlns:pstcn="http://burningbird.net/postcon/elements/1.0/">

<rdfs:Class rdf:about="http://burningbird.net/postcon/elements/1.0/Article">
  <rdfs:subClassOf rdf:resource="http://www.w3.org/2000/01/rdf-schema#Resource"/>
</rdfs:Class>

<rdf:Property rdf:about="http://burningbird.net/postcon/elements/1.0/title">
  <rdfs:domain rdf:resource="http://burningbird.net/postcon/elements/1.0/Article" />
</rdf:Property>

<rdf:Property rdf:about="http://burningbird.net/postcon/elements/1.0/author">
  <rdfs:domain rdf:resource="http://burningbird.net/postcon/elements/1.0/Article" />
</rdf:Property>
</rdf:RDF>
```

In this document, `Article` is defined as an `rdf:Resource` (subclass of the Resource class), and each property of `Article` (`title` and `author`) is related to it through the use of the RDF Schema *domain* constraint (discussed in the later section "Refining RDF Vocabularies with Constraints").

The Article class and its associated properties are associated with the Resource and Property classes, respectively, through the `subClassOf` property. This and other core RDF properties are discussed next.

Demonstrations of the RDF Schema Properties

The RDF specification's purpose is purely to define resources and associated facts, and then provide a way to allow these resource/fact mappings to interact. This is accomplished through capturing statements about the resource, with each statement consisting of a specific property such as `title` and `author` for the `Article` resource. The RDF Schema is no exception—statements about each resource are captured as individual properties. The only difference between the two is that one is an instance of business data (such as `Article`), and the other is metadata (related to the RDF model).

Following are the core properties (from both the RDF and RDFS namespaces) that are essential to the RDF Schema:

- rdfs:subClassOf
- rdfs:seeAlso
- rdfs:member
- rdfs:label
- rdf:subject
- rdf:object
- rdf:rest
- rdfs:range

- rdfs:subPropertyOf
- rdfs:isDefinedBy
- rdfs:comment
- rdf:type
- rdf:predicate
- rdf:first
- rdfs:domain
- rdf:value

The rdf:value property was described in Chapter 3. The rdf:subClassOf property identifies a class that is a subclass of another. For instance, in Example 5-2, Article is a subclass of the more generic Resource class, which all resources belong to. Article could also be a subclass of another class such as WebPage, which is, in turn, a subclass of Resource, as demonstrated in the following RDF/XML snippet:

```
<rdfs:Class rdf:ID="WebPage">
  <rdfs:subClassOf rdf:resource="http://www.w3.org/2000/01/rdf-schema#Resource"/>
</rdfs:Class>

<rdfs:Class rdf:ID="Article">
  <rdfs:subClassOf rdf:resource="http://burningbird.net/schema#WebPage"/>
</rdfs:Class>
```

The use of inheritance within the RDF Schema classes allows us to define superclasses such as WebPage. New subclasses of WebPage then not only inherit the properties and constraints of the superclass Resource, they also inherit the additional properties and constraints from WebPage.

The rdfs:subPropertyOf property is used when one property is a refinement of another property. For instance, in the Article schema, one of the properties is author. This property could be further refined to specify whether an author is a primary or secondary author, via the primaryAuthor and secondaryAuthor subproperties, respectively. Example 5-3 shows the use of this property refinement through the rdfs: subPropertyOf property.

Example 5-3. RDF Schema example of property refinement

```
<?xml version="1.0"?>
<rdf:RDF
  xmlns:rdf="http://www.w3.org/1999/02/22-rdf-syntax-ns#"
  xmlns:rdfs="http://www.w3.org/2000/01/rdf-schema#"
  xmlns:pstcn="http://burningbird.net/postcon/elements/1.0/">

<rdfs:Class rdf:about="http://burningbird.net/postcon/elements/1.0/Article">
  <rdfs:subClassOf rdf:resource="http://www.w3.org/2000/01/rdf-schema#Resource"/>
</rdfs:Class>
```

Example 5-3. RDF Schema example of property refinement (continued)

```
<rdf:Property rdf:about="http://burningbird.net/postcon/elements/1.0/title">
  <rdfs:domain rdf:resource="http://burningbird.net/postcon/elements/1.0/Article" />
</rdf:Property>

<rdf:Property rdf:about="http://burningbird.net/postcon/elements/1.0/author">
  <rdfs:domain rdf:resource="http://burningbird.net/postcon/elements/1.0/Article" />
</rdf:Property>

<rdf:Property rdf:about="http://burningbird.net/postcon/elements/1.0/primaryAuthor">
  <rdfs:domain rdf:resource="http://burningbird.net/postcon/elements/1.0/Article" />
  <rdfs:subPropertyOf rdf:resource="http://burningbird.net/postcon/elements/1.0/author" />
</rdf:Property>

<rdf:Property rdf:about="http://burningbird.net/postcon/elements/1.0/secondaryAuthor">
  <rdfs:domain rdf:resource="http://burningbird.net/postcon/elements/1.0/Article" />
  <rdfs:subPropertyOf rdf:resource="http://burningbird.net/postcon/elements/1.0/author" />
</rdf:Property>
</rdf:RDF>
```

The `rdfs:seeAlso` property is used to identify another resource that contains additional information about the resource being described. An example of using this property could be the following RDF fragment, showing the relationship between an article and a document maintaining the history of the article, identified as a class called ArticleHistory:

```
<rdfs:Class rdf:about=" http://burningbird.net/postcon/elements/1.0/ArticleHistory">
  <rdfs:subClassOf rdf:resource="http://www.w3.org/2000/01/rdf-schema#Resource"/>
</rdfs:Class>

<rdfs:Class rdf:about=" http://burningbird.net/postcon/elements/1.0/Article">
  <rdfs:subClassOf rdf:resource="http://www.w3.org/2000/01/rdf-schema#Resource"/>
  <rdfs:seeAlso rdf:resource="http://burningbird.net/postcon/elements/1.0/
ArticleHistory" />
</rdfs:Class>
```

Within the RDFS vocabulary, `rdfs:seeAlso` is also used to link the vocabulary document with a second document:

```
<rdf:Description rdf:about="http://www.w3.org/2000/01/rdf-schema#">
  <rdfs:seeAlso rdf:resource="http://www.w3.org/2000/01/rdf-schema-more"/>
</rdf:Description>
```

With this, additional schema elements can be added to the vocabulary without having to edit or modify the original schema.

According to the RDF Schema Specification, `rdfs:seeAlso` can be refined through the `rdfs:subPropertyOf` property to provide additional information about the manner in which the one resource provides additional information about the second resource:

```
<rdf:Property rdf:about=" http://burningbird.net/postcon/elements/1.0/
historyProvidedBy">
  <rdf:type rdf:resource="http://www.w3.org/1999/02/22-rdf-schema#Property"/>
```

```
    <rdfs:subPropertyOf rdf:resource="http://www.w3.org/2000/01/rdf-schema#seeAlso" />
</rdf:Property>

<rdfs:Class rdf:about=" http://burningbird.net/postcon/elements/1.0/ArticleHistory">
  <rdfs:subClassOf rdf:resource="http://www.w3.org/2000/01/rdf-schema#Resource"/>
</rdfs:Class>

<rdfs:Class rdf:about=" http://burningbird.net/postcon/elements/1.0/Article">
  <rdfs:subClassOf rdf:resource="http://www.w3.org/2000/01/rdf-schema#Resource"/>
  <bbd:historyProvidedBy rdf:resource=" http://burningbird.net/postcon/elements/1.0/
ArticleHistory" />
</rdfs:Class>
```

The rdfs:isDefinedBy property identifies the namespace for the resource, preventing any ambiguity or confusion about namespace ownership. For example, if a resource is identified by a GUID (Globally Unique Identifier), the rdfs:isDefinedBy property could be attached to the Resource class, to provide the URI for the schema.

Within the RDFS Schema vocabulary, the rdf:Statement class is defined to be a part of the RDF syntax namespace:

```
<rdfs:Class rdf:about="http://www.w3.org/1999/02/22-rdf-syntax-ns#Statement">
  <rdfs:isDefinedBy rdf:resource="http://www.w3.org/1999/02/22-rdf-syntax-ns#"/>
  <rdfs:label xml:lang="en">Statement</rdfs:label>
  <rdfs:subClassOf rdf:resource="http://www.w3.org/2000/01/rdf-schema#Resource"/>
  <rdfs:comment>The class of RDF statements.</rdfs:comment>
</rdfs:Class>
```

However, the rdfs:Literal class is defined to be a part of the RDF Schema namespace:

```
<rdfs:Class rdf:about="http://www.w3.org/2000/01/rdf-schema#Literal">
  <rdfs:isDefinedBy rdf:resource="http://www.w3.org/2000/01/rdf-schema#"/>
  <rdfs:label xml:lang="en">Literal</rdfs:label>
  <rdfs:comment>This represents the set of atomic values, eg. textual strings.</rdfs:
comment>
</rdfs:Class>
```

The rdfs:member property is a superproperty for each numbered container element (such as _1, _2, and so on).

 At the time of this writing, the RDF Working Group is working to resolve whether rdfs:member should be a member of rdfs:ContainerMembershipProperty. Check the RDF Schema specification for final resolution of this issue.

Two properties provide human readability to an RDF model. The rdfs:comment property is used to provide documentation of resources, and rdfs:label provides a readable version of the resource's name. In addition, you can attach the XML attribute xml:lang to the rdfs:label element and provide different labels for different languages.

You can add comments to an RDF/XML document using XML comments such as the following:

```
<!–Class defining Web articles–>
<rdfs:Class rdf:about="http://burningbird.net/postcon/elements/1.0/Article">
  <rdfs:subClassOf rdf:Resource="http://www.w3.org/2000/01/rdf-schema#Resource"/>
</rdfs:Class>
```

However, to formally attach documentation to an element in such a way that the documentation itself can be easily accessible through RDF parsers or other automated processes, then you need to have RDF Schema elements that can be used specifically for schema documentation. These elements are `rdfs:comment` and `rdfs:label`. The `rdfs:comment` provides a description of the resource, while the `rdfs:label` provides a human-readable version of the name.

Adding documentation to Example 5-3 results in the RDF/XML shown in Example 5-4. As you can see, just a few extra lines can provide considerable information.

Example 5-4. Using RDF Schema documentation elements

```
<?xml version="1.0"?>
<rdf:RDF
  xmlns:rdf="http://www.w3.org/1999/02/22-rdf-syntax-ns#"
  xmlns:rdfs="http://www.w3.org/2000/01/rdf-schema#"
  xmlns:pstcn="http://burningbird.net/postcon/elements/1.0/">

<rdfs:Class rdf:about="http://burningbird.net/postcon/elements/1.0/Article">
  <rdfs:subClassOf rdf:resource="http://www.w3.org/2000/01/rdf-schema#Resource"/>
  <rdfs:comment>Unique Online article</rdfs:comment>
  <rdfs:label xml:lang="en">Article</rdfs:label>
</rdfs:Class>

<rdf:Property rdf:about="http://burningbird.net/postcon/elements/1.0/title">
  <rdf:type rdf:resource="http://www.w3.org/1999/02/22-rdf-schema#Property"/>
  <rdfs:domain rdf:resource="http://burningbird.net/postcon/elements/1.0/Article" />
  <rdfs:comment>Online Article Title</rdfs:comment>
  <rdfs:label xml:lang="en">Title</rdfs:label>
</rdf:Property>

<rdf:Property rdf:about="http://burningbird.net/postcon/elements/1.0/author">
  <rdf:type rdf:resource="http://www.w3.org/1999/02/22-rdf-schema#Property"/>
  <rdfs:domain rdf:resource="http://burningbird.net/postcon/elements/1.0/Article" />
  <rdfs:comment>Primary author of article</rdfs:comment>
  <rdfs:label xml:lang="en">Author</rdfs:label>
</rdf:Property>

</rdf:RDF>
```

When viewing the schema in Example 5-3, you can understand what's being described because you have this chapter to provide information. However, in real life, a vocabulary and schema may not have associated documentation, or the link between the documentation and the vocabulary may not be maintained. By providing both comments and a readable label, you're providing information to the users about exactly what's being defined. This is no different than providing inline documentation and using good naming practices within code among application developers.

The `rdf:type` property defines the type of resource. As mentioned earlier, all resources are of type `Resource`, as well as being a more granular type, such as `Article`. The type property designates that the resource being referenced is an instance of this class.

Within an RDF/XML document, the `rdf:type` is usually assumed and isn't explicitly given. However, you can explicitly use the `rdf:type` property to remove any possibility of confusion between the RDF/XML document and N-Triples or an RDF graph generated from the document. This holds true for RDF Schema vocabulary documents. For instance, you can attach an `rdf:type` property to the `author` property to refine the definition, though its use in a schema is usually redundant.

```
<rdf:Property rdf:about="http://burningbird.net/postcon/elements/1.0/author">
  <rdf:type rdf:resource="http://www.w3.org/1999/02/22-rdf-schema#Property"/>
  <rdfs:domain rdf:resource="http://burningbird.net/postcon/elements/1.0/Article" />
  <rdfs:comment>Primary author of article</rdfs:comment>
  <rdfs:label xml:lang="en">Author</rdfs:label>
  <rdf:type rdf:resource="http://www.w3.org/1999/02/22-rdf-syntax-ns#Property" />

</rdf:Property>
```

The `rdf:subject`, `rdf:predicate`, and `rdf:object` properties are used with reification to explicitly define an RDF statement. In addition, the `rdf:first` and `rdf:next` properties are used to explicitly define the relationships within a collection. Since both reification and collections are covered in depth in Chapter 4, I won't repeat the details here.

The remaining two properties, `rdfs:domain` and `rdfs:range`, are described in the next section.

Refining RDF Vocabularies with Constraints

Within RDF Schema, constraints define class associations for properties. In addition, there are subclasses of both Property and Resource that are specific to constraints.

In Example 5-4, the `rdfs:domain` property was used to associate a property with the resource it modified. It was used with both the `author` and `title` properties to associate them with the `Article` resource. The RDF Schema property is further constrained to be used only with properties by specifying an `rdfs:domain` of `Property` for the `rdfs:domain` itself.

An RDF property can be used for more than one resource type. Something such as `title` can then be used for `Article` but can also be used for `Person` (a person's work title), as well as something such as `Painting` (title of a painting). The only limitation is the domain scope. The rdfs:range property is used to specify the classes the property can reference as values. Unlike the domain element, only one RDF range constraint can be attached to any property—equivalent to the restriction in most programming languages that a variable can be of only one data type, constraining the allowable values that the variable can contain.

To specify more than one class as range constraint for a property (more than one data type if you will), you can use a master class for all classes that will be designated by a specific range and then use inheritance to extend the class with subclasses.

In Example 5-5, a new class is added to the example schema called Directory. This class has one property, contains, which is used to identify web resources the directory contains. A new contains property is created and tied back to the class through the rdfs:domain property.

The web resources can be articles or examples; to allow both in the new contains range, a master class, WebPage, is created; it is then refined through the use of rdfs:subClassOf to create Article and Example classes. The master class is used as the value for the rdfs:range property of the contains class.

Example 5-5. Using RDF Schema constraints to refine an RDF schema

```
<?xml version="1.0"?>
<rdf:RDF
  xmlns:rdf="http://www.w3.org/1999/02/22-rdf-syntax-ns#"
  xmlns:rdfs="http://www.w3.org/2000/01/rdf-schema#"
  xmlns:pstcn="http://burningbird.net/postcon/elements/1.0/">

<rdfs:Class rdf:about="http://burningbird.net/postcon/elements/1.0/WebPage">
  <rdfs:subClassOf rdf:resource="http://www.w3.org/2000/01/rdf-schema#Resource"/>
</rdfs:Class>

<rdfs:Class rdf:about="http://burningbird.net/postcon/elements/1.0/Article">
  <rdfs:subClassOf rdf:resource="http://burningbird.net/postcon/elements/1.0/WebPage"/>
</rdfs:Class>

<rdfs:Class rdf:about="http://burningbird.net/postcon/elements/1.0/Example">
  <rdfs:subClassOf rdf:resource="http://burningbird.net/postcon/elements/1.0/WebPage"/>
</rdfs:Class>

<rdfs:Class rdf:about="http://burningbird.net/postcon/elements/1.0/Directory">
  <rdfs:subClassOf rdf:resource="http://www.w3.org/2000/01/rdf-schema#Resource"/>
</rdfs:Class>

<rdf:Property rdf:about="http://burningbird.net/postcon/elements/1.0/contains">
  <rdfs:domain rdf:resource="http://burningbird.net/postcon/elements/1.0/Directory" />
  <rdfs:range rdf:resource="http://burningbird.net/postcon/elements/1.0/WebPage" />
</rdf:Property>

</rdf:RDF>
```

RDF Schema Alternatives

RDF isn't the only specification related to describing schemas. XML documents (and their SGML predecessors) have long been validated through the use of Document Type Declarations (DTDs), described in the first release of the XML specification and still in heavy use. DTDs generally define how elements relate to one another within a schema; for example, they allow applications to check whether a specific element is required or one or more elements can be contained within another.

While useful for validating how elements within a schema relate to one another, DTDs have long had their critics. First of all, DTDs are based on a syntax totally unrelated to XML. This forces a person to become familiar with not one but two syntaxes in order to create a valid as well as well-formed XML document. The following DTD fragment defines an Items element, its child item, and the contents of item:

```
<!ELEMENT Items (item*)>
<!ELEMENT item (productName, quantity, USPrice, comment?, shipDate?)>
<!ATTLIST item
    partNum CDATA #REQUIRED>
<!ELEMENT productName (#PCDATA)>
<!ELEMENT quantity (#PCDATA)>
<!ELEMENT USPrice (#PCDATA)>
<!ELEMENT comment (#PCDATA)>
<!ELEMENT shipDate (#PCDATA)>
```

As you can see, the DTD syntax is fairly intuitive; however, syntactic elegance or not, DTDs do not provide the same type of functionality as the RDF specification. XML DTDs define how elements within a vocabulary relate to one another, not how they relate to the world at large, and the description of their contents is pretty vague. #PCDATA and its attribute cousin, CDATA, just mean "text." RDF provides a means of recording data within a global context, not just how elements in one specific vocabulary relate to one another.

Another mechanism to record schemas is defined by the W3C XML Schema 1.0 Specification. This specification is more closely related to the functionality used to define a relational table or to describe an object in object-oriented development. Schemas are used to define elements in relation to one another, as with the DTD syntax; it goes beyond DTDs, though, by providing a means of recording data types about the elements and attributes—a functionality long needed with XML vocabularies, as shown in the following fragment based on the specification:

```
<xsd:element name="Items">
 <xsd:complexType name="Items">
  <xsd:sequence>
   <xsd:element name="item" minOccurs="0" maxOccurs="unbounded">
    <xsd:complexType>
     <xsd:sequence>
      <xsd:element name="productName" type="xsd:string"/>
      <xsd:element name="quantity">
```

```
    <xsd:simpleType>
     <xsd:restriction base="xsd:positiveInteger">
      <xsd:maxExclusive value="100"/>
     </xsd:restriction>
    </xsd:simpleType>
   </xsd:element>
   <xsd:element name="USPrice"  type="xsd:decimal"/>
   <xsd:element ref="comment"   minOccurs="0"/>
   <xsd:element name="shipDate" type="xsd:date" minOccurs="0"/>
  </xsd:sequence>
  <xsd:attribute name="partNum" type="SKU" use="required"/>
 </xsd:complexType>
   </xsd:element>
  </xsd:sequence>
 </xsd:complexType>
</xsd:element>
```

As you can see, W3C XML Schema is an effective specification for defining XML elements, their relationships, and much more information about associated data types than DTDs provide.

A third approach, RELAX NG Compact Syntax, offers a combination of DTD readability and W3C XML Schema data typing, though it also has a mathematical foundation that in some ways has more in common with RDF than with DTDs or W3C XML Schema. The same example in RELAX NG Compact Syntax looks like:

```
Items = element Items { item* }
item =
  element item {
    att.partNum, productName, quantity, USPrice, comment?, shipDate?
  }
att.partNum = attribute partNum { text }
productName = element productName { text }
quantity = element quantity { xsd:positiveInteger {maxExclusive="100"}}
USPrice = element USPrice { xsd:decimal }
comment = element comment { text }
shipDate = element shipDate { xsd:date }

start = Items
```

All of these schema approaches facilitate automated processing of XML. Still, the various XML Schema tools can't replace the functionality provided by the RDF specification. To overgeneralize, XML tools are concerned with describing markup representations and their contents, while RDF tools are concerned with describing models. You can get a model from a representation or vice versa, but the two approaches focus on different things.

The RDF specification defines information about data within a particular context. It provides a means of recording information at a metadata level that can be used regardless of the domain. RDF's relationship with XML is that XML is used to serialize an RDF model; RDF is totally unconcerned whether XML is valid (that is, conforming to a DTD, RELAX NG description, or W3C XML Schema) as long as the

XML used to serialize an RDF model is well formed. In addition, concepts such as data types and complex and simple element structures—focal points within the W3C XML Schema—again focus on XML as used to define data, primarily for data interchange; they have nothing to do with recording data about data in order to facilitate intelligent web functionality.

## CHAPTER 6

Creating an RDF Vocabulary

Unlike other W3C specifications, such as HTML, you're not going to see RDF documents consisting solely of the elements that have been described in Chapters 3 through 5. Yes, there is a defined syntax for RDF, as reviewed in Chapters 3 and 4, and there is an RDF Schema, explored in Chapter 5. However, RDF isn't used to model business-specific resources directly because there are no domain-specific elements within the specification. Instead, RDF creates domain-specific vocabularies that are then used to model the resources, with an added advantage of having access to RDF-specific parsers and automated processes.

What kinds of vocabularies can be created? A better question is: what kinds of business resources can be described using a syntax/schema such as RDF? And the answer is: any business resource. The number of possible vocabularies is limitless, constrained only by each industry's need for interoperable vocabularies.

In this chapter you'll have a chance to see how a vocabulary is created and validated against the RDF syntax and schema. Once the elements for the vocabulary are defined, they'll then be compared against an existing web resource domain vocabulary, the Dublin Core, to look for matches.

First, though, let's take a closer look at what I mean when I say "RDF Vocabulary."

How RDF Vocabularies Differ from XML Vocabularies

RDF is a way of recording information about resources; RDF, as serialized using XML, is a way of recording information about a specific business domain using a set of elements defined within the rules of the RDF data model/graph and the constraints of the RDF syntax, vocabulary, and semantics.

RDF recorded in XML is a very powerful tool—it's been used to document events within a heterogeneous application environment, to describe publications, to record an environmental thesaurus, and so on. By using XML, you have access to a great number of existing XML applications such as parsers and APIs, even relational and Lightweight Directory Access Protocol (LDAP) data sources that are XML-capable. However, what do you get when you use RDF? Why not use XML directly?

As mentioned in previous chapters, RDF provides the same level of functionality to XML as the relational data model adds to commercial database systems. RDF provides a predefined grammar that can be used to consistently record business domain information in such a way that any business domain can have a vocabulary in RDF that can be processed with a host of RDF-based tools and frameworks.

Consider the environmental thesaurus I just mentioned. This is a joint effort between the California Environmental Resource Evaluation System (CERES) and the National Biological Information Infrastructure (NBII). This partnership was formed to create a common environmental vocabulary and the tools necessary to work with this vocabulary. One of the efforts of this project is to document this vocabulary using RDF.

Within the RDF vocabulary, the project has defined a class called Term that has several properties, such as Source, Category, and Status, attached to it. Instead of using RDF, the project could have recorded this information directly within XML; however, if they did this, they then would have to define the concept of "class" and "property" in order to record relationships such as "Source is a property of Term." In addition, the project would also have to create code to process the XML in such a way that the Source element is processed as a property of Term rather than an arbitrary related element that happens to be nested within the Term element. Lastly, the group would need to create a schema to support these new objects so that the XML document matches the constraints documented in this schema.

For the latter requirement, a Document Type Definition (DTD) file won't work, as DTDs primarily control nesting and frequency of occurrence of elements; XML Schema won't work, as it is concerned more with data types and other constraints rather than the metalanguage nature of "class" and "property." RELAX NG is more easily processed than either of those, but again it is solving different problems.

As you can use XML to serialize the contents of a relational database, you can use XML to serialize the contents of an RDF-based model—but XML isn't a replacement because XML is nothing more than a syntax. You need a metalanguage vocabulary to be able to use XML to record business domain information in such a way that any business can be documented, and RDF provides this capability.

However, don't take my word for it; try it yourself in the next several sections when you have a chance to see how a vocabulary is created.

Defining the Vocabulary: Business and Scope

As the Web has matured, more and more of the posted content is aging beyond usefulness. In many cases, this aged content is just deleted from a web site, resulting in

"404 Page not found" errors when you click through to the content from some search engine or via a link from another web page. Hitting a missing page is particularly frustrating if you've come to the page because of a description associated with it that exactly fits your current interest, and you don't even know why the page was deleted or if the resource might exist somewhere else.

A further problem with maturing web sites is that site structure doesn't remain constant—due to the use of new technologies or new directions in content management, resources may be moved around at the site or even moved to new domains. When you access the content, the less-than-helpful sites return with something along the lines of:

```
404 Not Found
We're sorry, the file that you requested does not exist or has moved.
```

Well, which is it? Is the page missing, or was the request invalid because the content's moved? If you get this message as a result of clicking on a link from another site, is it because the content's really been deleted or moved, or because the linking site made a mistake with the link? Is the site that owns the content using a new system of cataloging its resources, breaking existing links?

Other sites provide a page with a forwarding message and a link to redirect you to the new content. As important as these redirections are, though, the reasons behind the move may be additional information that can be useful in determining whether the resource is worth pursuing through what could end up being a chain of redirections, with each link in the chain reflecting a different move.

Unfortunately, the reasons for the move aren't maintained with the redirection in most cases.

Another problem is aging content that *isn't* deleted. With this type of page, you could be halfway through reading it only to realize that it talks about a product or technology that's been obsolete for years. There's nothing to indicate the relevance of the page, and external factors associated with the page, such as the page title or label, may not provide enough context to determine whether the resource is useful for your purposes or not.

 Netscape's support of Dynamic HTML (DHTML) for the company's browser is a classic case of content being under one label—DHTML—with two drastically different implementations based on browser version. DHTML for Version 4.x of Netscape won't work with the current Netscape 6.x products and vice versa. The only way to determine whether a page titled "Working with DHTML in Netscape" is useful for your purposes is to read it and hope you know enough about the subject to know whether you're wasting your time.

Content management systems such as FrontPage, Vignette, and others help with creating, posting, and managing the original content, but do not help provide information about the context of the resource. meta tags can be attached to each HTML resource providing copyright information, keywords, or authorship, but nothing regarding the expected life expectancy of the resource or its move history, including reasons for the move, unless you put this information into the description—an approach that isn't standardized and therefore not useful.

These systems are as helpless as web browsers at determining whether a 404 error occurred because of a typo, a relocation, or a resource no longer being maintained at the site.

What's needed is a content system that takes over after the content management systems have finished their task of posting the content: a postcontent information system that can be accessed by a runtime application and provide information about the resource to the resource consumers. Such a system must provide information that is useful for humans and is also usable by automated processes.

We'll use this type of system to demonstrate how to create an RDF vocabulary and, eventually, how to use the vocabulary just created. For simplicity in this chapter (and later in the book), I'll refer to this system as *PostCon*.

Defining the Vocabulary: Elements

How to start defining the vocabulary for this type of system? Compatible with most application efforts, the first step to creating the vocabulary is to define the business domain elements and their properties of interest within the given business scope.

The PostCon Domain Elements

Defining the business elements for a new system is the same process whether the domain is being defined for use within a more traditional relational database or within a system with data defined and managed through RDF-capable processes. Following from existing data modeling techniques, you first describe the major entities and their properties, then describe how these entities are related to one another.

PostCon has one major or root element, the web site resource; the system is interested in this resource from six different perspectives:

- What is the content's bio—who wrote it, who owns it, when was it created, and what are its subject and topic?
- What is the content's relevancy—has it been updated for new circumstances and does it have a date beyond which it is no longer pertinent?
- What is the content's history of movement—has it been deleted? If so, why? Has it moved? If so, why, and where is it now?

- What are the content's related resources—has it been replaced? Are other resources related to it? Are other resources dependent on it, or is it dependent on other resources?

- If the resource no longer exists, are there replacements? Why are they replacements?

- What are the presentation characteristics of the content? Its type? Does it conform to any standard? Does it require specialized user agents? Are there any dependencies?

The set of PostCon objects consists of a web resource, its bio, a movement associated with the resource, presentation and type information, and other related resources. Each object is then described by a set of properties. Many of these are compatible with HTML meta tag elements such as Title and Content and should be synchronized with the values included within the HTML; others are unique to the system.

The main system elements are then described by a set of properties, as defined in Table 6-1.

Table 6-1. PostCon system domain elements and their properties

Element	Property	Description
Content	Unique Content ID	To identify content
	Biography	Content biographical information
	Relevancy	Relevancy of content
	History	History of content movement
	Related	Related content
	Presentation	Content type and presentation
Content bio	Title	Resource's title
	Resource Abstract	Excerpt from resource if applicable
	Resource Description	Description of Resource
	Creation Date	Date resource was first created
	Content Author	Person or organization responsible for creating content
	Content Owner	Person or organization who owns copyright on content
Relevancy	Content Status	Current status of content
	Subject	Subject/topic of resource (may duplicate)
	Relevancy Expiration	Date when content is aged beyond usefulness
	References	External resources referenced in content
	Referenced by	External resources that reference content
History	Movement	Location at end of movement
	Reason	Reason for movement
	Date	Date of movement

Element	Property	Description
	Type	Type of movement
Related	Related Resource	Resource URI
	Reason	Reason for relationship
Recommendation	Recommended Resource	URI of recommended replacement
	Title	Title of replacement
	Reason	Reason for recommendation
Presentation	Format	Format of resource
	Conformity	Standards/specifications resource conforms to (may repeat)
	Requires	Resource dependencies (may repeat)—may have associated type of requirement as well as required resource (may repeat)

The Unique Resource ID (URI) is defined once for the content and follows it regardless of the content's current location. The Resource Title property is equivalent to the HTML Title element, and the Resource Description is equivalent to the Description meta tag, which contains a short abstract of the resource's contents:

```
<meta name="description" content="Dynamic Earth site focuses on
science and the world and universe around us. You can never know too much">
```

The material within the content attribute is used for the Resource Description content. The Content Author is equivalent to the Author meta tag, and the Content Owner is equivalent to the Copyright meta tag:

```
<meta name="author" content="Shelley Powers">
<meta name="copyright" content="&copy; 1997-2003 Burningbird">
```

The Content Status for the web resource contains information about the current status of the document, such as whether it has been deleted or is still active. The Relevancy Expiration is a date when the content author expects the resource contents to become dated and no longer viable. The Requires property also provides information about the viability of the content, such as being dependent on Version 1.0 of a specific product release.

The History of the resource tracks its movement throughout the network, as well as the date and reason for the move. This is particularly useful when providing information about deleted content. The Related material provides information about replacement URLs for content that is no longer viable, and the Recommendation material covers additional recommended material complementary to the material, while the Presentation reflects information necessary to "consume" the resource, as it were.

For a specific web resource, there is one Resource bio, Relevancy, History, and Presentation sections, but many related items. Additionally, within the History section there can be many movements. This and the domain information are then used to prototype the RDF vocabulary, as described next.

Prototyping the Vocabulary

Before creating a formal RDFS document for the new vocabulary, you should prototype the model with several different instances of it, to ensure that the results corroborate the expected outcome. During this process, check the validity of your data with the RDF Validator, which validates the result against the standard and also provides an edged graph and N-Triples breakdown of the RDF.

 You can access the RDF Validator at *http://www.w3.org/RDF/ Validator/*.

As a test case for the PostCon vocabulary, information about the giant squid articles introduced in Chapters 2 through 4 is recorded using the domain elements from the last section. The articles are particularly useful as test cases because they have been moved about, are related to each other, reference, and are referenced by external resources. About the only thing that the articles don't demonstrate is when a web resource has been deleted, and we'll test this out with another document later.

When creating a new vocabulary, the first thing to do is define the URI for the vocabulary namespace. By convention, this should be the URL of the RDFS document when it is eventually made. In the case of PostCon, I used the following URL for the namespace:

```
http://burningbird.net/postcon/elements/1.0/
```

This is actually fairly descriptive—this is the location of the set of PostCon Version 1.0 vocabulary elements. When the RDFS document for the vocabulary is finished, it will be dropped into this location primarily for use by utilities that make use of it for RDF/ XML exploration (covered in Chapter 7).

 There is no requirement as to the structure of the URI for a namespace, nor does the RDFS document have to exist—but it is good practice to use a consistent namespace and to create the document and place it in the URL of the namespace.

Next up is determining what the URI of the web resource is. We could actually create an identifier for our resources, but my preference for the PostCon system is just to use it as the identifier the URL of the resource when it was first defined within the PostCon RDF/XML vocabulary. What's important is that it be consistent and unique— any other requirements are purely system dependent, not RDF/XML dependent.

I used the first document in the article series as the test case, and since it was located within the domain *burningbird.net* and within the *articles* subdirectory, its URI became:

```
http://burningbird.net/articles/monsters1.htm
```

However, to simplify the model, xml:base (explained in Chapter 3) is used and set to a value of http://burningbird.net/articles, and the resource URI is set to monsters1.htm.

The other top-level predicates are added sans their predicates to give a relatively flat model at this point. Example 6-1 shows the RDF/XML at this stage.

Example 6-1. First cut of PostCon vocabulary, with scalar values

```
<?xml version="1.0"?>
<rdf:RDF
  xmlns:rdf="http://www.w3.org/1999/02/22-rdf-syntax-ns#"
  xmlns:pstcn="http://burningbird.net/postcon/elements/1.0/"
  xml:base="http://burningbird.net/articles/">

  <rdf:Description rdf:about="monsters1.htm">
     <pstcn:bio />
     <pstcn:relevancy />
     <pstcn:presentation />
     <pstcn:history />
     <pstcn:related />
  </rdf:Description>

</rdf:RDF>
```

Next, we'll start adding the other predicates to the model, but first, there's one change we want to make to the model. As it is currently defined, we have the resource, but we don't necessarily know what it is. It is a web resource, but by the model's definition it could be any other resource that can be defined by an arbitrary URI, including a person, a place, or a thing. To refine the model, then, we'll add an rdf:type predicate to it, with a value of http://burningbird.net/postcon/elements/ 1.0/Resource. However, to make the model as simple as possible, we'll use an RDF/ XML shortcut (detailed in "The rdf:type Property" in Chapter 3) and replace the rdf: Description block with a reference to this new class:

```
<pstcn:Resource>
     <pstcn:bio />
     <pstcn:relevancy />
     <pstcn:presentation />
     <pstcn:history />
     <pstcn:related />
</pstcn:Resource>
```

The directed graph that results from this change, as shown in Figure 6-1, is no different than if we had used the more formal rdf:Description block with the associated rdf:type predicate.

Next we'll start adding the predicates, beginning with pstcn:bio. Since RDF/XML requires a striped syntax of node-arc-node-arc, and rdf:bio is acting as an arc, rdf: bio's contents must be redefined as a blank node—a resource without a URI. Adding an rdf:Description block to rdf:bio and then adding its predicates as shown in Example 6-2 accomplishes redefining rdf:bio as a blank node. The predicates are

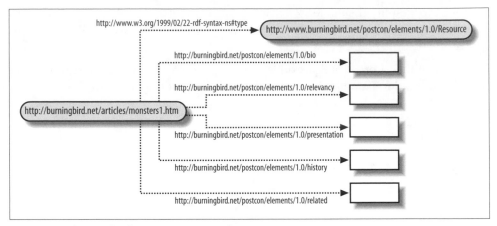

Figure 6-1. The graph of our PostCon example

named the same as the attributes defined in Table 6-1, but converted to QNames per
the RDF/XML requirement. Changes to the RDF/XML are boldfaced.

Example 6-2. Adding in the pstcn:bio predicates

```
<?xml version="1.0"?>
<rdf:RDF
  xmlns:rdf="http://www.w3.org/1999/02/22-rdf-syntax-ns#"
  xmlns:pstcn="http://burningbird.net/postcon/elements/1.0/"
  xml:base="http://burningbird.net/articles/">

  <pstcn:Resource rdf:about="monsters1.htm">
     <pstcn:bio>
        <rdf:Description>
           <pstcn:title>Tale of Two Monsters: Legends</pstcn:title>
     <pstcn:abstract>
           When I think of "monsters" I think of the creatures of
           legends and tales, from the books and movies, and
           I think of the creatures that have entertained me for years.
     </pstcn:abstract>
           <pstcn:description>
           Part 1 of four-part series on cryptozoology, legends,
           Nessie the Loch Ness Monster and the giant squid.
           </pstcn:description>
     <pstcn:dateCreated>1999-08-01T00:00:00-06:00</pstcn:dateCreated>
     <pstcn:author>Shelley Powers</pstcn:author>
     <pstcn:owner>Burningbird Network</pstcn:owner>
        </rdf:Description>
     </pstcn:bio>
     <pstcn:relevancy />
     <pstcn:presentation />
     <pstcn:history />
     <pstcn:related />
  </pstcn:Resource>

</rdf:RDF>
```

The `rdf:bio` resource isn't given a URI because one doesn't exist for it. The resulting graph shows a computer-generated blank node identifier assigned to the resource.

Again, in the interests of simplifying the model as much as possible, another RDF/XML shortcut is applied to the model. In this case, the attribute `rdf:parseType` is added to the `pstcn:bio` element, and its value is set to "Resource". Doing this, we can eliminate the `rdf:Description` block:

```
<pstcn:bio rdf:parseType="Resource">
    <pstcn:title>Tale of Two Monsters: Legends</pstcn:title>
    <pstcn:abstract>
      When I think of "monsters" I think of the creatures of
      legends and tales, from the books and movies, and
      I think of the creatures that have entertained me for years.
    </pstcn:abstract>
    <pstcn:description>
     Part 1 of four-part series on cryptozoology, legends,
     Nessie the Loch Ness Monster and the giant squid.
    </pstcn:description>
    <pstcn:dateCreated>1999-08-01T00:00:00-06:00</pstcn:dateCreated>
    <pstcn:author>Shelley Powers</pstcn:author>
    <pstcn:owner>Burningbird Network</pstcn:owner>
</pstcn:bio>
```

Though simplified with this syntactic change, the resulting directed graph of the model at this point, as shown in Figure 6-2, is equivalent to the longer, more formal syntax.

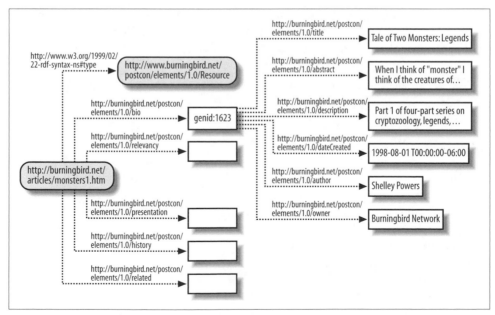

Figure 6-2. RDF directed graph of model defined in Example 6-2

Though the resulting XML is simpler when using one of the established shortcuts, it doesn't necessarily reflect either the N-Triples or the directed graph of the model. This could be confusing for people new to RDF/XML. When documenting your model, you'll most likely want to start with the more formal RDF/XML syntax and then demonstrate the vocabulary with instances that use the shortcuts.

In Figure 6-2, I show the bio properties grouped via a blank node. Coming from a relational database background, my first inclination is to group related properties into a resource and link this back to the primary resource, rather than "flatten" the model and include each property as a direct attribute of the original resource. I follow this approach with RDF, primarily because, in my opinion, it leads to cleaner RDF processing—whether that processing occurs manually or through automation.

If I had listed each of the "grouped" properties directly with the resource, there's no breakdown for *relevancy* or for the resource's *bio*. If a specific process was interested only in the biographical elements, each bio-related attribute would then have to be defined as biographically related to highlight it from the other properties. Now, if the bio-related properties were defined within one specific RDF "entity" (resource), it's a simple matter to process only bio properties just by processing all elements within the designated bio resource. Whether you're generating RDF through an API, consuming it with an RDF parser, or visually looking at an RDF document, grouping the properties through derived resources makes sense.

The other groupings of attributes, such as relevancy and presentation, are completed in the same manner as bio and I won't cover all that here. However, the Related predicate is handled differently and is therefore covered in the next section.

The PostCon vocabulary is used as a test case in all the examples for the rest of the book.

Adding Repeating Values

Not all recorded values occur as single properties within the PostCon vocabulary—a web resource can move many times, and there can be more than one recommended resource to replace an outdated item. The vocabulary must be able to handle repeating properties. Within the RDF specification, you can use the same predicate in multiple statements, such as the following:

```
<pstcn:related rdf:resource="monsters2.htm" />
<pstcn:related rdf:resource="monsters3.htm" />
<pstcn:related rdf:resource="monsters4.htm" />
```

The distinguishing aspect of these statements then becomes the object, the predicate value. Attached to the primary resource, this syntax states that there are three related resources for the entity being defined. It also states that there's no order to the resources, and the only point of connectivity between the resources is that they're related, in some way, to the original entity. There is neither an implicit nor an explicit grouping between the items.

At this point, the RDF/XML just shows the three related resources, and the resulting directed graph would show these items with ovals drawn around the objects as well as the resource. However, if I wanted to include additional information about the relationship between the related resources and the resource being defined in the document, I could do so in a couple of ways.

First, I can define the related resource using the `rdf:parseType="Resource"` setting as I did with `pstcn:bio`. The problem with this is that each of the related resources actually does have a URI, and using `rdf:parseType`, I'd lose this information. Instead, what I'll use is the `rdf:resource` attribute. This allows me to specify the URI for the resource.

Since these resources are related but separate from the main resource, I tend to want my model to reflect this, so I'll define the related resources as separate resources, related only through the URI. Example 6-3 shows the RDF/XML for the PostCon instance with the three related resources, each of them defined using the `pstcn:Resource` class, and each including the related resource attributes of `title` and `reason`.

Example 6-3. Adding in related PostCon resources

```
<?xml version="1.0"?>
<rdf:RDF
  xmlns:rdf="http://www.w3.org/1999/02/22-rdf-syntax-ns#"
  xmlns:pstcn="http://burningbird.net/postcon/elements/1.0/"
  xml:base="http://burningbird.net/articles/">

<pstcn:Resource rdf:about="monsters1.htm">

    <pstcn:bio rdf:parseType="Resource">
        <pstcn:title>Tale of Two Monsters: Legends</pstcn:title>
        <pstcn:abstract>
         When I think of "monsters" I think of the creatures of
         legends and tales, from the books and movies, and
         I think of the creatures that have entertained me for years.
        </pstcn:abstract>
        <pstcn:description>
         Part 1 of four-part series on cryptozoology, legends,
         Nessie the Loch Ness Monster and the giant squid.
        </pstcn:description>
        <pstcn:dateCreated>1999-08-01T00:00:00-06:00</pstcn:dateCreated>
        <pstcn:author>Shelley Powers</pstcn:author>
        <pstcn:owner>Burningbird Network</pstcn:owner>
    </pstcn:bio>
```

Example 6-3. Adding in related PostCon resources (continued)

```
    <pstcn:related rdf:resource="monsters2.htm" />
    <pstcn:related rdf:resource="monsters3.htm" />
    <pstcn:related rdf:resource="monsters4.htm" />

  </pstcn:Resource>

  <pstcn:Resource rdf:about="monsters2.htm">
    <pstcn:title>Cryptozooloy</pstcn:title>
    <pstcn:reason>First in the Tale of Two Monsters series.</pstcn:reason>
  </pstcn:Resource>
  <pstcn:Resource rdf:about="monsters3.htm">
    <pstcn:title>A Tale of Two Monsters: Architeuthis Dux </pstcn:title>
    <pstcn:reason>Second in the Tale of Two Monsters series.</pstcn:reason>
  </pstcn:Resource>
  <pstcn:Resource rdf:about="monsters4.htm">
    <pstcn:title>Nessie, the Loch Ness Monster </pstcn:title>
    <pstcn:reason>Fourth in the Tale of Two Monsters series.</pstcn:reason>
  </pstcn:Resource>

</rdf:RDF>
```

Since the predicates associated with each related resource are simple and nonrepeating, I'm going to apply another shortcut to simplify the model—simple nonrepeating predicates can be listed as attributes on the resource:

```
  <pstcn:Resource rdf:about="monsters2.htm"
        pstcn:title="Cryptozooloy"
        pstcn:reason="First in the Tale of Two Monsters series." />
  <pstcn:Resource rdf:about="monsters3.htm"
        pstcn:title="A Tale of Two Monsters: Architeuthis Dux"
        pstcn:reason="Second in the Tale of Two Monsters series." />
  <pstcn:Resource rdf:about="monsters4.htm"
        pstcn:title="Nessie, the Loch Ness Monster"
        pstcn:reason="Fourth in the Tale of Two Monsters series." />
```

The resulting RDF/XML and directed graph are the same. The only difference this change makes is to make the XML simpler and a little easier to read. It's also more comfortable for people familiar with XML, though, as stated earlier, it does tend to obscure the RDF constructs.

Another reason to use this shortcut is that, if I preferred not to list the resources separately, I could list them as is with the predicates redefined as attributes, directly back into main resource. You couldn't do this using the `rdf:resource` attribute because you couldn't add formalized predicates to the block without generating errors. You would have to use the more formal node-arc-node by defining the predicate (`pstcn:related`), which would contain the `rdf:Description` block, which would then contain the related predicates:

```
  <pstcn:related>
    <rdf:Description rdf:about="monsters3.htm"
        pstcn:title="A Tale of Two Monsters: Architeuthis Dux"
```

```
        pstcn:reason="Second in the Tale of Two Monsters series." />
   </pstcn:related>
```

However, you can add predicates to the related resources that have been defined through the use of pstcn:Resource, by using the predicates as attributes shortcut, as demonstrated in Example 6-4.

Example 6-4. Embedding related resources directly in main resource

```
<?xml version="1.0"?>
<rdf:RDF
  xmlns:rdf="http://www.w3.org/1999/02/22-rdf-syntax-ns#"
  xmlns:pstcn="http://burningbird.net/postcon/elements/1.0/"
  xml:base="http://burningbird.net/articles/">

<pstcn:Resource rdf:about="monsters1.htm">

   <pstcn:bio rdf:parseType="Resource">
      <pstcn:title>Tale of Two Monsters: Legends</pstcn:title>
   <pstcn:abstract>
      When I think of "monsters" I think of the creatures of
      legends and tales, from the books and movies, and
      I think of the creatures that have entertained me for years.
   </pstcn:abstract>
      <pstcn:description>
      Part 1 of four-part series on cryptozoology, legends,
      Nessie the Loch Ness Monster and the giant squid.
      </pstcn:description>
   <pstcn:dateCreated>1999-08-01T00:00:00-06:00</pstcn:dateCreated>
   <pstcn:author>Shelley Powers</pstcn:author>
   <pstcn:owner>Burningbird Network</pstcn:owner>
   </pstcn:bio>

   <pstcn:Resource rdf:resource="monsters2.htm"
      pstcn:title="Cryptozooloy"
      pstcn:reason="First in the Tale of Two Monsters series." />
   <pstcn:Resource rdf:resource="monsters3.htm"
      pstcn:title="A Tale of Two Monsters: Architeuthis Dux"
      pstcn:reason="Second in the Tale of Two Monsters series." />
   <pstcn:Resource rdf:resource="monsters4.htm"
      pstcn:title="Nessie, the Loch Ness Monster"
      pstcn:reason="Fourth in the Tale of Two Monsters series." />

   </pstcn:Resource>
</rdf:RDF>
```

In some ways, this demonstrates that you either commit to using formal syntax all the way, or you commit to using abbreviated (shortcut) syntax all the way—at least for one complete RDF construct, such as the related items. Since my reasons for wanting to list the related resources separately remain, even though the RDF/XML and resulting directed graph are identical, I'll continue to use the approach demonstrated in Example 6-3.

If I want to show that predicates are related to one another in some way beyond just being related to the defined entity, I'll use a container to group the items and then attach that container to the entity. The next section describes how.

Adding a Container

The PostCon vocabulary considers movements of the web resource related to one another. The first movement occurs when the resource is added to the web site; the second and each additional movement are related to one another by the date and time of the movement. Infinite numbers of movements are possible.

To group like items that are related to one another as well as to the main resource, I could use either an RDF Container or a Collection. Both provide the grouping-of-related-items semantics that I need, but the relationship and number of items within the grouping differ based on which construct I use. And that's how I'll determine which to use.

As described in Chapter 4, a Container is a group of related items that has no nth point—in other words, it could possibly contain an infinite number of items. A Collection, on the other hand, always has an endpoint, the implicit `rdf:nil`. Use of Collection creates the assumption that the grouping is of a finite number of objects.

Additional tool-based semantics are associated with containers and collections—such as sequence with `rdf:Seq` and so on—but these aren't enforced within the RDF data model/graph, so I won't depend on them to make my decision about what to use. Instead, I'll rely on the one factor that is semantically defined in the RDF graph: whether the number of items in the group is infinite. Since I determined that a web resource can have infinite movements, I will choose an RDF Container.

I now face additional choices, such as which container type to use. There is no enforcement of the Container differences within RDF, but there is a general assumption about behavior attached to each, so I'll want to pick the RDF Container type (`Seq`, `Bag`, or `Alt`) that fits my vocabulary model.

Since each movement is unique, the `Bag` type isn't a good fit because an implicit assumption associated with it is that items can be duplicated. Nor is the `Alt` type a good fit, because it implicitly represents items that are alternatives to each other. The best fit is `Seq`, which has implicit associated semantics of related items in a sequence, from first to last. This fits `history` particularly well.

Each movement has its own URI representing the movement itself, so each one can be identified distinctly. Because of this, my preference is, again, to list these out separately, related to the main resource through the container. Example 6-5 shows the PostCon vocabulary after adding in the `Seq` container. Note that I created a new class for the movement, `pstcn:Movement`. I couldn't use `pstcn:Resource`, because the movements really aren't resources. I could have also left the resources defined in generic `rdf:Description` blocks, but I prefer to embed as much information into the model as possible, and defining the new class—Movement—provides a type to go with each movement definition, independent of the relationship defined by history earlier in the main resource.

Example 6-5. PostCon vocabulary instance showing Movement and related resources

```
<?xml version="1.0"?>
<rdf:RDF
  xmlns:rdf="http://www.w3.org/1999/02/22-rdf-syntax-ns#"
  xmlns:pstcn="http://burningbird.net/postcon/elements/1.0/"
  xml:base="http://burningbird.net/articles/">

  <pstcn:Resource rdf:about="monsters1.htm">

<!-biography of resource->
    <pstcn:bio rdf:parseType="Resource">
      <pstcn:title>Tale of Two Monsters: Legends</pstcn:title>
      <pstcn:abstract>
        When I think of "monsters" I think of the creatures of
        legends and tales, from the books and movies, and
        I think of the creatures that have entertained me for years.
      </pstcn:abstract>
      <pstcn:description>
        Part 1 of four-part series on cryptozoology, legends,
        Nessie the Loch Ness Monster and the giant squid.
      </pstcn:description>
      <pstcn:dateCreated>1999-08-01T00:00:00-06:00</pstcn:dateCreated>
      <pstcn:author>Shelley Powers</pstcn:author>
      <pstcn:owner>Burningbird Network</pstcn:owner>
    </pstcn:bio>

<!-related resources->
    <pstcn:related rdf:resource="monsters2.htm" />
    <pstcn:related rdf:resource="monsters3.htm" />
    <pstcn:related rdf:resource="monsters4.htm" />

<!-resource movements->
    <pstcn:history>
      <rdf:Seq>
        <rdf:_1 rdf:resource="http://www.yasd.com/dynaearth/monsters1.htm" />
        <rdf:_2 rdf:resource="http://www.dynamicearth.com/articles/monsters1.htm" />
        <rdf:_3 rdf:resource="http://burningbird.net/articles/monsters1.htm" />
      </rdf:Seq>
    </pstcn:history>

  </pstcn:Resource>

<!-related resource defintions->
  <pstcn:Resource rdf:about="monsters2.htm">
    <pstcn:title>Cryptozooloy</pstcn:title>
    <pstcn:reason>First in the Tale of Two Monsters series.</pstcn:reason>
  </pstcn:Resource>
  <pstcn:Resource rdf:about="monsters3.htm">
```

```
        <pstcn:title>A Tale of Two Monsters: Architeuthis Dux (Giant Squid)</pstcn:title>
        <pstcn:reason>Second in the Tale of Two Monsters series.</pstcn:reason>
    </pstcn:Resource>
    <pstcn:Resource rdf:about="monsters4.htm">
        <pstcn:title>Nessie, the Loch Ness Monster </pstcn:title>
        <pstcn:reason>Fourth in the Tale of Two Monsters series.</pstcn:reason>
    </pstcn:Resource>

<!-resource movement definitions->
    <pstcn:Movement rdf:about="http://www.yasd.com/dynaearth/monsters1.htm">
        <pstcn:movementType>Add</pstcn:movementType>
        <pstcn:reason>New Article</pstcn:reason>
        <pstcn:date>1998-01-01T00:00:00-05:00</pstcn:date>
    </pstcn:Movement>
    <pstcn:Movement rdf:about="http://www.dynamicearth.com/articles/monsters1.htm">
        <pstcn:movementType>Move</pstcn:movementType>
        <pstcn:reason>moved to dynamicearth.com domain</pstcn:reason>
        <pstcn:date>1999-10-31:T00:00:00-05:00</pstcn:date>
    </pstcn:Movement>
    <pstcn:Movement rdf:about="http://burningbird.net/articles/monsters1.htm">
        <pstcn:movementType>Move</pstcn:movementType>
        <pstcn:reason>Moved to burningbird.net</pstcn:reason>
        <pstcn:date>2002-11-01:T00:00:00-05:00</pstcn:date>
    </pstcn:Movement>

</rdf:RDF>
```

There is also something intriguing in this RDF/XML example—the actual resource is defined both as the document Resource and as a Movement (in fact, the last movement for the history since the resource was defined in the PostCon system before any additional movements were made). This is perfectly legitimate and results in an interesting directed graph of a resource that has an arc pointing back to itself, as demonstrated in Figure 6-3.

Also notice in the figure that the original resource now has two type properties associated with it: one for Resource and one for Movement. Again, this is perfectly legitimate RDF. In fact, the more knowledge we can put into the model, and the simpler the syntax, the better.

Adding in a Value

The example RDF/XML demonstrated to this point has focused on bio, history, and related resources. The other PostCon classes—Relevancy and Presentation—are treated the same as bio, except for one new construct: the Presentation's Required property. Unlike other properties defined in the document up to this point, Requires is neither a straight resource property nor is it a literal—it's a value that has an associated type that determines how the value is treated. The ideal RDF/XML construct to use to represent this is `rdf:value`.

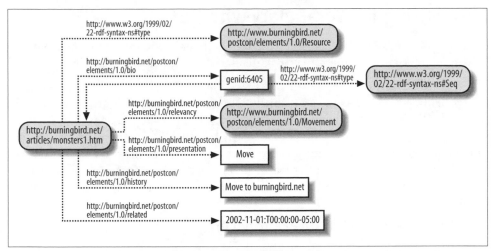

Figure 6-3. A resource containing a predicate whose value is the same URI as the original resource

Without replicating all of the Relevancy properties, the following RDF/XML demonstrates how `rdf:value` would work for `pstcn:requires`. The `pstcn:requires` property is defined with an `rdf:parseType` of `"Resource"`, and has two attributes: `pstcn:type`, which specifies the type of required resource, and `rdf:value`, which signals the actual value. Two resources are required:

```
<pstcn:presentation rdf:parseType="Resource">
    <pstcn:requires rdf:parseType="Resource">
        <pstcn:type>stylesheet</pstcn:type>
            <rdf:value>http://burningbird.net/de.css</rdf:value>
    </pstcn:requires>
    <pstcn:requires rdf:parseType="Resource">
        <pstcn:type>logo</pstcn:type>
        <rdf:value>http://burningbird.net/mm/dynamicearth.jpg</rdf:value>
    </pstcn:requires>
</pstcn:presentation>
```

The intended semantics for `rdf:value` are that it always references the actual value of the predicate—anything else is just definitive information about how that predicate is treated.

The rest of the vocabulary uses the same constructs as have been used to this point and is omitted for brevity. A complete example of the vocabulary is given later, after a few modifications are made to merge the vocabulary with the Dublin Core. In the meantime, though, testing the vocabulary demonstrated to this point with other web site test cases shows that it tests out with all the business domain data. At this point, we can be comfortable that the vocabulary matches the system needs. The next step is to formalize the vocabulary schema using RDF Schema.

Formalizing the Vocabulary with RDFS

Formally defined RDFS schemas aren't required for all RDF documents, but the schema approach guarantees that a particular RDF document is semantically and syntactically consistent across implementations.

RDFS defines which vocabulary elements are classes and which are properties. In addition, RDFS also matches a property with a specific element, as well as defining the range for each property. This is particularly helpful when defining properties that contain a range of elements, such as the pstcn:movementType property in the last section. RDFS also documents the type of literal that each property can reference—whether the property value is a string or a number, such as an integer.

What Is a Class and What Is a Property?

Determining what is a class and what is a property within the vocabulary is an interesting RDF Schema challenge. Your first reaction might be that an RDFS Class is equivalent to a relational data model Entity, but that doesn't hold.

In actuality, an RDFS Class is any item that can be used in place of an rdf:Description block, with an associated rdf:type, such as Movement or Resource. An RDFS Class is not a resource property, like bio, Presentation, or Relevancy.

 A quick test to double-check your use of RDFS Class versus RDFS Property for an item is to use ICS-FORTH's Validating RDF Parser (VRP), asking for a graph output on the test RDF/XML document. This tool actually identifies which elements it views as classes and which as properties. This tool is covered in Chapter 7.

Defining the Vocabulary Classes

To start, define the PostCon vocabulary classes. Table 6-1 shows that the classes mark the main objects defined within the table, as you would expect. Using RDFS, then, the main object of the vocabulary, Resource, is defined with the following RDF/XML syntax:

```
<rdfs:Class rdf:about="http://burningbird.net/postcon/elements/1.0/Resource">
 <rdfs:isDefinedBy rdf:resource="http://burningbird.net/postcon/elements/1.0/"/>
 <rdfs:subClassOf rdf:resource="http://www.w3.org/2000/01/rdf-schema#Resource"/>
 <rdfs:label xml:lang="en"> Web Resource</rdfs:label>
 <rdfs:comment xml:lang="en">
    Web resource managed with PostCon System
 </rdfs:comment>
</rdfs:Class>
```

This RDF/XML defines Resource to be an RDF Class, defined within the schema http://burningbird.net/postcon/elements/1.0/, which is a subclass of the RDF Resource type. Its human-readable label is Web Resource, and the comments provide a brief description of the item. Both label and comments have an `xml:lang` attribute defining the language. If you're providing multilingual support for your elements, repeat the label and comments but change the `xml:lang` attribute value.

 Though things such as label and comments aren't necessary for the schema, you should always include these. BrownSauce, a Java-based RDF browser (described in Chapter 7), provides this information to people browsing RDF/XML documents.

This class by itself demonstrates the need for namespaces within RDF/XML; the RDF vocabulary also has a Resource class. The same type of RDFS/XML is also applied to bio, Movement, Relevancy, and Presentation, all of which are defined as classes. All other elements are defined as properties.

Defining the Properties

Each property within the vocabulary is defined, including providing data type information, human-readable comments and labels, and a definition of the relationship between properties and classes. The latter is particularly important because it provides usage guidelines as well as understanding of the schema.

An example of a property definition for PostCon is the following, for type:

```
<rdf:Property rdf:about="http://burningbird.net/postcon/elements/1.0/type">
<rdfs:isDefinedBy rdf:resource="http://burningbird.net/postcon/elements/1.0/"/>
<rdfs:label xml:lang="en">Resource Type</rdfs:label>
<rdfs:comment>Type of Required Resource</rdfs:comment>
<rdfs:range rdf:resource="http://www.w3.org/2000/01/rdf-schema#Literal"/>
</rdf:Property>
```

The type element has a range that determines the type of values associated with it. In this case, the range is literal, meaning the element will contain literal values. In addition, there are two domains associated with the title that show the classes the property is associated with: bio and Movement.

The other properties are defined using almost the same schema, changing the label, comments, and domain as appropriate; the two properties history and related are different from the other properties, though, because they don't describe a literal. For instance, here is the definition for the related property:

```
<rdf:Property rdf:about="http://burningbird.net/postcon/elements/1.0/related">
<rdfs:isDefinedBy rdf:resource="http://burningbird.net/postcon/elements/1.0/"/>
<rdfs:label xml:lang="en"> Related Resource</rdfs:label>
<rdfs:comment xml:lang="en">
    Resources within PostCon system related to current resource
</rdfs:comment>
<rdfs:range rdf:resource="http://burningbird.net/postcon/elements/1.0/Resource"/>
<rdfs:domain rdf:resource="http://burningbird.net/postcon/elements/1.0/Resource"/>
</rdf:Property>
```

The predicate object associated with `related` is a resource of class Movement. Other than that, though, the definition is fairly close to how all the properties are defined.

The complete schema is shown in the next section. Note that testing the schema within the RDF Validator does prove that the RDF Schema is valid RDF/XML. The resultant RDF graph is a bit hard to read, though—all those references to the same RDFS classes.

Certain of the properties in the schema have an "allowable values are..." within them. There is currently no way to constrain allowable literals within the RDF Schema. However, since the schema is used more for human rather than machine interpretation, including this information within the comment is useful.

A vocabulary schema defines vocabulary elements and their relationship with one another and with the RDF and RDFS elements. For instance, since the PostCon schema document is a resource, using the PostCon vocabulary elements within the document to detail its creation is perfectly acceptable.

This approach is used within another widely used vocabulary, the Dublin Core (DC), which we will look at next and compare to the PostCon vocabulary. We'll also find that we can modify PostCon to make use of DC elements, simplifying it.

Integrating the Dublin Core

According to the mission statement, located at *http://www.dublincore.org/*:

> The Dublin Core Metadata Initiative is an open forum engaged in the development of interoperable online metadata standards that support a broad range of purposes and business models. DCMI's activities include consensus-driven working groups, global workshops, conferences, standards liaison, and educational efforts to promote widespread acceptance of metadata standards and practices.

The Dublin Core's primary purpose is to discover a metadata model that can be used to describe resources intelligently so that this information can be used in more efficient and intelligent resource searches, knowledge systems, and so on.

At first, this description of Dublin Core may position it as a competitive specification to RDF, but in reality, they're highly compatible. Dublin Core is an effort to define the business data of the Web, so to speak. RDF, on the other hand, is a way of recording this metadata so that it can be merged with other metadata defined for other businesses, not just the business of the Web. In other words, RDF is the methodology, and Dublin Core is one business employing the RDF methodology.

Since Dublin Core is an effort to define business data, serializing that data need not be done with RDF. The Dublin Core project provides an RDF/XML version of the data that it has defined, true. But it also provides one in simple, basic XML and one in HTML. However, it is the RDF/XML version we're interested in and will focus on at this time.

An Overview of the Dublic Core MetaData Element Set

The Dublin Core MetaData Element set (Version 1.1, found at *http://www.dublincore.org/documents/1999/07/02/dces/*) consists of a core set of elements that comprise what is known as simple Dublin Core. These elements are:

title
: A name given to the resource

creator
: An entity responsible for making the content of the resource

subject
: The topic of the content of the resource

description
: An account of the content of the resource

public
: An entity responsible for making the content available

contributor
: An entity responsible for making contributions to the content of the resource

date
: A date associated with an event in the life cycle of the resource

type
: The nature or genre of the content of the resource

format
: The physical or digital manifestation of the resource

identifier
: An unambiguous reference to the resource within a given context

source
: A reference to the resource from which the present resource is derived

language
: A language of the intellectual content of the resource

relation
: A reference to a related resource

coverage
: The extent or scope of the content of the resource

rights
: Information about rights held in and over the resource

Associated with the different entities is additional information, such as Language being derived from the two-character language code derived from the ISO 639 document (such as "EN" for English) and a date format for date (YYYY-MM-DD).

As you can see immediately, several DC elements could be used in place of PostCon elements. First, though, let's take a look at Dublin Core implemented as RDF/XML.

Dublin Core in RDF/XML

The Dublin Core vocabulary is one of the simplest, which is probably one reason it's so heavily used. The namespace for the elements is at:

```
http://purl.org/dc/elements/1.1/
```

If you go to this URL with your browser, you'll see an actual document, with a schema description for each element. The prefix usually given for the Dublin Core namespace within an RDF document is dc, which we'll use in this chapter.

I won't include the document here, nor will I discuss each element. However, some elements are of particular interest because they seem to map to a PostCon element. And if there's a way of reducing PostCon, we'll want to pursue it.

For instance, one element from PostCon that definitely looks to be in DC is title. The Dublin Core title is defined to be "a name given to the resource." Since our definition of title in PostCon is "resource's title," we have a match. Looking at the schema definition for the property we find:

```
<rdf:Property rdf:about="http://purl.org/dc/elements/1.1/title">
 <rdfs:label xml:lang="en-US">Title</rdfs:label>
 <rdfs:comment xml:lang="en-US">A name given to the resource.</rdfs:comment>
 <dc:description xml:lang="en-US">Typically, a Title will be a name by which the
resource is formally known.</dc:description>
 <rdfs:isDefinedBy rdf:resource="http://purl.org/dc/elements/1.1/" />
 <dcterms:issued>1999-07-02</dcterms:issued>
</rdf:Property>
```

There are some differences between this and the original PostCon title schema definition. For instance, the schema for the PostCon title listed the property's domains (that is, acceptable contexts for the property) to be the pstcn:Resource class (and indirectly to Movement, which is a subclass of pstcn:Resource). The DC doesn't list domains because it doesn't seek to limit what classes it can be used for, opening the door for us to use the property in PostCon.

Another difference is that DC is used directly to describe the property. Again, this won't adversely impact the use of title in PostCon. In fact, the additional information is helpful. Finally, there is another property assigned to a different namespace: dcterms:issued. Before we can determine whether this property will limit our use of title in PostCon, we'll have to take a closer look at this new schema.

 For more on Dublin Core in RDF/XML, see the pending recommendation "Expressing Simple Dublin Core in RDF/XML," authored by Dave Beckett, Eric Miller, and Dan Brickley, and found at *http://www. dublincore.org/documents/2001/11/28/dcmes-xml/*.

Qualified Dublin Core

All of the Dublin Core metadata elements are properties within the context of RDF. Within an RDF graph, that means that all of them radiate out from a single resource. Again, this makes the vocabulary attractive to use because it is so simple and uncomplicated. However, there are basic limitations to how broadly one can stretch any one element to meet a specific use. And by stretching meanings at all, we lose some refinement.

Sure, we can group all dates together, but do we want to?

So, the Dublin Core Working Group set out to define a set of qualifiers that limit or modify the meaning of the DC elements. Additionally, the group determined that the qualifiers belonged in one of two different categories: qualifiers for element refinement and qualifiers for encoding schema.

Element refinement qualifiers restrict the scope of the element. For instance, there is the general concept of date and then there is creation date (from PostCon), modified date, and so on. Those vocabularies that want such refinements can use things such as modified date and creation date. However, vocabularies (or applications) that don't care about the refinement can ignore it and just treat the qualified elements as date.

Element refinement qualifiers are based on the business of the schema rather than its implementation. Encoding schema qualifiers, though, exist purely to help with parsing and interpretation of the data. Again, date can have many interpretations as to what type of date is being recorded. By using encoding schema qualifiers, there's no confusion about what to expect for data within a specific date field.

When looking at Dublin Core, we can see uses for several of the elements, but when we look at the qualified Dublin Core implemented in RDF/XML, we find a strong match for several PostCon classes and properties.

First, the namespace for the qualified Dublin Core Schema is at *http://purl.org/dc/terms/*. The namespace prefix for the qualified Dublin Core is usually dcterms.

The first property that attracts attention is created, a qualifier on the date property. The created definition is:

```
<rdf:Property rdf:about="http://purl.org/dc/terms/created">
  <rdfs:label>Created</rdfs:label>
  <rdfs:comment>Date of creation of the resource.</rdfs:comment>
  <rdfs:subPropertyOf rdf:resource = "http://purl.org/dc/elements/1.1/date" />
  <rdfs:isDefinedBy rdf:resource="http://purl.org/dc/terms/" />
</rdf:Property>
```

The thing to focus on is the comment Date of creation of the resource. This exactly matches the description for the pstcn:creationDate property in PostCon. In the last section, we weren't sure how to handle the dcterms:issued, but now we know it's nothing more than an issued date, a further qualification of the specification for the title property.

Another set of properties that seemed similar to PostCon elements is the DC Relation property and the qualified replacers: `dcterms:isReplacedBy`, `dcterms:seeAlso`, `dcterms:references`, and so on. They're not used to replace PostCon's `related` property (and associated Resource class) though because the DC properties have built-in semantics that don't encompass all of PostCon's related property semantics. However, PostCon's `pstcn:dependencies` and DC's qualifier `dcterms:requires` seem to be a good match.

After the first glance, both the original Dublin Core elements and the qualified element set seem to have good replacements, or additions, to the PostCon vocabulary. And since both are defined within RDF, it will be simple to use them together in RDF/XML documents.

Mixing Vocabularies

After the first glance at the Dublin Core simple elements, I decided to replace the PostCon attributes demonstrated in this chapter with matching DC elements. These include the following replacements:

`pstcn:title`
    `dc:title`

`pstcn:author`
    `dc:creator`

`pstcn:owner`
    `dc:publisher`

`pstcn:abstract`
    `dcterms:abstract`

`pstcn:description`
    `dc:description`

`pstcn:creationDate`
    `dc:created`

`pstcn:date`
    `dc:date`

I also decided to add the `format` property, to provide the resource file type. Small changes, but they do reduce the size of the PostCon vocabulary, as well as allowing easier data sharing on these items.

To see how these two vocabularies work together, the RDF/XML for the sample `monsters1.htm` resource is provided in Example 6-6. The Dublin Core Schema namespaces are added to the top-level RDF element, and the `dc` and `dcterms` properties are used in place of the now-removed PostCon properties. In addition, both Relevancy and the Presentation resources have been added to complete the document.

Example 6-6. Mixing PostCon and DC vocabulary elements

```
<?xml version="1.0"?>
<rdf:RDF
  xmlns:rdf="http://www.w3.org/1999/02/22-rdf-syntax-ns#"
  xmlns:pstcn="http://burningbird.net/postcon/elements/1.0/"
  xmlns:dcterms="http://purl.org/dc/terms/"
  xmlns:dc="http://purl.org/dc/elements/1.1/"
  xml:base="http://burningbird.net/articles/">

  <pstcn:Resource rdf:about="monsters1.htm">

<!--Resource biographical information-->
    <pstcn:bio rdf:parseType="Resource">
        <dc:title>Tale of Two Monsters: Legends</dc:title>
        <dcterms:abstract>
            When I think of "monsters" I think of the creatures of
            legends and tales, from the books and movies, and
            I think of the creatures that have entertained me for years.
        </dcterms:abstract>
        <dc:description>
            Part 1 of four-part series on cryptozoology, legends,
            Nessie the Loch Ness Monster and the giant squid.
        </dc:description>
       <dc:created>1999-08-01T00:00:00-06:00</dc:created>
       <dc:creator>Shelley Powers</dc:creator>
       <dc:publisher>Burningbird Network</dc:publisher>
      </pstcn:bio>

<!--Resource's relevancy at time RDF/XML document was built-->
     <pstcn:relevancy rdf:parseType="Resource">
       <pstcn:currentStatus>Active</pstcn:currentStatus>
       <dcterms:valid>2003-12-01T00:00:00-06:00</dcterms:valid>
       <dc:subject>legends</dc:subject>
       <dc:subject>giant squid</dc:subject>
       <dc:subject>Loch Ness Monster</dc:subject>
       <dc:subject>Architeuthis Dux</dc:subject>
       <dc:subject>Nessie</dc:subject>
       <dcterms:isReferencedBy rdf:resource="http://www.pibburns.com/cryptozo.htm" />
       <dcterms:references rdf:resource="http://www.nrcc.utmb.edu/" />
      </pstcn:relevancy>

<!--Presentation/consumption information about resource-->
     <pstcn:presentation rdf:parseType="Resource">
        <dc:format>text/html</dc:format>
        <dcterms:conformsTo>XHTML 1.0 Strict</dcterms:conformsTo>
        <dcterms:conformsTo>CSS Validation</dcterms:conformsTo>
        <dcterms:requires>HTML User agent</dcterms:requires>
        <pstcn:requires rdf:parseType="Resource">
           <pstcn:type>stylesheet</pstcn:type>
           <rdf:value>http://burningbird.net/de.css</rdf:value>
        </pstcn:requires>
        <pstcn:requires rdf:parseType="Resource">
           <pstcn:type>logo</pstcn:type>
```

Example 6-6. Mixing PostCon and DC vocabulary elements (continued)

```
            <rdf:value>http://burningbird.net/mm/dynamicearth.jpg</rdf:value>
          </pstcn:requires>
        </pstcn:presentation>

<!--History of events of resource-->
      <pstcn:history>
        <rdf:Seq>
          <rdf:_1 rdf:resource="http://www.yasd.com/dynaearth/monsters1.htm" />
          <rdf:_2 rdf:resource="http://www.dynamicearth.com/articles/monsters1.htm" />
          <rdf:_3 rdf:resource="http://burningbird.net/articles/monsters1.htm" />
        </rdf:Seq>
      </pstcn:history>

<!--Resources internal to PostCon that are related to resource-->
      <pstcn:related rdf:resource="monsters2.htm" />
      <pstcn:related rdf:resource="monsters3.htm" />
      <pstcn:related rdf:resource="monsters4.htm" />
    </pstcn:Resource>

<!--Related resources-->
    <pstcn:Resource rdf:about="monsters2.htm">
      <dc:title>Cryptozooloy</dc:title>
      <pstcn:reason>First in the Tale of Two Monsters series.</pstcn:reason>
    </pstcn:Resource>
    <pstcn:Resource rdf:about="monsters3.htm">
      <dc:title>A Tale of Two Monsterss: Architeuthis Dux (Giant Squid)</dc:title>
      <pstcn:reason>Second in the Tale of Two Monsters series.</pstcn:reason>
    </pstcn:Resource>
    <pstcn:Resource rdf:about="monsters4.htm">
      <dc:title>Nessie, the Loch Ness Monster </dc:title>
      <pstcn:reason>Fourth in the Tale of Two Monsters series.</pstcn:reason>
    </pstcn:Resource>

<!--Resource events-->
    <pstcn:Movement rdf:about="http://www.yasd.com/dynaearth/monsters1.htm">
        <pstcn:movementType>Add</pstcn:movementType>
        <pstcn:reason>New Article</pstcn:reason>
        <dc:date>1998-01-01T00:00:00-05:00</dc:date>
    </pstcn:Movement>
    <pstcn:Movement rdf:about="http://www.dynamicearth.com/articles/monsters1.htm">
        <pstcn:movementType>Move</pstcn:movementType>
        <pstcn:reason>Moved to separate dynamicearth.com domain</pstcn:reason>
        <dc:date>1999-10-31:T00:00:00-05:00</dc:date>
    </pstcn:Movement>
    <pstcn:Movement rdf:about="http://www.burningbird.net/articles/monsters1.htm">
        <pstcn:movementType>Move</pstcn:movementType>
        <pstcn:reason>Collapsed into Burningbird</pstcn:reason>
        <dc:date>2002-11-01</dc:date>
    </pstcn:Movement>

</rdf:RDF>
```

Running this document through the RDF Validator generates the expected RDF graph and no error.

One thing that this exercise demonstrates is the need to keep a vocabulary small and then add to it. As you saw with Dublin Core, the group started with a small set of important elements and then extended this with a new set of qualifier elements. This is a good approach for you to follow with your vocabularies and is the approach that other groups such as the RSS Working Group (discussed in Chapter 13) used. Doing so, others are more likely to make use of your vocabulary, and it also decreases the chances for modification in the future. The complete RDF Schema for PostCon, after the Dublin Core elements have been identified, is actually quite small. It's shown in its entirety in Example 6-7.

Example 6-7. PostCon RDF Schema

```
<?xml version="1.0"?>
<rdf:RDF xml:lang="en"
    xmlns:rdf="http://www.w3.org/1999/02/22-rdf-syntax-ns#"
    xmlns:rdfs="http://www.w3.org/2000/01/rdf-schema#">

<rdfs:Class rdf:about="http://burningbird.net/postcon/elements/1.0/Resource">
 <rdfs:isDefinedBy rdf:resource="http://burningbird.net/postcon/elements/1.0/"/>
<rdfs:label xml:lang="en"> Web Resource</rdfs:label>
 <rdfs:comment xml:lang="en">
    Web resource managed with PostCon system
 </rdfs:comment>
 <rdf:type rdf:resource="http://www.w3.org/2000/01/rdf-schema#Resource" />
</rdfs:Class>

<rdfs:Class rdf:about="http://burningbird.net/postcon/elements/1.0/Movement">
 <rdfs:isDefinedBy rdf:resource="http://burningbird.net/postcon/elements/1.0/"/>
<rdfs:label xml:lang="en"> Web Resource Movement</rdfs:label>
 <rdfs:comment xml:lang="en">
    An event for the resource within the PostCon system
 </rdfs:comment>
</rdfs:Class>

<rdf:Property rdf:about="http://burningbird.net/postcon/elements/1.0/bio">
 <rdfs:isDefinedBy rdf:resource="http://burningbird.net/postcon/elements/1.0/"/>
 <rdfs:label xml:lang="en">Resource biography</rdfs:label>
 <rdfs:comment xml:lang="en">
    Biographical information for resource
 </rdfs:comment>
 <rdfs:range rdf:resource="http://burningbird.net/postcon/elements/1.0/Resource"/>
 <rdfs:domain rdf:resource="http://burningbird.net/postcon/elements/1.0/Resource"/>
</rdf:Property>

<rdf:Property rdf:about="http://burningbird.net/postcon/elements/1.0/relevancy">
 <rdfs:isDefinedBy rdf:resource="http://burningbird.net/postcon/elements/1.0/"/>
 <rdfs:label xml:lang="en">Resource Relevancy</rdfs:label>
 <rdfs:comment xml:lang="en">
    Biographical information for resource
```

Example 6-7. PostCon RDF Schema (continued)

```
  </rdfs:comment>
  <rdfs:range rdf:resource="http://burningbird.net/postcon/elements/1.0/Resource"/>
  <rdfs:domain rdf:resource="http://burningbird.net/postcon/elements/1.0/Resource"/>
 </rdf:Property>

<rdf:Property rdf:about="http://burningbird.net/postcon/elements/1.0/presentation">
  <rdfs:isDefinedBy rdf:resource="http://burningbird.net/postcon/elements/1.0/"/>
  <rdfs:label xml:lang="en">Resource Presentation</rdfs:label>
  <rdfs:comment xml:lang="en">
     Information related to relevancy of resource
  </rdfs:comment>
  <rdfs:range rdf:resource="http://burningbird.net/postcon/elements/1.0/Resource"/>
  <rdfs:domain rdf:resource="http://burningbird.net/postcon/elements/1.0/Resource"/>
 </rdf:Property>

<rdf:Property rdf:about="http://burningbird.net/postcon/elements/1.0/history">
  <rdfs:isDefinedBy rdf:resource="http://burningbird.net/postcon/elements/1.0/"/>
  <rdfs:label xml:lang="en"> Web Content History</rdfs:label>
  <rdfs:comment xml:lang="en">
     History of movement of content within system
  </rdfs:comment>
  <rdfs:range rdf:resource="http://burningbird.net/postcon/elements/1.0/Resource"/>
  <rdfs:domain rdf:resource="http://burningbird.net/postcon/elements/1.0/Resource"/>
 </rdf:Property>

<rdf:Property rdf:about="http://burningbird.net/postcon/elements/1.0/currentStatus">
  <rdfs:isDefinedBy rdf:resource="http://burningbird.net/postcon/elements/1.0/"/>
  <rdfs:label xml:lang="en">Current Status</rdfs:label>
  <rdfs:comment>Current status of document (allowable values of Active and Inactive)</rdfs:
comment>
  <rdfs:range rdf:resource="http://www.w3.org/2000/01/rdf-schema#Literal"/>
  <rdfs:domain rdf:resource="http://postcon/elements/1.0/Relevancy"/>
 </rdf:Property>

<rdf:Property rdf:about="http://burningbird.net/postcon/elements/1.0/reason">
  <rdfs:isDefinedBy rdf:resource="http://burningbird.net/postcon/elements/1.0/"/>
  <rdfs:label xml:lang="en">Reason</rdfs:label>
  <rdfs:comment>Reason</rdfs:comment>
  <rdfs:range rdf:resource="http://www.w3.org/2000/01/rdf-schema#Literal"/>
  <rdfs:domain rdf:resource="http://postcon/elements/1.0/Resource"/>
 </rdf:Property>

<rdf:Property rdf:about="http://burningbird.net/postcon/elements/1.0/movementType">
  <rdfs:isDefinedBy rdf:resource="http://burningbird.net/postcon/elements/1.0/"/>
  <rdfs:label xml:lang="en">Movement Type</rdfs:label>
  <rdfs:comment>Type of Movement (allowable values of Move, Add, Remove)</rdfs:comment>
  <rdfs:range rdf:resource="http://www.w3.org/2000/01/rdf-schema#Literal"/>
  <rdfs:domain rdf:resource="http://postcon/elements/1.0/Movement"/>
 </rdf:Property>

<rdf:Property rdf:about="http://burningbird.net/postcon/elements/1.0/related">
  <rdfs:isDefinedBy rdf:resource="http://burningbird.net/postcon/elements/1.0/"/>
```

Example 6-7. PostCon RDF Schema (continued)

```
<rdfs:label xml:lang="en"> Related Resource</rdfs:label>
<rdfs:comment xml:lang="en">
    Resources within PostCon system related to current resource
</rdfs:comment>
<rdfs:range rdf:resource="http://burningbird.net/postcon/elements/1.0/Resource"/>
</rdf:Property>

<rdf:Property rdf:about="http://burningbird.net/postcon/elements/1.0/requires">
<rdfs:isDefinedBy rdf:resource="http://burningbird.net/postcon/elements/1.0/"/>
<rdfs:label xml:lang="en">Resource Requirement</rdfs:label>
<rdfs:comment xml:lang="en">
    External resource required by current resource
</rdfs:comment>
<rdfs:range rdf:resource="http://burningbird.net/postcon/elements/1.0/Resource"/>
</rdf:Property>

<rdf:Property rdf:about="http://burningbird.net/postcon/elements/1.0/type">
<rdfs:isDefinedBy rdf:resource="http://burningbird.net/postcon/elements/1.0/"/>
<rdfs:label xml:lang="en">Resource Type</rdfs:label>
<rdfs:comment>Type of Required Resource</rdfs:comment>
<rdfs:range rdf:resource="http://www.w3.org/2000/01/rdf-schema#Literal"/>
</rdf:Property>

</rdf:RDF>
```

The schema is in RDF/XML and can be validated. Once validated, it can be embedded within an outer HTML or XHTML document in the location of the schema URI or left as a pure RDF/XML document in same location. The main reason for doing this (it's not required) is to give people the opportunity to review the schema to better understand the vocabulary. In addition, another reason to do this is that some tools, such as BrownSauce (which we'll look at in detail in Chapter 7), use the schema to provide better information about the RDF graph.

Using DC-dot to Generate DC RDF

Much about a document can be deleted directly from the document itself. The format, location, subject, author, and copyright from HTML meta tags and so on can all be derived from scraping the HTML for a particular web resource.

Based on this, an organization going by the abbreviation UKOLN, at the University of Bath in the UK, created the DC-dot generator. This online application will scrape a web resource, pull whatever information it can from it, and then return the result formatted in multiple ways, including RDF, XHTML meta tags, and straight XML.

 Access DC-dot at *http://www.ukoln.ac.uk/metadata/dcdot/*.

I decided to try this with the sample "Tale of Two Monsters" article. In the first page of the application, I entered the URL for the document, and checked both boxes to have the tool attempt to determine publisher and return RDF. The page returned has a first guess at the RDF/XML and provides a form that you can then use to modify the DC elements generated. Figure 6-4 displays the form you can use to modify the results.

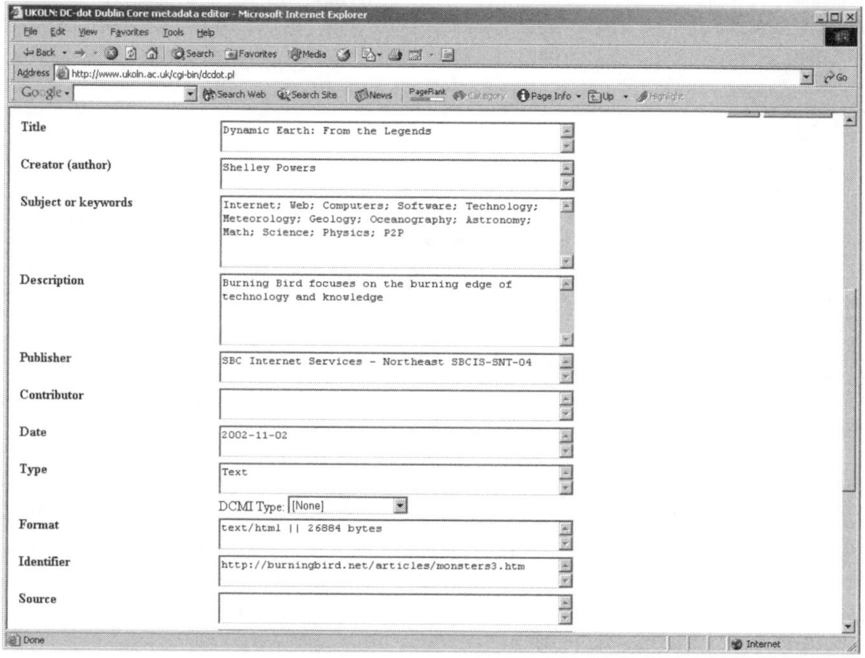

Figure 6-4. DC-dot format to modify results

With some modifications, the DC RDF/XML document generated is shown in Example 6-8.

Example 6-8. DC-dot-generated RDF/XML

```
<?xml version="1.0"?>
<!DOCTYPE rdf:RDF SYSTEM "http://purl.org/dc/schemas/dcmes-xml-20000714.dtd">

<rdf:RDF
  xmlns:rdf="http://www.w3.org/1999/02/22-rdf-syntax-ns#"
  xmlns:dc="http://purl.org/dc/elements/1.1/">
  <rdf:Description about="http://burningbird.net/articles/monsters3.htm">
    <dc:title>
      Tale of Two Monsters: Architeuthis Dux
    </dc:title>
    <dc:creator>
      Shelley Powers
```

Example 6-8. DC-dot-generated RDF/XML (continued)

```
    </dc:creator>
    <dc:subject>
      Internet; Web; Computers; Software; Technology;
      Meteorology; Geology; Oceanography; Astronomy; Math;
      Science; Physics; P2P
    </dc:subject>
    <dc:description>
      The Giant Squid and its relationship to mythology.
    </dc:description>
    <dc:publisher>
      Burningbird
    </dc:publisher>
    <dc:date>
      2002-01-20
    </dc:date>
    <dc:type>
      Text
    </dc:type>
    <dc:format>
      text/html
    </dc:format>
    <dc:format>
      8287 bytes
    </dc:format>
  </rdf:Description>
</rdf:RDF>
```

The generated RDF/XML validates with the RDF Validator, except for one element, boldfaced in the example code—the generator uses an unqualified about attribute, which, though allowed for existing vocabularies, is discouraged with new vocabularies and RDF/XML instances. However, this is a quick change to make.

Now that you've had a chance to try out RDF/XML, it's time to try out a few of the many, many tools and utilities and APIs that have been created specifically for processing RDF/XML.

CHAPTER 7

Editing, Parsing, and Browsing RDF/XML

Up to this point the only "moving parts" associated with RDF/XML have been those associated with the RDF Validator. Chances are good that this will always be your most important tool when working with RDF/XML. However, the RDF Validator isn't the only helpful tool, utility, or application for reading, validating, or writing serialized RDF. Several editors, parsers, browsers, and converters are available; we'll look at some of them in this chapter.

Though much of the technology associated with RDF and RDF/XML is geared toward developers, using many of the RDF/XML utilities requires little or no development experience. You may have to have to have certain software installed, but for the most part, it is either easy to install or is installed on your system.

All the applications and utilities in this chapter are a great way of getting familiar with RDF/XML whether you're a markup person, a developer, or just an interested bystander, because all the applications focus on either reading or creating RDF/XML—not on the development necessary to get to that point.

BrownSauce

After you've worked with RDF/XML for a while, you can read the formatted data and the structures quite easily. However, many people prefer to use a visual tool of some form for this purpose. There are graphical tools and editors, which I'll discuss later, but for now I want to demonstrate BrownSauce, a specialized RDF/XML browser.

One of the most useful tools I used while writing this book was BrownSauce, a Java-based RDF/XML browser created by Damian Steer. It's web based but can run locally on your desktop even if you don't have a web server installed; the only requirement is a Java Runtime Environment (JRE). BrownSauce parses RDF/XML documents and transforms them into a very readable format. One of its better features is its addition of hypertext links from the properties and classes in the RDF/XML document to the actual vocabulary schema definition in a separate page.

BrownSauce is open source and based on Jena (which is covered in the next chapter). However, you don't have to be Java literate to use BrownSauce. You do need support for the Java Runtime, such as 1.4 (find this at *http://javasoft.com*), but once that's installed, BrownSauce provides all the other Java classes you'll need. Download BrownSauce at *http://brownsauce.sourceforge.net/*. The version I used in the book is 0.1.2, running on Windows 2000 and Linux.

Once you've downloaded and installed BrownSauce, following the installation instructions, start the Java-based server that allows you to access the application by double-clicking on *run.bat* if you're running a Windows system or by running *run.sh* in a shell if you're a Unix or Mac OS X user. BrownSauce starts in port 8080 by default so you'll access the browser (typically) using:

```
http://localhost:8080/brownsauce/brownsauce.html
```

When the main BrownSauce page opens, you're shown two rows of form fields. The first row contains fields for entering a source and a resource URI. The first two fields enable browsing for a specific RDF resource within a given RDF/XML document. This tends to be what I use. For instance, to look at the example RDF/XML document used in the previous chapters, I'll enter the following values:

```
Source: http://burningbird.net/articles/monsters1.rdf
Resource: http://burningbird.net/articles/monsters1.htm
```

The page that opens, shown in Figure 7-1, displays all the predicates for the resource and their associated values.

As you can see from the figure, the display is quite easy to read, making effective use of whitespace. All non-hypertext-linked values are literals from the model—those items that would be drawn with a rectangular box within an RDF directed graph. What's interesting is that BrownSauce looked for a subproperty of rdfs:label—in this case the dc:title attribute from the main resource—and actually used different CSS styling in the page to make it stand out. (Yet another reason to make use of existing vocabularies such as Dublin Core as much as possible: many tools will already be aware of them and able to treat them specially.)

In addition, BrownSauce also made other subtle modifications to the values it found to make the content more readable. As an illustration, the pstcn:currentStatus predicate was displayed as Current Status in the document. The label was, again, pulled from the rdfs:label property within the PostCon schema—another reason to make sure your RDF Schema document is up-to-date and accessible.

BrownSauce also resolves some of the more complex RDF/XML constructs. For instance, the rdf:Seq that lists the history of a specific resource defined in the document is shown only by the predicate name, with hypertext link items to each event's resource for additional information. In addition, the use of rdf:value, which is a structured resource, is resolved to the type information (pstcn:type) and an object reference to the actual value itself.

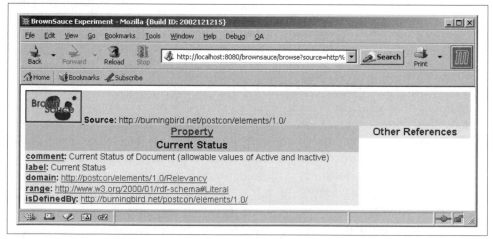

Figure 7-1. BrownSauce opening page for monsters1.rdf RDF/XML document

All of the predicates are hypertext linked. If you click on one of them, information from the schema for the item is displayed. Clicking on Current Status opens a new page with schema information for the status element, as shown in Figure 7-2.

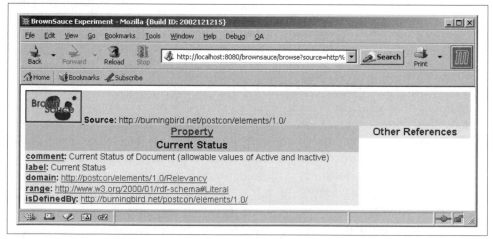

Figure 7-2. Schema definition for PostCon currentStatus property

BrownSauce loads all the schemas from all the vocabularies, so no matter what predicate you click, you should find the schema definition if one has been provided. And if `rdfs:comment` and `rdfs:label` predicates are used, these will be shown also. (Yet another reason to make sure you use RDFS predicates rather than Dublin Core to describe schema elements, as some vocabularies have done.)

You can modify BrownSauce's appearance by modifying the accompanying *bs.css* file. Schemas are cached, which makes reading additional documents using the same schemas quicker.

BrownSauce doesn't provide parsed access to data, nor does it allow you to edit it. What it does do is provide a human-readable format for examining RDF/XML documents. In particular, if you're defining domain data using RDF/XML, BrownSauce allows the domain experts who may not be RDF literate a chance to look at the data without having to be comfortable with either XML or RDF/XML. No matter how comfortable you are with RDF/XML, BrownSauce is a great tool to test your documents, your vocabulary, and the vocabulary's associated schema.

Parsers

RDF/XML parsers are usually included as part of a broader API. For instance, Jena has a parser, as do other APIs in other languages. Parsers aren't typically accessed directly, however, because you generally want to do something else with all that data after parsing it into an application-specific stream of data.

However, accessing parsers directly can be handy for a couple of reasons. The primary reason is to validate an RDF/XML document—a compliant RDF/XML parser should return meaningful error messages and warnings when it encounters erroneous or suspicious RDF/XML. Another reason to run a parser directly is to create another serialization of the RDF/XML, but in a different format, such as a set of N-Triples. When I'm creating a new RDF application, I run my example RDF/XML documents through an N-Triples parser to get the N-Triples; I then use these to help with my coding of the application.

 I parse RDF/XML into triples because most RDF APIs provide methods for working with triples, not the higher-level construct view. As an example, instead of creating an RDF container directly, you'll usually have to create all the triples that represent the statements underlying the container. This is demonstrated more clearly in the next several chapters.

In this section, we'll take a quick look at some parsers, beginning with ARP, the parser that forms the core of the well-used RDF Validator.

ARP2

ARP stands for Another RDF/XML Parser. ARP2 is the second generation of this parser, which has been modified to work with the newest RDF specifications. ARP is part of the Jena Toolkit, discussed in Chapter 8, but is also a separate installation in its own right. You can download and install ARP without having to download and install Jena. However, you have to have Java installed, at least JRE 1.4 or above.

 ARP is installed with Jena, or you can access it directly at *http://www.hpl.hp.com/semweb/arp.htm*. If you do download and install ARP as a separate processor, intending it to coexist with a separate installation of Jena, make sure that you don't have the separate ARP in your classpath, or you could have problems working with Jena.

Normally ARP is used within another application, but there is one class that you can access at the command line as a method of testing the viability of your RDF/XML document—the NTriple class. Once ARP2 is installed, you can run NTriple from the command line thus:

```
java com.hp.hpl.jena.rdf.arp.NTriple http://burningbird.net/articles/monsters1.rdf
```

NTriple produces either a listing of N-Triples from the RDF/XML, or produces errors if there's something wrong with the syntax. A partial sampling of the command-line output from the parser of the file shown in the command line is given in Example 7-1.

Example 7-1. Sample output from triples generated by ARP

```
http://burningbird.net/articles/monsters1.htm> <http://www.w3.org/1999/02/22-rdf-syntax-
ns#type> <http://burningbird.net/postcon/elements/1.0/Resource> .
_:jARP1 <http://purl.org/dc/elements/1.1/title> "Tale of Two Monsters: Legends" .
_:jARP1 <http://purl.org/dc/terms/abstract> "\n          When I think of \"monsters\" I
think of the creatures of \n          legends and tales, from the books and movies, and
\n          I think of the creatures that have entertained me for years.\n     \t  " .
_:jARP1 <http://purl.org/dc/elements/1.1/description> "\n          Part 1 of four-part
series on cryptozoology, legends, \n          Nessie the Loch Ness Monster and the giant
squid.\n          " .
_:jARP1 <http://purl.org/dc/elements/1.1/created> "1999-08-01T00:00:00-06:00" .
_:jARP1 <http://purl.org/dc/elements/1.1/creator> "Shelley Powers" .
_:jARP1 <http://purl.org/dc/elements/1.1/publisher> "Burningbird Network" .
<http://burningbird.net/articles/monsters1.htm> <http://burningbird.net/postcon/elements/
1.0/Bio> _:jARP1 .
_:jARP2 <http://burningbird.net/postcon/elements/1.0/currentStatus> "Active" .
_:jARP2 <http://purl.org/dc/terms/valid> "2003-12-01T00:00:00-06:00" .
_:jARP2 <http://purl.org/dc/elements/1.1/subject> "legends" .
_:jARP2 <http://purl.org/dc/elements/1.1/subject> "giant squid" .
_:jARP2 <http://purl.org/dc/elements/1.1/subject> "Loch Ness Monster" .
_:jARP2 <http://purl.org/dc/elements/1.1/subject> "Architeuthis Dux" .
_:jARP2 <http://purl.org/dc/elements/1.1/subject> "Nessie" .
_:jARP2 <http://purl.org/dc/terms/isReferencedBy> "http://www.pibburns.com/cryptozo.htm" .
```

Example 7-1. Sample output from triples generated by ARP (continued)

```
_:jARP2 <http://purl.org/dc/terms/references> "http://www.nrcc.utmb.edu/" .
<http://burningbird.net/articles/monsters1.htm> <http://burningbird.net/postcon/elements/
1.0/Relevancy> _:jARP2 .
```

Notice that the parser returns annotated text, showing line returns and maintaining the integrity of the text as it found it in the document.

 The output from ARP demonstrates one of the dangers of manually creating RDF/XML—preservation of special characters and whitespace. It's pretty common to break lines or line characters up when you type something manually, but such whitespace will be retained unnecessarily when the RDF/XML is read in by a parser such as ARP. If you create RDF/XML manually, drop whitespace unless it's an integral part of the text.

The NTriple command format is:

```
java <class-path> com.hp.hpl.jena.arp.NTriple ( [ [ -[xstfu]][ -b xmlBase -[eiw]
NNN[,NNN...] ] [ file ] [ url ] )...
```

Note, though, that with the release of ARP2 that I downloaded (which was alpha), I had to change the classpath to *com.hp.hpl.jena.rdf.arp.NTriple*. NTriple can work with files on a filesystem or accessed through a URL. The other options for NTriple are given in Table 7-1.

Table 7-1. NTriple options

Option	Description
-b *URI* or -b *URL*	Set XML base to URI or absolute URL.
-r	Document is completely RDF/XML (not embedded) and may not have rdf:RDF tags.
-t	No triples, errors only.
-x	Lax mode, suppress warnings.
-s	Strict mode, transform most warnings to errors.
-u	Allow unqualified attributes.
-f	All errors are final and processing stops when it reaches first.
-n	Show line numbers for triples.
E NNN[,NNN]	Treat specified warnings as errors.
-I NNN[,NNN]	Ignore numbered error/warning conditions.

In particular, if you're working with the new RDF/XML specification constructs, such as rdf:nodeID or rdf:datatype, you may want to test it with ARP, suppressing triples. Example 7-2 shows an RDF/XML document that's actually generated by Jena. It features the newer rdf:nodeID attribute, which breaks down on older parsers. However, I modified the file to change one of the legitimate uses of rdf:resource to rdf:about (in bold).

Example 7-2. RDF/XML document with one error

```
<rdf:RDF
  xmlns:rdf='http://www.w3.org/1999/02/22-rdf-syntax-ns#'
  xmlns:NS0='http://burningbird.net/postcon/elements/1.0/'
  xmlns:dc='http://purl.org/dc/elements/1.0/'
 >
  <rdf:Description rdf:nodeID='A0'>
    <dc:creator>Shelley Powers</dc:creator>
    <dc:publisher>Burningbird</dc:publisher>
    <dc:title xml:lang='en'>Tale of Two Monsters: Legends</dc:title>
  </rdf:Description>
  <rdf:Description rdf:about='http://burningbird.net/articles/monsters1.htm'>
    <NS0:related rdf:about='http://burningbird.net/articles/monsters2.htm'/>
    <NS0:related rdf:resource='http://burningbird.net/articles/monsters3.htm'/>
    <NS0:Bio rdf:nodeID='A0'/>
  </rdf:Description>
</rdf:RDF>
```

Running the NTriple application with the -t option returns the following error from this file:

```
C:\>java com.hp.hpl.jena.rdf.arp.NTriple -t c:\writing\rdfbook\java\pracRDFThird
.rdf

Error: file:/c:/writing/rdfbook/java/pracRDFThird.rdf[12:77]: {E201} Syntax error
when processing attribute rdf:about.
Cannot have attribute rdf:about in this context.
```

As you can see, ARP2 not only finds the error, it also gives you the location of the error and the reason the error occurs.

ARP2 works from the command line only, but if you're more interested in a parser with a GUI frontend, you might want to try out ICS-FORTH's Validating RDF Parser.

ICS-FORTH Validating RDF Parser

The ICS-FORTH Validating RDF Parser (VRP), like ARP, is part of a suite of tools but can also be downloaded separately. In addition, again like ARP, the only requirement to run the tool is a Java Runtime Environment installed, JRE 1.4 or up.

 You can download ICS-FORTH's Validating RDF Parser from the following location: *http://athena.ics.forth.gr:9090/RDF/*. You can also get access to it as part of the RDFSuite.

VRP is a set of Java classes that you can use within your own Java classes. However, the parser also comes with a Swing-based GUI frontend that you can use directly without having to touch any code. To access the GUI for the parser, once you've downloaded and unzipped the file containing the source, you're ready to start using it. Start up the parser by typing the following line:

```
java -classpath <path to VRP directory>/classes GUI.VRPGUI
```

The page that opens has two text input fields, one for an input file and one for recording the results. Below these are a set of checkboxes that switch on specific tests, such as ones for checking the syntax, checking for class hierarchy loops, and so on. Figure 7-3 shows the tool after I validated the test document (at *http://burningbird.net/articles/monsters1.rdf*), asking for validation only and having the tool test the syntax and class and property hierarchy loops. VRP can also open an HTML or XHTML document with RDF/XML embedded in it (as described in Chapter 3).

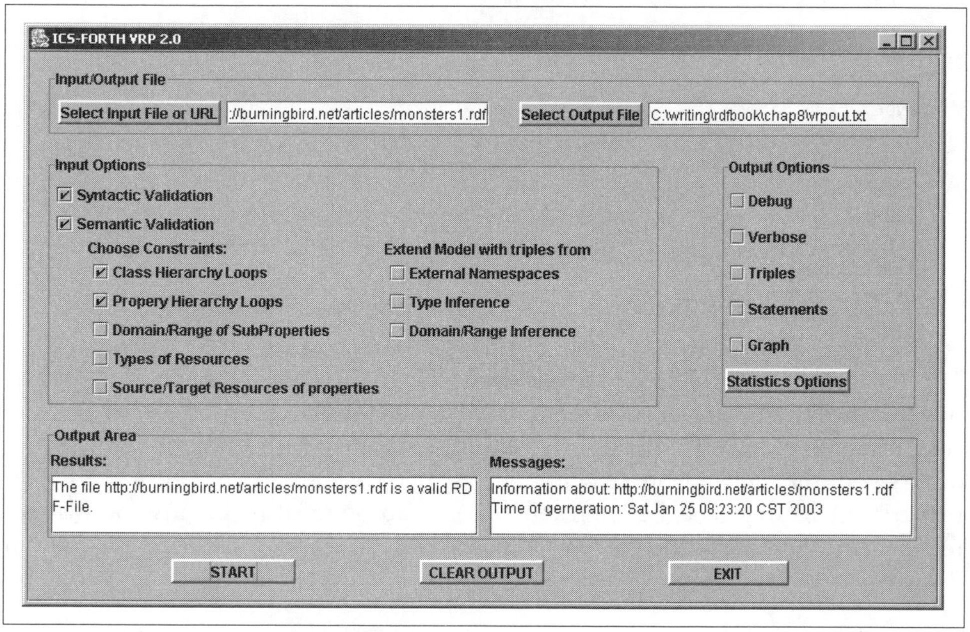

Figure 7-3. ICS-FORTH's Validating RDF Parser (VRP) standalone application

As you can see from the image, VRP has several input and output options. For instance, I can run the test again, this time checking the Triples, Statements, and Graph options for output. The tool first asks me for permission to overwrite the output file and then runs the tests, printing output to the Results window in the application as well as to the file. The Graph option provides a text description of what would be the RDF directed graph rather than a true graphical representation. A sampling from this file, the classes as defined in the RDFS graph output, are shown in Example 7-3. Note that the information associated with each schema class, such as the isDefinedBy, comment, and label information, isn't showing in the graph, though we know it to be present in the schema.

Example 7-3. VRP graph results describing document's classes

```
The classes of the Model:
http://burningbird.net/postcon/elements/1.0/#Movement
    subClassOf: []
    comment: []
    label: []
    seeAlso: []
    isDefinedBy: []
    value: []
    type: []
http://www.w3.org/1999/02/22-rdf-syntax-ns#Seq
    subClassOf: []
    comment: []
    label: []
    seeAlso: []
    isDefinedBy: []
    value: []
    type: []
http://burningbird.net/postcon/elements/1.0/#Resource
    subClassOf: []
    comment: []
    label: []
    seeAlso: []
    isDefinedBy: []
    value: []
    type: []
```

The version of the tool I used expands the absolute URIs for the classes and properties by converting them to URI fragments, such as #Resource and #Movement, before concatenating them to the URI. The base URI is specified with a trailing slash, just as occurs with the Dublin Core schema. The relative URIs should not have been "corrected" to URI fragments before resolution into absolute URIs. Because of this correction, the schema elements could not resolve correctly (as they did within BrownSauce).

 VRP generates Unix-style line-feeds. If you're using the product in Windows, make sure you view the result using a test reader that compensates for this. For example, use Wordpad not Notepad.

This could be why the tool didn't pick up the schema information for the items, or why it may not open related schema documents. Hard to say. One thing the tool does do is correctly resolve the RDF classes in the document, as compared to the RDF properties. This can be very helpful when you're creating an RDF Schema for a vocabulary and do not recall which elements are classes and which are properties.

The checks you can perform on a specific document are:

Syntax check
Checks whether the RDF/XML of the document conforms to the updated RDF/XML specification.

Semantic check: class hierarchy loop
Checks for loops in subclass hierarchy (parent class identifying itself as child of child class and so on).

Semantic check: property hierarchy loop
Same as previous but for properties.

Semantic check: domain/range of subproperties
A property's domain and range are a sum of its subproperties' domains and ranges.

Semantic check: resources of properties
Source/target property values should be instances of domain/range of property.

Semantic check: types of resources
Assigned RDF or XML type.

Extend model: external namespace
Connects to external namespaces to merge in their triples.

Extend model: type inference
Infer type of resource.

Extend model: domain/range inference
Infer domain/range from superproperty.

The semantic check for types of resources failed with all models I tested this against, including Dublin Core, RSS, and FOAF (Friend of a Friend) RDF/XML documents. This check is looking for a specific type information for each resource, something not available in most models. However, the example PostCon vocabulary file (at *http:// burningbird.net/articles/monsters1.rdf*) did pass all other tests. When I selected the option to include external namespace triples, the model again failed, but the results as a graph were quite interesting.

The results include information from the schema for PostCon, such as the following for the pstcn:movementType property:

```
http://burningbird.net/postcon/elements/1.0/movementType
    range: [http://www.w3.org/2000/01/rdf-schema#Literal]
    domain: [http://postcon/elements/1.0/Movement]
    subPropertyOf: []
    links:
    comment: [Type of Movement (allowable values of Move, Add, Remove)]
    label: [Movement Type]
    seeAlso: []
    isDefinedBy: [http://burningbird.net/postcon/elements/1.0/]
    value: []
    type: [http://www.w3.org/1999/02/22-rdf-syntax-ns#Property]
```

Notice the links property and that it has no value. However, later in the document, you'll see the graph for pstcn:movementType:

```
http://burningbird.net/postcon/elements/1.0/#movementType
    range: []
```

```
        domain: []
        subPropertyOf: []
        links: (http://www.yasd.com/dynaearth/monsters1.htm, Add) (http://www.
    dynamicearth.com/articles/monsters1.htm, Move) (http:/burningbird.net/articles/
    monsters1.htm, Move)
        comment: []
        label: []
        seeAlso: []
        isDefinedBy: []
        value: []
        type: []
```

Again, the automatic use of fragment identifiers breaks the information up; however, combine both blocks and you have a relatively good idea of all the dimensions
of the PostCon property `pstcn:movementType`.

In addition to Graph, other VRP outputs are:

Debug
> Shows tokens generated by Lexar, the lexicon analyzer

Verbose
> Details actions VRP takes

Triples
> Model triples

Statements
> Model statements

Statistic options
> Provides other information such as number of resources, statements, and time
> taken for some of the processes

I would definitely consider running VRP against an in-progress vocabulary while
you're designing your schema and then try it with External Namespaces as a test
with some of your models as a check on the schema.

Editors

As I stated earlier, after some time you can become comfortable enough with RDF/
XML to read and write the documents manually. But why bother? If you need to
manually write an RDF/XML document, you're better off doing so with a specialized RDF editor.

IsaViz

One of the more popular editors is IsaViz, a visual RDF/XML editing tool written in
Java. In fact, like so many other RDF/XML tools, it makes use of many of the Jena
classes, making Jena the most commonly used API of all (which is why it has its own
chapter).

You can access documentation and software for IsaViz at *http://www. w3.org/2001/11/IsaViz/*. By the time this book hits the streets, the version of IsaViz will be compliant with the released RDF specifications as described earlier in the book.

Once you've downloaded and installed IsaViz, you can run it using *run.sh* on Unix or OS X or *run.bat* on Windows. Several windows open, each containing a portion of the GUI for the application. Since IsaViz is such a graphical tool, much of this section is going to be pretty pictures, demonstrating different aspects of the tool.

IsaViz opens as a new project; you can either manually start creating a new RDF model or import one in either N-Triples format or from RDF/XML. We'll start with importing the test RDF/XML document into the editor, just to see how it works. You can import an existing document by selecting File, and then Import, and then selecting whether to Merge the model into the existing project or Replace it. Since the existing project doesn't have any model elements, I picked Replace and then provided the URL for the RDF/XML document.

In a surprisingly short amount of time, IsaViz loaded the model and displayed an RDF graph of it in the graph frame, as shown in Figure 7-4.

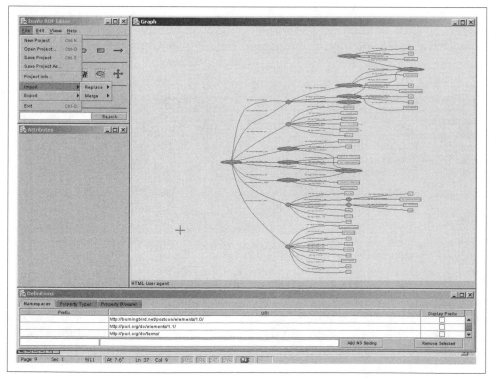

Figure 7-4. Importing monsters1.rdf RDF/XML document into IsaViz project

The full view of the model is a bit hard to read, but if you right-click on portions of the model in the Graph frame, the focus changes and the view zooms in so that you can look at the details. Left-clicking on any of the items in the model displays attribute information about the item in the Attributes frame. The complete listing of properties is shown at the bottom, in the Definitions frame. Project and model management is managed in the last frame, the Editor.

Clicking on the model, zooming in to the top resource, and left-clicking displays attribute information, as shown in Figure 7-5.

Figure 7-5. Attributes for resource

Clicking the Delete button removes the resource from the model, and clicking Show Properties opens another window with a listing of all resource properties, as shown in Figure 7-6. In the picture, the only properties that show are those that belong to the immediate resource.

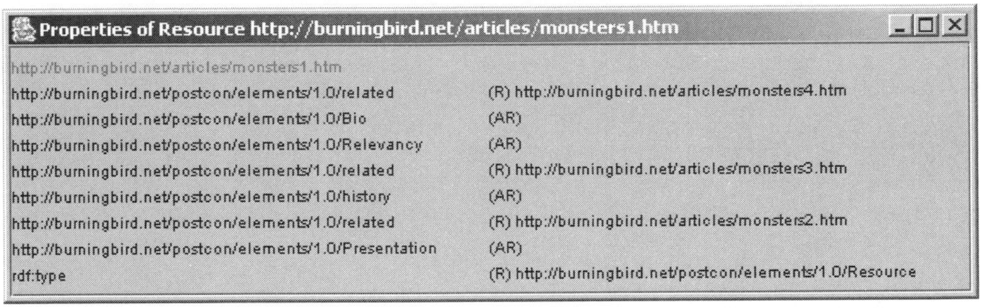

Figure 7-6. Properties for resource

The bottom frame window of IsaViz contains three tabbed windows, one showing the namespaces in the model, one showing the property types, and one showing the properties for the selected resource. You don't have to click on the resource within the graph to select it—you can also use the Edit menu in the IsaViz Editor window and search for a specific resource or object value.

You can zoom in on the model, by clicking the Shift key and then right-clicking in the model and dragging to the top to zoom in and to the bottom to zoom out. Holding the Shift key and clicking on a specific item also recenters the window on that item. To move around the model, right-click anywhere on it and drag to the top, bottom, right, or left to move in that direction.

If you want to select a portion of the graph, click the Select icon in the IsaViz Editor window and then click on whatever you want to select. If you want to select a resource and all of its predicates, hold the Shift down as you select the item. The selected items are highlighted in a bold outline, as shown in Figure 7-7.

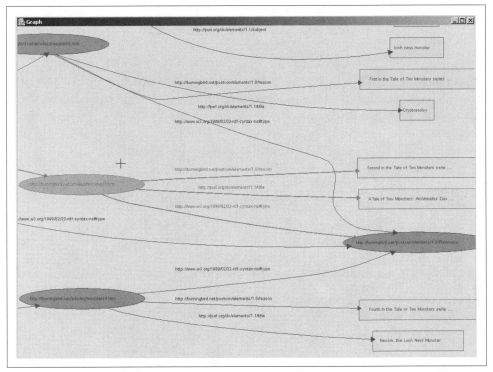

Figure 7-7. Selected path within the RDF directed graph

In addition to examining the model, you can also edit or add to it. As stated earlier, delete an item by selecting it and then clicking Delete from the Attributes view. You can add a new resource, property, or literal by clicking on the appropriate item in the IsaViz Editor window, shown in Figure 7-8, and then clicking on the model. A definition window opens, and you can add the URI or value or predicate URI for the item.

To add a predicate between the subject oval and the object, select the arrow icon, click first on the resource and then on the object—the arc between the nodes is drawn.

Once you're all finished with the project, you can save for further edits, or you can export multiple views of it. IsaViz allows you to export an RDF/XML file, an N-Triples

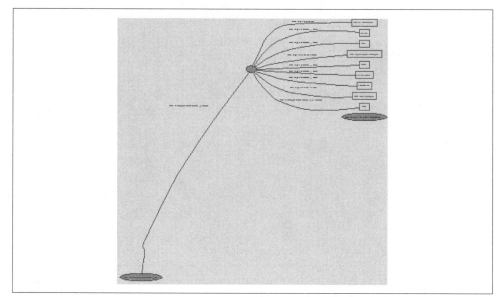

Figure 7-8. IsaViz Editor window with Resource selected

file, a PNG graphic, or an SVG graphic. Figure 7-9 shows the directed graph for the article RDF/XML after all but one predicate has been deleted from the top-level resource, exported as a PNG file.

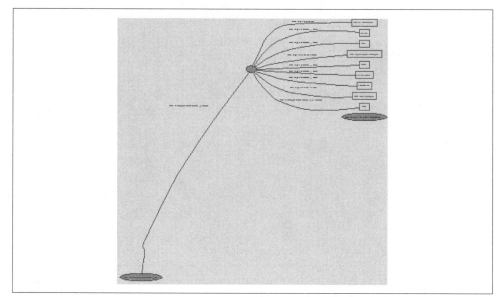

Figure 7-9. Exported PNG file of directed graph after modifications

IsaViz is an absolutely essential tool to have if you're working with RDF.

RDF Editor in Java

As with many other applications and utilities, the RDF Editor in Java (referred to as REJ from this point) derives much of its RDF processing power from Jena. On top of

Jena's functionality is a simple, easy-to-use text-based RDF editing tool that's compatible with X11 and Windows.

 You can download the RDF Editor in Java from SourceForge at *http://sourceforge.net/projects/rdfeditor/.*

REJ has a simple interface, which makes it fairly simple to learn how to use. It opens with the RDF/XML-specific tags and namespace already inserted into a blank document. You can continue to add to the model in the page, or you can open an existing model.

Just to see how the tool works, I opened the test RDF/XML document. To the right of the document window is a little ruler. If you move the glider, the element selected changes, as shown in Figure 7-10.

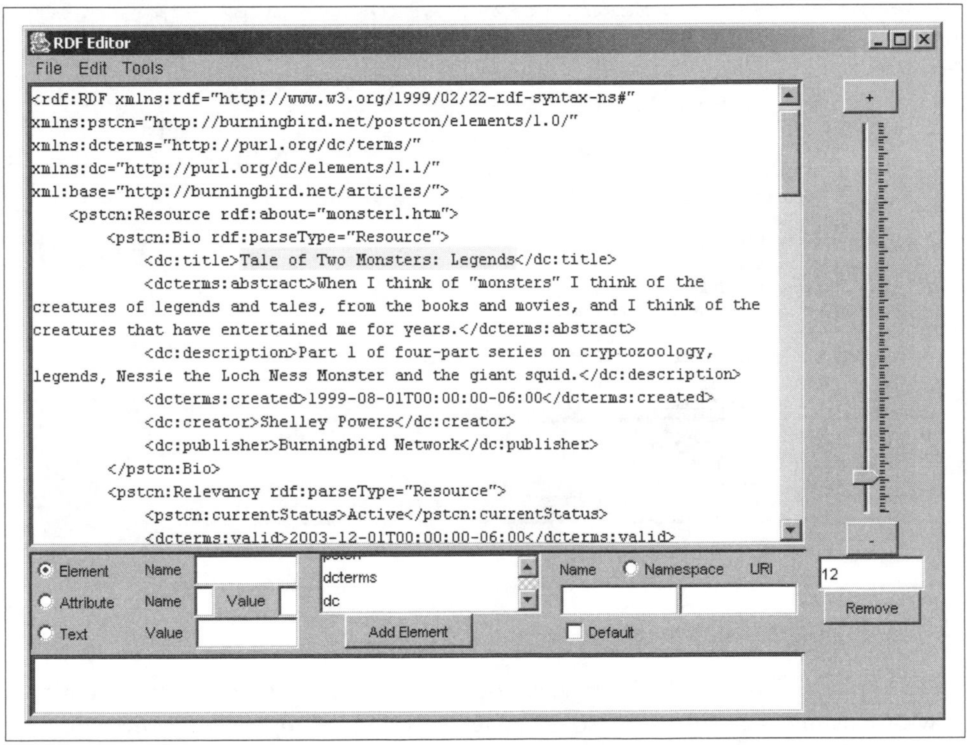

![RDF Editor screenshot showing an RDF/XML document]

Figure 7-10. Selecting specific component in RDF/XML document

You can also move the selection by clicking the plus (+) button to move up, and the minus (-) button to move the selection down. The element's position relative to the rest of the page is shown in the window below the ruler.

Once an element is selected, you can delete it and replace the element. For instance, in Figure 7-10, clicking the Remove button removes the text. Clicking on the Text radio button to the left of the control bar at the bottom sets the page up for accepting a literal. Once the value is entered in the field next to the Text radio button, I click the button next to it, which is now labeled PCDATA, and the text is inserted into the document at that point.

You can also add new elements, attributes, namespaces—all using the control bar at the bottom, which changes to fit whatever option you're in, as shown in Figure 7-11. Once you've added the new element, you can then add literals, other elements, and attributes to it.

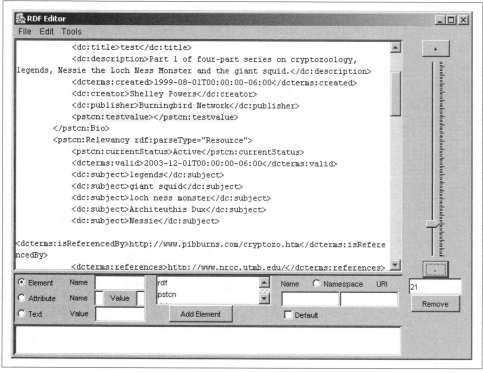

Figure 7-11. Adding a new element to the model

Once you're finished with the model, you can save the RDF/XML document to a new or existing file. You can also generate an N-Triples report from the model by selecting Tools and then selecting the N-Triples Report. The results are printed out in the bottom window and can also be saved.

Not a lot of bells and whistles, but REJ is a good choice if you're already comfortable with RDF/XML.

## CHAPTER 8

Jena: RDF in Java

Hewlett-Packard's Semantic Web team has been quietly working on Jena—a full-featured Java API for RDF—about as long as work has been progressing on RDF itself. In fact, the cochair of the RDF Working Group is Brian McBride, one of the creators of Jena.

Jena is an open source API and toolkit, accessible at Source Forge (*http://sourceforge. net/projects/jena*) or at *http://www.hpl.hp.com/semweb/jena.htm*. In addition, there's a Jena developers' discussion forum at *http://groups.yahoo.com/group/jena-dev/*.

Overview of the Classes

Included with the Jena toolkit are the dependencies and installation instructions, which I won't repeat here. I have worked with Jena on Linux (Red Hat), FreeBSD, and Windows; the examples included with Jena and the examples in this chapter work equally well in all environments. The only requirement is that you use JRE 1.2 or above.

A description of the many Java classes included with Jena is included with the installation (as Javadocs). I won't cover all of them here, only those most critical to understanding the underlying architecture in Jena.

 I used Jena 1.6.1 in this chapter, but by the time this book is out, Jena 2.0 should be available. The Jena developers are refactoring many of the classes, changing class structure as well as making modifications to the API itself. These changes will break these examples, unfortunately. However, the concepts behind the examples should stay the same, and the book support site will have updated example source.

The Underlying Parser

Included within the Jena toolset is an RDF parser, ARP (an acronym for Another RDF Parser), accessible as a standalone product. You had a chance to look at and work with ARP in Chapter 7, so I won't go into additional detail here, since it works in the background with no further intervention necessary on our part. Our work begins once the RDF data is loaded into a model.

Though not covered in this book, Jena also includes an N3 (Notation3) parser.

The Model

Jena's API architecture focuses on the RDF model, the set of statements that comprises an RDF document, graph, or instantiation of a vocabulary. A basic RDF/XML document is created by instantiating one of the model classes and adding at least one statement (triple) to it. To view the RDF/XML, read it into a model and then access the individual elements, either through the API or through the query engine.

The `ModelMem` class creates an RDF model in memory. It extends `ModelCom`—the class incorporating common model methods used by all models—and implements the key interface, `Model`. In addition, the DAML class, `DAMLModelImpl`, subclasses `ModelMem`.

The `ModelRDB` class is an implementation of the model used to manipulate RDF stored within a relational database such as MySQL or Oracle. Unlike the memory model, `ModelRDB` persists the RDF data for later access, and the basic functionality between it and `ModelMem` is opening and maintaining a connection to a relational database in addition to managing the data. An interesting additional aspect of this implementation, as we'll see later in the section "In-Memory Versus Persistent Model Storage," is that you can also specify how the RDF model is stored within a relational database—as a flat table of statements, as a hash, or through stored procedures.

Once data is stored in a model, the next step is querying it.

One major change with Jena 2.0 is the addition of the `ModelFactory` to create new instances of models.

The Query

You can access data in a stored RDF model directly using specific API function calls, or via RDQL—an RDF query language. As will be demonstrated in Chapter 10, querying data using an SQL-like syntax is a very effective way of pulling data from an RDF model, whether that model is stored in memory or in a relational database.

Jena's RDQL is implemented as an object called Query. Once instantiated, it can then be passed to a query engine (`QueryEngine`) and the results stored in a query result (`QueryResult` and various implementations: `QueryResultsFormatter`,

`QueryResultsMem`, and `QueryResultsStream`). To access specific returned values, program variables are bound to the result sets using the `ResultBinding` class.

Once data is retrieved from the RDF/XML, you can iterate through it using any number of iterators. Once you query data using the Query object, or if you access all RDF/XML elements of a specific class, you can assign the results to an iterator object and iterate through the set, displaying the results or looking for a specific value. Each of several different iterator classes within Jena is focused on specific RDF/XML classes, such as `NodeIterator` for general RDF nodes (literal or resource values), `ResIterator`, and `StmtIterator`.

DAML+OIL

Starting with later versions of Jena, support for DAML+OIL was added to the tool suite. DAML+OIL is a language for describing ontologies, a way of describing constraints and refinements for a given vocabulary that are beyond the sophistication of RDFS. Much of the effort on behalf of the Semantic Web is based on the Web Ontology Language at the W3C, which owes much of its effort to DAML+OIL. The principle DAML+OIL class within Jena, outside of the `DAMLModel`, is the `DAMLOntology` class. I won't be covering the DAML+OIL classes in this chapter, but the creators of Jena provide a tutorial that demonstrates them and is included in the documents you get when you download Jena.

Ontologies, DAML+OIL, and the W3C ontology language effort, OWL, are described in Chapter 12.

Creating and Serializing an RDF Model

Automating the process of creating an RDF/XML document is actually a fairly simple process, but you have to understand first how your RDF triples relate to one another. One approach to using Jena to generate RDF/XML for a particular vocabulary is to create a prototype document of the vocabulary and run it/them through the RDF Validator. Once the RDF/XML validates, parse it into N-Triples, and use these to build an application that can generate instances of a model of a given vocabulary, each using different data.

For the purposes of this chapter, I'm using Example 6-6 from Chapter 6 for a demonstration. This particular document, duplicated in this chapter's source, records the history and status of an article from one of my web sites. It makes a good example because it demonstrates the relationships that can appear within the PostCon vocabulary, and therefore makes a fine prototype for building an application that will build new versions of PostCon RDF/XML documents.

The examples in this chapter are, for the most part, working with the in-memory model from Jena. This model doesn't require the reader to have Berkeley DB, MySQL, or any other database installed.

Very Quick Simple Look

At its simplest, you can create an RDF model, create a single resource, add a couple of properties and then serialize it, all with just a few lines of code. So to get started, we'll do just that.

In Example 8-1, a new model is created, with the resource and one predicate repeated with two different objects. To create this model, an in-memory memory model is instantiated first, then an instance of an RDF resource using the Jena Resource class. Two instances of Property are created and attached to the module using addProperty, forming two complete RDF statements. The first parameter in the addProperty method is the Property instance, the second the actual property value. Once the model is built, it's printed out to standard output using the Jena PrintWriter class. For now, the values used within the model are all hardcoded into the application.

Example 8-1. Creating an RDF model with two statements, serialized to RDF/XML

```
import com.hp.hpl.mesa.rdf.jena.mem.ModelMem;
import com.hp.hpl.mesa.rdf.jena.model.*;
import com.hp.hpl.mesa.rdf.jena.common.PropertyImpl;
import java.io.FileOutputStream;
import java.io.PrintWriter;


public class pracRdfFirst extends Object {

    public static void main (String args[]) {
        String sURI = "http://burningbird.net/articles/monsters1.htm";
        String sPostcon = "http://www.burningbird.net/postcon/elements/1.0/";
        String sRelated = "related";
      try {
         // Create an empty graph
         Model model = new ModelMem( );

         // Create the resource
         Resource postcon = model.createResource(sURI);

         // Create the predicate (property)
         Property related = model.createProperty(sPostcon, sRelated);

         // Add the properties with associated values (objects)
         postcon.addProperty(related,
                         "http://burningbird.net/articles/monsters3.htm");
         postcon.addProperty(related,
                         "http://burningbird.net/articles/monsters2.htm");
```

```
        // Print RDF/XML of model to system output
        model.write(new PrintWriter(System.out));

    } catch (Exception e) {
        System.out.println("Failed: " + e);
    }
  }
}
```

Once compiled, running the application results in the following output:

```
<rdf:RDF
  xmlns:rdf='http://www.w3.org/1999/02/22-rdf-syntax-ns#'
  xmlns:NS0='http://www.burningbird.net/postcon/elements/1.0/'
 >
  <rdf:Description rdf:about='http://burningbird.net/articles/monsters1.htm'>
    <NS0:related>http://burningbird.net/articles/monsters3.htm</NS0:related>
    <NS0:related>http://burningbird.net/articles/monsters2.htm</NS0:related>
  </rdf:Description>
</rdf:RDF>
```

The generated RDF validates within the RDF Validator, producing the graph shown in Figure 8-1.

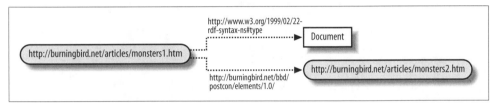

Figure 8-1. RDF model with one resource and two statements

At this point, we can continue creating and adding properties to the model directly in the application. However, the problem with creating the Property and Resource objects directly in the application that builds the models is that you have to duplicate this functionality across all applications that want to use the vocabulary. Not only is this inefficient, it adds to the overall size and complexity of an application. A better approach would be one the Jena developers demonstrated when they built their vocabulary objects: using a Java wrapper class.

 Though omitted in Example 8-1 and other examples, you should close the memory model and free the resources using the `model.close()` method.

Encapsulating the Vocabulary in a Java Wrapper Class

If you look at your Jena installation, in the directory source code directory under the following path, you'll find several Java classes in the vocabulary directory, */com/hp/ hpl/mesa/rdf/jena/vocabulary*.

The classes included wrap Dublin Core (DC) RDF, VCARD RDF, and so on. By using a wrapper class for the properties and resources of your RDF vocabulary, you have a way of defining all aspects of the RDF vocabulary in one spot, an approach that simplifies both implementation and maintenance.

 The location of the vocabulary classes will change in Version 2.0.

In this section, we'll create a vocabulary class for PostCon, using the existing Jena vocabulary wrapper classes as a template, The PostCon wrapper class consists of a set of static strings holding property or resource labels and a set of associated RDF properties, as shown in Example 8-2. As complex as the example RDF file is, you may be surprised by how few entries there are in this class; PostCon makes extensive use of other RDF vocabularies for much of its data collection, including Dublin Core, which has a predefined vocabulary wrapper class included with Jena (DC.java).

Example 8-2. POSTCON vocabulary wrapper class

```
package com.burningbird.postcon.vocabulary;

import com.hp.hpl.mesa.rdf.jena.common.ErrorHelper;
import com.hp.hpl.mesa.rdf.jena.common.PropertyImpl;
import com.hp.hpl.mesa.rdf.jena.common.ResourceImpl;
import com.hp.hpl.mesa.rdf.jena.model.Model;
import com.hp.hpl.mesa.rdf.jena.model.Property;
import com.hp.hpl.mesa.rdf.jena.model.Resource;
import com.hp.hpl.mesa.rdf.jena.model.RDFException;

public class POSTCON extends Object {

    // URI for vocabulary elements
    protected static final String uri = "http://burningbird.net/postcon/elements/1.0/";

    // Return URI for vocabulary elements
    public static String getURI()
    {
        return uri;
    }

    // Define the property labels and objects
        static final String    nbio = "bio";
    public static       Property bio = null;
        static final String    nrelevancy = "relevancy";
    public static       Property relevancy = null;
        static final String    npresentation = "presentation";
    public static       Resource presentation = null;
        static final String    nhistory = "history";
    public static       Property history = null;
        static final String    nmovementtype = "movementType";
```

Example 8-2. POSTCON vocabulary wrapper class (continued)

```
public static       Property movementtype = null;
     static final String   nreason = "reason";
public static       Property reason = null;
     static final String   nstatus = "currentStatus";
public static       Property status = null;
     static final String   nrelated = "related";
public static       Property related = null;
     static final String   ntype = "type";
public static       Property type = null;
     static final String   nrequires = "requires";
public static       Property requires = null;


// Instantiate the properties and the resource
static {
    try {

        // Instantiate the properties
        bio          = new PropertyImpl(uri, nbio);
        relevancy    = new PropertyImpl(uri, nrelevancy);
        presentation = new PropertyImpl(uri, npresentation);
        history      = new PropertyImpl(uri, nhistory);
        related      = new PropertyImpl(uri, nrelated);
        type         = new PropertyImpl(uri, ntype);
        requires     = new PropertyImpl(uri, nrequires);
        movementtype = new PropertyImpl(uri, nmovementtype);
        reason       = new PropertyImpl(uri, nreason);
        status       = new PropertyImpl(uri, nstatus);

    } catch (RDFException e) {
        ErrorHelper.logInternalError("POSTCON", 1, e);
    }
}


}
```

At the top of the example code, after the declarations, is a static string holding the URI of the PostCon element vocabulary and a method to return it. Following these is a list of declarations for each property, including a Property element and the associated label for each.

> Note that the two PostCon RDF classes Resource and Movement are not included. The reason is that I'm using the Jena Resource class to define them and then adding rdf:type to define the type of the resource. The resulting RDF graph is the same—only the syntax is different.

Once the properties are defined in the code, they are instantiated, and the file is saved and compiled. To import this class, use the following in your Java applications:

```
import com.burningbird.postcon.vocabulary.POSTCON;
```

At this point, the PostCon vocabulary wrapper class is ready for use. We rewrite the application in Example 8-1, except this time we'll use the POSTCON wrapper class, as shown in Example 8-3. In addition, we'll cascade the addProperty calls directly in the function call to create the resource (createResource), to keep the code compact, as well as to show a more direct connection between the two.

Example 8-3. Using wrapper class to add properties to resource

```java
import com.hp.hpl.mesa.rdf.jena.mem.ModelMem;
import com.hp.hpl.mesa.rdf.jena.model.*;
import com.hp.hpl.mesa.rdf.jena.vocabulary.*;
import com.burningbird.postcon.vocabulary.POSTCON;
import java.io.FileOutputStream;
import java.io.PrintWriter;

public class pracRDFSecond extends Object {


    public static void main (String args[]) {

        // Resource names
        String sResource = "http://burningbird.net/articles/monsters1.htm";
        String sRelResource1 = "http://burningbird.net/articles/monsters2.htm";
        String sRelResource2 = "http://burningbird.net/articles/monsters3.htm";

        try {
            // Create an empty graph
            Model model = new ModelMem( );

            // Create the resource
            //    and add the properties cascading style
            Resource article
              = model.createResource(sResource)
              .addProperty(POSTCON.related, model.createResource(sRelResource1))
              .addProperty(POSTCON.related, model.createResource(sRelResource2));

            // Print RDF/XML of model to system output
            model.write(new PrintWriter(System.out));

        } catch (Exception e) {
            System.out.println("Failed: " + e);
        }
    }
}
```

As you can see, using the wrapper class simplified the code considerably. The new application is saved, compiled, and run. The output from this application is shown in Example 8-4. Again, running it through the RDF Validator confirms that the serialized RDF/XML represents the model correctly and validly.

Example 8-4. Generated RDF/XML from serialized PostCon submodel

```
<rdf:RDF
  xmlns:rdf='http://www.w3.org/1999/02/22-rdf-syntax-ns#'
  xmlns:NSO='http://burningbird.net/postcon/elements/1.0/'
 >
  <rdf:Description rdf:about='http://burningbird.net/articles/monsters1.htm'>
    <NSO:related rdf:resource='http://burningbird.net/articles/monsters2.htm'/>
    <NSO:related rdf:resource='http://burningbird.net/articles/monsters3.htm'/>
  </rdf:Description>
</rdf:RDF>
```

You've probably noted by now that Jena generates namespace prefixes for the vocabulary elements. As you'll see later, you can change the prefix used for namespaces. However, the specific prefix used is unimportant, except perhaps for readability across models when the same vocabulary is used in multiple places, such as the Dublin Core vocabulary.

Adding More Complex Structures

As has been demonstrated, adding literal or simple resource properties for a specific RDF resource in a model is quite uncomplicated with Jena. However, many RDF models make use of more complex structures, including nesting resources following the RDF node-edge-node pattern. In this section, we'll demonstrate how Jena can just as easily handle more complex RDF model structures and their associated RDF/XML.

 Much of the code shown in this chapter came about through development of the PostCon application (RDF Web Content Information System), discussed throughout the book. You can download the source for the Java-based implementation of PostCon at SourceForge (*http://rdfcontent.sourceforge.net/*).

The `pstcn:bio` property is, itself, a resource that does not have a specific URI—a blank node, or *bnode*. Though not a literal, it's still added as a property using `addProperty`.

In Example 8-5, a new resource representing the article is created and the two related resource properties are added. In addition, a new resource is created for bio, and several properties are added to it; these properties are defined within the DC vocabulary, and I used the DC wrapper class to create them. Once the resource is implemented, I attach it to a higher-level resource using `addProperty`.

Example 8-5. Adding a blank node to a model

```
import com.hp.hpl.mesa.rdf.jena.mem.ModelMem;
import com.hp.hpl.mesa.rdf.jena.model.*;
import com.hp.hpl.mesa.rdf.jena.vocabulary.*;
import com.burningbird.postcon.vocabulary.POSTCON;
import java.io.FileOutputStream;
import java.io.PrintWriter;

public class pracRDFThird extends Object {

    public static void main (String args[]) {

// Resource names
String sResource = "http://burningbird.net/articles/monsters1.htm";
String sRelResource1 = "http://burningbird.net/articles/monsters2.htm";
String sRelResource2 = "http://burningbird.net/articles/monsters3.htm";
String sType = "http://burningbird.net/postcon/elements/1.0/Resource";

try {
 // Create an empty graph
 Model model = new ModelMem( );

 // Create the resource
 // and add the properties cascading style
 Resource article
 = model.createResource(sResource)
 .addProperty(POSTCON.related, model.createResource(sRelResource1))
 .addProperty(POSTCON.related, model.createResource(sRelResource2));

 // Create the bio bnode resource
 // and add properties
 Resource bio
 = model.createResource( )
 .addProperty(DC.creator, "Shelley Powers")
 .addProperty(DC.publisher, "Burningbird")
 .addProperty(DC.title, model.createLiteral("Tale of Two Monsters: Legends", "en"));

 // Attach to main resource
 article.addProperty(POSTCON.bio, bio);

 // Print RDF/XML of model to system output
  model.write(new PrintWriter(System.out));

        } catch (Exception e) {
            System.out.println("Failed: " + e);
        }
    }
}
String sResource = "http://burningbird.net/articles/monsters1.htm";
String sRelResource1 = "http://burningbird.net/articles/monsters2.htm";
```

I could have used the cascade approach to add the bio directly to the document resource as it was being created. However, creating bio separately and then adding it

---

to the top-level resource is, in my opinion, easier to read, and the resulting RDF model and serialized RDF/XML is identical. The results of the application are shown in Example 8-6. As you can see, Jena uses `rdf:nodeID` and separates out the resource, rather than nesting it. This is nothing more than convenience and syntactic sugar—the resulting RDF graph is still equivalent in meaning.

Example 8-6. Generated RDF/XML demonstrating more complex structures

```
<rdf:RDF
  xmlns:rdf='http://www.w3.org/1999/02/22-rdf-syntax-ns#'
  xmlns:NSO='http://burningbird.net/postcon/elements/1.0/'
  xmlns:dc='http://purl.org/dc/elements/1.0/'
 >
  <rdf:Description rdf:nodeID='A0'>
    <dc:creator>Shelley Powers</dc:creator>
    <dc:publisher>Burningbird</dc:publisher>
    <dc:title xml:lang='en'>Tale of Two Monsters: Legends</dc:title>
  </rdf:Description>
  <rdf:Description rdf:about='http://burningbird.net/articles/monsters1.htm'>
    <NSO:related rdf:resource='http://burningbird.net/articles/monsters2.htm'/>
    <NSO:related rdf:resource='http://burningbird.net/articles/monsters3.htm'/>
    <NSO:bio rdf:nodeID='A0'/>
  </rdf:Description>
</rdf:RDF>
```

The example demonstrates how to implement the striped XML quality of RDF, which has a node-edge-node-edge pattern of nesting. Another RDF pattern that Post-Con supports is a container holding the resource's history, which is implemented in the later section titled "Creating a Container."

Creating a Typed Node

The RDF model created to this point shows the top-level resource as a basic `rdf:Description` node, with a given URI. However, in the actual RDF/XML, the top-level node is what is known as a typed node, which means it is defined with a specific `rdf:type` property.

Implementing a typed node in Jena is actually quite simple, by the numbers.

First, the POSTCON wrapper class needs to be modified to add the new resource implementation. To support this, two new Jena classes are imported into the POSTCON Java code:

```
import com.hp.hpl.mesa.rdf.jena.common.ResourceImpl;
import com.hp.hpl.mesa.rdf.jena.model.Resource;
```

Next, the document resource definition is added:

```
// add the one resource
      static final String   nresource = "resource";
  public static       Resource resource = null;
```

Finally, the resource is instantiated:

```
resource = new ResourceImpl(uri+nresource);
```

Once the wrapper class is modified, the typed node information is implemented within the Jena code, as shown in Example 8-7.

Example 8-7. Adding an rdf:type for the top-level document resource

```java
import com.hp.hpl.mesa.rdf.jena.mem.ModelMem;
import com.hp.hpl.mesa.rdf.jena.model.*;
import com.hp.hpl.mesa.rdf.jena.vocabulary.*;
import com.burningbird.postcon.vocabulary.POSTCON;
import java.io.FileOutputStream;
import java.io.PrintWriter;

public class chap1005 extends Object {


    public static void main (String args[]) {

        // Resource names
        String sResource = "http://burningbird.net/articles/monsters1.htm";

        try {
            // Create an empty graph
            Model model = new ModelMem( );

            // Create the resource
            //    and add the properties cascading style
            Resource article
              = model.createResource(sResource)
                    .addProperty(RDF.type, POSTCON.resource);

            // Print RDF/XML of model to system output
            model.write(new PrintWriter(System.out));

        } catch (Exception e) {
            System.out.println("Failed: " + e);
        }
    }
}
```

The resulting RDF/XML:

```xml
<rdf:RDF
  xmlns:rdf='http://www.w3.org/1999/02/22-rdf-syntax-ns#'
 >
  <rdf:Description rdf:about='http://burningbird.net/articles/monsters1.htm'>
    <rdf:type rdf:resource='http://burningbird.net/postcon/elements/1.0/Resource'/>
  </rdf:Description>
</rdf:RDF>
```

is equivalent to the same RDF/XML used in the sample document:

```
<pstcn:Resource rdf:about="monsters1.htm">
...
</pstcn:Resource>
```

Both result in the exact same RDF model, shown in Figure 8-2.

Figure 8-2. RDF model of typed (document) node

Creating a Container

As discussed earlier in the book, an RDF container is a grouping of related items. There are no formalized semantics for a container other than this, though tools and applications may add additional semantics based on type of container: Alt, Seq, or Bag.

The PostCon vocabulary uses an `rdf:Seq` container to group the resource history, with the application-specific implication that if tools support this concept, the contained items are sequenced in order, from top to bottom, within the container:

```
<pstcn:history>
  <rdf:Seq>
    <rdf:_1 rdf:resource="http://www.yasd.com/dynaearth/monsters1.htm" />
    <rdf:_2 rdf:resource="http://www.dynamicearth.com/articles/monsters1.htm" />
    <rdf:_3 rdf:resource="http://burningbird.net/articles/monsters1.htm" />
  </rdf:Seq>
</pstcn:history>
```

For tools that don't support my additional container semantics, the items can be sequenced by whatever properties are associated with each contained resource—the date, URI, movement type, or even random sequencing:

```
<rdf:Description rdf:about="http://www.yasd.com/dynaearth/monsters1.htm">
    <pstcn:movementType>Add</pstcn:movementType>
    <pstcn:reason>New Article</pstcn:reason>
    <dc:date>1998-01-01T00:00:00-05:00</dc:date>
</rdf:Description>
```

RDF containers are just a variation of typed node and can be implemented directly just by using the same code shown to this point. After all, a container is nothing more than a blank node with a given `rdf:type` (such as `http://www.w3.org/1999/02/22-rdf-syntax-ns#Seq`) acting as the subject for several statements, all with the same predicate and all pointing to objects that are resources. You could emulate containers directly given previous code. However, it's a lot simpler just to use the APIs.

In Example 8-8, an RDF container, an rdf:Seq, is created and three resources are added to it. Each of the resources has properties of its own, including pstcn: movementType, reason (both of which are from POSTCON), and date (from DC). Once completed, the rdf:Seq is then added to the document resource.

Example 8-8. Adding the history container to the model

```
import com.hp.hpl.mesa.rdf.jena.mem.ModelMem;
import com.hp.hpl.mesa.rdf.jena.model.*;
import com.hp.hpl.mesa.rdf.jena.vocabulary.*;
import com.burningbird.postcon.vocabulary.POSTCON;
import java.io.FileOutputStream;
import java.io.PrintWriter;

public class pracRDFFifth extends Object {


    public static void main (String args[]) {

        // Resource names
        String sResource = "http://burningbird.net/articles/monsters1.htm";
        String sHistory1 = "http://www.yasd.com/dynaearth/monsters1.htm";
        String sHistory2 = "http://www.dynamicearth.com/articles/monsters1.htm";
        String sHistory3 = "http://www.burningbird.net/articles/monsters1.htm";

        try {
            // Create an empty graph
            Model model = new ModelMem( );

            // Create Seq
            Seq hist = model.createSeq( )
                .add (1, model.createResource(sHistory1)
                .addProperty(POSTCON.movementtype, model.createLiteral("Add"))
                .addProperty(POSTCON.reason, model.createLiteral("New Article"))
                .addProperty(DC.date, model.createLiteral("1998-01-01T00:00:00-05:00")))
                .add (2, model.createResource(sHistory2)
                .addProperty(POSTCON.movementtype, model.createLiteral("Move"))
                .addProperty(POSTCON.reason, model.createLiteral("Moved to separate
                    dynamicearth.com domain"))
                .addProperty(DC.date, model.createLiteral("1999-10-31:T00:00:00-05:00")))
                .add (3, model.createResource(sHistory3)
                .addProperty(POSTCON.movementtype, model.createLiteral("Move"))
                .addProperty(POSTCON.reason, model.createLiteral("Collapsed
                    into Burningbird"))
                .addProperty(DC.date, model.createLiteral("2002-11-01:T00:00:00-5:00")));

            // Create the resource
            //    and add the properties cascading style
            Resource article
              = model.createResource(sResource)
              .addProperty(POSTCON.history, hist);
```

Example 8-8. Adding the history container to the model (continued)

```
                // Print RDF/XML of model to system output
                RDFWriter writer = model.getWriter();
                writer.setNsPrefix("pstcn", "http://burningbird.net/postcon/elements/1.0/");
                writer.write(model, new PrintWriter(System.out),
                    "http://burningbird.net/articles" );

        } catch (Exception e) {
            System.out.println("Failed: " + e);
        }
    }
}
```

Another new item added with this code is the `RDFWriter.setNsPrefix` method, which defines the prefix so that it shows as `pstcn` rather than the default of `NS0`. This isn't necessarily important—whatever abbreviation used is resolved to the namespace within the model—but it does make the models easier to read if you use the same QName all the time.

As described in Chapter 4, a container is a grouping of like items, and there are no additional formal semantics attached to the concept of container. Now, the fact that I used `rdf:Seq` could imply that the items within the container should be processed in order, from first to last. However, this is up to the implementation to determine exactly how an `rdf:Seq` container is processed outside of the formal semantics within the RDF specifications.

What's interesting is that, within Jena, a container is treated exactly as the typed node that I described earlier—which means that the generated RDF/XML, as shown in Example 8-9, shows the `rdf:Seq` as its typed node equivalent, rather than in the container-like syntax shown in the example source.

Example 8-9. Generated RDF/XML showing container defined as typed node

```
<rdf:RDF
  xmlns:rdf='http://www.w3.org/1999/02/22-rdf-syntax-ns#'
  xmlns:pstcn='http://burningbird.net/postcon/elements/1.0/'
  xmlns:dc='http://purl.org/dc/elements/1.0/'
 >
  <rdf:Description rdf:about='http://burningbird.net/articles/monsters1.htm'>
    <pstcn:history rdf:nodeID='A0'/>
  </rdf:Description>
  <rdf:Description rdf:about='http://www.dynamicearth.com/articles/monsters1.htm'>
    <pstcn:movementType>Move</pstcn:movementType>
    <pstcn:reason>Moved to separate dynamicearth.com domain</pstcn:reason>
    <dc:date>1999-10-31:T00:00:00-05:00</dc:date>
  </rdf:Description>
  <rdf:Description rdf:about='http://www.burningbird.net/articles/monsters1.htm'>
    <pstcn:movementType>Move</pstcn:movementType>
    <pstcn:reason>Collapsed into Burningbird</pstcn:reason>
    <dc:date>2002-11-01:T00:00:00-5:00</dc:date>
  </rdf:Description>
```

```
  <rdf:Description rdf:nodeID='A0'>
    <rdf:type rdf:resource='http://www.w3.org/1999/02/22-rdf-syntax-ns#Seq'/>
    <rdf:_1 rdf:resource='http://www.yasd.com/dynaearth/monsters1.htm'/>
    <rdf:_2 rdf:resource='http://www.dynamicearth.com/articles/monsters1.htm'/>
    <rdf:_3 rdf:resource='http://www.burningbird.net/articles/monsters1.htm'/>
  </rdf:Description>
  <rdf:Description rdf:about='http://www.yasd.com/dynaearth/monsters1.htm'>
    <pstcn:movementType>Add</pstcn:movementType>
    <pstcn:reason>New Article</pstcn:reason>
    <dc:date>1998-01-01T00:00:00-05:00</dc:date>
  </rdf:Description>
</rdf:RDF>
```

I prefer the Jena implementation of the container because it implies nothing about container-like behavior that doesn't exist within the RDF specifications. The generated RDF/XML provides a clearer picture of a set of like resources, grouped for some reason, and then added as a property to another resource. No more, no less.

Now that we've had a chance to build RDF models and view the serialized RDF/XML from them, we'll take a look at parsing and accessing data in existing RDF/XML documents.

> One type of RDF statement I haven't demonstrated is a reified statement, primarily because I don't use reified statements within my applications. However, if you need reification for your own effort, you can find a couple of example Java applications that build reified statements within the Jena Toolkit.

Parsing and Querying an RDF Document

Once an RDF/XML document is created, it serves no useful purpose unless the data in the document can be parsed and queried. In many ways, the advantage to something like RDF/XML is that the data is structured in specific ways, making it easier to access different data with the same code.

This section will take a look at opening an existing RDF/XML document, both within the filesystem and through the Internet, and accessing the data contained within the documents.

Just Doing a Basic Dump

When accessing the data within an RDF/XML document, you'll want to access the data in two different ways—accessing specific pieces of data or accessing all of it for alternative presentation. For instance, most of the tools discussed in Chapters 14 and 15 are interested in all the data within an RDF/XML document, data that is then transformed in one way or another.

One of the most common ways of "dumping" the data within an RDF/XML document (outputting all the data in a new format) is to print it out in N-Triples format. This was demonstrated with the parser attached with the Jena Toolkit, ARP. However, another way of looking at the data is to dump out a listing of objects of one type or another.

In Example 8-10, the PostCon RDF file for the demonstration article is accessed and opened into a memory model using the read method; this method takes the URL of the file as its parameter. Once the model is loaded, the listObjects method is called on the model object and assigned to a nodeIterator. This object is just one of the many different iterators that Jena provides: nodeIterator, stmtIterator, ResIterator, and so on. Each of these is specialized to provide access to specific Jena object types. In the example, once the nodeIterator is populated, it's traversed, and all of the RDF objects—the property "values"—are printed out using the simple toString base method.

Example 8-10. Basic dump of objects, printing out object values

```
import com.hp.hpl.mesa.rdf.jena.mem.ModelMem;
import com.hp.hpl.mesa.rdf.jena.model.*;

public class pracRDFSixth extends Object {

public static void main (String args[]) {

String sUri = args[0];

try {

    // Create memory model, read in RDF/XML document
    ModelMem model = new ModelMem( );
    model.read(sUri);

    // Print out objects in model using toString
    NodeIterator iter = model.listObjects();
    while (iter.hasNext()) {
        System.out.println("  " + iter.next().toString());
    }

    } catch (Exception e) {
            System.out.println("Failed: " + e);
    }
  }
}
```

The application is run against the *monsters1.rdf* example file:

```
java pracRDFSixth http://burningbird.net/articles/monsters1.rdf
```

This is probably one of the simplest Jena applications you can write and test to make sure that a model is loaded correctly. Instead of objects, you could also dump out the subjects (`ResIterator` and `listSubjects`) or even the entire statement (`StmtIterator` and `listStatements`). The functionality is relatively the same, except for the `iterator` and the `fetch` method called.

Accessing Specific Values

Instead of listing all statements or all objects, you can fine-tune the code to list only subjects, statements, or objects matching specific properties, using the property implementations created within the wrapper classes, such as POSTCON.

To access all objects that have the PostCon related property, the POSTCON wrapper class is added to the import section:

```
import com.burningbird.postcon.vocabulary.POSTCON;
```

Next, the `listObjectsOfProperty` method is used instead of `listObjects`:

```
NodeIterator iter = model.listObjectsOfProperty(POSTCON.related);
```

That's it to access all objects given a specific property. As you can see, the wrapper class is handy for more than just creating a model.

To access all the statements for a given resource, first access the resource from the model and then list all the properties associated with that resource. In Example 8-11, all of the statements are accessed for the top-level resource contained within the document. Traversing the list of statements, the subject is accessed and printed out (both namespace and local name), followed by the predicate (again, namespace and local name), and finally the object.

Example 8-11. Printing out each statement triple for a given RDF/XML document

```
import com.hp.hpl.mesa.rdf.jena.mem.ModelMem;
import com.hp.hpl.mesa.rdf.jena.model.*;
import com.burningbird.postcon.vocabulary.POSTCON;

public class pracRDFSeventh extends Object {

public static void main (String args[]) {

String sUri = args[0];
String sResource = args[1];

try {

    // Create memory model, read in RDF/XML document
    ModelMem model = new ModelMem();
    model.read(sUri);

    // Find resource
    Resource res = model.getResource(sResource);
```

```
    // Find properties
    StmtIterator iter = res.listProperties();

    // Print out triple - subject | property | object
    while (iter.hasNext()) {
        // Next statement in queue
        Statement stmt = iter.next();

        // Get subject, print
        Resource res2 = stmt.getSubject();
        System.out.print(res2.getNameSpace() + res2.getLocalName());

        // Get predicate, print
        Property prop = stmt.getPredicate();
        System.out.print(" " + prop.getNameSpace() + prop.getLocalName());

        // Get object, print
        RDFNode node = stmt.getObject();
        System.out.println(" " + node.toString() + "\n");
    }

    } catch (Exception e) {
            System.out.println("Failed: " + e);
    }
 }
}
```

Running this application outputs the triple for each statement for the document, including application-generated object values for blank nodes:

```
http://burningbird.net/articles/monsters1.htm
http://www.w3.org/1999/02/22-rdf-syntax-ns#type http://burningbird.net/postcon/
elements/1.0/Resource

http://burningbird.net/articles/monsters1.htm
http://burningbird.net/postcon/elements/1.0/bio
anon:a9ae05:f2ecfdc9db:-7fff

http://burningbird.net/articles/monsters1.htm http://burningbird.net/postcon/
elements/1.0/relevancy
anon:a9ae05:f2ecfdc9db:-7ff7

http://burningbird.net/articles/monsters1.htm http://burningbird.net/postcon/
elements/1.0/presentation
anon:a9ae05:f2ecfdc9db:-7fec

http://burningbird.net/articles/monsters1.htm
http://burningbird.net/postcon/elements/1.0/history
anon:a9ae05:f2ecfdc9db:-7fde

http://burningbird.net/articles/monsters1.htm
http://burningbird.net/postcon/elements/1.0/related
http://burningbird.net/articles/monsters2.htm
```

```
http://burningbird.net/articles/monsters1.htm
http://burningbird.net/postcon/elements/1.0/related
http://burningbird.net/articles/monsters3.htm

http://burningbird.net/articles/monsters1.htm
http://burningbird.net/postcon/elements/1.0/related
http://burningbird.net/articles/monsters4.htm
```

Note in the code that the variation of getObject used is the one returning an RDFNode object. The reason is that other variations work only if the object is a literal and throw exceptions if a nonliteral is found. Since some of the objects in this document are resources, the RDFNode method works best.

As can be seen from the examples, querying the data in an RDF/XML document doesn't have to be difficult—you just have to remember the triple nature of the statements in RDF/XML.

 One of the most powerful aspects of Jena is the ability to use a query language—RDQL—to query an RDF model to data that matches given patterns. This is explored in Chapter 10.

In-Memory Versus Persistent Model Storage

All the examples to this point have used the memory model, but Jena also provides the capability to persist data to relational database storage. The databases supported are MySQL, PostgreSQL, Interbase, and Oracle. Within each database system, Jena also supports differing storage layouts:

Generic
> All statements are stored in a single table, and resources and literals are indexed using integer identifiers generated by the database.

GenericProc
> Similar to generic, but data access is through stored procedures.

MMGeneric
> Similar to generic but can store multiple models.

Hash
> Similar to generic but uses MD5 hashes to generate the identifiers.

MMHash
> Similar to hash but can store multiple models.

The first step of storing a model in a database is to create the structure to store the data. The tables must be created in an already existing database, which has been formatted and had tables added. This code needs to be run once. After the database structure is created, it can then be opened directly in another application or used within the same application.

In Example 8-12, I'm storing two models in the database using a different name for each. In addition, I'm also creating the JDBC connection directly rather than having DBConnection create it for me. The model used is based on a MySQL database, using the MMGeneric layout. I'm not using the slightly more efficient hash method (MMHash), primarily because the generic layout is the better one to take if you're thinking of accessing the data directly through JDBC rather than through Jena.

 At the time of this writing, using DBConnection to make the JDBC connection is failing in the second application to access the same database. Creating an instance of the JDBC connection and passing it in as a parameter to DBConnection averts this failure.

Once the database is formatted, two RDF/XML documents are opened and stored in two separate models within the database.

Example 8-12. Persisting two RDF/XML models to a MySQL database

```
import com.hp.hpl.mesa.rdf.jena.model.*;
import com.hp.hpl.mesa.rdf.jena.rdb.ModelRDB;
import com.hp.hpl.mesa.rdf.jena.rdb.DBConnection;
import java.sql.*;

public class pracRDFEighth extends Object {


public static void main (String args[]) {

// Pass two RDF documents, connection string,
String sUri = args[0];
String sUri2 = args[1];
String sConn = args[2];
String sUser = args[3];
String sPass = args[4];

try {
  // Load driver class
  Class.forName("com.mysql.jdbc.Driver").newInstance();

  // Establish connection - replace with your own conn info
  Connection con = DriverManager.getConnection(sConn, "user", "pass");
  DBConnection dbcon = new DBConnection(con);

  // Format database
  ModelRDB.create(dbcon, "MMGeneric", "Mysql");

  // Create and read first model
  ModelRDB model1 = ModelRDB.createModel(dbcon, "one");
  model1.read(sUri);
```

Example 8-12. Persisting two RDF/XML models to a MySQL database (continued)

```
    // Create and read second model
    ModelRDB model2 = ModelRDB.createModel(dbcon, "two");
    model2.read(sUri2);


    } catch (Exception e) {
            System.out.println("Failed: " + e);
    }
 }
}
```

The application expects the following command line:

```
    java pracRDFEighth firstrdffile secondrdffile connect_string username password
```

You'll need to adjust the database connection string, username, and password to fit your environment. In the example, instead of reading the two models into separate databases, I could also have read them into the same database.

Once the model data is persisted, any number of applications can then access it. In Example 8-13, I'm accessing both models, dumping all of the objects in the first and writing out triples from the second.

Example 8-13. Accessing RDF models stored in MySQL database

```
import com.hp.hpl.mesa.rdf.jena.model.*;
import com.hp.hpl.mesa.rdf.jena.rdb.ModelRDB;
import com.hp.hpl.mesa.rdf.jena.rdb.DBConnection;
import java.sql.*;

public class pracRDFNinth extends Object {


public static void main (String args[]) {

String sConn = args[0];
String sUser = args[1];
String sPass = args[2];

try {
  // load driver class
  Class.forName("com.mysql.jdbc.Driver").newInstance();

    // Establish connection - replace with your own conn info
      Connection con = DriverManager.getConnection(sConn, sUser, sPass);
    DBConnection dbcon = new DBConnection(con);

    // Open two existing models
    ModelRDB model1 = ModelRDB.open(dbcon, "one");
    ModelRDB model2 = ModelRDB.open(dbcon, "two");
```

Example 8-13. Accessing RDF models stored in MySQL database (continued)

```
    // Print out objects in first model using toString
    NodeIterator iter = model1.listObjects();
    while (iter.hasNext()) {
        System.out.println("  " + iter.next().toString());
    }

    // Print out triples in second model - find resource
    Resource res = model2.getResource("http://burningbird.net/articles/monsters1.htm");

    // Find properties
    StmtIterator sIter = res.listProperties();

    // Print out triple - subject | property | object
    while (sIter.hasNext()) {
        // Next statement in queue
        com.hp.hpl.mesa.rdf.jena.model.Statement stmt = sIter.next();

        // Get subject, print
        Resource res2 = stmt.getSubject();
        System.out.print(res2.getNameSpace() + res2.getLocalName());

        // Get predicate, print
        Property prop = stmt.getPredicate();
        System.out.print(" " + prop.getNameSpace() + prop.getLocalName());

        // Get object, print
        RDFNode node = stmt.getObject();
        System.out.println(" " + node.toString() + "\n");
    }

} catch (Exception e) {
        System.out.println("Failed: " + e);
    }
  }
}
```

Jena uses a highly normalized data model for the RDF statements. In addition to accessing the data through the Jena API, you can also access it directly using whatever database connectivity you prefer. However, I recommend that you access the data for read-only purposes and leave updates to the Jena API.

## CHAPTER 9

RDF and Perl, PHP, and Python

There is commonality among many of the APIs that manipulate RDF/XML, regardless of the programming language in which the API is implemented. Usually a new model is created, some form of storage mechanism is assigned to it, and statements are added to it by first creating the resource, predicate, and object associated with the statement, and then creating the statement itself. This similarity of procedure is one of the advantages to the metadata structure of RDF—a fundamental data structure transcends implementation. This basic data structure was apparent in the last chapter, which manipulated RDF using Java. This same data structure and similarity of actions are also apparent in this chapter, which looks at working with RDF/XML using what I call the three Ps of programming.

If you've worked on web development, particularly within a Unix environment, chances are you've used at least one of the three Ps: Perl, PHP, or Python. Perl has become ubiquitous across most Unix environments (which now include Mac OS X); with the help of ActiveState, Perl is also fairly common in Windows. PHP is now beginning to rival ASP as the web scripting language of choice, especially since PHP is designed to work with Apache, the most widely used web server in the world. Python is much newer, but is increasing in popularity at a rapid pace due to the extremely loyal following it has attracted.

Considering the popularity of these three languages, it's not a surprise that each boasts more than one language-based RDF/XML API or other technology. It would be difficult to find and cover every Perl-, PHP-, and Python-based RDF/XML API. Instead, in this chapter, I focus on the APIs that have had recent updates and/or are most widely used. This includes the APIs I've used in my own projects, noted in the discussions.

The online book support site lists download locations for the most recent PHP, Perl, and Python RDF/XML tools, utilities, and APIs. For more on Perl, see the Perl resource site at *http://perl.com*. The main Python site is *http://python.org*, and PHP's main site is *http://php.net*.

RDF/XML and Perl

There would seem to be a natural fit between Perl, a language known for its parsing and pattern-matching capability, and RDF. When I went searching for Perl APIs, I was surprised to find that several I discovered had not been updated for months (sometimes years) or were seriously incomplete. However, I was able to find a couple of Perl APIs that are active, are being supported, and provide much of the functionality necessary for working with the RDF data model through RDF/XML.

 The W3C had a Perl library that included an RDF Parser, *perllib*, found at *http://www.w3.org/1999/02/26-modules/*. However, there hasn't been a solid release of the Perl modules associated with it in quite some time, and the only activity that's occurred in relation to it is buried in the CVS files for the API. Because there hasn't been a release of the API in some time, I decided not to include it in this chapter.

Ginger Alliance PerlRDF

I found the Ginger Alliance Perl APIs by searching for RDF within CPAN, the repository of Perl on the Internet (accessible at *http://perl.com*). The organization provides Perl modules that can parse, store, and query Notation3 (RDF::Notation3) as well as RDF/XML (RDF::Core), but we'll cover only the RDF/XML module in this book.

Updates to PerlRDF

Be aware that at the time of this writing, PerlRDF has not been updated to reflect all of the new constructs released with the newest RDF Working Group documents. However, I was assured by the author that PerlRDF is still being fully supported, and the group had every intention of ensuring it meets the new RDF specifications as soon as they release. The version used in this chapter was released in October 2002.

You can download the Ginger Alliance Perl modules from CPAN or access them directly at the organization's web site (at *http://www.gingerall.cz/charlie/ga/xml/p_rdf.xml*). The examples in this chapter were created with RDF::Core 2.0, and installation instructions are contained within the source files. Both APIs work with Perl 5 and should be platform independent. The source is licensed under Mozilla Public License 1.1 and the GNU General Public License.

The RDF::Core modules for RDF/XML allow you to parse and store an existing RDF/XML document, add to it, and query it using function calls, as well as serialize a new or modified model. You can store the module in memory, within a PostgreSQL database or in Berkeley DB.

Model Persistence and Basic Querying

RDF models can be built within the code or parsed in from an external file. First, though, you have to create a storage mechanism to store the data. PerlRDF gives you a choice of storing a model in memory or in a Berkeley DB or PostgreSQL database. The RDF::Core::Storage object manages the memory access, and it has three different implementations for the three different storage mechanisms.

RDF::Core::Storage::Memory manages in-memory storage. This object won't persist after the Perl application terminates or goes out of scope, and the only unique method is new, which takes no parameters:

```
require RDF::Core::Storage::Memory;
my $storage = new RDF::Core::Storage::Memory;
```

The RDF::Core Berkeley DB object, RDF::Core::Storage::DB_File, utilizes the existing Berkeley Database DB_File Perl module for much of its functionality. DB_File uses the tie function to bind the DB object functions to the database file on disk, hiding much of the detail of database management. Unlike the memory method, the DB_File object's new method takes several parameters:

Name
> The name used as the first part of the name for several files, to support the structures necessary to store the RDF model.

Flags, Mode
> Equivalent to the flags and mode used with the Berkeley DB dbopen method. Examples of flags are O_RDONLY, O_RDRW, and O_CREAT. By default, O_RDONLY and O_RDRW are used. The default mode is 0666.

MemLimit
> Controls the number of statements returned within an enumerator (to be discussed) if nonzero.

Sync
> Number of wire transfer processes to complete before synchronizing memory data with storage or zero to not force synchronization.

In the following code, a storage object is instantiated, set to the current directory with the name of rdfdata, and given a MemLimit set to 500 statements; all other values are set to default:

```
require RDF::Core::Storage::DB_File;
my $storage = new RDF::Core::Storage::DB_File(Name =>'./rdfdata',
                                              MemLimit => 5000,
                                             );
```

The last storage mechanism supported in RDF::Core, RDF::Core::Storage::PostGres uses the PostgreSQL data store to persist the RDF model. Its new method takes the following options:

ConnecStr
> PostgreSQL connection string

DBUser, DBPassword
> Database user and password

Model
> Distinguish between models (can store than one model in PostgreSQL database)

After a storage object is instantiated, the methods to manipulate its data are the same regardless of the underlying physical storage mechanism.

Building an RDF Model

A basic procedure is used with PerlRDF to create a new RDF model. First, create the storage mechanism; next, create the model and each of the components of an RDF statement, assigning them to a new statement. Finally, add the statement to the model. That's all you need to add a new triple to an RDF model. The power of this Perl module is in its simplicity of use.

To demonstrate this, Example 9-1 shows a simple application that creates a new model using a Berkeley database, adds a couple of statements for the same resource, and then serializes the model to RDF/XML. The first statement adds an rdf:type of PostCon Resource to the main resource; the second adds a movement type predicate. Note that predicate objects are created directly from the subject object, though the two aren't associated within the model until they're added to the model. Also note that literals are specific instances of Perl objects, in this case RDF::Core:: Literal.

Example 9-1. Creating simple RDF graph with two statements

```
use strict;

require RDF::Core::Storage::Memory;
require RDF::Core::Model;
require RDF::Core::Statement;
require RDF::Core::Model::Serializer;
require RDF::Core::Literal;

# create storage object
my $storage = new RDF::Core::Storage::Memory;
my $model = new RDF::Core::Model (Storage => $storage);

my $subject =
  new RDF::Core::Resource('http://burningbird.net/articles/monsters1.rdf');
my $predicate =
  $subject->new('http://www.w3.org/1999/02/22-rdf-syntax-ns#type');
my $object =
  new RDF::Core::Resource('http://burningbird.net/postcon/elements/1.0/Resource');
my $statement = new RDF::Core::Statement($subject, $predicate, $object);
$model->addStmt($statement);
```

Example 9-1. Creating simple RDF graph with two statements (continued)

```
$model->addStmt(new RDF::Core::Statement($subject,
                $subject->new('http://burningbird.net/postcon/elements/1.0/movementType'),
                new RDF::Core::Literal('Move')));

my $xml = '';
  my $serializer = new RDF::Core::Model::Serializer(Model=>$model,
                                                    Output=>\$xml
                                                    );

  $serializer->serialize;
  print "$xml\n";
```

Running this application results in the following RDF/XML:

```
<rdf:RDF
xmlns:rdf="http://www.w3.org/1999/02/22-rdf-syntax-ns#"
xmlns:a="http://burningbird.net/postcon/elements/1.0/"
>
<rdf:Description about="http://burningbird.net/articles/monsters1.rdf">
<rdf:type rdf:resource="http://burningbird.net/postcon/elements/1.0/Resource"/>
<a:movementType>Move</a:movementType>
</rdf:Description>
</rdf:RDF>
```

PerlRDF hasn't been updated to reflect the W3C's recommendation to qualify all attributes; in this case about should become rdf:about. However, this isn't an error, and the most that happens when testing this in the RDF Validator is that you'll get a warning:

```
Warning: {W101} Unqualified use of rdf:about has been deprecated.[Line = 5, Column =
72]
```

It was a simple matter to fix this directly, within the Serializer.pm. In both instances of an "about" element being printed out (contained within quotes, use your text editor's search function to find these), replace "about" with "rdf:about". The rest of the examples in this chapter reflect this change.

Additional statements can be built and added on using the same approach. If the statement can be modeled as a particular N-Triple, it can be added as a statement to the model using RDF::Core, including blank nodes.

In Example 9-2, the code will add the N-Triples statements equivalent to the newer RDF construct, rdf:value. From *monsters1.rdf*, this looks like the following using the more formalized syntax:

```
<pstcn:presentation rdf:parseType="Resource">
    <pstcn:requires rdf:parseType="Resource">
        <pstcn:type>stylesheet</pstcn:type>
        <rdf:value>http://burningbird.net/de.css</rdf:value>
    </pstcn:requires>
</pstcn:presentation>
```

Technically, no specific method is included in RDF::Core for creating the formalized rdf:value syntax, but one's not needed as long as you can add statements for each N-Triple that results when the syntax is broken down into triples. In the case of rdf:value, the N-Triples for the rdf:value construct associated with the stylesheet in *monsters1.rdf* are (from the RDF Validator):

```
_:jARP24590 <http://burningbird.net/postcon/elements/1.0/type> "stylesheet" .
_:jARP24590 <http://www.w3.org/1999/02/22-rdf-syntax-ns#value>
"http://burningbird.net/de.css" .
_:jARP24589 <http://burningbird.net/postcon/elements/1.0/requires> _:jARP24590 .
<http://burningbird.net/articles/monsters1.htm> <http://burningbird.net/postcon/
elements/1.0/presentation> _:jARP24589 .
```

Breaking this down into actions, first a blank node must be created and added as a statement with the resource monsters1.htm and a given predicate of http://burningbird.net/postcon/elements/1.0/presentation. This blank node is then used as the resource for the next statement that's added, which adds another blank node, this one with the predicate of http://burningbird.net/postcon/elements/1.0/requires. In this example, the RDF::Core object NodeFactory creates the blank nodes for both.

Next, the second blank node that was created is used to add the next statement, with a predicate of http://www.w3.org/1999/02/22-rdf-syntax-ns#value and value of http://burningbird.net/de.css. The last statement has a predicate of http://burningbird.net/postcon/elements/1.0/type and a value of stylesheet. Since blank nodes created by NodeFactory are RDF::Core::Resource objects, they can also create predicates for each of the statements.

Example 9-2. Adding rdf:value as N-Triples to the model

```
use strict;

require RDF::Core::Storage::Memory;
require RDF::Core::Model;
require RDF::Core::Statement;
require RDF::Core::Model::Serializer;
require RDF::Core::Literal;
require RDF::Core::NodeFactory;

# create storage object
my $storage = new RDF::Core::Storage::Memory;
my $model = new RDF::Core::Model (Storage => $storage);

# new subject and new resource factory
my $subject =
  new RDF::Core::Resource('http://burningbird.net/articles/monsters1.rdf');
my $factory =
  new RDF::Core::NodeFactory(BaseURI=>'http://burningbird.net/articles/');

# create bnode for presentation
my $bPresentation = $factory->newResource;
```

Example 9-2. Adding rdf:value as N-Triples to the model (continued)

```
# create bnode for requires
my $bRequires = $factory->newResource;

# add presentation
my $predicate =
  $subject->new('http://burningbird.net/postcon/elements/1.0/presentation');
my $statement =
  new RDF::Core::Statement($subject, $predicate, $bPresentation);
$model->addStmt($statement);

# add requires
$model->addStmt(new RDF::Core::Statement($bPresentation,
                $bPresentation->new('http://burningbird.net/postcon/elements/1.0/requires'),
                $bRequires));

# add rdf:value
$model->addStmt(new RDF::Core::Statement($bRequires,
           $bRequires->new('http://www.w3.org/1999/02/22-rdf-syntax-ns#value'),
                      new RDF::Core::Literal('http://burningbird.net/de.css')));

# add value type
$model->addStmt(new RDF::Core::Statement($bRequires,
                $bRequires->new('http://burningbird.net/postcon/elements/1.0/type'),
                new RDF::Core::Literal('stylesheet')));

my $xml = '';
my $serializer = new RDF::Core::Model::Serializer(Model=>$model,
                                                  Output=>\$xml
                                                  );

$serializer->serialize;
print "$xml\n";
```

Running the application results in the following RDF/XML output:

```
<rdf:RDF
xmlns:rdf="http://www.w3.org/1999/02/22-rdf-syntax-ns#"
xmlns:a="http://burningbird.net/postcon/elements/1.0/"
>
<rdf:Description rdf:about="http://burningbird.net/articles/monsters1.htm">
<a:presentation>
<rdf:Description>
<a:requires>
<rdf:Description>
<rdf:value>http://burningbird.net/de.css</rdf:value>
<a:type>stylesheet</a:type>
</rdf:Description>
</a:requires>
</rdf:Description>
</a:presentation>
</rdf:Description>
</rdf:RDF>
```

Plugging this into the RDF Validator and asking for N-Triples output returns the following N-Triples:

```
_:jARP24933 <http://www.w3.org/1999/02/22-rdf-syntax-ns#value>
"http://burningbird.net/de.css" .
_:jARP24933 <http://burningbird.net/postcon/elements/1.0/type> "stylesheet" .
_:jARP24932 <http://burningbird.net/postcon/elements/1.0/requires> _:jARP24933 .
<http://burningbird.net/articles/monsters1.htm> <http://burningbird.net/postcon/
elements/1.0/presentation> _:jARP24932 .
```

This maps back to the original N-Triples that we used to build the statements in the first place. As the generated N-Triples demonstrate, the subgraph of the *monsters1.rdf* directed graph that's specific to the use of rdf:value is identical to using the more formalized syntax for this construct. Regardless of the complexity of the model, the same procedure can be used to add all statements.

In addition to building a model from scratch, you can also read RDF models in from external resources such as an RDF/XML document, demonstrated in the next section.

Parsing RDF/XML Documents

Using RDF::Core to parse and query an RDF file is much simpler than creating an RDF model within code, something true of all APIs and parsers used in this book.

Whether you build the RDF model directly in the code or read it in, you still have to create a storage object and attach it to a model before you can start adding statements. However, when you read in a model from an external source, you can use the RDF::Core::Model::Parser object to read in the RDF/XML directly and generate the appropriate statements.

 One major different between reading RDF statements in from an RDF/XML file and reading a file in using a parser is that the API may not support all the current constructs within the RDF/XML document, especially if you're using some of the more specialized XML shortcuts. As you read in the data, you may run into problems. If this happens, then you'll want to modify the RDF/XML, transforming the shortcut to the more formalized syntax to reflect the N-Triples that the parser can process.

To demonstrate how simple it is to read in an RDF/XML document, the code in Example 9-3 reads in the *monsters1.rdf* file, storing it in a Berkeley DB *datastore*. The application then calls getStmts on the model, returning an RDF::Core::Enumerator object, which is used to print out the N-Triples defined within the document.

Example 9-3. Parsing in RDF/XML document and then printing out N-Triples from model

```
use strict;

require RDF::Core::Model;
require RDF::Core::Model::Parser;
```

Example 9-3. Parsing in RDF/XML document and then printing out N-Triples from model

```
require RDF::Core::Enumerator;
require RDF::Core::Statement;
require RDF::Core::Storage::DB_File;

# create storage
my $storage = new RDF::Core::Storage::DB_File(Name =>'./rdfdata',
                                              MemLimit => 5000,
                                              );

# create model and map to storage
my $model = new RDF::Core::Model (Storage => $storage);

# define parser options and parse external RDF/XML document
my %options = ( Model => $model,
              Source => "/home/shelleyp/www/articles/monsters1.rdf",
              SourceType => 'file',
              BaseURI => "http://burningbird.net/",
              InlineURI => "http://burningbird.net/"
              );
my $parser = new RDF::Core::Model::Parser(%options);
$parser->parse;

# enumerate through statements, printing out labels
my $enumerator = $model->getStmts;
my $statement = $enumerator->getFirst;
while (defined $statement) {
   print $statement->getLabel."\n";
   $statement = $enumerator->getNext
}

# close enumerator
$enumerator->close;
```

The Berkeley DB file prefix is rdfdata, and several files will be generated with this prefix. The options for the parser include the file location for the RDF/XML document, the fact that it's being read in as a file and not a URL, and a base and an inline URI. The base URI is used to resolve relative URIs, while the inline URI is for blank node resources. RDF::Core generates a blank node identifier consisting of this inline URI and a separate number for each blank node within the document.

When the application is run, the N-Triples are printed out to system output, which can then be piped to a file to persist the output. A sampling of these N-Triples representing the subgraph we've been using for the example, the rdf:value syntax, is:

```
<http://burningbird.net/articles/monsters1.htm> <http://burningbird.net/postcon/
elements/1.0/presentation> <http://burningbird.net/3> .
<http://burningbird.net/3> <http://burningbird.net/postcon/elements/1.0/requires>
<http://burningbird.net/4> .
<http://burningbird.net/4> <http://burningbird.net/postcon/elements/1.0/type>
"stylesheet".
<http://burningbird.net/4> <http://www.w3.org/1999/02/22-rdf-syntax-ns#value> "http:/
/burningbird.net/de.css" .
```

Though the blank node identifiers are different from those generated by the RDF Validator, the statements are equivalent.

Now that the RDF/XML document has been read in, we can access it within the database to perform more selective queries.

Querying RDF with RDF::Core

In the last section, the code read the RDF/XML into a persistent Berkeley Database. Instead of going back against the document, we'll use the database for queries in the next examples.

You might want to see how many statements have a given predicate. To count statements matching a specific value in any one of the triple components, use countStmts, passing in appropriate search parameters for subject, predicate, and object. The number of statements found matching the given values is returned. Passing an undefined parameter signals that any value found for the specific items is a match. In Example 9-4, we're interested in only the statements that use the predicate http:// burningbird.net/postcon/elements/1.0/reason. The code loads the database and accesses the countStmts directly on the RDF::Core::Storage object (the Model object has a countStmts function, too).

Example 9-4. Count of statements matching a specific predicate

```
use strict;

require RDF::Core::Storage::DB_File;
require RDF::Core::Resource;

# load model from storage
my $storage = new RDF::Core::Storage::DB_File(Name =>'./rdfdata',
                                              MemLimit => 500);

# objects must be defined
my $subject;
my $object;

# initiate predicate
my $predicate =
  new RDF::Core::Resource('http://burningbird.net/postcon/elements/1.0/reason');

# get count of statements for predicate and print
my $val = $storage->countStmts($subject, $predicate, $object);
print $val . "\n";
```

When run, the application returns a value of 6, matching the number of statements that have the given predicate. If you're interested only in statements with a given predicate and subject, you could define the subject object in addition to the predicate:

```
my $subject = new RDF::Core::Resource("http://burningbird.net/articles/monsters4.
htm");
```

The value then returned is 1, for one record found matching that combination of subject and predicate.

 You'll also need to add in the RDF::Core::Literal class if you want to match on the subject in this example.

If you're interested in finding data to go with the count of statements, you can modify the code to use the method getStmts instead, returning an enumerator, which you can then traverse to get the data you're interested in.

The RDF::Core classes also support a more sophisticated querying capability similar to RDQL (discussed in detail in the next chapter). As with RDQL, the query language supported with RDF::Core supports select, from, and where keywords for the results, source, and search parameters. Three objects process RDQL queries in RDF::Core:

RDF::Core::Functions
> A mapping between a row of data and a function handler

RDF::Core::Evaluator
> An evaluator object passed to the query to be used to evaluate the specific query

RDF::Core::Query
> A query object

The RDF::Core::Functions class contains a package of functions used to drill down to specific schema elements within the query set. It's instantiated first, taking optional instances of the model being queried, an instance of the RDF Schema model, and a factory object.

The RDF::Core::Evaluator class is what evaluates a specific query, passed in as a string, formed from RDQL. When it's instantiated, it can take an instance of the model being queried, the instance of the Functions class, as well as the factory class and a hash containing namespaces and their associated prefixes, or it can default for a default namespace. The last option is a reference to a function defined in the code to be called for each row returned in the query set. If this isn't provided, then the result is returned as an array of rows.

The RDF::Core::Query class pulls the other objects and the query string together, returning an array of rows (statements) matching the query or passing the row to a function defined within the function object to process each row. The documentation included with RDF::Core::Query provides a description of the query language supported with RDF::Core including examples.

 Another excellent Perl-based RDF API is RDFStore, written by Alberto Reggiori. This API is based on the Stanford Java API created by Sergey Melnik. Access it at *http://rdfstore.sourceforge.net/*.

RDF API for PHP

Few languages have achieved faster acceptance than PHP. ISPs now install support for PHP when they install Apache, so most people have access to this server-side tag-based scripting language. And where there's scripting, there's support for RDF. PHP boasts two RDF APIs: the RDF API for PHP and the RDF-specific classes within the PHP XML classes. The latter is covered in the next chapter; this chapter focuses on the RDF API for PHP, which I'll refer to as RAP for brevity.

 The RDF API for PHP (RAP) home page is at *http://www.wiwiss.fu-berlin.de/suhl/bizer/rdfapi/*. The SourceForge project for the API is at *http://sourceforge.net/projects/rdfapi-php/*.

Basic Building Blocks

The RAP classes are split into three main packages: model, syntax, and util. The model package includes all the classes to create or read specific elements of an RDF model, including reading or creating complete statements from a model or their individual components. These classes are:

BlankNode
> Used to create a blank node, to get the bnode identifier, or check equality between two bnodes

Literal
> Support for model literals

Model
> Contains methods to build or read a specific RDF model

Node
> An abstract RDF node

Resource
> Support for model resources

Statement
> Creating or manipulating a complete RDF triple

RAP doesn't, at this time, support persistence to a database such as MySQL or Berkeley DB, but you can serialize the data through RdfSerializer, which is one of the two syntax classes. To read a serialized model, you would then use the other syntax class, RdfParser.

The util class Object is another abstract class with some general methods overloaded in classes built on it, so it's of no interest for our purposes. However, the RDFUtil class provides some handy methods, including the method writeHTMLTable to output an RDF/XML document in nice tabular form.

Building an RDF Model

Creating a new RDF model and adding statements to it using RAP is extremely easy. Start by creating a new RDF graph (data model) and then just add statements to it, creating new resources or literals as you go. The best way to see how to create a new graph is to look at a complete example of creating a model and then outputting the results to a page.

In the first example of this API, the path from the top-level resource all the way through the first movement is created as a subgraph of the larger *monsters1.rdf* model. Since movements in this model are coordinated through an RDF container, `rdf:Seq`, information related to the container must also be added to ensure that the generated RDF/XML maps correctly to the original RDF/XML of the full model. The N-Triples for just this path, as generated by the RDF Validator, are:

```
<http://burningbird.net/articles/monsters1.htm>
<http://www.w3.org/1999/02/22-rdf-syntax-ns#type> <http://burningbird.net/postcon/
elements/1.0/Document> .
<http://burningbird.net/articles/monsters1.htm> <http://burningbird.net/postcon/
elements/1.0/history> _:jARP31427 .
_:jARP31427 <http://www.w3.org/1999/02/22-rdf-syntax-ns#type>
<http://www.w3.org/1999/02/22-rdf-syntax-ns#Seq> .
_:jARP31427 <http://www.w3.org/1999/02/22-rdf-syntax-ns#_1> <http://www.yasd.com/
dynaearth/monsters1.htm> .
<http://www.yasd.com/dynaearth/monsters1.htm> <http://burningbird.net/postcon/
elements/1.0/movementType> "Add" .
```

In the script, the first two lines map the RDF API directories and should reflect your own installation. This test script was built on a Linux box, which the path to the API reflects. Following the global directory definitions, a new model, as well as the top-level resource (since this will be used more than once in the page), is created. Added to the new model is a new statement consisting of the top-level resource as the subject, a new resource created for the predicate, and the object. In this case, the top-level resource is defined as a PostCon Document class.

Following the initial statement, a blank node is created to represent the `rdf:Seq` object using the label `history`, and a type resource identifying it as `rdf:Seq` is added to the model. The first of the movements is added using the container element URI and giving as object the URI of the movement object. In the last statement, the `movementType` property is added for this resource, as shown in Example 9-5. To observe the resulting model, it's serialized using the `RDFUtil::writeHTML` class, to generate a table of statements. And then the model is serialized to RDF/XML, using the `RDFSerializer` class.

Example 9-5. Creating an RDF model using RDF API for PHP and serializing it to the page

```php
<?php
define("RDFAPI_INCLUDE_DIR", "./../api/");
include(RDFAPI_INCLUDE_DIR . "RDFAPI.php");
```

Example 9-5. Creating an RDF model using RDF API for PHP and serializing it to the page (continued)

```
// New Model, set base URI
$model = new Model();
$model->setBaseURI("http://burningbird.net/articles/");

// first statement
$mainsource = new Resource("monsters1.htm");
$model->add(new Statement($mainsource, $RDF_type,
             new
Resource("http://burningbird.net/postcon/elements/1.0/Document")));

$history = new BlankNode("history");
$model->add(new Statement($mainsource,
               new
Resource("http://burningbird.net/postcon/elements/1.0/history"),
               $history));

// Define RDF Bag
$model->add(new Statement($history, $RDF_type, $RDF_Seq));

$movement = new Resource("http://www.yasd.com/dynaearth/monsters1.htm");
$model->add(new Statement($history,
               new Resource(RDF_NAMESPACE_URI . "_1"),
               $movement));

$model->add(new Statement($movement,
           new
Resource("http://burningbird.net/postcon/elements/1.0/movementType"),
           new Literal("Add", "en")));

// Output as table
RDFUtil::writeHTMLTable($model);

file://Serialize and output model
$ser = new RDFSerializer();
$ser->addNamespacePrefix("pstcn",
"http://burningbird.net/postcon/elements/1.0/");
$rdf =& $ser->serialize($model);
echo "<p><textarea cols='110' rows='20'>" . $rdf . "</textarea>";

file://Save the model to a file
$ser->saveAs($model,"rdf_output.rdf");

?>
```

When this script is included within HTML and accessed via the Web, the result looks similar to Figure 9-1.

If you want to persist the serialized result of the model, use PHP's own file I/O functions to save the generated RDF/XML to a file. Note that the figure shows bnodes as URI, which isn't proper format. However, this is an internally generated value that has no impact on the validity of the RDF/XML.

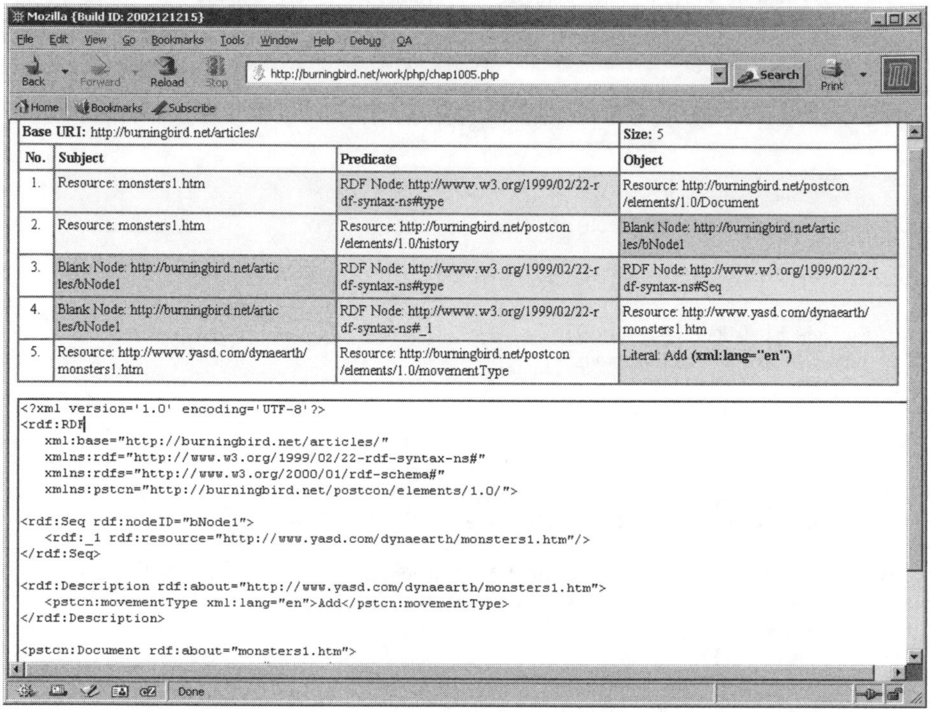

Figure 9-1. Page resulting from running PHP script in Example 9-5

Example 9-6 contains the script to open this serialized RDF/XML and iterate through it (this script was provided by the RAP creator, Chris Bizer).

Example 9-6. Iterating through the serialized RDF/XML created in Example 9-5

```php
<?php

// Include RDF API
define("RDFAPI_INCLUDE_DIR", "./../api/");
include(RDFAPI_INCLUDE_DIR . "RDFAPI.php");

// Create new Parser
$parser = new RdfParser();

// Parse document
$model =& $parser->generateModel("rdf_output.rdf");

// Get StatementIterator
$it = $model->getStatementIterator();

// Traverse model and output statements
while ($it->hasNext()) {
   $statement = $it->next();
```

Example 9-6. Iterating through the serialized RDF/XML created in Example 9-5 (continued)

```
    echo "Statement number: " . $it->getCurrentPosition() . "<BR>";
    echo "Subject: " . $statement->getLabelSubject() . "<BR>";
    echo "Predicate: " . $statement->getLabelPredicate() . "<BR>";
    echo "Object: " . $statement->getLabelObject() . "<P>";
}

?>
```

You can add or subtract statements on a given model, check to see if the model contains a specific statement, and even find the intersection or combination of multiple models, using the Model class. However, one of the most frequent activities you'll likely do is query the model.

Querying a Model

The Model class in RAP has a couple of different methods you can use to find information. For instance, the `findVocabulary` method returns all triples from a given vocabulary, as identified by a namespace. This is rather handy if your document combines elements from many different namespaces.

Two other methods allow for more fine-grained queries: `find` and `findRegex`.

The `find` method takes three parameters: subject, predicate, and object. Passing in null for a specific parameter matches any value for that component in the triple. The `findRegex` method uses a Perl-style regular expression to check for a match in any of the components. Both methods return a new Model, which you can print out using the `RDFUtil` method `writeHTMLTable`. However, if you want to print the data out using your own approach or want to print out only specific components in the resulting triple, you'll have to do a little more work, and will use private methods and members of the RAP class. This makes me hesitant to use RAP for querying.

What I've done is mix PHP classes when working with RDF. I use RAP to create RDF models, and I then use the PHP XML classes, described in the next chapter, to persist the RDF/XML to a database and to use RDQL queries to query that database.

RDF and Python: RDFLib

It would be difficult not to see the natural fit between Python and RDF. Of course, Python programmers would say the same happens with all uses of Python, but when you see how quick and simple it is to build an RDF/XML model from scratch using the Python RDF library, RDFLib, you might think about switching regardless of what language you normally use.

RDFLib was created by Daniel Krech. Download the most recent release of RDFLib at *http://rdflib.net*. I used RDFLib 1.2.3 on Windows 2000 when writing this section. RDFLib requires Python 2.2.1 or later. Additional software is required if you want to use the rdflib.Z informationStore, providing support for contexts in addition to persistent triples.

RDFLib is actually a part of a larger application framework, Redfoot, discussed in Chapter 12. However, RDFLib is a separate, fully RDF functional API. If there's any additional need with the API, it's documentation, which is quite scarce for the product. However, the libraries are so intuitive, one could almost say that the documentation isn't needed.

All the unique components of an RDF model have been defined as Python objects in RDFLib:

RDFLib.URIRef
> A resource with a URI

RDFLib.BNode
> A resource without a URI

RDFLib.Literal
> A literal

RDFLib.Namespace
> Manage a namespace

TripleStore
> In-memory triple store

In addition, `RDFLib.constants` contains definitions for the RDF properties such as type and value.

Example 9-7 implements a subgraph of the test RDF/XML document (*monsters1.rdf*) defined in the following snippet of XML:

```
<pstcn:Resource rdf:about="monsters1.htm">
   <pstcn:presentation rdf:parseType="Resource">
      <pstcn:requires rdf:parseType="Resource">
         <pstcn:type>stylesheet</pstcn:type>
         <rdf:value>http://burningbird.net/de.css</rdf:value>
      </pstcn:requires>
   </pstcn:presentation>
</pstcn:Resource>
```

To begin, a `Namespace` object is created for the PostCon namespace, in addition to a `TripleStore` used for the model in progress. Following this, the top-level resource is created using `URIRef`, which is then added as a triple with the RDF type and the Post-Con `Document` type. After that, it's just a matter of creating the appropriate type of object and adding more triples. Note that `Namespace` manages the namespace annotations for all of the objects requiring one, such as all of the predicates. At the end, the triples are printed out to standard output, and the model is serialized to RDF/XML.

Example 9-7. Building a graph using RDFLib

```
from rdflib.URIRef import URIRef
from rdflib.Literal import Literal
from rdflib.BNode import BNode
from rdflib.Namespace import Namespace
from rdflib.constants import TYPE, VALUE

# Import RDFLib's default TripleStore implementation
from rdflib.TripleStore import TripleStore

# Create a namespace object
POSTCON = Namespace("http://burningbird.net/postcon/elements/1.0/")

store = TripleStore()

store.prefix_mapping("pstcn", "http://http://burningbird.net/postcon/elements/1.0/")

# Create top-level resource
monsters = URIRef(POSTCON["monsters1.htm"])

# Add type statement
store.add((monsters, TYPE, POSTCON["Document"]))

# Create bnode and add as statement
presentation = BNode();
store.add((monsters, POSTCON["presentation"],presentation))

# Create second bnode, add
requires = BNode();
store.add((presentation, POSTCON["requires"], requires))

# add two end nodes
type = Literal("stylesheet")
store.add((requires, POSTCON["type"],type))

value = Literal("http://burningbird.net/de.css")
store.add((requires, VALUE, value))

# Iterate over triples in store and print them out
for s, p, o in store:
    print s, p, o

# Serialize the store as RDF/XML to the file subgraph.rdf
store.save("subgraph.rdf")
```

Just this small sample demonstrates how simple RDFLib is to use. The generated RDF/XML looks similar to the following, indentation and all, which is a nice little feature of the library.

```
<?xml version="1.0" encoding="UTF-8"?>
<rdf:RDF
   xmlns:rdfs="http://www.w3.org/2000/01/rdf-schema#"
   xmlns:n4="http://burningbird.net/postcon/elements/1.0/"
```

```
      xmlns:pstcn="http://http://burningbird.net/postcon/elements/1.0/"
      xmlns:rdf="http://www.w3.org/1999/02/22-rdf-syntax-ns#"
  >
      <n4:Document rdf:about="http://burningbird.net/postcon/elements/1.0/monsters1.htm">
        <n4:presentation>
          <rdf:Description>
            <n4:requires>
              <rdf:Description>
                <n4:type>stylesheet</n4:type>
                <rdf:value>http://burningbird.net/de.css</rdf:value>
              </rdf:Description>
            </n4:requires>
          </rdf:Description>
        </n4:presentation>
      </n4:Document>
  </rdf:RDF>
```

Testing this in the RDF Validator results in a directed graph equivalent to the sub-graph found in the larger model, and equivalent to the graph generated earlier in the chapter with the Perl modules.

You can also load an existing RDF/XML document into a TripleStore and then run queries against the triples. Example 9-8 contains a small Python application that loads *monsters1.rdf* into a TripleStore and then looks for all subjects of class Movement. These are passed into an inner loop and used to look up the movement type for each Movement.

Example 9-8. Finding all movements and movement types in RDF/XML document

```python
from rdflib.Namespace import Namespace
from rdflib.constants import TYPE

# Import RDFLib's default TripleStore implementation
from rdflib.TripleStore import TripleStore

# Create a namespace object
POSTCON = Namespace("http://burningbird.net/postcon/elements/1.0/")
DC = Namespace("http://purl.org/dc/elements/1.1/")

store = TripleStore()
store.load("http://burningbird.net/articles/monsters1.rdf");

# For each pstcn:Movement print out movementType
for movement in store.subjects(TYPE, POSTCON["Movement"]):
    for movementType in store.objects(movement, POSTCON["movementType"]):
        print "Moved To: %s Reason: %s" % (movement, movementType)
```

This application prints out the movement resource objects as well as the movement types:

```
Moved To: http://burningbird.net/burningbird.net/articles/monsters1.htm Reason:
Move
Moved To: http://www.yasd.com/dynaearth/monsters1.htm Reason: Add
Moved To: http://www.dynamicearth.com/articles/monsters1.htm Reason: Move
```

The TripleStore document *triple_store.html* in the RDFLib documentation describes the TripleStore.triples method and the variations on it that you can use for queries. The method used differs but the basic functionality remains the same as that just demonstrated.

 Another open source and Python-based RDF API is 4RDF and its Versa query language, a product of Fourthought. 4RDF is part of 4Suite, a set of tools for working with XML, XSLT, and RDF. More information is available at *http://fourthought.com*.

## CHAPTER 10

Querying RDF: RDF as Data

RDF as a model for metadata and RDF/XML as a way of serializing the model are interesting, but the power of the specifications lies in our ability to access the data easily, using techniques we're familiar with from other data models, such as the relational data model discussed in Chapter 6.

It is only natural that techniques used for one data model should be adapted for use with another; so the method for accessing the relational data model, Structured Query Language (SQL), is used in a similar manner with RDF/XML through language techniques such as SquishQL, RDQL, RQL, and others.

Many of the query languages and schemas mentioned in this chapter are also covered in an online document at *http://www.w3.org/2001/11/ 13-RDF-Query-Rules*. In addition, if your interest is more inclined to RDF as data (or to the more logical side of RDF), check out the *www-rdf-rules* discussion list at *http://lists.w3.org/Archives/Public/www-rdf-rules/*.

RDF and the Relational Data Model

RDF and the relational data model are both metadata models, so it's natural to want to see how the one can work with the other. Stanford took a look at different designs of tables for storing RDF data in an online paper located at *http://www-db.stanford. edu/~melnik/rdf/db.html*. With some differences based on data types and the ability to store multiple models, most of the schemas demonstrated were basically the same—store the model as triples, with or without support for additional information such as namespace or model identifier.

An updated document comparing RDBMS and Semantic Web data is located at *http://www.w3.org/2001/sw/Europe/reports/scalable_rdbms_ mapping_report/*.

If you look at implementations that store RDF within relational databases, these simple overlay schemas are used, for the most part, by all of them. For instance, Jena gives you a couple of different options in database storage; the first is whether multiple models are supported, and the second is whether a hash is used to generate the identifiers for the resources. However, the basic structure of the database is the same—a table for storing statements, with secondary tables storing literals (which could get quite large), resources, and namespaces.

Siderean Software's Seamark server (covered in Chapter 15) also uses a basic layout for storing its data, with separate tables for resource and literal and another table pulling together the triples (in addition to specific information about accessing the model). However, other applications, such as Plugged In Software's Tucana Knowledge Store, use a data storage schema that is built from the ground up based on RDF, and make no use of relational data stores at all.

Another online white paper that discusses the relational data model and RDF directly is "Relational Databases and the Semantic Web" at *http://www.w3.org/DesignIssues/RDB-RDF.html*.

Roots: rdfDB QL

One of the earliest persistent data stores for RDF was R.V. Guha's rdfDB, a database built from the ground up to store RDF data. This database, written in C and primarily tested within a Linux environment, uses a specialized language derived from SQL, a language he called "…a high level SQLish query language," to manipulate and query RDF data within the database.

You can download a copy of rdfDB at *http://guha.com/rdfdb/*. Note that there has been little activity with this database in the last few years; I'm including coverage of it here primarily for historical perspective.

In Guha's language, you can create a database, insert or delete rows from it, and query it. A row in his language would be an RDF triple, in the format of arc-source-target, somewhat different from N-Triples and other languages that portray an RDF triple as source-arc-target. However, the principles are the same.

For instance, to insert a row, use the following syntax (taken from Guha's sample session online):

```
insert into test1 (type DanB Person), (name DanB 'Dan Brickley') </>
```

If the result is successful, the database returns 0; otherwise, a negative value representing the type of error that occurred with the statement is returned.

The data is queried by forming a select statement that provides a variable or variables for resulting data, a from clause giving the database name, and a where clause made up of triples in the format of arc-source-target, with placeholders in the position of unknown values. Again from the sample he provides at his web site:

```
select ?x from test1 where (worksFor ?x W3C) (name ?x ?y) </>
```

The results are returned on separate lines, variables mapped to values:

```
?x = DanC ?y = 'Dan Connolly'
?x = DanB ?y = 'Dan Brickley'
```

Though Guha's rdfDB was the precursor to much of the effort in querying RDF, he hasn't worked on the database recently. However, others took up the effort he pioneered and have since worked to enhance and improve on it. Among these is the Inkling database and SquishQL, an open source effort that included contributions from Leigh Dobbs, Libby Miller, and Dan Brickley.

Inkling and SquishQL

Unlike rdfDB, written in C in a Linux environment, the Inkling database was written in Java, originally on Linux and Solaris and most recently hosted and tested on Mac OS X, using several Java JDBC classes. Though I've tried it only on the Mac OS X environment myself, it should work in other environments that have Java installed. An additional requirement for Inkling is an installation of PostgreSQL, as it uses this database for persistent storage (unlike rdfDB, which manages its own storage).

 You can view documentation and test the Inkling database online at *http://swordfish.rdfweb.org/rdfquery/*. You can also download source code for Inkling at this site. Note that Inkling uses PostgreSQL for its persistent data store. If you don't want to install Inkling to your own system, you can also use the online test application, running it against your own persisted RDF/XML documents available on the Web.

Once you've downloaded the Inkling installation file, you'll first need to make sure that you have a database called *test* created, and that you've run the SQL commands contained in the *inklingsqlschema.psql* file. You'll also need to set *JAVA_HOME*. In the Mac OS X environment, *JAVA_HOME* is set to */Library/Java/Home* if you're using the Java installations that are designed specifically for Mac OS X.

The data structure loaded into the PostgreSQL database is relatively simple—one table containing pointers (hashed values) to the actual values in a second table. A flag specifies if the value is a resource or an actual object. If I have anything to disagree with about this design, it's the combination of resources and objects in one table. Resource URIs are typically Unicode character strings most likely not more than a few hundred characters or so in length. Objects (literals), though, can be large. My test file used in many of the other examples in this book (*http://burningbird.net/articles/monsters1.rdf*) has objects that can be several thousand characters in length. Normally, a better design would have been to separate out the known resources into a separate table or even two tables—one for predicates, one for subjects. However, that's a personal preference.

You can access several demonstration applications installed with Inkling or the online application. You can also use a set of Java classes that support the application directly. Of particular interest in these is a JDBC driver created specifically for Inkling-formatted data, allowing you to query data using a SquishQL-formatted query whether the data is in PostgreSQL database. However, we're more interested at this point in the queries, which we'll focus on in the rest of this section.

 The example file used throughout this chapter is from Example 6-6—
monsters1.rdf.

The SquishQL supported in Inkling has strong ties to SQL. A simple query is similar to the following:

```
SELECT ?subject
FROM http://burningbird.net/articles/monsters1.rdf
WHERE (dc::subject ?x ?subject)
USING dc FOR http://purl.org/dc/elements/1.1/
```

In this query, triples form a where clause, leading with the predicate, followed by subject and then by object. If the query uses a variable as placeholder, all values in that field are returned. For this example, all `dc:subject` predicates are returned regardless of specific subject or object value.

The query is being made against a file rather than the default database (and can be accessed remotely via a URL), which is noted in the FROM clause. The SELECT clause lists the value or values returned, and the USING clause gives a mapping between the predicate URI and the abbreviation for the URI. It's important to note that the using clause isn't a namespace prefix, but a way of providing abbreviations for longer URIs. This could mean a specific namespace but isn't limited only to namespaces formally identified within the RDF/XML document.

The variables begin with a question mark and consist of characters, with no spaces. Figure 10-1 shows both this query and the output format as given in the Inkling online query application.

After submitting the form, a second page opens up displaying the results:

```
The subject is Loch Ness Monster
The subject is giant squid
The subject is legends
The subject is Architeuthis Dux
The subject is Nessie
```

You can also make more complex queries. For instance, to find all uses of `pstcn: reason` associated with movements, rather than with related resources, you can join query triples to return specific predicates for given resources that are themselves

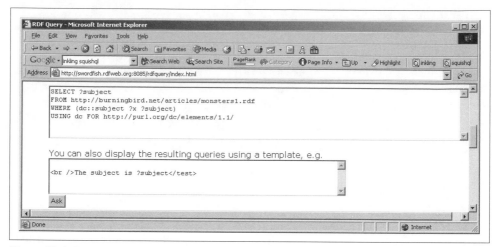

Figure 10-1. Preparing to run a query against the test RDF document

identified by other predicates; in this case, a predicate of rdf:type of http://
burningbird.net/postcon/elements/1.0/Movement, as shown in Example 10-1.

Example 10-1. Finding all reasons for movements within test RDF/XML document

```
SELECT ?resource ?value
FROM http://burningbird.net/articles/monsters1.rdf
WHERE (rdf::type ?resource "http://burningbird.net/postcon/elements/1.0/Movement")
      (pstcn::reason ?resource ?value)
USING pstcn FOR http://burningbird.net/postcon/elements/1.0/
      rdf FOR http://www.w3.org/1999/02/22-rdf-syntax-ns#
```

In this example, the first triple looks for all resources with a given rdf:type of http://
burningbird.net/postcon/elements/1.0/Movement. These are then passed into the second triple in the subject field, fine-tuning the reasons returned to those associated
with movement resources. In the example, predicates from two namespaces are used,
as shown in the using clause. In addition, two values are returned in the select clause
and printed out:

```
The reason for the movement to http://www.dynamicearth.com/articles/monsters1.htm is
Moved to separate dynamicearth.com domain
The reason for the movement to http:/burningbird.net/articles/monsters1.htm is
Collapsed into Burningbird
The reason for the movement to http://www.yasd.com/dynaearth/monsters1.htm is New
Article
```

This combining of triple patterns is known as following one specific *path* within an
RDF model, of node-arc-node-arc-node and so on. You can add additional triple patterns to travel further down the path until you reach the data you're after, no matter
how deeply nested within the model. The key is to use a variable assigned data in
one triple pattern—such as a subject or object value—as one of the constraints in the
next triple pattern and so on.

In addition to filtering based on triple pattern matching, you can also use more traditional query constraints such as the less-than (<) and greater-than (>) operators and equality (= and ~). All of the comparison operators work with integers except for the string equality operator (~).

In Example 10-2, the string equality operator is used to return a resource from a movement on a specific date.

Example 10-2. Find movement resource where movement occurred on a specific date

```
SELECT ?resource
FROM http://burningbird.net/articles/monsters1.rdf
WHERE (rdf::type ?resource "http://burningbird.net/postcon/elements/1.0/Movement")
      (dc::date ?resource ?date)
AND ?date ~ "1999-10-31:T00:00:00-05:00"
USING pstcn FOR http://burningbird.net/postcon/elements/1.0/
      rdf FOR http://www.w3.org/1999/02/22-rdf-syntax-ns#
      dc FOR http://purl.org/dc/elements/1.1/
```

The example just shown is a variation of about the most complex query you'll see with RDF, regardless of specific query language. Variations of the queries just add additional constraints, namespaces, sources (such as multiple documents), and so on. But the basic structure given in the following remains the same:

```
SELECT variables
FROM source
WHERE (triple clause)
USING namespace mapping
```

The type of query language demonstrated, beginning with rdfDB and continuing with SquishQL, is the one that's formed the basis of one of the more popular RDF/XML query languages, RDQL, demonstrated in the next section.

RDQL

The RDQL language is based on the earlier work of Guha's RDFDB QL and SquishQL, with some relatively minor differences. Its popularity is ensured because of its use within Jena, probably the most widely used RDF API.

RDQL supports the different clauses of select, from, where, and using (with some exceptions) as SquishQL. Additionally, RDQL can change based on the implementation and whether you're using a Java API such as Jena, a PHP class such as the PHP XML classes, or a Perl module such as RDFStore. However, though the syntax varies within the clauses, the concepts remain the same.

Variables are in the format of a question mark, followed by other characters, just as in SquishQL:

```
?<identifier>
```

However, one difference between SquishQL and RDQL occurs in the select clause, which requires commas rather than spaces to separate all variables.

The from, or source, clause, can be omitted with RDQL depending on the implementation. For instance, in Jena, the source of the RDF/XML can be specified and loaded separately through a separate class method or can be given directly in the query. However, in the PHP RDF/XML classes, the from clause must be provided within the query. The same applies to RDFStore, which also requires that the URL be surrounded by angle brackets.

The *where* clause (or triple pattern clause) differs in that the pattern follows the more traditional subject-predicate-object ordering, and URIs are differentiated from literals by being surrounded by angle brackets. However, the way that triple patterns are combined to form more complex queries is the same in RDQL and SquishQL.

RDQL has greater sophistication in incorporating comparison semantics with the triple pattern within the constrain clause. The use of AND is the same, but other operators—such as the OR operator (||), bitwise operators (& and |), and negation (!)—are supported.

Within Jena, there is no using clause because the namespaces for the resources are included with the resource rather than being listed as a separate namespace. However, the PHP XML classes support using, as does RDFStore.

Jena's RDQL and the Query-O-Matic

In addition to the rich set of Java classes that allow access to individual triples as well as the ability to build complex RDF/XML documents (as described in Chapter 8) Jena also provides specialized classes for use with RDQL:

Query
> The Query class manages the actual query, enabling the building of a query through an API or passed as a string.

QueryExecution
> Query engine interface.

QueryEngine
> The actual execution of the query (the intelligence behind the query process).

QueryResults
> The iterator that manages the results.

ResultBinding
> Mapping from variables to values.

In addition to these standard classes, newer implementations of Jena also support some newer classes, such as a `QueryEngineSesame` class, which works against the Sesame RDF repository (discussed at the end of the chapter).

The use of the classes is very straightforward. Use `Query` to build or parse the query, which is then passed to `QueryEngine` for processing. The results are returned to the `QueryExecution` class, which provides methods to access the results, which are assigned to `QueryResults`. To access individual items in the results, the data is bound to program variables using `ResultsBinding`.

To demonstrate how Jena works with RDQL, I created a dynamic query application, which I call the Query-O-Matic, building it in Java as a Tomcat JSP application.

The Query-O-Matic

The Query-O-Matic is a two-page application, with the first HTML page containing a form and the second JSP page processing the form contents. It's built using Jena 1.6, and managed with Tomcat. The source code is included as part of the example code for the book.

 The Query-O-Matic does require that you have knowledge of Tomcat and JSP-based applications. If you don't, you can still work with the code, but you'll need to provide a different interface for it. You can get more details about Jena's RDQL support in the RDQL tutorial at *http://www.hpl.hp.com/semweb/doc/tutorial/RDQL/index.html*.

To create the application, the Jena *.jar* files must be copied to the common library or to the application-specific WEB-INF lib directory. I copied them to the common library location because I use Jena for several applications.

The first page is nothing special, an HTML form with three fields:

- The first field is a text input field to hold the URL of the RDF/XML document.
- The second field is a textarea to hold the actual query.
- The third field is another text input file to hold the variable that's printed out.

Figure 10-2 shows the page containing the form, as well as links to sample RDF/XML documents.

In the JSP page, the form values are pulled from the HTTP request. The URL is used to load the document; once it is loaded, the query is run against the document using the Jena `QueryEngine` class. To iterate through the results, another class, `QueryResults`, is created, and each record returned from the query is then bound to a specific object, in order to access a specific value. The result value that's passed from the form is polled from the object and the value is printed out, as shown in Example 10-3. Once all values are processed, the result set is closed.

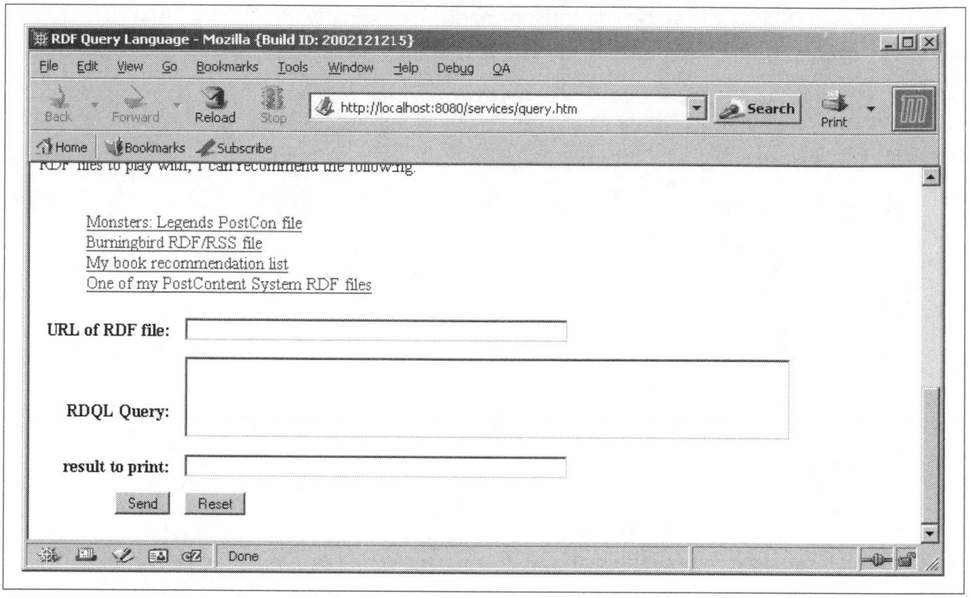

Figure 10-2. Form to capture RDQL parameters

Example 10-3. Java/JSP code to dynamically process RDQL query using Jena

```
<html>
<%@ page import="com.hp.hpl.mesa.rdf.jena.mem.*,
                 java.io.File,
                 java.util.*,
                 com.hp.hpl.mesa.rdf.jena.model.*,
                 com.hp.hpl.mesa.rdf.jena.common.*,
                 com.hp.hpl.jena.util.*,
                 com.hp.hpl.jena.rdf.query.*,
                 com.hp.hpl.jena.rdf.query.parser.*" %>

<body>

<%
  ModelMem model;

  try {
  model = new ModelMem( );
  String sUri = request.getParameter("uri");
  String sQuery = request.getParameter("query");
  String sResult = request.getParameter("result");

  model.read(sUri);

  // query string
  Query query = new Query(sQuery);

  query.setSource(model);
```

Example 10-3. Java/JSP code to dynamically process RDQL query using Jena (continued)

```
    QueryExecution qe = new QueryEngine(query) ;
    QueryResults results = qe.exec( );
    out.print("<h1>test</h1>");

      for ( Iterator iter2 = results ; iter2.hasNext( ) ; ) {
          ResultBinding env = (ResultBinding)iter2.next( ) ;
                Object obj = env.get(sResult);
                out.print(obj.toString( ));
                out.print("<br>");
      }

    // close results
    results.close( ) ;
    }
    catch (Exception e) {
      out.print(e.toString( ));
    }


%>
<br>
</font>
</body>
</html>
```

Once the two pages and supporting Jena *.jar* files are installed into Tomcat, we're ready to try out some RDQL in the Query-O-Matic.

Trying out the Query-O-Matic

The simplest test of the Query-O-Matic is to run an RDQL variation of the first query made with Inkling/SquishQL, which is to find all the dc:subject predicates in the RDF/XML document and print out the associated object values. The contents of the form are given in Example 10-4.

Example 10-4. RDQL query to find dc:subject in RDF/XML document

```
uri: http://burningbird.net/articles/monsters1.rdf
query: SELECT ?subject
          WHERE (?x, <dc:subject>, ?subject)
          USING dc FOR <http://purl.org/dc/elements/1.1/>
result: subject
```

Comparing this with the SquishQL example shows that both are basically the same with minor syntactic differences. When the form is submitted and the query processed, the results returned are exactly the same, too.

Another slightly more complicated query is shown in Example 10-5, which demonstrates traversing two arcs in order to find a specific value.

Example 10-5. More complex query traversing two arcs

```
SELECT ?value
WHERE (?resource, <rdf:type>, <pstcn:Movement>),
(?resource, <pstcn:reason>, ?value)
USING pstcn FOR<http://burningbird.net/postcon/elements/1.0/>,
     rdf FOR <http://www.w3.org/1999/02/22-rdf-syntax-ns#>
```

Notice that object values that are resources are treated the same as the subject and predicate values, with angle brackets around the URI (or the QName). The only type of value that doesn't have angle brackets is literals.

A slightly more complicated query more fully demonstrates the filtering capability of the triple pattern. To better understand how this query works, take a look at the N-Triples of the statements of the subgraph from the *monsters1.rdf* example:

```
<http://burningbird.net/articles/monsters1.htm> <http://www.w3.org/1999/02/22-rdf-
syntax-ns#type> <http://burningbird.net/postcon/elements/1.0/Resource> .
<http://burningbird.net/articles/monsters1.htm> <http://burningbird.net/postcon/
elements/1.0/presentation> _:jARP10030 .
_:jARP10030 <http://burningbird.net/postcon/elements/1.0/requires> _:jARP10032 .
_:jARP10032 <http://burningbird.net/postcon/elements/1.0/type> "logo" .
_:jARP10032 <http://www.w3.org/1999/02/22-rdf-syntax-ns#value> "http://burningbird.
net/mm/dynamicearth.jpg" .
_:jARP10030 <http://burningbird.net/postcon/elements/1.0/requires> _:jARP10031 .
_:jARP10031 <http://burningbird.net/postcon/elements/1.0/type> "stylesheet" .
_:jARP10031 <http://www.w3.org/1999/02/22-rdf-syntax-ns#value> "http://burningbird.
net/de.css" .
```

These are the statements we'll be querying with the code shown in Example 10-6. Within the query, the `pstcn:presentation` arc is followed from the main resource (`monsters1.htm`) to get the object/resource for it (a blank node). Then, the `pstcn:requires` predicate arc is followed to get the two required presentation bnodes. However, we're interested only in the one whose `pstcn:type` is `"stylesheet"`. Once we have that, then we'll access the value of the stylesheet. The path I just highlighted in the text is also highlighted in the example.

Example 10-6. Using triple pattern as a filter

```
SELECT ?value
WHERE (?x, <pstcn:presentation>, ?resource),
(?resource, <pstcn:requires>, ?resource2),
(?resource2, <pstcn:type>, "stylesheet"),
(?resource2, <rdf:value>, ?value)
USING pstcn FOR       <http://burningbird.net/postcon/elements/1.0/>,
     rdf FOR <http://www.w3.org/1999/02/22-rdf-syntax-ns#>
```

The result from running this query is:

```
http://burningbird.net/de.css
```

Exactly what we wanted to get.

I used a triple pattern to find the specific required presentation resource, rather than a conditional filter, because I wasn't going to be querying among the end values—I'm actually modifying the query within the path to the end statement. If I wanted to find specific values using a conditional filter, I would list triple patterns up until I returned all of the statements of interest and then use the filter on these statements to find specific values.

A demonstration of this is shown in Example 10-7, where a date is returned for a movement with movement type of "Add". Notice that equality is denoted by the eq operator rather than using nonalphabetic characters such as ==, common in several programming languages.

Example 10-7. Returning date for movement of type "Add"

```
SELECT ?date
WHERE
(?resource, <rdf:type>, <pstcn:Movement>),
(?resource, <pstcn:movementType>, ?value),
(?resource, <dc:date>, ?date)
AND (?value eq "Add")
USING pstcn FOR        <http://burningbird.net/postcon/elements/1.0/>,
    rdf FOR <http://www.w3.org/1999/02/22-rdf-syntax-ns#>,
    dc for <http://purl.org/dc/elements/1.1/>
```

Regardless of the complexity of the query, the Query-O-Matic should be able to process the results. Best of all, you can then take the query and add it to your own code and know that it's been pretested.

However, if you're not a big fan of Java, then you may be interested in the PHP version of Query-O-Matic, Query-O-Matic Lite.

PHP Query-O-Matic Lite

If you've worked with PHP and with XML, then you're familiar with the PHP XML classes. These classes provide functionality to process virtually all popular uses of XML, including RDF/XML. The two packages of interest in this chapter are RDQL and RDQL_DB.

 The PHP XML class main web page is at *http://phpxmlclasses. sourceforge.net/*. This section assumes you are familiar with working with PHP.

As you can imagine from the package names, RDQL provides RDQL query capability within the PHP environment, and RDQL_DB provides persistent support for it. They're both so complete that the PHP version of Query-O-Matic (Lite) took less than 10 lines of code, hence the *Lite* designation. But before we look at that, let's take a close look at the classes themselves.

There are four classes within the RDQL package, but the one of interest to us is RDQL_query_document. This class has one method, rdql_query_url, which takes as a string a contained query string and returns an array of associative arrays with the results of the query. The RDQL_DB package provides two classes of particular importance to this chapter: RDQL_db, which controls all database actions, and RDQL_query_db, which acts the same as RDQL_query_document, taking a string and returning the results of a query as an array of results. RDQL_DB makes use of RDQL for query parsing and other shared functionality.

To use RDQL_DB, you'll need to preload the database structure required by the package. This is found in a file called *rdql_db.sql* in the installation. At this time, only MySQL is supported, and the file is loaded at the command line:

```
mysql databasename < rdql_db.sql
```

 You must, of course, have the ability to modify the database in order to create tables in it. Follow the MySQL documentation if you have problems loading the RDQL tables.

The RDQL table structure is quite simple. Two tables are created: rdf_data contains columns for each member of an RDF triple as well as information about each, and rdf_documents keeps track of the different RDF/XML documents that are loaded into the database. Unlike the PHP classes discussed in Chapter 9, the PHP RDQL and RDQL_DB packages provide functionality to parse, load, and persist existing RDF/XML documents and to use RDQL to query them, but neither provides functionality to modify or create an RDF/XML document.

At the time of this writing, the PHP XML classes had not been updated to include the new RDF/XML constructs. Because of this, the example RDF/XML document used for most of the book, *monsters1.rdf*, can't be parsed cleanly. Instead, another RDF/XML document was used. This document is reproduced in Example 10-8 so that you can follow the demonstration more easily.

Example 10-8. Resume RDF/XML document

```
<?xml version="1.0"?>
<rdf:RDF
  xmlns:rdf="http://www.w3.org/1999/02/22-rdf-syntax-ns#"
  xmlns:bbd="http://burningbird.net/resume/elements/1.0/"
  xml:base="http://burningbird.net/shelley_powers/resume/" >

  <rdf:Description rdf:about="http://burningbird.net/shelley_powers/">
    <bbd:bio rdf:resource="bio"/>
    <bbd:job rdf:resource="job" />
    <bbd:education rdf:resource="education" />
    <bbd:experience rdf:resource="experience" />
    <bbd:skills rdf:resource="skills" />
    <bbd:references rdf:resource="references" />
```

Example 10-8. Resume RDF/XML document (continued)

```
    </rdf:Description>

    <rdf:Description rdf:about="bio">

        <bbd:firstname>Shelley</bbd:firstname>
        <bbd:lastname>Powers</bbd:lastname>
        <bbd:city>St. Louis</bbd:city>
        <bbd:state>Missouri</bbd:state>
        <bbd:country>US</bbd:country>
        <bbd:homephone> - </bbd:homephone>
        <bbd:mobile> - </bbd:mobile>
        <bbd:workphone> - </bbd:workphone>
        <bbd:email>shelleyp@burningbird.net</bbd:email>
    </rdf:Description>

    <rdf:Description rdf:about="job">
        <bbd:position>Software Engineer</bbd:position>
        <bbd:position>Technical Architect</bbd:position>
        <bbd:experience>16+ years</bbd:experience>
        <bbd:permorcontract>Contract</bbd:permorcontract>
        <bbd:start>2002-09-29</bbd:start>
        <bbd:relocate>No</bbd:relocate>
        <bbd:travel>yes</bbd:travel>
        <bbd:location>St. Louis, Missouri</bbd:location>
        <bbd:status>full</bbd:status>
        <bbd:rateusdollars>100</bbd:rateusdollars>
        <bbd:unit>hour</bbd:unit>
        <bbd:worklocation>both</bbd:worklocation>
        <bbd:idealjob>I'm primarily interested in contract positions with a
                    fairly aggressive schedule; I like to be in an energetic
                    environment. My preferred work is technology architecture,
                    but I'm also a hands-on senior software developer.
        </bbd:idealjob>

    </rdf:Description>

    <rdf:Description rdf:about="education">
        <rdf:_1>
            <rdf:Description rdf:about="degree1">
                <bbd:degree>AA</bbd:degree>
                <bbd:discipline>Liberal Arts</bbd:discipline>
                <bbd:date>1981-06-01</bbd:date>
                <bbd:gpa>3.98</bbd:gpa>
                <bbd:honors>High Honors</bbd:honors>
                <bbd:college>Yakima Valley Community College</bbd:college>
                <bbd:location>Yakima, Washington</bbd:location>
            </rdf:Description>
        </rdf:_1>
        <rdf:_2>
            <rdf:Description rdf:about="degree2">
                <bbd:degree>BA</bbd:degree>
                <bbd:discipline>Psychology</bbd:discipline>
```

Example 10-8. Resume RDF/XML document (continued)

```
            <bbd:date>1986-06-01</bbd:date>
            <bbd:gpa>3.65</bbd:gpa>
            <bbd:honors>Magna cum laude</bbd:honors>
            <bbd:honors>Dean's Scholar</bbd:honors>
            <bbd:college>Central Washington University</bbd:college>
            <bbd:location>Ellensburg, Washington</bbd:location>
          </rdf:Description>
        </rdf:_2>
        <rdf:_3>
          <rdf:Description rdf:about="degree3">
            <bbd:degree>BS</bbd:degree>
            <bbd:discipline>Computer Science</bbd:discipline>
            <bbd:date>1987-06-01</bbd:date>
            <bbd:gpa>3.65</bbd:gpa>
            <bbd:college>Central Washington University</bbd:college>
            <bbd:location>Ellensburg, Washington</bbd:location>
          </rdf:Description>
        </rdf:_3>
      </rdf:Description>


    <rdf:Description rdf:about="experience">
      <rdf:_1>
        <rdf:Description rdf:about="job1">
            <bbd:company>Boeing</bbd:company>
            <bbd:title>Data Architect</bbd:title>
            <bbd:title>Information Repository Modeler</bbd:title>
            <bbd:title>Software Engineer</bbd:title>
            <bbd:title>Database Architect</bbd:title>
            <bbd:start>1987</bbd:start>
            <bbd:end>1992</bbd:end>
            <bbd:description>
At Boeing I worked as a developer for the Peace Shield Project (FORTRAN/Ingres on VAX/
VMS).  Peace Shield is Saudi Arabia's air defense system. At the end of the project, I
moved into a position of Oracle DBA and provided support for various organizations.  I
worked with Oracle versions 5.0 and 6.0, and with SQL Forms, Pro*C, and OCI. I was also
interim information modeler for Boeing Commercial's Repository, providing data modeling
and design for this effort.
From the data group, I moved into my last position at Boeing, which was for the Acoustical
and Linguistics group, developing applications for Windows using Microsoft C, C++, the
Windows SDK, and using Smalltalk as a prototype tool. The object-based applications we
created utilized new speech technology as a solution to business needs including a speech
driven robotic work order system.
            </bbd:description>
          </rdf:Description>
        </rdf:_1>
      </rdf:Description>

    <rdf:Description rdf:about="skills">
      <rdf:_1>
        <rdf:Description rdf:about="java">
          <bbd:level>Expert</bbd:level>
```

Example 10-8. Resume RDF/XML document (continued)

```
        <bbd:years>6</bbd:years>
        <bbd:lastused>now</bbd:lastused>
      </rdf:Description>
    </rdf:_1>
    <rdf:_2>
      <rdf:Description rdf:about="C++">
        <bbd:level>Expert</bbd:level>
        <bbd:years>8</bbd:years>
        <bbd:lastused>2 years ago</bbd:lastused>
      </rdf:Description>
    </rdf:_2>
  </rdf:Description>

</rdf:RDF>
```

 The PHP XML classes may have been updated to reflect the most recent RDF specifications by the time this book is published.

To demonstrate both the persistence capability and the query functionality of the PHP XML classes, Example 10-9 shows a complete PHP page that opens a connection to the database, loads in a document, queries the data, and then removes the document from persistent storage.

Example 10-9. Application to read in resume RDF/XML document and run query against it

```php
<?
mysql_connect("localhost","username","password");
mysql_select_db("databasename");
?>
<html>
<head>
  <title>RDQL PHP Example</title>
</head>
<body>
<?php
include_once("C:\class_rdql_db\class_rdql_db.php");

# read in, store document
$rdqldb = new RDQL_db();
$rdqldb->set_warning_mode(true);
$rdqldb->store_rdf_document("http://weblog.burningbird.net/resume.rdf","resume");
# build and execute query
$query='SELECT ?b
FROM <resume>
WHERE (?a, <bbd:title>, ?b)
USING bbd for <http://www.burningbird.net/resume_schema#>';

#parse and print results
```

```
$rows = RDQL_query_db::rdql_query_db($query);
if (!empty($rows)) {
    foreach($rows as $row) {
        foreach($row as $key=>$val) {
            print("$val<p>");
        }
    }
}
else {
    print("No data found");
}

# data dump and delete document from db
$data = $rdqldb->get_rdf_document("resume");
print("<h3>General dump of the data</h3>");
print($data);

$rdqldb->remove_rdf_document("resume");
?>
</div>
</body>
</html>
```

This example is running in a Windows environment, and the path to the PHP class is set accordingly. The method get_rdf_document returns the RDF/XML of the document contained within the database. To print out the elements as well as the data, modify the string before printing:

```
$data=str_replace("<","&lt;",$data);
$data=str_replace(">","&gt;",$data);
print ($data);
```

As the example demonstrates, parsing and querying an RDF/XML document with the PHP XML classes is quite simple, one of the advantages of a consistent metadata storage and query language.

The code for Query-O-Matic Lite is even simpler. The first page with the HTML form has just one field, querystr, a textarea input field. When the form is submitted, the second page accesses this string, strips out any slashes, and then passes the string directly to the PHP class to process the query, as is shown in Example 10-10. In this example, the RDQL class is used and the document is opened directly via URL, rather than being persisted to a database first. In addition, unlike Query-O-Matic, Lite allows multiple variables in the select clause—each is printed out with spaces in between, and each row is printed on a separate line.

Example 10-10. Code for PHP RDF/XML Query-O-Matic Lite

```
<html>
<head>
```

Example 10-10. Code for PHP RDF/XML Query-O-Matic Lite (continued)

```
   <title>RDFQL Query-O-Matic Light</title>
</head>
<body>
<?php

include_once("class_rdql.php");
$querystr=stripslashes($_GET['querystr']);
$rows = RDQL_query_document::rdql_query_url($querystr);
if (empty($rows)) die("No data found for your query");

foreach($rows as $row) {
      foreach($row as $key=>$val) {
         print("$val ");
      }
  print ("<br /><br />");
  }
?>
</body>
</html>
```

Even accounting for the HTML in the example, Query-O-Matic Lite is one of the smallest PHP applications I've created. However, as long as the underlying RDF/XML parser (class_rdf_parser) can parse the RDF/XML, you can run queries against the data.

Figure 10-3 shows the first page of Query-O-Matic Lite, with an RDQL query typed into the query input text box.

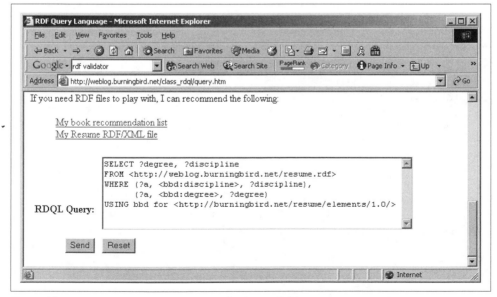

Figure 10-3. Entering an RDQL query into the Query-O-Matic

The query, shown in Example 10-11, accesses all degrees and disciplines within the document and prints them out.

Example 10-11. RDQL query accessing disciplines and degrees from resume RDF/XML document

```
SELECT ?degree, ?discipline
FROM <http://weblog.burningbird.net/resume.rdf>
WHERE (?a, <bbd:discipline>, ?discipline),
      (?a, <bbd:degree>, ?degree)
USING bbd for <http://burningbird.net/resume/elements/1.0/>
```

The results of running this query are:

```
AA Liberal Arts
BA Psychology
BS Computer Science
```

The PHP XML classes also support conditional and Boolean operators for filtering data once a subset has been found with the triple patterns. It's just that the set of operators differs from those for Jena, as there has been no standardization of RDQL across implementations...yet. In addition, you can list more than one document in the from/source clause, and the data from both is then available for the query.

I loaded several RDF/RSS files (for more on RSS, see Chapter 13) from my web sites and then created a query that searched for all entries after a certain time (the start of 2003) and printed out the date/timestamp, title, and link to the article. Example 10-12 contains the RDQL for this query.

Example 10-12. Complex RDQL query

```
SELECT ?date, ?title, ?link
FROM <http://weblog.burningbird.net/index.rdf>
     <http://articles.burningbird.net/index.rdf>
     <http://rdf.burningbird.net/index.rdf>
WHERE (?a, <rdf:type>, <rss:item>),
      (?a, <rss:title>, ?title),
      (?a, <rss:link>, ?link),
      (?a, <dc:date>, ?date)
AND ?date > '2002-12-31'
USING rss for <http://purl.org/rss/1.0/>,
      dc for <http://purl.org/dc/elements/1.1/>
```

The data from all RDF/XML files was joined, the query made and filtered, and the resulting output met my expectations. Not only that, but the process was quite quick, as well as incredibly easy—a very effective demonstration of the power of RDF, RDF/XML, and RDQL.

Sesame

Sesame is, to quote the web site where it's supported, "...an Open Source RDF Schema-Based Repository and Querying Facility." It's a Java JSP/Servlet application that I downloaded and installed on my Windows box, running it with a standalone Tomcat server (Version 4.1.18).

 The Sesame web site, including source for the product and documentation, is at *http://sesame.aidministrator.nl/*.

Once I worked through an installation problem having to do with an extraneous angle bracket in the *web.xml* file definition for an Oracle database installation (something the creators of Sesame have said will be fixed), getting the application to run was a piece of cake—just start Tomcat.

I installed Sesame with support for MySQL. Once I started it (see instructions), the first thing I did was load in the *monsters1.rdf* test document, accessed through the URL online. The document loaded fairly quickly, though the tool didn't provide feedback that it was finished loading.

After loading, I explored the database entries by accessing the Explore menu option (at the top of the page) and then specifying *http://burningbird.net/articles/monsters1. htm* as the URI to start the exploration with (the top-level resource for the test document). The page that opened is shown in Figure 10-4. Quite a nice layout, with each predicate/object defined as a hypertext link that takes you to more information about the object. Like BrownSauce, covered in Chapter 7, Sesame provides a nice RDF/XML browser.

Two other options at the top of the Sesame page allow you to query the data using RDQL (the same RDQL explored in this chapter) or using Sesame's RQL (RDF Query Language). I accessed the RDQL page first and tried the RDQL query defined earlier in Example 10-7:

```
SELECT ?date
WHERE
(?resource, <rdf:type>, <pstcn:Movement>),
(?resource, <pstcn:movementType>, ?value),
(?resource, <dc:date>, ?date)
AND (?value eq "Add")
USING pstcn FOR        <http://burningbird.net/postcon/elements/1.0/>,
     rdf FOR <http://www.w3.org/1999/02/22-rdf-syntax-ns#>,
     dc for <http://purl.org/dc/elements/1.1/>
```

Note that this query is looking for a date (dc:date) for the resource movement where the movement was equivalent to the resource being added ("Add"). Figure 10-5 shows the result of running this query, which was evaluated in an amazingly short amount of time—seemingly instantaneous.

RQL is similar in concept to RDQL, though not surprisingly it has a different syntax, as well as different features and functionality. For instance, using the online repository querying capability, you can easily find all RDF classes within the

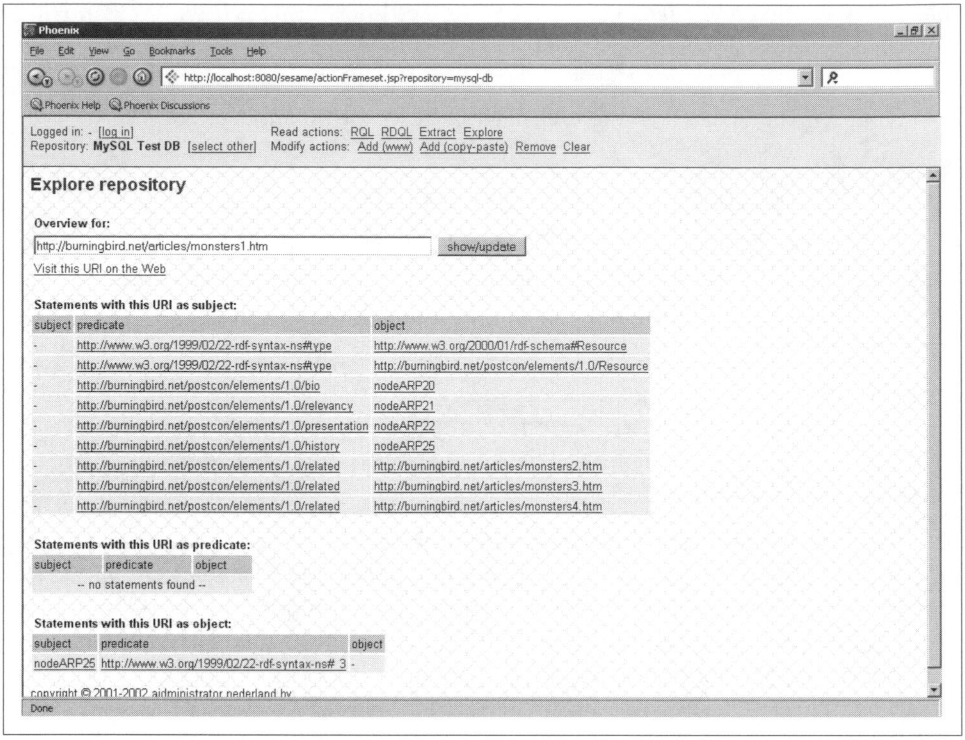

Figure 10-4. *RDF/XML test document, explored in Sesame*

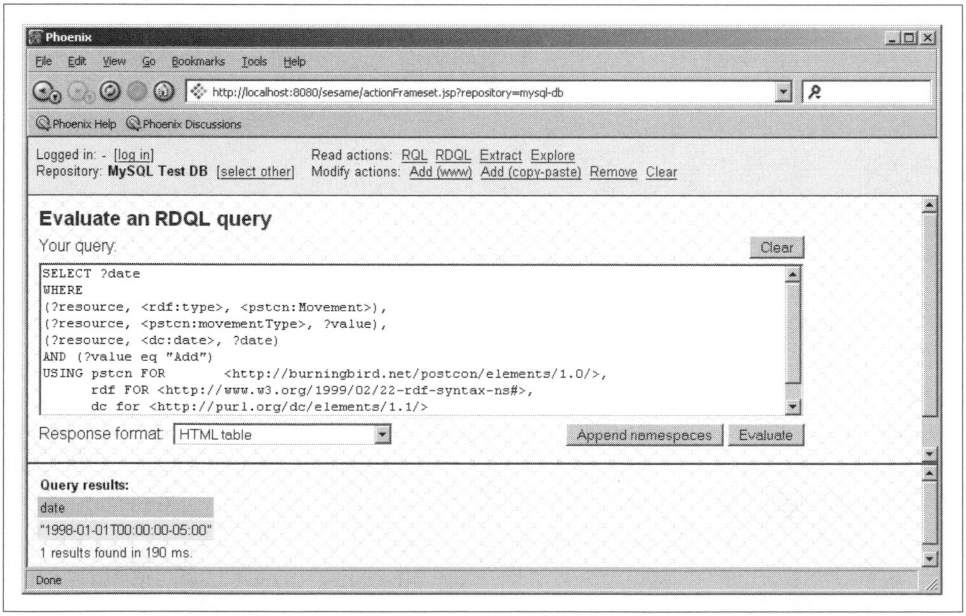

Figure 10-5. *Running RDQL query and viewing the result*

repository just by typing `Class` as the query (by itself with no other characters). For the test document, the result is:

```
http://www.w3.org/1999/02/22-rdf-syntax-ns#Property
http://www.w3.org/2000/01/rdf-schema#Resource
http://www.w3.org/2000/01/rdf-schema#Literal
http://www.w3.org/2000/01/rdf-schema#Class
http://burningbird.net/postcon/elements/1.0/Resource
http://www.w3.org/1999/02/22-rdf-syntax-ns#Seq
http://burningbird.net/postcon/elements/1.0/Movement
```

The PostCon classes of `Movement` and `Resource` are found, as are the RDF class `Seq` and the RDFS classes of `Property`, `Resource`, `Literal`, and `Class`. A variation of this query is `Property`, to get a listing of all properties in the repository.

To get more selective in your information querying, to find the source and target for a specific property, you would provide the full URI of the property. For instance, to find the source and target for the predicate `movementType`, I typed in the following:

```
http://burningbird.net/postcon/elements/1.0/movementType
```

This returned the following:

```
http://www.yasd.com/dynaearth/monsters1.htm  "Add"
http://www.dynamicearth.com/articles/monsters1.htm "Move"
http://burningbird.net/articles/monsters1.htm "Move"
```

As with RDQL, you can build complex queries using joins and conditional operations. It's here that there's a great deal of similarity between RDQL and RQL. In the following, the source and target for the `movementType` property is queried using a more formalized SQL-like query like RDQL uses:

```
select X, Y
from {X} http://burningbird.net/postcon/elements/1.0/movementType {Y}
```

Conditional operators are provided in a where clause following the `select from` clause, as the following demonstrates finding a specific source whose `movementType` is equal to `"Add"`:

```
select X
from {X} http://burningbird.net/postcon/elements/1.0/movementType {Y}
where Y = "Add"
```

To join queries, use a period between the query results. In the following RQL query, all objects that have a property of `http://burningbird.net/postcon/elements/1.0/related` are queried and then joined with another query that finds the titles of the related resources:

```
select *
from http://burningbird.net/postcon/elements/1.0/related {X}. http://purl.org/dc/
elements/1.1/title {Y}
```

The result from this query is:

```
http://burningbird.net/articles/monsters2.htm  "Cryptozooloy"
http://burningbird.net/articles/monsters3.htm "A Tale of Two Monsters: Architeuthis
Dux (Giant Squid)"
http://burningbird.net/articles/monsters4.htm "Nessie, the Loch Ness Monster "
```

You can see a great deal of similarity between the two query languages, and I like both equally well, though I'll admit to a slight preference for the simplicity of RQL.

Of course, being able to query a repository via a predefined interface isn't going to help you build an application. Sesame comes with a Java API for both server and client functions, including being able to run RDQL and RQL queries against the repository. I won't cover either in this chapter, as both are quite nicely documented at the Sesame web site, and documentation is included with the downloaded property.

One additional feature of Sesame is the repositories support for different protocols for querying the data, using SOAP and the Java RMI in addition to invoking services using HTTP. Again, these are very well documented, including examples, at the Sesame site and in the downloaded product. In addition, as was mentioned earlier in the chapter, you can also use the Sesame repository as the persistent datastore with the Jena Java API.

## CHAPTER 11

A Brief Look at Additional RDF Application Environments

The previous chapters have provided a reasonably detailed look at several APIs created in some of the more popular programming languages today: Java, PHP, Python, and Perl. However, as popular as these languages are, they're not the only ones implementing APIs for processing RDF/XML. There are APIs created in LISP and C, Ruby, Tcl, even .NET-enabled APIs written in C#.

Additionally, some APIs are released as part of a larger framework—APIs connected with a repository or other higher-level functionality. Technically, these frameworks do provide language-based APIs. However, their size and complexity tend to make them a bit much for those looking only for a set of objects to create and/or read an RDF/XML document.

In this chapter, we'll take a look—briefly, because we want to get into some uses of RDF—at some of the odd-language APIs as well as the more complex frameworks. To start, we'll look at APIs written in that new kid on the block: C#.

RDF and C#

When Microsoft went to its new .NET architecture, one of the products released with the architecture was the Common Language Runtime (CLR), a programming language platform capable of supporting different programming languages. The first language released was C#, a hybrid between C++ and Java.

 If you're running Linux, you don't need .NET to compile C# code; you can also compile the code using the C# compiler provided with Mono, an open source CLR alternative. Download Mono at Ximian's Mono site, *http://www.go-mono.com/*.

When I was looking around for application environments that support RDF/XML, I checked for a C# or .NET-based environment, not really expecting to find anything.

However, I found more than one product, including an easy-to-install, lightweight C# parser named Drive.

 Drive can be downloaded at *http://www.daml.ri.cmu.edu/drive/news. html*. According to a news release at the site, the API has been updated to the newest RDF specification.

Drive is a relatively uncomplicated API, providing three major classes:

Softagents.Drive.RDFEdge

Represents an edge (arc) within an RDF graph. Variables include m_Sourcenode and m_Destnode, representing the source and destination node of the arc, respectively.

Softagents.Drive.RDFGraph

Stores and manages the entire graph.

Softagents.Drive.RDFNode

Represents a node within an RDF graph. Variables include m_Edges, with all arcs associated with the node. Methods include getEdges, getIncomingEdges, getOutgoingEdges, and so on.

To work with a graph, first create an instance of RDFGraph, reading in an RDF/XML document. Once it is read in, you can then query information from the graph, such as accessing a node with a URI and then querying for the edges related to that node.

Example 11-1 shows a small application that pulls the URL for a RDF/XML document from the command line and then loads this document in a newly created RDFGraph object. Next, the RDFGraph method getNode is called, passing in the URI for the resource and getting back an RDFNode object instantiated to that object. The getEdges method is called on the node returning an ArrayList of RDFEdge objects. The URI and local name properties for each of the edges are accessed and then printed out to the console. Finally, at the end, another RDFGraph method, PrintNTriples, is called to print out all of the N-Triples from the model.

Example 11-1. Printing out the edges for a given node using Drive C# parser

```
/*****************************************************************************
 * PracticalRDF
 *****************************************************************************/
using System;
using Softagents.Drive;
using System.Collections;

namespace PracticalRDF
{
    /// PracticalRDF
    ///
    public class PracticalRDF
    {
        [STAThread]
        static void Main(string[] args)
```

```
{
        string[] arrNodes;

        // check argument count
    if(args.Length <1)
    {
        Console.WriteLine("Usage:Practical <inputfile.rdf>");
        return;
    }

        //read in RDF/XML document
    RDFGraph rg = new RDFGraph();
        rg.BuildRDFGraph(args[0]);

        // find specific node
    RDFNode rNode = rg.GetNode("http://burningbird.net/articles/monsters1.htm");
    System.Collections.ArrayList arrEdges = rNode.GetEdges();

        // access edges and print
        foreach (RDFEdge rEdge in arrEdges) {
            Console.WriteLine(rEdge.m_lpszNameSpace + rEdge.m_lpszEdgeLocalName);
            }

        // dump all N-Triples
    Console.WriteLine("\nN Triples\n");
    rg.PrintNTriples();

    }
    }
}
```

After compilation, the application is executed, passing in the name of the RDF/XML document:

```
PracticalRDF http://burningbird.net/articles/monsters1.rdf
```

The parser does return warnings about a possible redefinition of a node ID for each of the major resources, but this doesn't impact on the process:

```
Warning: Possible redefinition of Node ID=http://burningbird.net/articles/monsters1.
htm! Ignoring.
Warning: Possible redefinition of Node ID=http://burningbird.net/articles/monsters2.
htm! Ignoring.
Warning: Possible redefinition of Node ID=http://burningbird.net/articles/monsters3.
htm! Ignoring.
Warning: Possible redefinition of Node ID=http://burningbird.net/articles/monsters4.
htm! Ignoring.
Warning: Possible redefinition of Node ID=http://www.yasd.com/dynaearth/monsters1.
htm! Ignoring.
Warning: Possible redefinition of Node ID=http://www.dynamicearth.com/articles/
monsters1.htm! Ignoring.
```

All of the predicates directly attached to the top-level node within the document are found and returned:

```
http://burningbird.net/postcon/elements/1.0/relevancy
http://burningbird.net/postcon/elements/1.0/history
http://burningbird.net/postcon/elements/1.0/bio
http://www.w3.org/1999/02/22-rdf-syntax-ns#type
http://burningbird.net/postcon/elements/1.0/related
http://burningbird.net/postcon/elements/1.0/related
http://burningbird.net/postcon/elements/1.0/related
http://burningbird.net/postcon/elements/1.0/presentation
```

Drive cannot handle query-like processing of the data, using an RDQL language. However, there are methods for adding edges to a node and nodes to a graph if you're interested in building an RDF graph from scratch or modifying an existing one.

Wilbur — RDF API CLOS

It's been many years since I used LISP, but I wasn't surprised to find at least one RDF implementation based on it: Wilbur, written none by none other than the legendary Ora Lassila, coeditor of the original RDF Model & Syntax Specification and the person whose name appears in many RDF/XML tutorials.

 Wilbur is Nokia's RDF Toolkit for CLOS. Documentation and source can be downloaded from the SourceForge location at *http://wilbur-rdf. sourceforge.net/docs/*.

Wilbur has parsers capable of working with RDF, DAML (an ontology language discussed in more detail in Chapter 12), and straight XML, with the addition of an RDF API, in addition to an HTTP client and frame system built on RDF and DAML+OIL.

The APIs supported by Wilbur are documented online, but there are no examples or screenshots. There may be examples and additional documentation within Wilbur; however, since I didn't have support for CLOS, I couldn't try out the applications or the development tool. However, I wanted to include a reference to it for the sake of comprehensive coverage of language support for RDF.

Overview of Redland — a Multilanguage-Based RDF Framework

Though the majority of RDF/XML APIs are based on Perl, Python, Java, and PHP, several are in other language-based APIs, including ones in C# and CLOS, as discussed in the last section. For instance, if you're interested in working with Tcl, XOTcl—based on MIT's OTcl—has RDF/XML-processing capability (*http://media. wu-wien.ac.at/*). Additionally, Dan Brickley has created an experimental RDF system written in Ruby called RubyRDF (at *http://www.w3.org/2001/12/rubyrdf/intro.html*).

And if you're interested in a system that supports Tcl as well as Ruby, and Perl, and Python, and Java, and so on, then you'll want to check out Redland.

One of the older applications supporting RDF and RDF/XML, and one consistently updated to match effort in the RDF specification is Redland—a multilanguage API and data management toolkit. Unlike most of the other APIs discussed in this book, Redland has a core of functionality exposed through the programming language C, functionality that is then wrapped in several other programming languages including Python, Perl, PHP, Java, Ruby, and Tcl. This API capability is then mapped to a scalable architecture supporting data persistence and query.

Because of its use of C, Redland is port and platform dependent; it has been successfully tested in the Linux, BSD, and Mac OS X environments. At the time of this writing, Version 0.9.12 of Redland was released and installed cleanly on my Mac OS X. When writing this section, I tested the C objects, as well as the Python and Perl APIs, the most stable language wrappers in Redland.

 The main Redland web site is at *http://www.redland.opensource.ac.uk/*. The RDF/XML parser used by Redland, Raptor, can be downloaded and used separately from the framework. Redland is licensed under LGPL and MPL licenses.

Working with the Online Tools

To quickly jump into Redland and its capabilities, there are online demonstrations of several aspects of the framework and its component tools. One online tool is an RSS Validator, which validates any RSS 1.0 (RDF/RSS) file. RSS is described in detail in Chapter 13, but for now, I'll use the validator to validate an RDF/XML file built from several other combined RSS files. Figure 11-1 shows the results of running the RSS Validator against the file.

Another validator is an N-Triples Validator, which makes a nice change from RDF/XML validators. There's also a parser test page, as well as an online database that you can actually manipulate as you test Redland's capabilities with a persistent store. I created a new database called *shelley* and loaded in my test RDF/XML file, *monsters1.rdf*. I could then query the data using Redland's query triple or by printing out the data and clicking on any one of the triples to access it. The latter is particularly useful because the query that would return the statement is generated and printed out, giving you a model to use for future queries.

As an example of a triple query in Redland, the following returns all statements that match on the PostCon reason predicate:

```
?-[http://burningbird.net/postcon/elements/1.0/reason]->?
```

The format for the triple pattern is:

```
[subject]-[predicate]->[object]
```

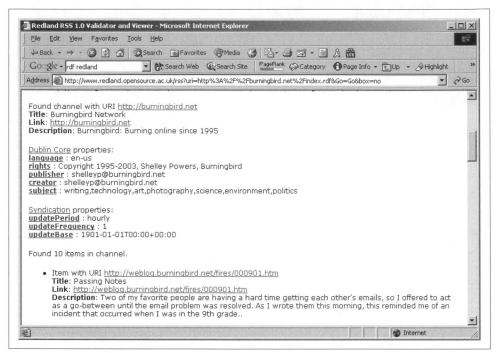

Figure 11-1. Output of Redland RSS Validator

for resource objects and the following for strings:

```
[subject]-[predicate]->"object"
```

Use the question mark to denote that the application is supposed to match on any data within that triple component.

Working with the Redland Framework

The Redland site contains documentation for the core C API, as well as the primary wrappers: Perl, Python, and Java. The API Reference covers the C API, and each wrapper has a separate page with information specific to that wrapper language. For instance, if you access the Perl page, you'll find a table of application objects; next to each object is a link to the documentation page for the core Redland function (written in C), such as librdf_node, and next to that is a link to the associated language class.

Clicking on the C version of the object opens a page with a listing of all the functions that class supports. Clicking on any of those opens a page that describes how the function works and the parameters it accepts. Clicking on the language wrapper object provides a page of documentation about the object, formatted in a manner similar to other documentation for that language. For instance, Figure 11-2 shows the documentation page for the Perl Statement object, including the traditional Synopsis.

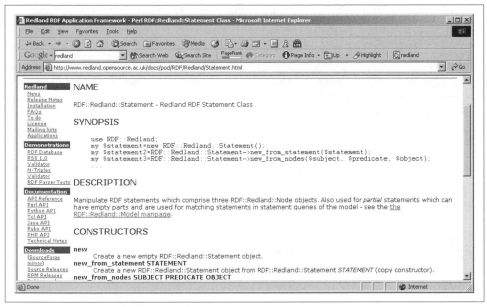

Figure 11-2. Documentation for the Perl Redland object, Statement

However, the Python documentation was a real eye-opener, following a traditional Python documentation approach (*pydoc*) as shown in Figure 11-3.

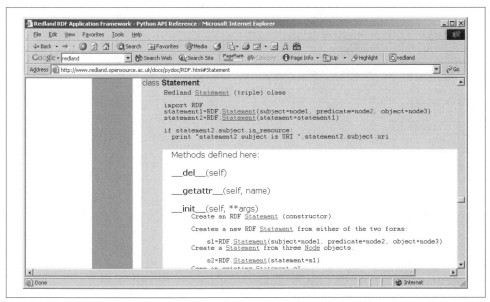

Figure 11-3. Documentation for the Python Redland object, Statement

Normally I wouldn't spend space in a book showing documentation, but I was intrigued by Redland's use of language-specific documentation style to document different wrappers. In addition to the style, though, the documentation demonstrates how the object is used in an application, which is critical for learning how to use the API correctly.

Redland has persistent database support through the Berkeley DB, if you have access to it, or you can use the memory model. You specify which storage mechanism to use when you create the storage for the RDF model you're working with. In addition, you can also specify what parser you want to use, choosing from several, including Raptor, the parser that comes with Redland, which you can use independent of Redland. Other parsers you can use are SiRPAC, Repat, RDFStore, and so on.

To use Redland, program your application using the native API or whichever of the wrappers you're comfortable in, compile it, and run it, in a manner similar to those shown in Chapter 10. The main difference is that the language wrappers are wrappers—behind the scenes, they invoke the functionality through the native API classes. Table 11-1 shows the main Redland classes, focusing on two languages I'm most comfortable with, Perl and Python, in addition to the native API.

Table 11-1. Mapping between Perl, Python, and C classes in Redland

Native C API class	Perl class	Python class	Description
librdf_model	RDF::Redland::Model	RDF.Model	Set of statements (triples) comprising a unique model
librdf_storage	RDF::Redland::Storage	RDF.Storage	Storage for the model (persistent or memory)
librdf_statement	RDF::Redland::Statement	RDF.Statement	One complete triple
librdf_node	RDF::Redland::Node	RDF.Node	RDFnode (resource or literal)
librdf_parser	RDF::Redland::Parser	RDF.Parser	Parses serialized RDF/XML into either a stream or a model
librdf_stream	RDF::Redland::Stream	RDF.Stream	Contains stream of RDF statements
librdf_serializer	RDF::Redland::Serializer	RDF.Serializer	Serializes the model using a specific mime type such as "ntriples" or "rdfxml"
librdf_iterator	RDF::Redland::Iterator	RDF.Iterator	Supports iteration of nodes from a query
librdf_uri	RDF::Redland::URI	RDF.Uri	Generates URIs
	RDF::Redland::World	RDF.World	Wrapper class to start and stop Redland environment

There are other classes in each wrapper, but the ones shown in Table 11-1 are the ones of primary interest.

A Quick Demo

I created two small applications, one in Perl, one in Python, to demonstrate the interchangeability of languages within the Redland framework.

The Perl application, shown in Example 11-2, creates a new Berkeley DB datastore and attaches it to a model. The application then adds a statement, opens the example RDF/XML document located on the filesystem, and parses it into the model using the Redland parser method parse_as_stream. Once loaded, it serializes the model to disk as a test and then flushes the storage to disk.

Example 11-2. Perl example loading data into storage

```
!/usr/bin/perl
#
use RDF::Redland;

# create storage and model
my $storage=new RDF::Redland::Storage("hashes", "practrdf",
                                      "new='yes',hash-type='bdb',dir='/Users/shelleyp'");
die "Failed to create RDF::Redland::Storage\n" unless $storage;
my $model=new RDF::Redland::Model($storage, "");
die "Failed to create RDF::Redland::Model for storage\n" unless $model;

# add new statement to model
my $statement=RDF::Redland::Statement->new_from_nodes(RDF::Redland::Node->new_from_uri_
string("http://burningbird.net/articles/monsters1.htm"),
                                         RDF::Redland::Node->new_from_uri_
string("http://burningbird.net/postcon/elements/1.0/relatedTo"),
                                         RDF::Redland::Node->new_from_uri_
string("http://burningbird.net/articles/monsters5.htm"));
die "Failed to create RDF::Redland::Statement\n" unless $statement;
$model->add_statement($statement);
$statement=undef;

# open file for parsing
# RDF/XML parser using Raptor
my $uri=new RDF::Redland::URI("file:monsters1.rdf");
my $base=new RDF::Redland::URI("http://burningbird.net/articles/");

my $parser=new RDF::Redland::Parser("raptor", "application/rdf+xml");
die "Failed to find parser\n" if !$parser;

# parse file
$stream=$parser->parse_as_stream($uri,$base);
my $count=0;
while(!$stream->end) {
  $model->add_statement($stream->current);
  $count++;
  $stream->next;
}
$stream=undef;
```

Example 11-2. Perl example loading data into storage (continued)

```
# serialize as rdf/xml
my $serializer=new RDF::Redland::Serializer("rdfxml");
die "Failed to find serializer\n" if !$serializer;
$serializer->serialize_model_to_file("prac-out.rdf", $base, $model);
$serializer=undef;

warn "\nDone\n";

# force flush of storage to disk
$storage=undef;
$model=undef;
```

Once the data is stored in the database from the first application, the second application opens this store and looks for all statements with dc:subject as predicate. Once they are found, the application prints these statements out. When finished, it serializes the entire model to a stream, and then prints out each statement in the stream, as shown in Example 11-3.

Example 11-3. Python application that accesses stored RDF/XML and prints out statements

```
import RDF

storage=RDF.Storage(storage_name="hashes",
                    name="practrdf",
                    options_string="hash-type='bdb',dir='/Users/shelleyp'")
if not storage:
  raise "new RDF.Storage failed"

model=RDF.Model(storage)
if not model:
  raise "new RDF.model failed"

# find statement
print "Printing all matching statements"
statement=RDF.Statement(subject=None,
                        predicate=RDF.Node(uri_string="http://purl.org/dc/elements/1.1/
subject"),
                        object=None)
stream=model.find_statements(statement);

# print results
while not stream.end():
  print "found statement:",stream.current()
  stream.next();

# print out all statements
print "Printing all statements"
stream=model.serialise()
while not stream.end():
  print "Statement:",stream.current()
  stream.next()
```

When the first application is run, the new database is created. However, the second application just opens the persisted datastore created by the first Perl application.

 Example 11-3 reads the RDF/XML document in from the local filesystem rather than remotely via the URL. In the OS 10.2.4 environment, the examples were tested in; trying to read a file remotely did result in a Bus error.

Redfoot

Redfoot is another multicomponent application. If you reviewed the Python section of Chapter 9, you saw one of the components—an RDF parser and API written in Python called RDFLib—in use. In addition to RDFLib, Redfoot also provides a lightweight HTTP server in addition to a scriptlike language the creator of Redfoot calls Hypercode.

 Information and the source code for Redfoot can be found at *http://redfoot.net*. Download RDFLib separately at *http://rdflib.net*. Check the documentation to review the requirements for Redfoot, first, before installing

Redfoot has an HTTP listener that by default listens in on port 80, so if you have another web server running, you may want to shut it off, first. When running locally, access the RDFLib page through *http://localhost*.

After Redfoot is running, you can administer Redfoot by setting the document root, managing contexts, or editing a weblog (Redfoot also provides a basic weblogging tool). Document root controls where all persisting information is stored. The framework supports multiple RDF/XML models—the *contexts* of the tools. Redfoot has several included with the default installation. You can also add additional ones, as I did with the example file at *http://burningbird.net/articles/monsters1.rdf*. I added the file by specifying its URL within the Add Contexts admin page. From this same admin page, you can also add weblog entries into a weblog; however, the weblog editing features of Redfoot are fairly basic compared to other specialized weblogging tools.

From the main admin page you can access several examples, including an RDF Navigator that seems to allow you to build an RDF model, search on it, and so on. It's difficult to tell exactly how to use the application, though, because there's no documentation for it. The Recipes and the FOAF application, though, are intuitively easy to use. Figure 11-4 shows a page from the Recipes application.

As stated earlier, Redfoot uses its own scripting language it calls Hypercode. Hypercode is Python that's embedded within a CDATA block in an RDF/XML document

Figure 11-4. Example page from Recipes application

that contains information about how to initialize the data. For instance, Example 11-4, from the application's Hello World example, reports back "Hello World" to the browser.

Example 11-4. Snippet from Hello World Redfoot application

```
<rdf:Description rdf:about="http://localhost:8080/">
    <rdfs:label>Hello World</rdfs:label>
    <red:facet>
      <red:Facet>
        <rdfs:label>Hello World Facet</rdfs:label>
        <red:outer rdf:resource="http://redfoot.net/2002/11/09/redsite#outer"/>
        <red:code>
          <red:Python>
            <rdfs:label>Redsite Outer page</rdfs:label>
            <red:codestr>
<![CDATA[

response.write("""

<p>Hello World!</p>

""")

]]>
```

Example 11-4. Snippet from Hello World Redfoot application (continued)

```
        </red:codestr>
      </red:Python>
    </red:code>
  </red:Facet>
 </red:facet>
</rdf:Description>
```

```
</rdf:RDF>
```

In this example, information about the code is defined using RDF/XML and then implemented within the Python block. Interesting, but again the documentation is quite sparse. Redfoot is an application you'll want to check out only if you like to explore, feel comfortable with minimum documentation, and have a great fondness for Python.

CHAPTER 12
Ontologies: RDF Business Models

Since the focus of this book is more on the practical usage of RDF than the more theoretical Semantic Web, I wasn't sure about covering *ontologies*. After all, in a white paper at Stanford University, Tom Gruber described ontology thus:

> An ontology is a specification of a conceptualization.

It's a bit difficult to determine how to incorporate a discussion of a concept based on such an elusive definition into a book that begins with *Practical*. However, looking at examples of ontologies, in particular OIL, DAML+OIL, and the W3C's current OWL (Web Ontology Language) effort, it seemed to me that ontologies do fit into a book with *Practical* in the title, because an ontology is really the definition of the business rules associated with a vocabulary. In other words: ontologies are business models. According to the Web Ontology Language (OWL) Use Cases and Requirements document:

> An ontology formally defines a common set of terms that are used to describe and represent a domain. Ontologies can be used by automated tools to power advanced services such as more accurate Web search, intelligent software agents and knowledge management

Following on the relational model analogy discussed in earlier chapters, if RDF is analogous to the relational data model and SQL is analogous to RDF/XML, then ontologies built on RDF/XML are equivalent to large architected business applications such as SAP, PeopleSoft, and Oracle's Financial and Warehouse applications. This equation definitely opened a home for ontologies in this book, and this chapter is it.

 Tom Gruber's paper at Stanford is at *http://www-ksl.stanford.edu/kst/what-is-an-ontology.html*. The OWL Use Cases and Requirements document is at *http://www.w3.org/TR/webont-req/*. The W3C's OWL effort is accessible at the W3C Web Ontology site at *http://www.w3.org/2001/sw/WebOnt/*.

Why Ontology?

Since we spent two chapters discussing how to create RDF vocabularies using a combination of RDF and RDFS elements (Chapters 5 and 6), you may be wondering why we would need an ontology on top of this. What can ontology provide that the RDF Schema doesn't?

RDFS imposes fairly loose constraints on vocabularies. For instance, there's nothing in the schema that restricts the cardinality of a specific property or that provides information that two properties are disjoint (i.e., can't use one when using the other). An ontology language such as OWL adds additional constraints that increase the accuracy of implementations of a given vocabulary. More than that, though, they allow additional information to be inferred about the data, though it may not be specifically recorded.

RDFS provides properties, such as subClassOf, that define relationships between two classes—one is a subclass of, or inherits from, a second class. This also applies to an ontology language, but it can add additional class characteristics, such as its uniqueness, that aren't defined within RDFS.

We can develop a vocabulary, an ontology if you will, using just RDFS, but it won't be as precise or as comprehensive as one that also incorporates ontological elements from DAML+OIL/OWL; the more precise you are with data specification, the better off you'll be.

Brief History of the Ontology Movement

The current ontology effort at the W3C is OWL, which was rooted in the DAML (DARPA Agent Markup Language) project—specifically the ontology language originating from this project: DAML+OIL.

Though you'll see DAML+OIL, OIL (Ontology Inference Layer) originated separately in Europe starting in 1997. It was preceded by SHOE (Simple HTML Ontology Extensions) in 1995. OIL is particularly relevant in a book on RDF because it was the first ontology based on RDF as well as the XML Schema.

The first release of DARPA's DAML was in 2000, following early standardization work on the part of the W3C. One year after DAML was released, a joint ontology language, DAML+OIL, was released. An early press release on DAML+OIL appearing in the *Cover Pages* (at *http://xml.coverpages.org/ni2001-03-28-a.html*), said the following:

> The reference description document characterizes DAML+OIL as "a semantic markup language for Web resources." It builds on earlier W3C standards such as RDF and RDF Schema, and extends these languages with richer modeling primitives.

The first version of DAML+OIL was released in December of 2000, and the current version was released in March 2001. At the time, one of the primitives that DAML+OIL provided was *data typing*, which the first RDF specification didn't provide.

What's interesting with DAML+OIL is that the classes and properties and their relation to each other as defined in the document are extremely similar to those shown in RDFS (as described in Chapter 5). For instance, a `daml:Class` element categorizes elements that are classes. There is also the concept of property, defined through `daml:ObjectProperty`, but there is a conceptual difference between class and property in DAML+OIL and class and property in RDFS. However, exactly what this conceptual difference is has been the focus of considerable debate within the Semantic Web community.

In the *www-rdf-logic* mailing list, a thread started once about the difference between `rdfs:Class` and `daml:Class` (at *http://lists.w3.org/Archives/Public/www-rdf-logic/2002Mar/0017.html*). Exactly when does one use `rdfs:Class` and when does one use `daml:Class`?

General consensus tends to support the view that RDFS describes metadata, including DAML+OIL itself. However, one should use DAML+OIL elements to define actual instances of data, such as elements as they are defined in my PostCon vocabulary. This does make sense and supports the view that I have of DAML+OIL as compared to RDFS: that DAML+OIL is a way of describing a generalized business model, such as those defined in PeopleSoft and SAP, while RDFS is the metalanguage that defines DAML+OIL, equivalent to the relational data model used to define the databases that support PeopleSoft and SAP.

Unfortunately, this view hasn't received complete concurrence from all parties, and there is considerable bleed-through of the use of one schema over the other or, said another way, lack of clarity between the layers of the architecture, using the parlance of the community that works closely with ontologies and RDF.

The W3C entered the picture more fully when it formed the Semantic Web Activity Group in February 2001 and followed up with the creation of the Ontology Working Group. An announcement in August 2001 revealed the intent of incorporating the work of the DAML and OIL groups into the W3C Semantic Web activities (from *http://lists.w3.org/Archives/Public/www-rdf-logic/2001Aug/0014.html*):

> The current international collaboration between DAML and OIL groups on a Web ontology layer is expected to become a part of this W3C Activity.

Though not necessarily a part of the effort, DAML+OIL provided the foundation for the W3C ontology effort. The Web Ontology (WebOnt) Working Group was formally launched in November 2001, and work began on defining the language necessary for an ontology layer—OWL, the Web Ontology Language.

This chapter primarily focuses on OWL, but you can review the earlier DAML+OIL specifications at *http://www.w3.org/TR/daml+oil-reference*. In particular, a sample ontology at *http://www.w3.org/TR/daml+oil-walkthru/daml+oil-ex.daml* provides a good snapshot of the state of DAML+OIL at the time the work on OWL began. Lastly, the DAML Ontology Library has a listing of ontologies defined using DAML+OIL, at *http://www.daml.org/ontologies/*. A DAML+OIL-to-OWL converter is at *http://www.mindswap.org/2002/owl.html*.

OWL Use Cases and Requirements

As with most W3C efforts, you can track the progress of work within any one activity by the state and version of the documents released. The first document released by the WebOnt group on OWL listed a set of requirements for an ontology language, followed by documents for test cases, abstract syntax and semantics, and, finally, a language reference and user guide.

The roots for OWL exist in the OWL Use Cases and Requirements document, released in July 2002 and recently updated. According to this document, we've been working with ontologies all along by using vocabularies such as ones I've used in the book like Dublin Core and PostCon. These are ontologies because they define the data for a specific knowledge domain, which is what the Use Case and Requirements document defines as ontology.

Specifically, ontology encompasses four concepts:

- Classes
- Relationships between classes
- Properties of classes
- Constraints on relationships between the classes and properties of the classes

When you consider that these concepts can be used, equally, with RDF and RDFS, you can see why there is some confusion about where RDFS ends and OWL begins. The Use Cases document, while demonstrative of applications facilitated by the use of an ontology, didn't exactly help with clarifying when to use OWL and when to use RDFS, other than suggesting use of RDFS for defining OWL and then using OWL for everything else.

One interesting example of an OWL use case is the ontology web portal, *OntoWeb*, at *http://ontoweb.aifb.uni-karlsruhe.de/*.

In addition to use cases, design goals given in the document were:

- Ontologies must be sharable, so that more than one business within a particular business domain could use the same ontology defined for that domain.

- Evolving ontologies should be given version numbers and the schema defining the ontology given a separate URI for each new version (such as PostCon with its *http://burningbird.net/postcon/elements/1.0/version*). Ontologies would then be related through the use of `rdfs:subClassOf`.

- Ontologies must be interoperable.

- Inconsistencies in ontologies must be detected automatically to prevent them from occurring.

- Ontologies must balance expressivity and scalability.

- Ontologies must be consistent with other standards.

- Internationalization must be supported.

None of the use cases or design goals is overwhelmingly complex, except possibly testing for inconsistencies. The next document in the series released by the working group then contained test cases to see if the OWL met the various design goals.

 The most recent version of the Use Cases and Requirements document can be found at *http://www.w3.org/TR/webont-req/*.

OWL Specifications

OWL has no shortage of associated documents:

- Requirements for a Web Ontology Language
- Web Ontology Language (OWL) Guide Version 1.0
- OWL Web Ontology Language 1.0 Reference
- Web Ontology Language (OWL) Abstract Syntax and Semantics
- Web Ontology Language (OWL) Test Cases
- Feature Synopsis for OWL Lite and OWL

We just looked at the Requirements document. The other documents somewhat mirror their counterparts over at the RDF Working Group, with the OWL Guide being comparable to the RDF Primer, the OWL Reference to the Syntax document, and the OWL Abstract Syntax and Semantics document to a combination of the RDF Concepts and Semantics documents. The test cases for both are similar; though the OWL feature synopsis doesn't necessarily map to an existing RDF document, it seems similar to a reference card for OWL.

After reviewing the use cases and requirements governing the design of OWL, the next document to review to better understand OWL would be the guide. Just as does its counterpart in RDF, the RDF Primer, the guide provides a general overview of OWL and the associated effort.

OWL Guide 1.0

A further clarification of ontology is provided in the OWL Guide, when it describes how an ontology differs from an XML Schema. According to the guide:

> An ontology differs from an XML schema in that it is a knowledge representation, not a message format.

This is an important point. XML Schemas and message-based uses of XML focus on specific pieces of data and specific uses of data, such as sending a message and processing its results. Nothing within basic XML or within the XML Schema allows one to derive information outside of the context of the specific use. For instance, the tool I used to maintain a weblog might support SOAP requirements that allow me to publish a new posting, but nothing associated with the SOAP request allows me, or anyone, to learn more about that specific posting, or even the weblog, other than what's included within the transaction. OWL differs from XML Schema (as well as SOAP and many of the other uses of XML) in that it allows you to record data about an object outside of any specific transaction associated with that data. It allows you to record knowledge. OWL (and by its association, RDF) focuses on data rather than process.

The guide provides an overview of three different types of OWL:

OWL Lite

Supports simple classifications, allowing only cardinalities (member count) of 0 or 1 and only minimal constraints. An example would be a taxonomy.

OWL DL

Supports more complex ontologies, but with some guarantees, such as processing finishing in finite time, restricting elements to be one type, and so on. According to the guide, it's called DL, meaning "description logics."

OWL Full

Full support for maximum freedom of RDF, with no computational guarantees and the possibility of indefinite processing time.

These specific designations have more to do with what certain tools can and will support, which of course influences the design and implementation of a specific ontology. Looking at PostCon's RDFS definition, PostCon could be ported to an ontology, with any restrictions and constraints added to it fitting comfortably within those allowed by OWL DL.

The rest of the guide then covers the basic components of OWL. Later, as we review each of these, I'll demonstrate the concepts by porting PostCon over to OWL, to supplement the example of the Wine ontology used within the OWL document.

 At this point, you may want to take a look at a tutorial on OWL, "Ontology Development 101: A Guide to Creating Your First Ontology," found at *http://www.ksl.stanford.edu/people/dlm/papers/ontology-tutorial-noy-mcguinness-abstract.html.*

OWL Reference 1.0

The OWL Reference document provides the formal specification of the language. It is equivalent to the XML specification for RDF/XML covered in Chapters 3 and 4. However, unlike the RDF document, the OWL documents are a work in progress and far from complete.

The section of most interest in the reference is the one covering the language structure. Unlike RDF, the OWL vocabulary is quite large. Like RDF, though, it makes use of elements from RDFS (and from RDF).

The Reference document can be found at *http://www.w3.org/TR/owl-ref/*. The prefix for the OWL namespace used in the OWL documents is owl, a convention I'll follow in this chapter. OWL is based on RDF and RDFS, which means it must first and foremost validate as proper RDF/XML.

The Reference document breaks the structure of OWL down into separate components, most of which are already familiar to you from previous chapters, such as the concepts of classes, properties, and enumerations (collections). The section later in this chapter titled "Basic Constructs of OWL" provides an overview of these items. However, OWL also has several concepts unique to it, such as the Boolean combination of class expressions and property restrictions, which add the additional layer of reasoning you would expect for a language defining a business domain. These warrant a closer examination, which occurs in the section titled "Bits of Knowledge: More Complex OWL Constructs."

You'll sometimes find reference to owl:Thing in the document, but it doesn't show in any formal definition of elements, though it is listed as a term. This element represents the class of all classes and is an artifact of the DAML+OIL effort from which OWL is derived.

OWL Abstract Syntax and Semantics

The Abstract Syntax and Semantics document provides a breakdown of the model theoretical axioms and rules guiding the implementation and interpretation of OWL. It provides a semantic definition of what is a "fact" within OWL, as well as a high-level overview of how OWL differs from DAML+OIL and how OWL Lite differs from the full-featured OWL.

The WebOnt is considering making a minor modification to the name of this document, changing it to Semantics and Abstract Syntax.

A major difference between OWL and OWL Lite is the inclusion of what the document calls OWL descriptions. The formal definition of a description is:

```
< description> ::= <classID>
                 | <restriction>
                 | unionOf( {<description>} )
                 | intersectionOf( {<description>} )
                 | complementOf( <description> )
                 | oneOf({<individualID>} )
```

Primarily, an OWL description is one of a class identifier, a property restriction, or a complex class association. These descriptions enhance the reasoning inherent within OWL ontology—reasoning that goes beyond that allowed in RDFS.

Regarding the separation of OWL and OWL Lite in this chapter, for the most part the section titled "Basic Constructs of OWL" applies to both OWL and OWL Lite, though the data typing discussed in the section is beyond OWL Lite. Additionally, the property restrictions covered in "Bits of Knowledge: More Complex OWL Constructs" apply to both. However, the discussion about complex classes in this section applies purely to the fully featured OWL, as these make up most of the options from the OWL description just provided.

Another section in the Abstract document, "RDFS-Compatible Model-Theoretic Semantics," provides a semantic description of the relationship between OWL and RDFS. Though much of the section is given over to theorems and proofs, the first part provides a basic overview describing the compatibility between the two. In particular, it describes the differences between OWL Full and OWL DL.

This chapter focuses on OWL Lite and OWL Full. You'll want to check out the Abstract document for more information on OWL DL. The latest document can be found at *http://www.w3.org/TR/owl-semantics/*.

Feature Synopsis for OWL Lite and OWL

The Feature Synopsis document provides a summary of features for OWL and OWL Lite. It makes a good "in a nutshell" review of the material and is definitely worth a read as you learn more about OWL.

Access the recent version of the Synopsis document at *http://www.w3. org/TR/owl-features/*.

Basic Constructs of OWL

In this section, we'll look at the basic elements of OWL, those that exist regardless of the ontology being defined. If you're familiar with RDFS (as covered in Chapter 5), most of these should be familiar to you. Specifically, in this section we'll cover the following OWL elements:

- owl:Class
- owl:DatatypeProperty
- owl:imports
- owl:Ontology
- rdfs:range
- rdfs:subPropertyOf

- owl:Datatype
- rdfs:domain
- owl:ObjectProperty
- rdf:Property
- rdfs:subClassOf
- owl:versionInfo

RDF Schema and OWL are compatible, which is why you'll see RDFS elements within the OWL element set. However, the direction of this compatibility is one way—only from RDF and RDF to OWL; you won't see OWL elements within the RDF Schema.

You start an OWL ontology with the header, covered next.

OWL Header

The first component is the outer OWL block, delimited by owl:Ontology, containing version information (through owl:versionInfo) and an imports section (through owl:imports). The imports section includes an rdf:resource attribute that points to a separate RDF resource providing definitions used with the ontology. This could include the complete schema for the ontology.

Redefining PostCon as an OWL ontology rather than a vocabulary defined directly in RDFS, the OWL header would be similar to the following:

```
<rdf:RDF
    xmlns:pstcn="http://burningbird.net/postcon"
    xmlns:owl ="http://www.w3.org/2002/07/owl#"
    xmlns:rdf ="http://www.w3.org/1999/02/22-rdf-syntax-ns#"
    xmlns:rdfs="http://www.w3.org/2000/01/rdf-schema#"
    xmlns:dc="http://purl.org/dc/elements/1.1/"
    xmlns:xsd ="http://www.w3.org/2000/10/XMLSchema#">
<owl:Ontology rdf:about="http://burningbird.net/postcon">
  <owl:comment>PostContent Management</owl:comment>
  <owl:versionInfo>
       $Id: Overview.html,v 1.2 2002/11/08 16:42:25 connolly Exp $
  </owl:versionInfo>
  <dc:creator>Shelley Powers</dc:creator>
  <dc:title>PostCon</dc:title>
</owl:Ontology>
</rdf:RDF>
```

The namespaces are familiar as is the use of the outer rdf:RDF opening and closing tags. However, note that I used a different namespace for PostCon. I'm not defining a schema for the existing RDF vocabulary—I'm creating a new ontology, from the ground up, using RDF/XML and based on the business domain behind the vocabulary.

New material introduced in the header is the outer Ontology block to contain the ontological definitions and the version information elements, as well as the ontology comments. This section could also have included an import statement, to import another ontology, but none is defined for PostCon at this moment. Importing differs from inclusion of a namespace by incorporating that ontology's assertions into the ontology currently being defined, therefore making them part of the knowledge base on which the new ontology is being built.

The version information shown is one difference between RDF and OWL—OWL assumes that different versions of the ontology will be developed, therefore it's imperative to maintain this type of information with the document for each version.

Dublin Core elements are included in the header to provide title, creator, and other information, since this ontology is a published resource, and DC was designed to document metadata about published resources. It's not required—really, little of this material is required—but any extra information helps.

Between the OWL header and the final RDF closing tag is the definition of the classes and properties of the ontology itself.

OWL Classes and Individuals

Not unlike RDFS, OWL classes define entities via properties. The classes defined for the PostCon ontology should therefore be similar to those defined with RDFS in Chapter 6. What might be more apparent with OWL is the hierarchical nature of the classes.

In PostCon, there is a Resource, which is basically anything being tracked with the PostCon system. During the tracking process, the Resource moves from location to location, each of which is tracked as a movement. It still has all the characteristics of being a Resource; the movement doesn't change this. However, there are new characteristics associated with the item. The ResourceMovement, then, becomes a subclass of Resource. In addition, there are other resources that are related in some way to the Resource. RelatedResource is also defined as a subclass of Resource:

```
<owl:Class rdf:ID="Resource" />
<owl:Class rdf:ID="RelatedResource">
   <owl:subClassOf rdf:resource="#Resource" />
</owl:Class>
<owl:Class rdf:ID="ResourceMovement">
   <owl:subClassOf rdf:resource="#Resource" />
</owl:Class>
```

There are other possible classes within PostCon—for instance, different types of resources, such as photos, text documents, music, and video—each of which has different properties unique to the type of the object.

However, within the PostCon system, much of the uniqueness of each individual object can be described using the same properties. For instance, a requirement for viewing a video file is a browser plug-in that enables this, a requirement for a music file is the same, and so on. Each type of object has a requirement, and one property can capture this requirement for all the types. In this case, rather than each object type being a separate class, they're all instances of the same class. In ontological terms, each of these types of resource is an individual member of the class, rather than a subclass of it.

OWL Simple Properties and Complex Data Types

An OWL property is really not that much different from a property defined in RDFS. They share the same use of `rdfs:domain` and `rdfs:range`, but in addition, constraints that aren't defined in RDFS can be applied to OWL properties.

In PostCon, one property of a resource movement is its movement type information. The definition for it in OWL is very similar to what we would find in the RDF Schema:

```
<owl:ObjectProperty rdf:ID="movementType">
    <rdfs:domain rdf:resource="#ResourceMovement">
    <rdfs:range rdf:resource="" />
</owl:ObjectProperty>
```

The property `movementType` has a domain of `ResourceMovement`, which means that any resource with this property is a `ResourceMovement`. If a property inherits all the characteristics of another, it's a subproperty of the original, noted in OWL with the `subPropertyOf` property.

However, where RDFS and OWL differ, quite dramatically, is in data typing. Both specifications use XML Schema data types; both allow the use of data type within the schema definition (within the class definition for OWL, RDFS for RDF); and both allow annotation of instances with data type (individual for OWL, in actual properties in RDF). The two differ in that RDF limits data types to those types that can be referenced by URI, such as the predefined schema instances (in *http://www.w3.org/ TR/xmlschema-2/*). OWL extends the concept of data type to include creating classes of data types that are then used to constrain the range of properties.

To demonstrate, consider the `movementType` property just defined using `ObjectProperty`. The domain is `ResourceMovement`, and we could say it has a range of `rdf:Property`, which would be correct; however, it would also be too diffuse, because `movementType` has one other constraint attached to it: there are only three allowable values, "Add", "Drop", and "Move". Within RDFS there is nothing to automatically constrain the data used with `movementType` other than to use `xsd:string` to state it's a string and `rdf:Property` to state it's a property.

In OWL, though, we can do much more. Borrowing from the design of the data types for the example Wine ontology in the OWL Guide, I created a custom XML Schema data type definition file as follows:

```
<xsd:schema xmlns:xsd="http://www.w3.org/2001/XMLSchema"
        xmlns="http://burningbird.net/postcon/postcon-pstcn.xsd">
```

```
<xsd:simpleType name="movementTypes">
  <xsd:restriction base="xsd:string">
    <xsd:enumeration value="Add"/>
    <xsd:enumeration value="Drop"/>
    <xsd:enumeration value="Move"/>
  </xsd:restriction>
</xsd:simpleType>
 </xsd:schema>
```

This new simple type has a base restriction of `string`, but it also lists an enumeration of allowable values—"`Add`", "`Drop`", and "`Move`". To tie this into my ontology, I would then create a data typing class to represent this movement type:

```
<owl:Class rdf:ID="MovementType" />
```

I can then tie the *data type* restrictions to the `MovementType` class, using `DataTypeProperty`:

```
<owl:DataTypeProperty rdf:ID="movementTypeValue">
  <rdfs:domain rdf:resource="#MovementType" />
  <rdfs:range rdf:resource="pstcn:movementType"/>
</owl:DataTypeProperty>
```

Finally, I can complete the property definition for `movementType`, by adding an `rdf:range` that uses the new data type class:

```
<owl:ObjectProperty rdf:ID="movementType">
   <rdfs:domain rdf:resource="#ResourceMovement" />
   <rdf:range rdf:resource="#MovementType" />
</owl:ObjectProperty>
```

This seems a bit complex, but one restriction on allowable values for `rdf:range` is that they must be class values, such as `rdf:Property`. Using this approach, the RDF Schema requirements are met, but the greater needs of the ontology—being allowed to specify an enumeration of allowed items—are also met.

Bits of Knowledge: More Complex OWL Constructs

The example in the last section that allowed us to define a more complex data type for a specific property begins to demonstrate the divergence between RDFS and OWL—this ability to attach more nuances of meaning to the data being modeled, beyond nuances defined in RDF. Rightfully so—the relational data model provides the structure necessary to build generic data types that can manage all data; complex business models such as SAP and PeopleSoft use the relational model as a base for more complex models representing more specific business models. The two layers of relational data are complementary rather than competitive, just as the two layers of RDF/RDFS and OWL are complimentary rather than competitive.

The OWL elements we'll cover in this section are:

- `owl:allValuesFrom`
- `owl:complementOf`
- `owl:disjointWith`
- `owl:hasValue`
- `owl:InverseFunctionalProperty`
- `owl:maxCardinality`
- `owl:ObjectRestriction`
- `owl:onProperty`
- `owl:someValuesFrom`
- `owl:TransitiveProperty`

- `owl:cardinality`
- `owl:differentFrom`
- `owl:FunctionalProperty`
- `owl:intersectionOf`
- `owl:inverseOf`
- `owl:minCardinality`
- `owl:oneOf`
- `owl:Restriction`
- `owl:SymmetricProperty`
- `owl:unionOf`

The element names themselves indicate their functional value within OWL.

Increasing the Power of the Property

A property in RDF provides information about the entity it's describing, but the information tends to be somewhat linear. There are two types of information properties in an RDF record: an actual instance of data, such as a string containing a name or another resource, continuing the node-arc-node-arc-node path within the model.

In ontologies, properties can be much more active in their description of the knowledge described in the ontology with the aid of some enhancements built directly into the ontology language. OWL categorizes these property enhancements into characteristics and restrictions.

Property characteristics

Property characteristics increase our ability to record our understanding about the data we're describing in such a way that automated tools can infer much more of the reasoning we used when we pulled all this data together. In any model, there's a reason why we included this property or that entity, and not all of these reasons can be determined with the constructs supported in RDF or even with other data models such as the relational or object-oriented models.

To demonstrate the property characteristics, some new assumptions and additions to the existing PostCon ontology are made. In the current understanding of PostCon, a resource within the system would also exist as one resource on the server. However, there's nothing in the system that enforces this—a single web resource doesn't have to exist in one physical entity. For instance, an "article" such as the one used throughout the book, "Tale of Two Monsters: Legends" could be separated across many pages, but still be treated as a single entity within the system. To capture this information, a new property, partOf, can be defined and used as follows within the PostCon ontology:

```
<Resource rdf:ID="Section1">
  <partOf rdf:resource="#monsters1" />
```

```
  </Resource>
  <Resource rdf:ID="monsters1">
  </Resource>
```

With the new property, sections of an article can be split into further sections and so on, with each child section attached to the parent section through partOf.

This is an effective way to manage larger resources, but one thing lost with this structure is the fact that all of the sections ultimately roll up into one document, with each child section rolling up into the parent section, which may then roll up into another section and so on. However, OWL property characteristics provide a way to capture this type of information.

One property characteristic is the TransitiveProperty. The logic associated with this property is:

```
P(x,y) and P(y,z) implies P(x,z)
```

Using TransitiveProperty in PostCon would result in something similar to the following:

```
<owl:ObjectProperty rdf:ID="partOf">
  <rdf:type rdf:resource="owl:TransitiveProperty" />
  <rdfs:domain rdf:resource="&owl;Thing" />
  <rdfs:range rdf:resource="#Resource" />
</owl:ObjectProperty>

<Resource rdf:ID="sectionHeader1a">
  <partOf rdf:resource="sectionHeader1" />
</Resource>

<Region rdf:ID="sectionHeader1">
  <partOf rdf:resource="#monsters1" />
</Region>
```

The TransitiveProperty characteristic is attached to the property partOf. This property is used to attach the "sectionHeader1a" section to the parent section, "sectionHeader1". When the parent section is then attached to the main article, "monsters1", by the use of TransitiveProperty, the "sectionHeader1a" is also defined to be "part of" the top-level document. No special processing or understanding of the domain would be necessary to intuit this information because it's provided with the characteristic.

A second property characteristic is the SymmetricProperty. The logic for it is:

```
P(x,y) iff P(y,x)
```

With the new PostCon property, sections can be marked as peers to each other through the use of SymmetricProperty applied to a new predicate, sectionPeer:

```
<owl:ObjectProperty rdf:ID="sectionPeer">
  <rdf:type rdf:resource="&owl;SymmetricProperty" />
  <rdfs:domain rdf:resource="#Resource" />
  <rdfs:range rdf:resource="#Resource" />
</owl:ObjectProperty>
```

```
<Resource rdf:ID="sectionHeader1a">
  <partOf rdf:resource="#sectionHeader1" />
  <sectionPeer rdf:resource="#sectionHeader1b" />
</Resource>

<Resource rdf:ID="sectionHeader1b">
  <partOf rdf:resource="#sectionHeader1" />
  <sectionPeer rdf:resource="#sectionHeader1a" />
</Resource>
```

A third property characteristic is `FunctionalProperty`, with the logic:

```
P(x,y) and P(x,z) implies y = z
```

Earlier in the section on data types, we created a custom data type, `MovementType`, to specify that allowable values be within a given set. The data type was attached to a specific property, `movementType`, which then became functional (noted by `FunctionalProperty`) in that all movement types can be assigned only one value, and the value must be from the allowable types:

```
<owl:Class rdf:ID="MovementType" />

<owl:ObjectProperty rdf:ID="movementType">
    <rdf:type rdf:resource="&owl;FunctionalProperty" />
    <rdfs:domain rdf:resource="#ResourceMovement" />
    <rdf:range rdf:resource="#MovementType" />
</owl:ObjectProperty>
```

The `inverseOf` characteristic is pretty straightforward: a new property can be defined as the inverse of an existing property. The logic for it is:

```
P1(x,y) iff P2(y,x)
```

If `partOf` shows a child section's relationship to a parent section, then the property `hasChild` would define a parent section's relationship to one of its children:

```
<owl:ObjectProperty rdf:ID="hasChild">
    <owl:inverseOf rdf:resource="#partOf" />
</owl:ObjectProperty>
```

Finally, the last property characteristic is `InverseFunctionalProperty`, which combines the logic of both the `inverse` and the `FunctionalProperty`:

```
P(y,x) and P(z,x) implies y = z
```

We can consider `partOf` as functional (as defined by `FunctionalProperty`), because a section is part of another section, and that other section only (a functional constraint). And if `partOf` is functional, then the inverse functional equivalent of `partOf` would be the `hasChild` property:

```
<owl:ObjectProperty rdf:ID="partOf">
    <rdf:type rdf:resource="&owl;FunctionalProperty" />
</owl:ObjectProperty>

<owl:ObjectProperty rdf:ID="childOf">
    <rdf:type rdf:resource="&owl;InverseFunctionalProperty" />
```

```
    <owl:inverseOf rdf:resource="#partOf" />
  </owl:ObjectProperty>
```

Properties can be further refined through restrictions, discussed next.

Property restrictions

If property characteristics enhance reasoning by extending the meaning behind element relationships with each other, than property restrictions fine-tune the reasoning by restricting properties within specific contexts.

Returning to PostCon, the Resource class has two subclasses, ResourceMovement and
RelatedResource:

```
<owl:Class rdf:ID="Resource" />
<owl:Class rdf:ID="RelatedResource">
  <owl:subClassOf rdf:resource="#Resource" />
</owl:Class>
<owl:Class rdf:ID="ResourceMovement">
  <owl:subClassOf rdf:resource="#Resource" />
</owl:Class>
```

In the RDF Schema for PostCon, both of these classes would have "reason" as a
predicate, explaining the association between the classes. In addition,
ResourceMovement also has movementType.

Instead of having two different properties, we could have just the one—reason—
and then attach a property restriction—allValuesFrom—to it, restricting values for
this property to MovementType values only. The use of this restriction is demonstrated
in the following code:

```
<owl:Class rdf:ID="ResourceMovement">
  <owl:subClassOf rdf:resource="#Resource" />
  <rdfs:subClassOf>
   <owl:Restriction>
     <owl:onProperty rdf:resource="#reason" />
     <owl:allValuesFrom rdf:resource="#MovementType" />
   </owl:Restriction>
  </rdfs:subClassOf>
</owl:Class>
```

Restrictions differ from characteristics in that restrictions apply to a sub-set of the
data, rather than globally to all data. In this use of allValuesFrom, the restriction
applies to the reason property only when it's used within the ResourceMovement class,
not when its used in the RelatedResource class.

A less restricted version of allValuesFrom is someValuesFrom, used to specify that at
least one of the properties restricted, in this case reason, must point to a specific
MovementType.

Another restriction is cardinality. Cardinality indicates the exact number of individual instances of a property allowed within a class—not the maximum or minimum
number, but the exact number that must exist.

Returning to PostCon, each individual `ResourceMovement` can have one and only one `movementType` property. This restriction would be modeled in OWL with the following:

```
<owl:Class rdf:ID="ResourceMovement">
  <rdfs:subClassOf>
    <owl:Restriction>
      <owl:onProperty rdf:resource="#movementType"/>
      <owl:cardinality>1</owl:cardinality>
    </owl:Restriction>
  </rdfs:subClassOf>
</owl:Class>
```

According to the OWL Guide, OWL Lite can specify values of only 0 or 1 for the cardinality restriction. However, for OWL Full, in addition to the use of the cardinality restriction, `owl:maxCardinality` can be used to set an upper cardinality, while `owl:minCardinality` can be used to set the lower. Setting both defines a range.

The last property restriction is `hasValue`, used with a class to differentiate those with properties from a specific range. Again returning to `ResourceMovement`, the use of `hasValue` could be used to differentiate `ResourceMovement` from `RelatedResource`, by adding the restriction that `ResourceMovement` classes have a `movementType` pointing to the `MovementType` class:

```
<owl:Class rdf:ID="ResourceMovement">
  <rdfs:subClassOf>
    <owl:Restriction>
      <owl:onProperty rdf:resource="#movementType"/>
      <owl:hasValue rdf:resource="#MovementType" />
    </owl:Restriction>
  </rdfs:subClassOf>
</owl:Class>
```

The more uses of property characteristics and restrictions placed on objects in the ontology, the better able tools are to make strong inferences about the true meaning of the data being defined.

Complex Classes

More complex class relationships exist than just the simple hierarchy defined through the use of `subClassOf`. These relationships are managed through a set of properties that controls how one class relates to another. These class expressions, as OWL defines them, are based on typical set operations used elsewhere, such as in logic or math. All classes constructed using set operations, such as `intersectionOf`, are closed, explicitly stating the parameters of class membership for a specific class.

Intersection

An intersection of a class and one or more properties is created using the `intersectionOf` property. All members of a class defined with `intersectionOf` are explicitly defined by the intersection of the class membership and the property or properties specified.

One change that could be made to PostCon is to differentiate between types of resources, based on the assumption that different types of resources have different information associated with them. If we do classify resources in this manner, then we'll also want to explicitly state without equivocation which class each resource would belong in. In the following OWL definition, the new resource class, XMLResource, is restricted to members that belong to the Resource class and also belong to all things that are based on XML:

```
<owl:Class rdf:ID="XMLResource">
  <owl:intersectionOf rdf:parseType="Collection">
    <owl:Class rdf:about="#Resource" />
    <owl:Restriction>
      <owl:onProperty rdf:resource="#hasFormat" />
      <owl:hasValue rdf:resource="#XML" />
    </owl:Restriction>
  </owl:intersectionOf>
</owl:Class>
```

The XMLResource class consists of a class defining a set of properties, all of which can be used to describe something formatted as XML. The intersection would then be "Resource" and "things formatted as XML." The Collection parseType is a required attribute in the class definition because the class is being constructed to define a collection of like material.

Rather than base the intersection on a specific property, you can also just specify an intersection of classes. In the following, a new class, RSSXMLResource, is defined as the intersection between XMLResource and another new complex class, RSSResource:

```
<owl:Class rdf:ID="RSSXMLResource">
  <owl:intersectionOf rdf:parseType="Collection">
    <owl:Class rdf:about="#XMLResource" />
    <owl:Class rdf:about="#RSSResource" />
  </owl:intersectionOf>
</owl:Class>
```

Members of RSSXMLResource would be resources formatted as XML but based on some RSS vocabulary; RSS documents that are not XML formatted wouldn't be included, and neither would XML documents that aren't based on RSS. RSS 1.0 (RDF/RSS) would be a member of this class.

Union

The unionOf construct creates a class whose members combine the properties of both classes being joined. A demonstration of this is the following, which defines a new class, called WebpageResource. This combines the properties of XMLResource and a new class, HTMLResource:

```
<owl:Class rdf:ID="WebpageResource">
  <owl:unionOf rdf:parseType="Collection">
    <owl:Class rdf:about="#XMLResource" />
    <owl:Class rdf:about="#HTMLResouce" />
  </owl:unionOf>
</owl:Class>
```

XML, XHTML, and HTML pages would all be members of this class.

 As the guide notes, defining a class to be a subclass of two classes results in an intersection of the two classes. With `XMLResource` and `HTMLResource`, this would be an empty class because HTML, by its nature, is not an XML document.

Complement

A class that consists of all members of a specific domain that do not belong to a specific class can be created using the `complementOf` construct. Continuing our classification of PostCon resources, all web resources that aren't HTML, XML, or XHTML can be lumped into one class membership using a class definition like the following:

```
<owl:Class rdf:ID="WebResource" />
  <owl:Class rdf:ID="NotWebPage">
    <owl:complementOf rdf:resource="#WebpageResource" />
  </owl:Class>
```

According to the OWL documentation, `complementOf` is usually used with other set operations. With PostCon, this increasingly complex construct could be used to define a class that contains all members of resources that are not XML-formatted RSS with the following definition:

```
<owl:Class rdf:ID="NotRSSXMLResource">
  <owl:intersectionOf rdf:parseType="Collection">
    <owl:Class rdf:about="#Resource"/>
    <owl:Class>
      <owl:complementOf>
        <owl:Class rdf:ID="RSSXMLResource">
          <owl:intersectionOf rdf:parseType="Collection">
            <owl:Class rdf:about="#XMLResource" />
            <owl:Class rdf:about="#RSSResource" />
          </owl:intersectionOf>
        </owl:Class>
      </owl:complementOf>
    </owl:Class>
  </owl:intersectionOf>
</owl:Class>
```

If a circle were drawn around XML-formatted RSS files, everything outside of this circle that is a `Resource` would belong to `NotRSSXMLResource`.

Enumeration

An enumeration is a class with a predetermined, closed set of members. Applied to web resources, this could be an enumeration of graphics types supported at a particular web site, as shown in the following, using the OWL enumeration operator, `oneOf`:

```
<owl:Class rdf:ID="GraphicResource">
  <rdfs:subClassOf rdf:resource="#Resource"/>
```

```
    <owl:oneOf rdf:parseType="Collection">
      <owl:Thing rdf:about="#JPEG"/>
      <owl:Thing rdf:about="#PNG"/>
      <owl:Thing rdf:about="#GIF"/>
    </owl:oneOf>
  </owl:Class>
```

The list could, of course, be extended to include other graphics types. A member of
an enumerated class belongs to one, and only one, of the collection members.

Disjoint

Finally, the last complex class construction is the disjoint construct, which lists all of
the classes that a particular class is guaranteed not to be a member of. As an example, the following defines a new class, TextFile, guaranteed not to be a member of
the GraphicResource and VideoResource classes:

```
<owl:Class rdf:ID="TextFile">
  <rdfs:subClassOf rdf:resource="#Resource"/>
  <owl:disjointWith rdf:resource="#GraphicResource"/>
  <owl:disjointWith rdf:resource="#VideoResource"/>
</owl:Class>
```

The Complementary Nature of RDF and OWL

Previous sections barely skimmed the richness of OWL, though they have shown
that regardless of the complexity of the constructs, they remain valid RDF/XML. In
fact, if you open up the Wine ontology that the OWL group uses for its examples,
located at *http://www.w3.org/TR/owl-guide/wine.owl*, you'll find that it validates.
You'll want to turn on the graph option first, and you should be prepared to wait
because *wine.owl* is quite large.

So, when should you use just RDF Schema and when should you use OWL?

If you're defining a fairly simple vocabulary primarily for your own use (and I use
RDF/XML for a dozen different little applications at my site), and if you're concerned primarily with the striped nature of RDF/XML, you'll most likely want to just
define your vocabulary in RDF and RDFS.

However, if you're documenting a model of a specific domain and you hope to
encourage others to use it and, best of all, be able to use the data to make sophisticated queries, you're going to want to use OWL to take advantage of its many inferential enhancements.

Before we leave this chapter, we'll take a quick glance at a couple of editors specialized for ontologies. Take what you've learned in this chapter out for a spin.

Ontology Tools: Editors

Ontology editors can also be RDFS editors, but they usually have extended services and features to meet the increased demand in sophistication of the ontology. In this section, we'll look at two such editors: SMORE and Protégé.

SMORE—Semantic Markup, Ontology, and RDF Editor

Much of the effort on behalf of both RDF and OWL is predicated on the Semantic Web, so the lack of tools that connect traditional web creation tools such as a WYSI-WYG editor for HTML with support for newer technologies, such as an ontology editor, is rather surprising. However, SMORE—the Semantic Markup, Ontology, and RDF Editor—is an application that incorporates four separate applications into one to provide just such support. SMORE, another application written in Java, is one of the interesting products to come out of the Semantic Web Research Group, along with several converters, RDF scrapers, and other useful tools and utilities.

 The Semantic Web Research Group's web site is at *http://www. mindswap.org/*. You can download SMORE from *http://www. mindswap.org/~aditkal/editor.shtml*. The tool is freely available.

SMORE opens with an interface consisting of four separate windows within one frame. Each window contains a separate application: a web browser in one, a web ontology browser in another, a WYSIWYG HTML editor in a third, and a semantic data representation in the fourth. Figure 12-1 shows the tool just after it opens.

All four applications are integrated with one another. When examining the ontological class in the ontology browser, clicking on the source opens the RDF/XML for the class in the web browser; right-clicking on a term in the WYSIWYG HTML editor adds the term to the semantic data representation under development, and so on.

 Opening an HTML document in the editor caused the application to fail, throwing several Java exceptions. This should be fixed when this book hits the streets.

Documentation on using the tool can be found in Help.

Protégé

Protégé is a Java-based ontology editor that provides the mechanisms to create ontologies and then allows you to save them as plain text, into JDBC-accessible datastores, and as RDF/XML. Installation consists of downloading the tool and then

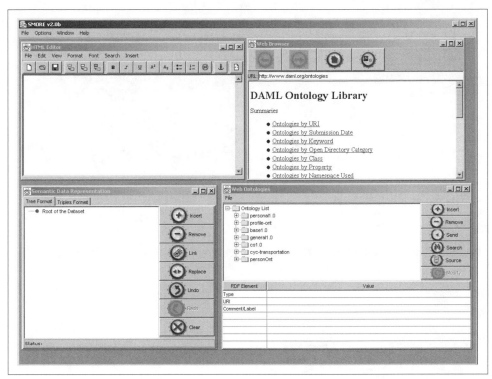

Figure 12-1. SMORE when it's first opened

clicking the installer that the Java applet in the installation page recommends for your system.

> The Protégé home page is at *http://protégé.standord.edu*, and the download page is at *http://protege.stanford.edu/download/prerelease/index.html*. The system has installers for, and been tested with, Windows, Mac OS X, AIX, Solaris, Linux, HP-UX, and generic Unix and other Java supportive platforms. I tested Version 1.8 for this chapter, within my Windows 2000 box. The extensive documentation can be viewed online at *http://protege.stanford.edu/useit.htm*l.

Figure 12-2 shows the editor when it's first opened up, with the existing demonstration project, Newspaper, loaded.

The tabbed interface allows you to define new classes and subclasses in the first page, in addition to adding properties (which the tool, in line with much of the ontology effort, calls *slots*). If a class has a key figure next to it, such as Person in Figure 12-2, clicking on the key displays or hides the class subclasses. Define a new

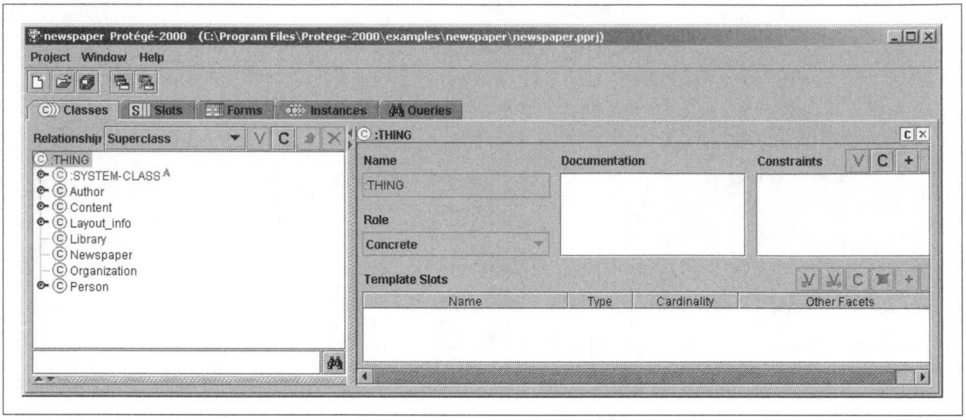

Figure 12-2. Screenshot of Protégé after it opens

class by clicking the high-level THING and then clicking the C toolbar item in the left toolbar, just over the Classes.

The next tab shows the slots (properties) defined in the ontology, as shown in Figure 12-3.

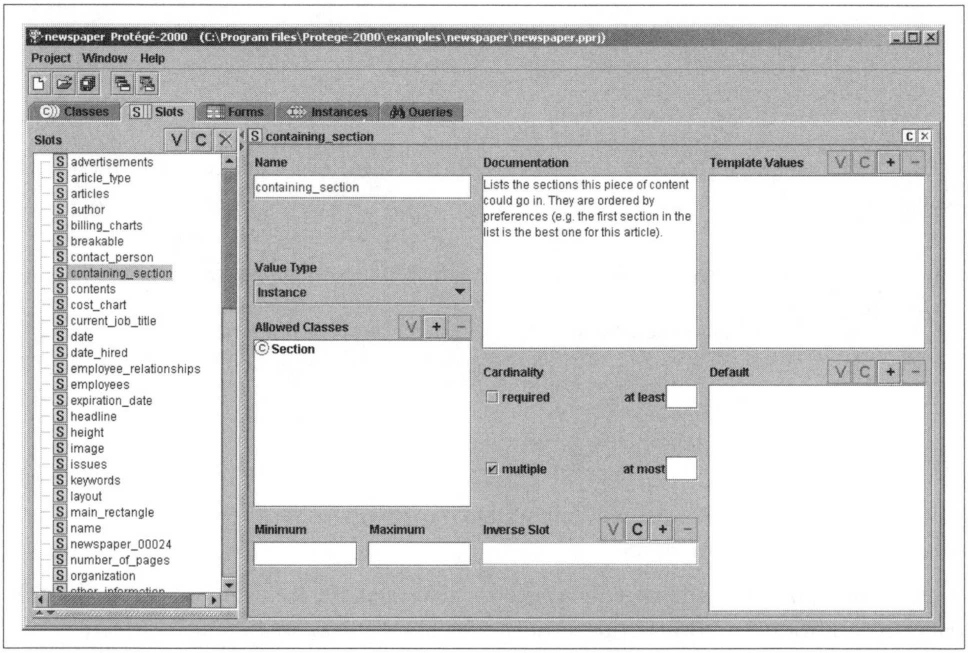

Figure 12-3. The Slots tab on the editor

For each property, you can specify a name, provide documentation, restrict the range of classes, specify its cardinality, and create an inverse slot (equivalent to the inverseOf property characteristic described before).

The next tab provides a form designer window that allows you to define a form used to record individual ontology members (instances). Clicking on a class in the left window opens the default (or saved customized) form in the right. At that point, you can do things such as move the form fields around, resize them, and so on.

The last tab is where the forms customized in the previous tab are displayed, allowing you to record instance data for the ontology. In addition, data that's already been recorded displays when the form is opened, as shown in Figure 12-4, including a mapping between a higher-level class instance and repeating properties. Note in the form that data entry doesn't have to be limited to plain text fields.

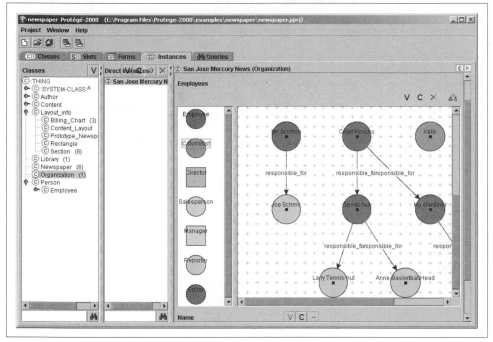

Figure 12-4. Tab to enter instance data

Finally, the last tab is used to enter queries about the data stored within the project. As with other query systems against RDF data described in earlier chapters, the queries are built as triples—subject, object, and predicate. Several can be combined, and a query can even be used as the object in a triple, as shown in Figure 12-5.

Again, the project can be saved at any time and can also be exported as the previously mentioned RDF/XML, JDBC, or text. In addition, the tool can also generate

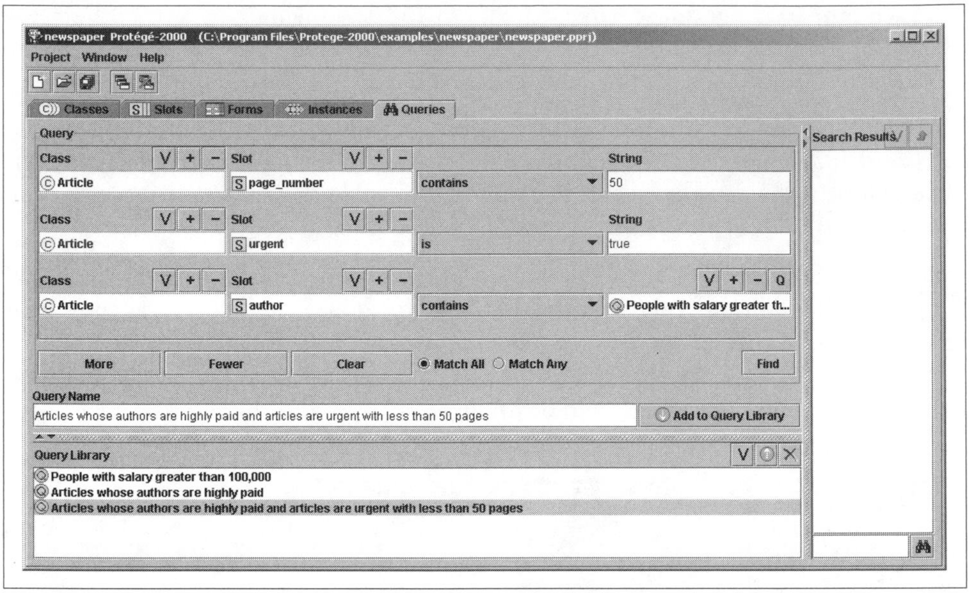

Figure 12-5. Queries tab with query made of three triples, one of which has a query as object

HTML of the contents, with all the proper hypertext links between classes, sub-classes, slots, and so on maintained. Additionally, there's a metrics function available from the Project menu that provides instance information.

This is one fun tool.

## CHAPTER 13

Subscription and Aggregation with RSS

If vocabularies such as the Dublin Core can be considered children of RDF, then RSS is the specification's rebellious teenager. RSS, or RDF Site Summary (and sometimes Rich Site Summary or Really Simple Syndication) is primarily used for syndication and aggregation. O'Reilly's news service, Meerkat, with its continuously updating news headlines, uses RSS for its data feeds.

RSS is also the most prevalent implementation of RDF in the world at this time, primarily through its use in weblogging and with popular online media outfits such as BBC News, Salon, Wired, and others. (If you're not familiar with weblogging, weblogs are online journals that are usually updated daily, with most recent entries showing at the top of the page in a reverse chronological order. Weblogging, or *blogging* as it's frequently termed, has increased in popularity in the last few years, and estimates now put the number of weblogs at more than 500,000 in the world.)

In order to keep up with your favorite news sources or weblogs, you can visit each one in turn, or you can subscribe to the site's syndication feed. This feed contains the most recent weblog entries, their titles, the URL for each entry, and a brief description of the article or posting, all documented in RSS.

This chapter takes a detailed look at the RSS specification and its history as well as example RSS feeds. In addition, the chapter will also take a look at popular aggregators—tools that process RSS—as well as examples of how to process the content.

 Access the RSS 1.0 specification at *http://purl.org/rss/1.0/*. The RSS Working Group's group discussion can be found at *http://groups. yahoo.com/group/rss-dev/*.

RSS: Quick History

Both a varied history and some controversy surround RSS. Rather than spend time on this in the book, I'll point you to a Yahoo group's RSS Development Group message that details much of it (at *http://groups.yahoo.com/group/rss-dev/message/1136*).

The concept of a providing data in a defined format in order to support news feeds and data channels didn't originate with RSS. For instance, the use of RSS—in any format—was predated by Microsoft's CDF, which I used at one time to provide data channels of my web sites.

RSS originally stood for RDF Site Summary and was a vocabulary of RDF/XML developed at Netscape several years ago for the company's implementation of channels. The use of RDF in RSS, as well as in earliest implementations of Mozilla, was due to R.V. Guha, an original RDF pioneer. When Netscape's attention was diverted to other matters—or should we say when AOL decided the support for RSS wasn't an effective profit center—RSS was left orphaned. This actually had a physical impact, because one result of this abandonment was Netscape pulling the DTD for RSS 0.9/0.91 that people used to use to validate their RSS XML.

Other people and companies took up the interest in the specification, including Userland's Dave Winer, a principal contributor to the earliest RSS specification. It was Winer's and Userland's use of RSS that sparked a growth of RSS, first within Userland, then eventually outside of the company.

These versions of RSS did not depend on RDF, but instead were based on an RSS-specific XML vocabulary. The specification released in December 2000, RSS 1.0, is based on RDF. One reason for switching back to an RDF base was to inherit the rich extensibility built into RDF, including the use of namespaces to handle element collision. The RSS Group saw in namespaces the answer to the problem of how to extend RSS without having to continually release new versions of the specification. Another reason is that the information included in RSS feeds—such as article title, author, excerpt and so on—is a rich source of information. By implementing RSS within an RDF framework, there's hope that the information can be merged with other RDF vocabularies and uses.

Today, RSS 1.0 is solidly RDF based. However, non-RDF RSS documents are currently in use throughout the Internet, primarily based on Userland's current RSS specification. The most recent such non-RDF specification was RSS 2.0, released late in 2002.

 For a more detailed and comprehensive look at RSS and its history as well as non-RDF implementations, please see the O'Reilly book *Content Syndication with XML and RSS*, by Ben Hammersley. Ben covers both branches of RSS, the RDF and the non-RDF versions.

RSS 1.0: A Quick Introduction

RSS 1.0 is an RDF vocabulary and as such must follow the rules and specifications associated with RDF. However, the developers of RSS 1.0 wanted to constrain the specification's XML syntax in order to simplify the development of tools and technologies to generate and consume RSS. Based on this, RSS always validates as proper RDF, but a non-RSS RDF model won't necessarily validate as proper RSS. Validation is constrained from RSS to RDF, but not the reverse.

Example 13-1 shows a portion of the RSS for my own weblog (generated by the weblogging tool Movable Type, found at *http://www.movabletype.org*).

Example 13-1. RSS 1.0 generated by Movable Type

```
<?xml version="1.0"?>

<rdf:RDF xmlns:rdf="http://www.w3.org/1999/02/22-rdf-syntax-ns#" xmlns:dc="http://purl.
org/dc/elements/1.1/" xmlns="http://purl.org/rss/1.0/">

<channel rdf:about="http://weblog.burningbird.net/">
<title>Burningbird</title>
<link>http://weblog.burningbird.net/</link>
<description></description>

<items>
<rdf:Seq>
<rdf:li rdf:resource="http://weblog.burningbird.net/archives/000472.php" />
<rdf:li rdf:resource="http://weblog.burningbird.net/archives/000471.php" />
</rdf:Seq>
</items>

</channel>

<item rdf:about="http://weblog.burningbird.net/archives/000472.php">
<title>Serendipity, all over again</title>
<description>When I wrote the previous posting, &quot;How Green is my
Valley&quot;, I referenced both my old hometown, Kettle Falls,
Washington, and a posting by Loren, otherwise known as In a Dark Time.
At the time that I read Loren's weblog,...
</description>
<link>http://weblog.burningbird.net/archives/000472.php</link>
<dc:subject>Virtual Neighborhood</dc:subject>
<dc:creator>shelley</dc:creator>
<dc:date>2002-08-23T15:07:57-06:00</dc:date>
</item>

<item rdf:about="http://weblog.burningbird.net/archives/000471.php">
<title>How Green is my Valley</title>
<description>The housing complex that I live in is quite large, with small
buildings consisting of a combination of townhomes and flats. One of the nicest
aspects of the place is all the trees and plants and green areas,
including our...
</description>
<link>http://weblog.burningbird.net/archives/000471.php</link>
<dc:subject>Mother Nature</dc:subject>
<dc:creator>shelley</dc:creator>
<dc:date>2002-08-23T12:49:24-06:00</dc:date>
</item>

</rdf:RDF>
```

In the example, two weblog entries are described. The required RDF enclosing tag is included, and each RSS item is defined first as an RDF container element, and later given a title and description, as well as entry author, subject (category), and date. The content is valid RDF, as you'll find if you run it through the RDF Validator (described in Chapter 3).

However, if you're used to working with RDF, you may notice that the primary element of interest in the document isn't defined using the RDF Description tag, as was demonstrated in many of the examples in previous chapters. Instead, a typed node of channel is used. The RSS Working Group used this approach to simplify processing of the RSS. By using a typed node, standard XML processing can pull information from this RSS file without having to be aware of any more complex RDF mechanisms. Additionally, the use of the typed node also ensures backward compatibility with RSS 0.9 (though not with RSS 0.91 and the other Userland RSS releases).

This RSS feed also makes use of one core RSS module, the specialized Dublin Core module, discussed later in the chapter.

A Detailed Look at the Specification

RSS is first and foremost valid RDF, requiring the enclosing RDF element. Other RSS-specific elements that are required are channel, title, link, and one or more item elements. The remaining RSS elements are optional.

 The RSS RDFS can be found at *http://web.resource.org/rss/1.0/schema. rdf/*. Examining this, you'll see that many of the RSS properties discussed in this section are actually subproperties of related DC properties, such as TITLE, URL, DESCRIPTION, and so on.

Certain allowable features of RDF are restricted within RSS, primarily to simplify the tool builder's task. For instance, at the time of this writing, repeating properties (or *subelements* as they are termed in the RSS spec), which are allowed in RDF, are restricted in RSS. This restriction means that you couldn't list multiple subelements of the higher-level item element, such as multiple DC subject entries (which would be a naturally occurring repetitive element). However, the RSS Working Group is working toward removing this restriction or at least having each RSS module writer explicitly specify where repeating properties are allowed.

Another RSS-specific restriction is that each higher-level element must have an rdf: about attribute (as shown in Example 13-1 for the item and channel elements), and the URI contained in this attribute must follow URL naming conventions (i.e., be an http, ftp, mailto, etc. type of URI). Remaining restrictions are based on the RSS elements, as discussed in the next several sections.

channel

The `channel` element surrounds the data being described in the document. It's equivalent to an RDF typed node and features starting and ending tags. The only required attribute is `rdf:about`, containing the URL of the resource being described:

```
<?xml version="1.0"?>

<rdf:RDF xmlns:rdf="http://www.w3.org/1999/02/22-rdf-syntax-ns#" xmlns:dc="http://
purl.org/dc/elements/1.1/" xmlns:sy="http://purl.o
rg/rss/1.0/modules/syndication/" xmlns="http://purl.org/rss/1.0/">

<channel rdf:about="http://weblog.burningbird.net/">
...
</channel>
...
</rdf:RDF>
```

You could extend the `channel` element with new attributes, and the element should still validate as both RDF and RSS. However, a better approach would be to check whether one of the RSS modules has the data elements you need to describe your data and to use that module instead. If not, you may want to consider submitting your own recommended modules (as described later in the section titled "Extending the Specification Through Modules").

title, link, and description

The `title`, `link`, and `description` elements are all required subelements of `channel`. The RSS specification has a recommended length for each: 40 characters or fewer for `title`, and 500 characters or fewer for `link` and `description`.

```
<?xml version="1.0"?>

<rdf:RDF xmlns:rdf="http://www.w3.org/1999/02/22-rdf-syntax-ns#" xmlns:dc="http://
purl.org/dc/elements/1.1/" xmlns:sy="http://purl.o
rg/rss/1.0/modules/syndication/" xmlns="http://purl.org/rss/1.0/">

<channel rdf:about="http://weblog.burningbird.net/">
<title>Burningbird</title>
<link>http://weblog.burningbird.net/</link>
<description></description>
...
</channel>
...
</rdf:RDF>
```

The elements are required, but they may contain no data, as the `description` element in this example demonstrates.

All three elements are PCDATA, which means the character data is parsed for things such as named entities (i.e., < for < and so on), but the data cannot contain child elements. This also means you *cannot* use markup in these elements. When a suggestion was made about including XHTML or some other form of XML within the `title` element, the RSS Working Group strongly recommended against this technique.

The `link` element doesn't necessarily repeat the URI of the item being described. Instead, it contains the URL of the HTML that contains the rendering of the item begin described (whether this is the channel, the image, or a specific item). For the vast majority of uses of RSS, the link duplicates the URL given as a URI in the `rdf:` `about` attribute. However, this can sometimes differ. For instance, a URI for a site might be:

```
http://somesite.com
```

but the link to the actual material might be:

```
http://www.somesite.com/index.html
```

The site may choose to use a different URI to represent the site contents, reflecting the independence of the URI from the actual URL. Why? Could be because the site wants to change the channel site at some point, perhaps linking it to:

```
http://channel.somesite.com/index.php
```

but the site URI remains the same, and therefore consistent.

`title`, `link`, and `description` are required subelements of `item`, `textinput`, and `image`, in addition to being subelements of `channel`.

items

The `items` element contains an `rdf:Seq` container, which contains a reference to each item described in the RSS document:

```
<?xml version="1.0"?>

<rdf:RDF xmlns:rdf="http://www.w3.org/1999/02/22-rdf-syntax-ns#" xmlns:dc="http://
purl.org/dc/elements/1.1/" xmlns:sy="http://purl.o
rg/rss/1.0/modules/syndication/" xmlns="http://purl.org/rss/1.0/">

<channel rdf:about="http://weblog.burningbird.net/">
<title>Burningbird</title>
<link>http://weblog.burningbird.net/</link>
<description></description>

<items>
<rdf:Seq>
<rdf:li rdf:resource="http://weblog.burningbird.net/archives/000472.php" />
<rdf:li rdf:resource="http://weblog.burningbird.net/archives/000471.php" />
</rdf:Seq>
</items>

</channel>
...
</rdf:RDF>
```

The `rdf:Seq` container is used for `items` to maintain the order of how the items are processed. News aggregators usually display news in reverse chronological order—latest news displayed at the top of the list—and the sequence helps maintain this order.

The RSS specification requires that there be at least one `item` listed in the `items` container. Though there is no upper limit specified for RSS 1.0, it's a good idea to restrict the number to 15 or fewer, to ensure backward compatibility with RSS .9x.

During recent discussions about the possibility of simplifying RSS 1.0, one specific area was targeted: `items`. Why? Most RSS generation tools and aggregators have problems with the RDF container. It wasn't so much that the concept of container was difficult, as it was having to list the items out first within `items` and then process the items again as individual `item` elements. However, without repeating properties, there was no way of managing multiply repeating elements except to use the container.

Several suggestions have been made to simplify the syntax, including to support repeating properties and to eliminate the use of `rdf:Seq`. Example 13-2 shows a different RSS 1.0 document; this one utilizes repeating properties and eliminates the use of the container, demonstrating how this could change the appearance of RSS 1.0 files.

Example 13-2. Simplified RDF/RSS syntax

```
<rdf:RDF xmlns:rdf="http://www.w3.org/1999/02/22-rdf-syntax-ns#" xmlns:dc="http://purl.
org/dc/elements/1.1/" xmlns="http://purl.org/
rss/1.0/">

<channel rdf:about="http://weblog.burningbird.net/">
<title>Burningbird</title>
<link>http://weblog.burningbird.net/</link>
<description></description>

<hasitem>
<item rdf:about="http://weblog.burningbird.net/archives/000514.php">
<link>http://weblog.burningbird.net/archives/000514.php</link>
<title>Myths About RDF/RSS</title>
<description>Lots of discussion about the direction that RSS is going to take,
which I think is good. However, the first thing that happens any time a
conversation about RSS occurs is people start questioning the use of RDF within the...</
description>
<dc:subject>Technology</dc:subject>
<dc:creator>shelley</dc:creator>
<dc:date>2002-09-06T00:53:16-06:00</dc:date>
</item>
</hasitem>
<hasitem>
<item rdf:about="http;//weblog.burningbird.net/archives/000515.php">
<link>http://weblog.burningbird.net/archives/000515.php</link>
<title>ThreadNeedle Status</title>
<description>I provided a status on ThreadNeedle at the QuickTopic discussion
```

Example 13-2. Simplified RDF/RSS syntax (continued)

```
group. I wish I had toys for you to play with, but no such luck. To those who
were counting on this technology...</description>
<dc:subject>Technology</dc:subject>
<dc:creator>shelley</dc:creator>
<dc:date>2002-09-06T00:19:28-06:00</dc:date>
</item>
</hasitem>
</channel>

</rdf:RDF>
```

I also created a small PHP program to process the simplified RDF/RSS, shown in
Example 13-3. The interesting thing about the code is that it also worked with Userland RSS as well as the original RSS 1.0, the point being that aggregators aren't the
tools that have problems with RDF containers—it's the generation end where things
get complicated.

*Example 13-3. PHP program to process RSS 1.0, RSS 0.9x, and simplified
RSS 1.0 content*

```php
<?php

$insideitem = false;
$tag = "";
$title = "";
$author = "";
$link = "";
$description = "";

function startElement($parser, $name, $attrs) {
        global $insideitem, $tag, $title, $author, $link, $description;
        if ($insideitem) {
                $tag = $name;
        } elseif ($name == "ITEM") {
                $insideitem = true;
        }
}

function endElement($parser, $name) {
        global $insideitem, $tag, $title, $author, $link, $description;
        if ($name == "ITEM") {
            printf("<p class='%s'>", trim($read));
            printf("<a class='%s' href='%s'><span style='font-weight: bold'>%s</span></a>
",
                        trim($read),trim($link),htmlspecialchars(trim($title)));
            printf("<br />by %s", htmlspecialchars(trim($author)));
            printf("<br />Description: %s", htmlspecialchars(trim($description)));
            printf("</p>");
            $title = "";
            $author = "";
            $link = "";
```

```
            $description = "";
            $insideitem = false;
        }
}

function characterData($parser, $data) {
        global $insideitem, $tag, $title, $link, $author, $description;
        if ($insideitem) {
        switch ($tag) {
                case "TITLE":
                $title .= $data;
                break;
                case "DC:CREATOR":
                $author .= $data;
                break;
                case "LINK":
                $link .= $data;
                break;
                case "DESCRIPTION":
                $description .= $data;
                break;
                }
        }
}

$xml_parser = xml_parser_create( );
xml_set_element_handler($xml_parser, "startElement", "endElement");
xml_set_character_data_handler($xml_parser, "characterData");
$fp = fopen("http://weblog.burningbird.net/index.rdf","r")
        or die("Error reading RSS data.");
while ($data = fread($fp, 4096))
        xml_parse($xml_parser, $data, feof($fp))
                or die(sprintf("XML error: %s at line %d",
                        xml_error_string(xml_get_error_code($xml_parser)),
                        xml_get_current_line_number($xml_parser)));
fclose($fp);
xml_parser_free($xml_parser);

?>
```

At this time, debate on simplification of RSS 1.0 is currently underway within the Working Group.

image

If there is an image associated with the HTML rendering of the item described in the channel, its URL and associated information are described in the image element with the required subelements: title, url, and link:

```
<image rdf:about="http://weblog.burningbird.net/mm/birdflame.gif">
    <title>Burningbird</title>
```

```
<link>http://weblog.burningbird.net</link>
<url>http://weblog.burningbird.net/mm/birdflame.gif</url>
</image>
```

With this RSS, the item described has a URI of `http://weblog.burningbird.net/mm/birdflame.gif`, a URL that's the same as the URI, a title of `Burningbird` (consider it to be equivalent to the ALT tag of an HTML IMG tag), and the URI of the page where the image is displayed.

textinput

The `textinput` element describes an XHTML `textinput` form element somehow associated with the RSS, such as a form submitting a subscription to an RSS feed. Though maintained for backward compatibility with RSS 0.9, the RSS Working Group is recommending that this element be deprecated for RSS 1.0—a wise decision in my opinion.

The `textinput` element doesn't provide useful information about the item being described, and its meaning is overloaded, as is mentioned in the RSS specification. For instance, is the element used to describe a form element to subscribe to a feed? Or is it being used for search? In addition, form elements for processing RSS data are inappropriate embedded within the data itself. This is equivalent to embedding an application form within the data the form accesses in an Oracle database.

However, if you do see the `textinput` element used, it requires `title`, `description`, `link`, and `name` subelements. The `name` subelement is unique to `textinput` and contains the XHTML form element's name.

item

RSS provides a method for describing groups of related items; each item within the specification is documented with the `item` tag. This tag is the key element, the heart and soul if you will, of RSS.

The required subelements for `item` are `title`, `description`, and `link`. Additional elements can be added using RSS modules, but these three subelements must be present for the RSS to validate as RSS:

```
<item rdf:about="http://weblog.burningbird.net/archives/000472.php">
<title>Serendipity, all over again</title>
<description>When I wrote the previous posting, &quot;How Green is my
Valley&quot;, I referenced both my old hometown, Kettle Falls,
Washington, and a posting by Loren, otherwise known as In a Dark Time.
At the time that I read Loren's weblog,...
</description>
<link>http://weblog.burningbird.net/archives/000472.php</link>
<dc:subject>Virtual Neighborhood</dc:subject>
<dc:creator>shelley</dc:creator>
<dc:date>2002-08-23T15:07:57-06:00</dc:date>
</item>
```

As you can see, there really aren't that many core elements within the RSS specification, as the Working Group decided to keep the specification simple and allow additions through the use of modules, discussed next.

Extending the Specification Through Modules

When writing a specification, or a standard, the authors can take one of two approaches: they can try to capture the entire world encompassed by the specification, a process that can take years, or they can create a specification that has a minimal set of elements and provide a mechanism to allow for extensions. The RSS Working Group opted for the latter option—start small, and provide a carefully defined extension mechanism. For RSS, the extension mechanism is the module.

RSS modules are sets of elements that are delimited from other modules through use of XML namespaces. Different modules can have the same element, and both can be used in RSS without fear of collision as long as each module has its own namespace. The following is the namespace declaration for the Syndication module:

```
xmlns:sy="http://purl.org/rss/1.0/modules/syndication/"
```

The use of namespaces in RSS is no different than the use of namespaces in more general RDF. The primary difference between the two is that new namespaces are generally used to define relatively complete RDF vocabularies.

According to the RSS 1.0 modules guide (found at *http://groups.yahoo.com/group/rss-dev/files/Modules/modules.html*), module designers should narrow the focus of their module to a specific need. The premise behind this is that many small modules are more manageable and more targeted than a few big, all-encompassing modules. The guidelines also recommend following a simple (flat) model for new modules over a rich (nested, complex) module whenever possible, so that modules are more easily mixed and managed together.

One final rule for module developers is a fairly significant one that has to do with the `rdf:parseType` attribute; if this attribute is set to a value of `"Literal"`, then it can contain any type of XML including non-RDF-compliant XML. The reason for this "loophole" in the RSS specification is to allow modules to be added without strict compliance to the rules governing the use of RDF.

An example of the use of `rdf:parseType` within RSS is the following, pulled from the modules guideline document:

```
<dc:creator rdf:parseType="Literal">
  <name>
    <firstname>John</firstname>
    <middle_initial>Q.</middle_initial>
    <lastname>Public</lastname>
  </name>
</dc:creator>
```

In this example, the data contained within the `dc:creator` element is treated as a literal and the RSS/RDF parsers will return all of the data as one large string.

 The use of `parseType="Literal"` cuts off the XML contained within the element from full integration into the RDF, because individual elements contained in the data aren't discretely accessible. In my opinion, this shortcut defeats the purpose of having a metalanguage.

The RSS Modules

RSS consists of three basic or core modules as well as the module extension mechanism just described. For the most part, the three core modules will fit most data needs. However, specialized business data and/or processing may require new elements.

Core: Syndication, Content, and Dublin Core

The Syndication module provides information, such as the update frequency of the data, for tool builders. Rather than an RSS aggregator having to test a data source at set time periods, it can access the Syndication data and update only when the data is scheduled to change.

Table 13-1 contains the Syndication elements. The namespace for Syndication is `xmlns:sy="http://purl.org/rss/1.0/modules/syndication/"`. The elements are sub-elements of the `channel` element, which means they apply to the data in the RSS document as a whole, rather than individual items.

Table 13-1. Syndication elements

Element	Purpose	Data
updatePeriod	Frequency of update of data	Hourly | daily | weekly | monthly | yearly
updateFrequency	Frequency of updates within time period	Integer
updateBase	Based date combined with period and frequency to determine updates	PCDATA

Example 13-4 shows a simplified RDF/RSS file demonstrating the use of the Syndication elements. This file is actually generated from a merge of several RDF/RSS files using an application built in Perl that I'll demonstrate later in the chapter. I've simplified the file to show only one item to restrict the size of the example. The Syndication elements are bolded.

Example 13-4. RSS demonstrating use of Syndication Elements

```
<rdf:RDF
 xmlns:rdf="http://www.w3.org/1999/02/22-rdf-syntax-ns#"
 xmlns="http://purl.org/rss/1.0/"
 xmlns:dc="http://purl.org/dc/elements/1.1/"
```

Example 13-4. RSS demonstrating use of Syndication Elements (continued)

```
  xmlns:taxo="http://purl.org/rss/1.0/modules/taxonomy/"
  xmlns:syn="http://purl.org/rss/1.0/modules/syndication/"
>

<channel rdf:about="http://burningbird.net">
    <title>Burningbird Network</title>
    <link>http://burningbird.net</link>
    <description>Burningbird: Burning online since 1995</description>
    <dc:language>en-us</dc:language>
    <dc:rights>Copyright 1995-2003, Shelley Powers, Burningbird</dc:rights>
    <dc:publisher>shelleyp@burningbird.net</dc:publisher>
    <dc:creator>shelleyp@burningbird.net</dc:creator>
    <dc:subject>writing,technology,art,photography,science,environment,politics</dc:
subject>
    <syn:updatePeriod>hourly</syn:updatePeriod>
    <syn:updateFrequency>1</syn:updateFrequency>
    <syn:updateBase>1901-01-01T00:00+00:00</syn:updateBase>
    <items>
        <rdf:Seq>
            <rdf:li rdf:resource="http://rdf.burningbird.net/archives/000853.htm" />
        </rdf:Seq>
    </items>
    <image rdf:resource="http://burningbird.net/mm/birdflame.gif" />
</channel>
<image rdf:about="http://burningbird.net/mm/birdflame.gif">
    <title>Burningbird</title>
    <url>http://burningbird.net/mm/birdflame.gif</url>
    <link>http://burningbird.net/</link>
    <dc:creator>Shelley Powers</dc:creator>
</image>
<item rdf:about="http://rdf.burningbird.net/archives/000853.htm">
    <title>Corrected chapters 6 and 9 uploaded</title>
    <link>http://rdf.burningbird.net/archives/000853.htm</link>
    <description>I found some small errors in the schema from chapters 6 and 9 and have
uploaded corrected chapters for both.
    </description>
    <dc:creator>yasd</dc:creator>
    <dc:date>2003-01-25T10:22:02-06:00</dc:date>
</item>
</rdf:RDF>
```

The Content module provides information about the format of the data contained in the RSS document. This includes space for comments about the data. The namespace declaration is xmlns:content="http://purl.org/rss/1.0/modules/content".

Table 13-2 lists the Content elements. Note that at the time of this writing, the content:encoded element hadn't yet been approved by the RSS Working Group.

Table 13-2. Content module elements

Element	Purpose	Data
items	Container for item	Subelement of RSS `item` or `channel`
item	Provides a description of containing element	PCDATA
format	Format of item	Empty element with `rdf:resource` pointing to URI of format
rdf:value	Used if URI is not provided with `content:item`	CDATA
encoding	Encoding of item	Optional empty element with `rdf:resource` pointing to URI of encoding format

The content:encoded element is used to wrap the individual RSS feed item as CDATA-encoded values. Rather than provide excerpts, content:encoded tends to have the entire article or item, rather than just one excerpt. Of course, one of the problems with something such as this is republication rights—if the complete article is provided in the RSS feed, can it be republished in an aggregation that is publicly accessible?

 The issue of republication and rights is covered when we look at Creative Commons licensing and its use of RDF/XML in Chapter 14.

The Dublin Core RSS module is an RSS-standardized version of the Dublin Core RDF (discussed in Chapter 6). The RSS namespace for this module is xmlns:dc="http://purl.org/dc/elements/1.1/". Though made available as part of the RSS specification, the elements as described in Chapter 6 are no different here, so I won't repeat the list. An example of their use with RSS can be seen in the RSS associated with my weblog feed:

```
<item rdf:about="http://weblog.burningbird.net/archives/000479.php">
<title>Today is for Working</title>
<description>
The best part of getting up early is watching the sun rise.
Today is for working, it is. Today is for nose down and
finishing tasks and making milestones. I've marked out in my mind tasks
to accomplish with each...
</description>
<link>http://weblog.burningbird.net/archives/000479.php</link>
<dc:subject>Life in General</dc:subject>
<dc:creator>shelley</dc:creator>
<dc:date>2002-08-26T05:13:03-06:00</dc:date>
</item>
```

The Dublin Core elements are also used in my Favorite Books application, described in the section titled "Build Your Own RSS Consumer."

Currently the Dublin Core elements usually contain CDATA values (i.e., string literals), but the data type definition for the elements is all PCDATA. The Working Group is looking at the possibility of merging the use of Dublin Core RSS elements with that of the Taxonomy module (discussed in the next section).

The Dublin Core elements are fully defined in the document, "Dublin Core Element Set, Version 1.1" located at *http://dublincore.org/documents/1999/07/02/dces/*.

Extended Modules

Several extended RSS modules describe information that ranges from discussion threads to companies to email and taxonomies. At the time of this writing, the only modules that have been accepted as standard are those just described: the core modules Syndication, Content, and Dublin Core.

Approved and pending modules can be found at *http://web.resource.org/rss/1.0/modules/* and as part of the *dmoz* Open Directory project, *http://dmoz.org/Reference/Libraries/Library_and_Information_Science/Technical_Services/Cataloguing/Metadata/RDF/Applications/RSS/Specifications/RSS1.0_Modules/*.

I won't list each individual module as none been accepted fully into the RSS 1.0 specification, and the list is changeable. However, before proceeding to look at the tools that work with RSS 1.0, I want to digress for a moment and talk about the concepts behind extended modules.

The idea of using modules to extend the RSS 1.0 specification, without having to modify or edit the specification directly, is a good one; new modules, such as one for *slashdot.com*-related data (mod_slash), mod_dcterms for Qualified Dublin Core metadata, and linking (mod_link) are based on this. By using namespaces to differentiate between the modules, one can easily add a new module without impacting on the others. However, this very simplicity is a danger in and of itself.

The whole purpose behind namespace support for RDF was to allow the combination of multiple RDF vocabularies without collision between vocabulary elements. The assumption behind this was that each vocabulary was both comprehensive and complete in its description of the business data the vocabulary defines.

However, there is a subtle difference between this original purpose for namespaces in RDF (and in XML) and their use in RSS 1.0. Rather than namespaces being seen as a way of combining rich and complete vocabularies, they're seen as a way of adding new data easily and quickly—and that's not always a good thing.

A case in point: during the discussions related to RDF/RSS (RSS 1.0) and non-RDF RSS (Userland RSS or RSS 2.0), one issue that came up was how to redirect RSS aggregators to new locations for feeds when the feeds were moved. Suggestions were made to use `mod_dcterms` for this purpose, but this wasn't necessarily compatible with the non-RDF RSS. Another suggestion was to create a module that contained one element for RDF RSS and one element for non-RDF RSS. This was a clear violation of both the concepts and the philosophy for namespaces within RDF (or within the larger world of XML).

The idea wasn't followed through on but does demonstrate the danger behind viewing modules as workarounds rather than complete and independent RDF vocabularies that can exist outside of the RSS 1.0 specification.

RSS Aggregators

Newspapers, magazines, and other traditional forms of publication are increasingly putting their data online. Add to this the steadily growing number of weblogs, and you have an enormous pool of information sources to draw on.

To help in this process, many of these publications publish RSS files providing headlines, entry links, and brief descriptions of newly published writing. News aggregators gather this data from numerous sources, presenting it to you in one page for quick perusal. If you see a story of interest, you can then click on the provided link to get to the publication.

This section takes a look at three popular aggregators: one Mac-only aggregator (NetNewsWire), one cross-platform desktop-based reader (AmphetaDesk), one web based (Meerkat), and one Mac-only aggregator (NetNewsWire). First, though, a brief discussion about RSS autodiscovery is in order.

 At its simplest, you can view RSS files in a web browser, formatting the data with an associated stylesheet, though you won't have the aggregation capability with this approach.

RSS Autodiscovery

How do you discover an RSS file, RDF based or otherwise? A person could embed a graphic or a link to the file in every page that has an associated RSS file, but this forces the person to add the button manually and the subscriber to go to the linked page and then add it as an RSS feed. A better approach is to use RSS autodiscovery.

RSS autodiscovery is enabled by adding a `link` element in your primary web page that provides the link to your syndication RSS. The HTML format is as follows:

```
<link rel="alternate" type="application/rss+xml" title="RSS" href="url/to/rss/file">
```

In my weblog, the autodiscovery is set to the following, using the XHTML version of `link`—the preferred approach:

```
<link rel="alternate" type="application/rss+xml" title="RSS" href="http://weblog.
burningbird.net/index.rdf" />
```

With autodiscovery, your readers can just provide the web page URL to the aggregator that supports autodiscovery, and the tool uses this to find the RSS file on its own. Note that the format of the link must be consistent—the only thing that should change is the URL to the RSS file. Also note that this link should go in your document's HEAD section.

AmphetaDesk

AmphetaDesk is a news aggregator that resides on your (Linux, Windows, or Mac OS) computer, and that touches RSS files at set frequencies looking for updates. Its creator is Kevin Hemenway, who goes by the pseudonym of Morbus Iff.

 AmphetaDesk is open source and freely available, supported only by donations (download and read more about the application at *http:// www.disobey.com/amphetadesk/* and the open source project at *http:// sourceforge.net/projects/amphetadesk/*).

In addition to creating software such as AmphetaDesk, Kevin is also a prolific author of both books and articles, primarily for O'Reilly. Kevin's main web site is at *disobey.com*.

AmphetaDesk is one of the simplest-to-use aggregators, but that's not its only appeal. AmphetaDesk is also customizable, from changing channels to changing the appearance to changing the code itself (AmphetaDesk is written in Perl).

Using AmphetaDesk

Once installed, running the application for the first time opens a web browser with a page containing preset aggregated news items. You can continue using the settings as is or you can customize the data. For instance, if you have several weblogs you're interested in keeping abreast of, you can add each of them as channels; the tool will track changes for you.

I customized AmphetaDesk by removing all of the preselected channels, and then added my own favorites. From the browser page I clicked the link labeled My Channels and then checked all of the boxes next to the items listed, as shown in Figure 13-1.

The channels are RSS files. To add new channels, you can specify the URL of the feed in the text box as shown in Figure 13-1, clicking the button labeled Add This Channel, or you can use RSS autodiscovery by providing the URL of the web page that contains the autodiscovery link. Additionally, you can use the built-in Add a Channels page that contains 9000+ prediscovered channels.

AmphetaDesk, like many other aggregators, supports adding a variation of a Subscribe link to your links toolbar on your browser, by dragging a link from a web page to the bar. I did this with my Mozilla browser. Now when I visit a page I'm interested in subscribing to, I just click the Subscribe link on the toolbar and the RSS feed for the site is added as a channel to my customized AmphetaDesk.

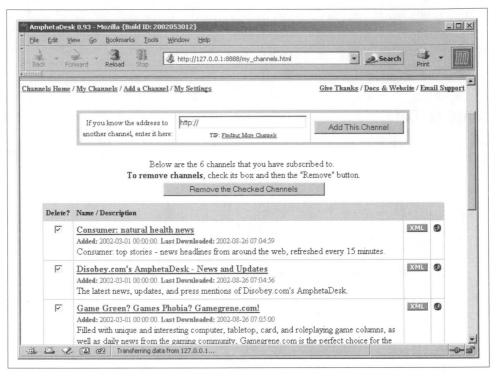

Figure 13-1. Customizing AmphetaDesk by removing existing channels

I visited several of my favorite news sources and weblogs and added each of them as an RSS channel. Next, I went to the application settings (accessible through the My Settings link) and further customized the tool by changing the time to check for updates to one hour (60 minutes). The application checks the RSS sources every 60 minutes and posts new entries to the Channels page.

More advanced customization

If you like to play around with your software, you can further customize Ampheta-Desk in several different ways. For instance, you can add a new "skin" to the application, which means controlling the look of the application by adjusting the templates the tool uses. However, use caution and always back up the files as you experiment. The documentation for customizing the application skin is included with the product.

If you're a developer, you can further customize the application, either working within the Source Forge project or creating your own customized version of AmphetaDesk. However, be forewarned that if you change the code base for your own installation, you'll need to merge the changed code in with new releases of AmphetaDesk. Find out more about AmphetaDesk code customization at *http://www.decafbad.com/twiki/bin/view/Main/AmphetaOutlines* and *http://www.cantoni.org/software/AmphetaDesk.html*

A particularly interesting aspect to AmphetaDesk is that you can modify the source code for the application and run it locally, without having Perl installed.

Meerkat

Meerkat is an online news aggregation support that can be customized, though customization is limited to querying from existing news sources. It's accessible online
and requires no installation on your machine—only a browser.

Access the main site at *http://oreillynet.com/meerkat/*. Meerkat was
written by Rael Dornfest, from O'Reilly.

After accessing the Meerkat site, the first page that opens is the application page. It
has a form at the top that allows you to pick predefined filters, labeled *Profiles/Mobs*.
Selecting one of the predefined filters limits the news headlines to just those that are
related to the filter. In Figure 13-2, the filter picked was labeled *Apache*, and the
news headlines were related to Apache-related items.

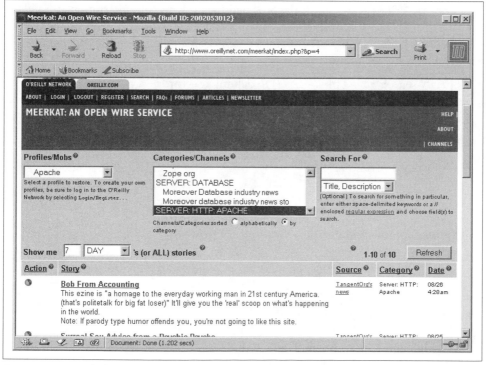

Figure 13-2. Meerkat news filtered on Apache-related items

You can also filter the results based on categories and channels or search for specific terms. Additionally, you can modify how many entries show by selecting a time frame. Clicking on the Refresh button updates the display after you've changed your selections.

I've been a Meerkat subscriber for more than a year, yet I hadn't accessed the site directly in months, not until I started working on this chapter. This seemingly contradictory statement can be explained by discussing the real power behind Meerkat—the ability to incorporate the Meerkat services into your own applications, web pages, or desktop.

Meerkat has exposed APIs, based on different technologies, to access the news feed (more on this at *http://www.oreillynet.com/pub/a/rss/2000/05/09/meerkat_api.html*). These *flavors*, as the different open APIs are called with Meerkat, allow you to incorporate the Meerkat into your like-flavored application.

For instance, I incorporate a JavaScript-based Meerkat feed into one of my web sites, using the following code:

```
<div style="font-size: 8pt; font-family: Times New Roman">
<script language="JavaScript"
src="http://meerkat.oreillynet.com/?p=1&_fl=js&_de=0">
</div>
```

This code describes a JavaScript-flavored news feed, with full descriptions turned off (to save space), using a profile of 1, which is all news stories. I could have further modified the feed by using other parameters. For instance, the following parameters impact which stories show:

s   Specify search, using plus sign (+) to delimit keywords

sw   To specify what is searched, such as title, description, and so on

c   To display a specific channel

t   To set time period of displayed items

p   To specify a particular profile

m   To specify a particular mob

i   To specify a particular story

In addition, the following parameters influence the display:

_fl

    Flavor

_de

    Whether descriptions are shown

_ca

    Whether category is shown

_ch

   Which channel the story came from

_da

   Story date

_dc

   The Dublin Core metadata associated with the stories

So, I can change my current setting to the following:

```
<div style="font-size: 8pt; font-family: Times New Roman">
<script language="JavaScript"
src="http://meerkat.oreillynet.com/?p=1&_fl=js&_de=1&t=1DAY">
</div>
```

Notice that the parameters are separated by the ampersand.

The setting just shown instructs Meerkat to give me the stories from profile 1, one day's worth, JavaScript formatted, and with full descriptions. All other parameters are set to their default settings. The result of this JavaScript embedded into a web page is shown in Figure 13-3.

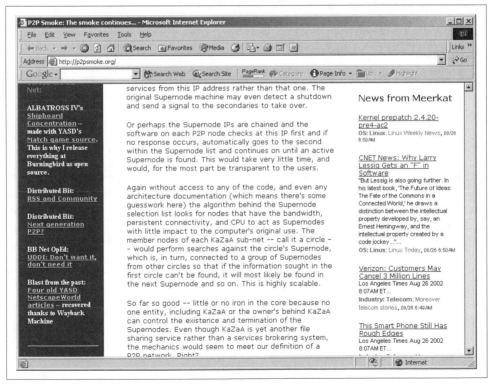

Figure 13-3. Meerkat display using JavaScript to access feed

You can see how uncomplicated the Meerkat feed is to access. Best of all, the feed uses CSS, so you can modify the display of the feed by incorporating CSS settings for predefined Meerkat values.

The Meerkat API has been ported for use with many languages and technologies including a raw RSS feed, XML, PHP, Sherlock plug-in, N3, HTML, and others. In addition, you can access Meerkat services using XML-RPC.

NetNewsWire and NetNewsWire Lite

An RSS aggregator, plus more, that is gaining considerable popularity with Mac OS X users is Ranchero Software's NetNewsWire and its lighter version, NetNewsWire Lite. I use it myself on my PowerBook and am very impressed with its ease of use. And as with so many other aggregation tools, you can do more than just read RSS feeds with the tool—with the commercial version still in beta when I wrote this book, you can edit weblog postings with the tool and use it to post them to your weblog.

 You can download NetNewsWire from *http://ranchero.com/ netnewswire/*. The RSS aggregator–only version is NetNewsWire Lite; the commercial version NetNewsWire is the one with the extra features such as weblog posting. I used the NetNewsWire beta 1.01b for this chapter.

When you first install and open NetNewsWire, it comes with only a few sites already subscribed. However, it's an easy matter to subscribe to new feeds, particularly if the web page that provides the feed supports autodiscovery.

Figure 13-4 shows NetNewsWire Pro with some of my favorite weblogs, including my own, subscribed.

You can use the tool to jump to unread items, or you can click on any of the subscriptions to display the current RSS contents. Clicking on any of these opens the excerpt associated with the item. To add new items, just click the Subscribe button and fill in the URL of the RSS file or the X(HTML) page that has the RSS autodiscovery entry. That's it. The tool will fill in the necessary information from the file, including the title associated with the RSS feed.

If you double-click on any one of the items, the actual page opens in your default browser, which you can set via your System Preferences.

You can also open the actual RSS XML of the feed in TextEdit as shown in Figure 13-5. This is a handy way of getting a little more familiar with RDF/RSS—by using the tool to take a look at RDF/RSS files out on the Web.

Other functionality NetNewsWire Pro supports includes the ability to create weblog postings, check their spelling, and then post directly from the tool.

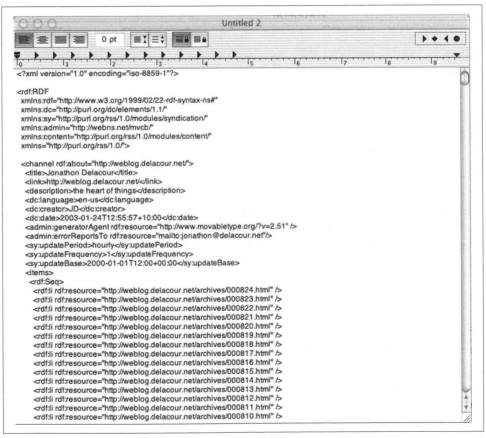

Figure 13-4. NetNewsWire Pro with a few subscribed RSS feeds

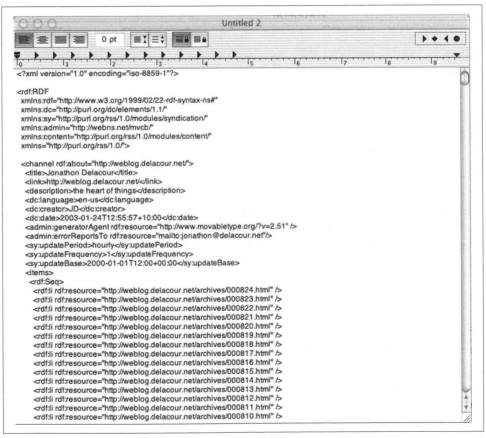

Figure 13-5. Examining a feed in TextEdit

Creating Your Own RSS Content

RSS allows you to aggregate like items, though you don't have to restrict this to web pages and news sources and things like that. For instance, one effective use of RSS would be to keep lists of multimedia recommendations such as books, music, and movies.

I use RSS to maintain a list of book recommendations from friends. For the most part, the RSS elements and the DC module define most of the data I want to capture, including the `dc:creator`, `dc:subject`, and the standard RSS `channel`, `items`, and `item`. However, within the core RSS 1.0 specification, a few useful fields are missing. Among these are elements to record who made the recommendation, the URL of her web site, whether the book has been read (or the movie has been viewed), and an URL of the review if any. Since the business I'm interested in documenting—book recommendations—isn't fully covered or predefined in any existing RDF vocabulary or within any existing RSS 1.0 module I could find, I created one of my own, with the following namespace:

```
xmlns:recs="http://burningbird.net/recommendations/elements/1.0/"
```

I then defined the following elements in the namespace:

recby
> Name of person who made the recommendation (optional), PCDATA

status
> Status of recommendation (required; 1=consumed, 0=unconsumed)

reclink
> URL of web site of recommendation or recommender (optional)

review
> URL of review (optional)

I asked around with some of my friends and ended up with a selection of book recommendations, which I then recorded in my newly extended RSS. Example 13-5 shows an abbreviated book recommendations list.

Example 13-5. Book recommendation RSS

```
<?xml version="1.0"?>

<rdf:RDF
xmlns:rdf="http://www.w3.org/1999/02/22-rdf-syntax-ns#"
xmlns:dc="http://purl.org/dc/elements/1.1/"
xmlns:sy="http://purl.org/rss/1.0/modules/syndication/"
xmlns:recs="http://burningbird.net/recommendations/elements/1.0/"
xmlns="http://purl.org/rss/1.0/">

<channel rdf:about="http://weblog.burningbird.net/books.rdf">
<title>Burningbird BookList</title>
<link>http://weblog.burningbird.net/books.rdf</link>
```

Example 13-5. Book recommendation RSS (continued)

```
<description>
Burningbird's To Be Read Booklist and Recommendations
</description>

<items>
<rdf:Seq>
<rdf:li rdf:resource="http://isbn.nu/0395489016" />
<rdf:li rdf:resource="http://isbn.nu/0446391301" />
<rdf:li rdf:resource="http://isbn.nu/0679454519" />
<rdf:li rdf:resource="http://isbn.nu/0743418174" />
<rdf:li rdf:resource="http://isbn.nu/0553211161" />
</rdf:Seq>
</items>

</channel>

<item rdf:about="http://isbn.nu/0446391301">
<title>Geek Love</title>
<description></description>
<dc:creator>Katherine Dunn</dc:creator>
<dc:subject>Fiction</dc:subject>
<dc:subject>Drama</dc:subject>
<dc:identifier>0446391301</dc:identifier>
<link>http://isbn.nu/0446391301/price/1</link>
<recs:recby>Denise Howell</recs:recby>
<recs:status>0</recs:status>
<recs:reclink>http://bgbg.blogspot.com/</recs:reclink>
</item>

<item rdf:about="http://isbn.nu/0743418174">
<title>Good in Bed</title>
<description></description>
<dc:creator>Jennifer Weiner</dc:creator>
<dc:subject>Fiction</dc:subject>
<link>http://isbn.nu/0743418174/price/1</link>
<recs:recby>Leesa</recs:recby>
<recs:read>unread</recs:read>
<recs:reclink>http://leesa.devfarm.com/</recs:reclink>
</item>

<item rdf:about="http://isbn.nu/0553211161">
<title>Leaves of Grass</title>
<description></description>
<dc:creator>Walt Whitman</dc:creator>
<dc:subject>Poetry</dc:subject>
<link>http://isbn.nu/0553211161/price/1</link>
<recs:recby>bumr</recs:recby>
<recs:read>unread</recs:read>
<recs:reclink>http://bumr.net/</recs:reclink>
</item>

<item rdf:about="http://isbn.nu/0679742115/">
```

Example 13-5. Book recommendation RSS (continued)

```
<title>Vox</title>
<description></description>
<dc:creator>Nicholson Baker</dc:creator>
<dc:subject>Fiction</dc:subject>
<link>http://isbn.nu/0679742115/</link>
<recs:recby>Karl aka Paradox1x</recs:recby>
<recs:reclink>http://www.paradox1x.org/html/books.shtml
  </recs:reclink>
<recs:read>unread</recs:read>
</item>

<item rdf:about="http://isbn.nu/0395489016">
<title>Let Us Now Praise Famous Men</title>
<description></description>
<dc:creator>James Agee, Walker Evans</dc:creator>
<dc:subject>Nonfiction</dc:subject>
<link>http://isbn.nu/0395489016</link>
<recs:recby>Jonathon Delacour</recs:recby>
<recs:reclink>http://weblog.delacour.net</recs:reclink>
<recs:status>1</recs:status>
<recs:review>http://weblog.burningbird.net/archives/000442.php
  </recs:review>
</item>

</rdf:RDF>
```

Though there is no description for each of the book items, the `description` elements are still listed because this element is mandatory. Of course, the next step to take would be to formalize the Recommendations module through the RSS Working Group, but for now, we'll accept it the way it is. In the next section, we'll look at a couple of different applications to process this data.

Build Your Own RSS Consumer

You don't have to use a prebuilt RSS aggregation tool or RSS consumer. Because of the restrictions and constraints placed on RSS, it's relatively simple to build your own application that processes RSS and displays the results. You can use technology that is designed for XML or RDF (demonstrated throughout the book), or you can use technology specifically designed for RSS.

To demonstrate, I created an application to process the book recommendation RSS feed shown in Example 13-5. It uses an RSS API written in Java to process the RSS (any RSS) from a JSP page.

I'm rather partial to J2EE applications and have a Tomcat installation at my web site. My first inclination when creating a new dynamic web application is to see if there is a Java API I can use within JSP pages. In the next example, an RSS specialized API is used—a brand new API called the Informa RSS Library, available at Source Forge (*http://sourceforge.net/projects/informa/*). This API provides Java classes that allow you to access specific pieces of RSS data, rather than having to write the XML parsing aspect of the code.

I downloaded the Java *.jar* files containing the code and added then to the *JAVA_ APP/WEB-INF/lib* subdirectory associated with the location of the JSP pages. I then restarted Tomcat in order to pick up the new libraries.

The Informa RSS Java libraries are added into the JSP page with an imports statement, as shown in Example 13-6.

Example 13-6. JSP imports section

```
<%@ page import="java.net.URL,
                 java.io.File,
                 java.util.*,
                 de.nava.informa.core.ChannelIF,
                 de.nava.informa.core.ChannelParserIF,
                 de.nava.informa.core.ItemIF,
                 de.nava.informa.impl.basic.ChannelBuilder,
                 de.nava.informa.parsers.RSS_1_0_Parser" %>
```

Next, within the HTML body of the JSP page, the RSS file is opened and the contents processed and printed out to the page, as shown in Example 13-7.

Example 13-7. Using RSS Java API to process RSS file

```
<%
        // get RSS file URL
        String sRDFUri = request.getParameter("uri");
        String sTitle = null;

        URL u = null;
        ChannelParserIF parser = null;
        ChannelIF channel = null;
        Collection cItems = null;
        Iterator iItems = null;
        String sError;

        try {
          u = new URL(sRDFUri);

          // create RSS 1.0 parser
          parser = new RSS_1_0_Parser(
                          new ChannelBuilder());

          // get channel
          channel = parser.parse(u);
          sTitle = channel.getTitle();

          // print title as header
          out.println("<h1>" + sTitle + "</h1>");
          cItems = channel.getItems();
```

Example 13-7. Using RSS Java API to process RSS file (continued)

```
        // get items collection
        iItems = cItems.iterator( );

        // iterate through collection and print out RSS elements`
        while (iItems.hasNext( )) {
           ItemIF item = (ItemIF)iItems.next( );
           out.print("<a href='");
           out.print(item.getLink( ));
           out.print("'>");
           out.print(item.getTitle( ));
           out.println("</a>");
           out.println("<br />");

   }
}
catch (Exception e) {
   sError = e.getMessage( );
   out.println(sError);
   }
%>
```

In the example, an RSS 1.0 parser is created to parse the RSS into memory. Once in memory the channel element is accessed and the title is pulled from the element and printed out. Next, the Java collection containing the RSS file's items is accessed and each item element is processed, pulling the data out for printing. The book recommendation item title and link are accessed and a list of hypertext-linked titles is printed out on the page, as shown in Figure 13-6.

A disadvantage to using a specialized RSS API is that different RDF vocabularies can't be used with the API—it's focused purely on RSS elements. However, an advantage to the RSS API is that any RSS file can be processed using the same JSP page.

Since the RSS file URL is passed to the JSP page from an HTML form element, instead of passing in the book recommendation RSS, I passed in my weblog's RSS 1.0 file. Figure 13-7 shows the page that results from reading in this file (with no change to the code).

Because RSS 1.0 is first and foremost RDF, you can also use any of the technologies and languages in the rest of the book to parse, or generate, the RSS demonstrated in this chapter, which is ultimately why RDF is such a handy thing for a software developer such as myself.

Merging RDF/RSS Files

In addition to reading RSS, you can also create applications that write it or that both read and write RDF/RSS. I use an application that does just this with my own Burningbird web sites.

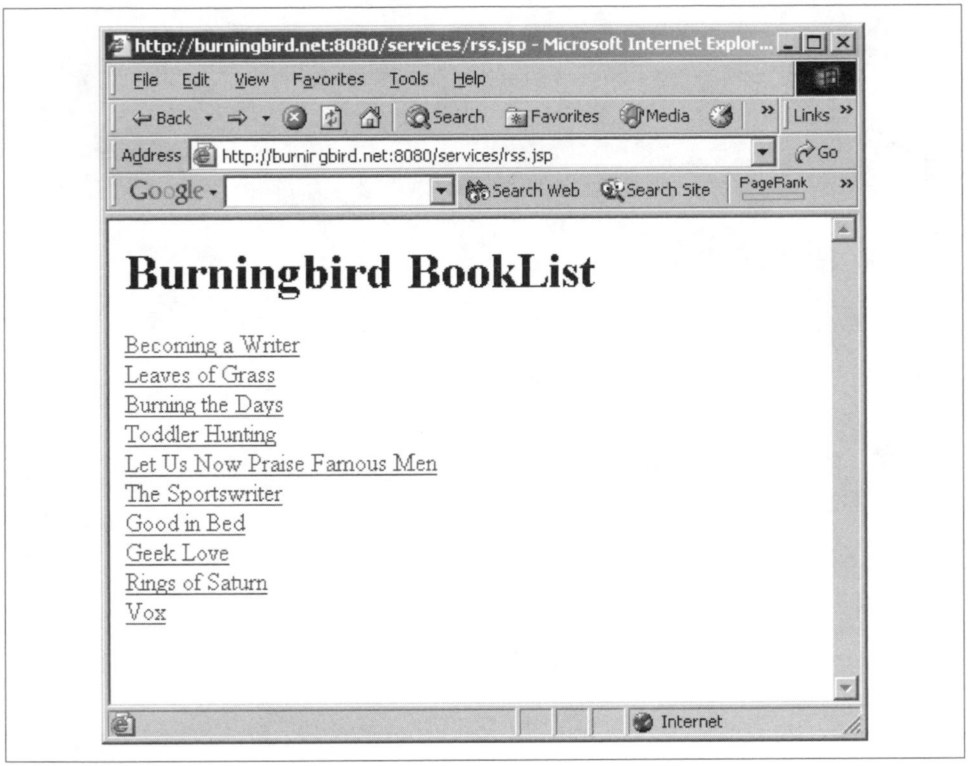

Figure 13-6. JSP- and Java-generated book list from RSS

I have several different types of sites at *burningbird.net*, each with its own RSS/RDF file. People could subscribe to each individual file, but I wanted to give my readers an option to subscribe to one main RDF/RSS file that contains the 10 most recent entries across the entire Burningbird network. To do this, I created an application in Perl that reads in the individual RSS files and merges all the items into one array. I then sorted the array in descending order by date, and "skimmed" the 10 most recent entries. Next, I used the data making up these entries to create a brand new RDF/RSS file, hosted at the main *http://burningbird.net/index.rdf* RSS file location.

Because I don't always have access to the most recent version of Python or access to a Tomcat server, I couldn't use either my Java- or my Python-based solution at my main web site. Instead, I wrote an application in Perl, making use of a very handy RSS Perl module, XML::RSS, originally developed by Jonathan Eisenzopf and now maintained at Source Forge.

You can access the source and documentation for using XML::RSS at *http://perl-rss.sourceforge.net/*.

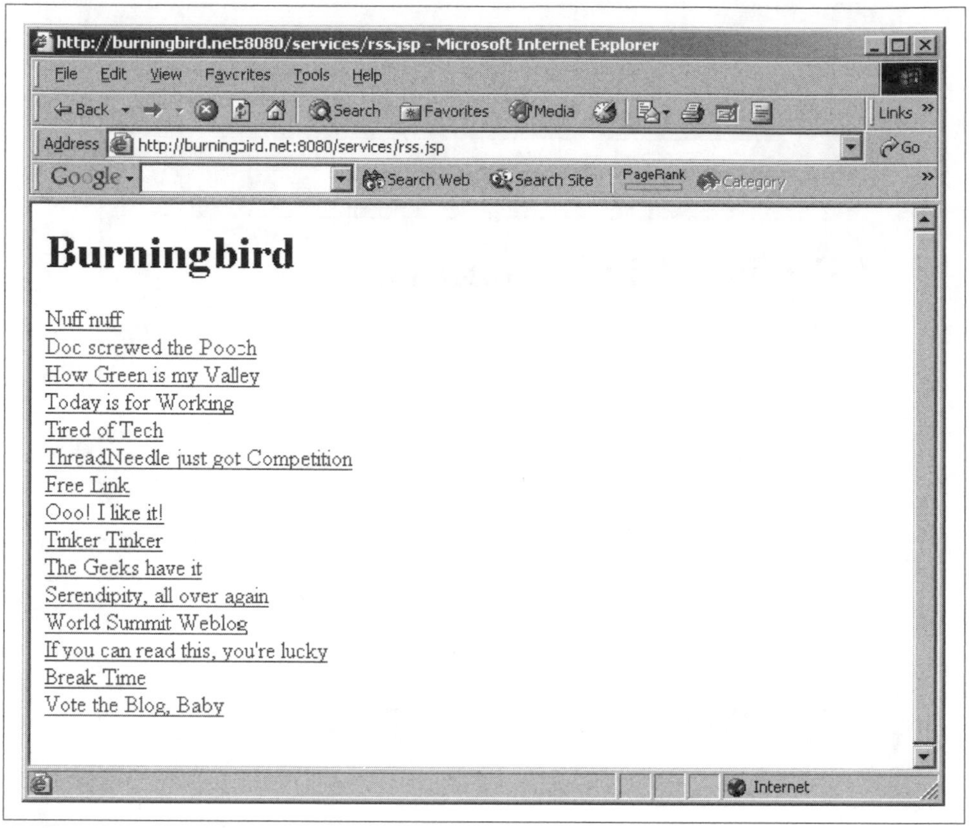

Figure 13-7. List of weblog entries pulled from weblog's RSS file

The XML::RSS Perl module provides an object that can read in an RSS file in either RDF/RSS format or the non-RDF format. The data is then accessible via associative arrays (or dictionaries for Pythonistas), using the RSS predicates as key to find each value. For instance, after reading in an RDF/RSS file, you can access the dc:date field for an individual item using code similar to the following:

```
$dt = $item->{'dc'}->{'date'};
```

All items are accessible as an associative array with the key items, and each individual item is accessible from it with item. Elements associated with a particular namespace, such as dc, form yet another associative array attached to each item.

The application starts by opening a file that contains the list of all of my *index.rdf* files and reading the filenames (each on a separate line) into an array:

```
my $rdffile = "/home/shelleyp/www/work/cronapp/indexfiles.txt";
open(DAT, $rdffile) || die("could not open");
my @files=<DAT>;
close(DAT);
```

The application cycles through all the files in the array, creating an instance of XML::
RSS to process the data in each. Each individual item within the file is loaded into an
associative array, using the item's timestamp as key:

```
foreach my $file (@files) {
  my $rss = new XML::RSS;

  $rss->parsefile($file);

    foreach my $item(@{$rss->{'items'}}) {
      my $dt = $item->{'dc'}->{'date'};
      $arry{$dt} = $item;
      }
}
```

A new RDF/RSS object is created and the header information is provided:

```
my $rss = new XML::RSS (version => '1.0');

$rss->channel(
    title       => "Burningbird Network",
    link        => "http://burningbird.net",
    description => "Burningbird: Burning online since 1995",
    dc => {
      subject   => "writing,technology,art,photography,science,environment,politics",
      creator   => 'shelleyp@burningbird.net',
      publisher => 'shelleyp@burningbird.net',
      rights    => 'Copyright 1995-2003, Shelley Powers, Burningbird',
      language  => 'en-us',
    },
    syn => {
      updatePeriod    => "hourly",
      updateFrequency => "1",
      updateBase      => "1901-01-01T00:00+00:00",
    },
);

$rss->image(
    title => "Burningbird",
    url   => "http://burningbird.net/mm/birdflame.gif",
    link  => "http://burningbird.net/",
    dc => {
      creator  => "Shelley Powers",
    },
);
```

Once the items are loaded, they're sorted in descending order, and a scalar array of
the timestamp keys is accessed in order to loop through only the top 10 (most
recent) items. As each item is accessed, it's used to build a new item within the new
RDF/RSS object. When the processing is finished, the generated RDF/RSS object is
serialized to a file. Example 13-8 shows the code for the complete application.

Example 13-8. Perl application that merges the entries from several different RDF/RSS files, creating a new RDF/RSS file from results

```perl
#!/usr/bin/perl -w

###################################################
# merge RDF/RSS files
# Author: Shelley Powers
###################################################

use lib '.';
use strict;
use XML::RSS;
use HTML::Entities;

# read in list of RDF/RSS files
my $rdffile = "/home/shelleyp/www/work/cronapp/indexfiles.txt";
open(DAT, $rdffile) || die("could not open");
my @files=<DAT>;
close(DAT);

# how many items to include
my $total = 10;

# array for all RSS items
my %arry;

# read in each RDF/RSS file, load into array
foreach my $file (@files) {
  my $rss = new XML::RSS;

  $rss->parsefile($file);

  foreach my $item(@{$rss->{'items'}}) {
    my $dt = $item->{'dc'}->{'date'};
    $arry{$dt} = $item;
    }
}

# sort descending order by timestamp
my @keys = reverse(sort(keys %arry));

# create new RDF/RSS file
# create header
my $rss = new XML::RSS (version => '1.0');
$rss->channel(
    title       => "Burningbird Network",
    link        => "http://burningbird.net",
    description => "Burningbird: Burning online since 1995",
    dc => {
      subject   => "writing,technology,art,photography,science,environment,politics",
      creator   => 'shelleyp@burningbird.net',
      publisher => 'shelleyp@burningbird.net',
      rights    => 'Copyright 1995-2003, Shelley Powers, Burningbird',
```

```perl
      language    => 'en-us',
    },
    syn => {
      updatePeriod      => "hourly",
      updateFrequency   => "1",
      updateBase        => "1901-01-01T00:00+00:00",
    },
 );

 $rss->image(
    title  => "Burningbird",
    url    => "http://burningbird.net/mm/birdflame.gif",
    link   => "http://burningbird.net/",
    dc => {
      creator  => "Shelley Powers",
    },
 );

# add items
my $i = 0;

while ($i < $total) {
  my $key = $keys[$i];

  # build new RSS item
  $rss->add_item(
      title          => encode_entities($arry{$key}->{'title'}),
      description    => encode_entities($arry{$key}->{'description'}),
      link           => $arry{$key}->{'link'},
      dc => {
          subject  => $arry{$key}->{'dc'}->{'subject'},
          creator  => $arry{$key}->{'dc'}->{'creator'},
          date     => $arry{$key}->{'dc'}->{'date'},
      },
  );
  $i++;
}
$rss->save('/home/shelleyp/www/index.rdf');
```

The application is then run as a scheduled hourly task, which is more than frequent enough.

As you can see, when you use a specialized API, regardless of the language, your task is greatly simplified. Trying to code this all by hand using regular expressions or even an XML processor would take at least twice as much code, and three times the work. You get a lot of return for a little investment in using a specialized XML vocabulary organized with the RDF metamodel.

## CHAPTER 14

A World of Uses: Noncommercial Applications Based on RDF

My first introduction to RDF didn't come about because I developed a sudden and overwhelming interest in the Semantic Web. My interest had more prosaic beginnings than that—through exposure to RDF/XML in Mozilla, an open source browser/application framework.

Then and now, RDF/XML formed the format for the table of contents (TOC)–based structures that formed favorites lists, the sidebar, and pretty much anything expressible in a table of contents infrastructure. One of the frustrating things about the effort, though, is that it seemed that the RDF/XML used by Mozilla kept changing. And it also seemed that I couldn't get the knack of using it correctly. So, I decided the only thing to do was access the RDF specifications directly and learn about RDF and RDF/XML from the source. The rest, as they say, is history, culminating in my writing this book.

One mark of a mature specification is its use within commercial products, and we'll look at commercial applications of RDF and RDF/XML in the next chapter. However, these commercial products are based, in principle and in spirit, on earlier open source and noncommercial applications built by a specification's earliest adopters. Without these uses of RDF, the path wouldn't be laid for the business use of RDF.

This chapter takes a look at some of what I classify as noncommercial uses of RDF and RDF/XML, open source or not. The applications included are just a sampling of those available and include applications that haven't been covered elsewhere in the book. The best place to start is Mozilla.

Mozilla

Mozilla started out as a redesign of Netscape's browser but ended up being more than anyone expected. It became an effort to develop a component-based architecture and framework for a development environment, on which Mozilla, the browser, was then implemented. Because of this underlying framework, other applications could use bits and pieces of Mozilla, or the underlying technology, for their own efforts.

Right from the start, Mozilla incorporated the use of RDF/XML to manage all TOC- and other tree-structured data, such as the favorites list, sidebar, and so on. As stated earlier, it was through Mozilla's work with RDF/XML that I was originally introduced to the specification—an introduction that colors my view of RDF as more of a "practical" specification then one necessary for Semantic Web efforts.

 You can download the most recent release of Mozilla at *http://mozilla. org*. Developer documentation is located at *http://mozilla.org/catalog/*, and a development forum and repository is at *http://www.mozdev.org/*.

Mozilla contains many components, but the one we'll focus on because of its association with RDF/XML is XUL (eXtensible User interface Language)—the component that controls the user interface, including all windowing and window components.

XUL Briefly

Rather than hardcode a user interface for each of the visual components of Mozilla, the Mozilla Working Group decided to use XML to define user interface components and then provide behind-the-scenes functionality to make these components active. By using this approach, rather than having to use some form of code to change or create a new application interface, you'd just create a new XML file, hooking in the appropriate functionality as needed.

For instance, the XML to create a window with two buttons would be as follows:

```
<?xml version="1.0"?>
<?xml-stylesheet href="chrome://global/skin/" type="text/css"?>
<window id="example-window" title="Example 2.2.1"
        xmlns:html="http://www.w3.org/1999/xhtml"
        xmlns="http://www.mozilla.org/keymaster/gatekeeper/there.is.only.xul">
<button label="Practical"/>
<button label="RDF"/>
</window>
```

Opening the window in Mozilla, or some other browser that supports XUL, would show a window similar to that in Figure 14-1. Of course, clicking on any of the buttons doesn't do anything at this point; you'll need to use a little scripting to add functionality.

Clicking on a button or a list item or opening or closing windows all trigger events that you can trap and use to perform some action, such as the following, added to a button to call a JavaScript function that's defined in an external file:

```
<button label="Open New Window" oncommand="openBrowser();" />
```

The script is then included in the XUL document with the script tag:

```
<script src="open.js" />
```

Mozilla has ways of connecting to the core functionality of the underlying engine through XPConnect, in addition to XBL (Extensible Binding Language), which offers

Figure 14-1. Window application with two functionality buttons created using XUL

a way of binding behaviors to an XUL widget. However, both of these are considerably beyond the scope of this book. What is within scope is RDF/XML's place in the Mozilla effort, through its use with templates, discussed next.

> The coverage of XUL and templates in this section is by necessity very light. Developing applications using the Mozilla components could fill an entire book. In fact, it has; see O'Reilly's *Creating Applications with Mozilla*.

XUL Templates

When building a new application interface, for the most part you'll add static components—adding the XML for one button, one browser window, one menu or toolbar, etc. However, you may also want to display a list or treeview based on larger amounts of data likely to change over time. In this case, you'll want to use an XUL template in your XML and then connect the template with an external RDF/XML datafile. Using this approach, the data in the RDF/XML file can change without your having to alter the XML for the user interface directly.

At its simplest, a template is nothing more than a set of rules that maps XUL components to RDF/XML elements, repeating the XUL components for each RDF/XML element found that matches the specific rule. Templates can be used with most XUL widgets, including listboxes and buttons, but one of the more common uses is binding RDF/XML data into a treeview.

A treeview control is actually a container for several other XUL widgets, each of which controls a different part of the treeview. The structure of the widgets is:

tree
> Outer treeview container

treecols
> Container for treecol widgets

treecol
> A column within the treeview

treechildren
    Container for the data rows

treeitem
    Controls the top row within the treeview and also the behavior of each other
    row within the treeview

treerow
    One individual row in the treeview

treecell
    One individual cell (cross-section between a unique column and a unique row)

Before showing you the XML for treeview as well as the RDF/XML data source,
Figure 14-2 shows an XUL application in development that's using a treeview to manage data in the left-most box in the page. This particular view is two columns, with a
category in the left column, and a title in the right. Clicking on any category opens up
the display and shows all the titles underneath. One of the rows can be selected and
the column widths altered by moving the sizing bar between the columns.

The first part of the XUL created is the tree definition. Among the attributes you can
define is one called datasources, and it's to this attribute that you assign an RDF/
XML document:

```
<tree flex="1" width="200" height="200"
      datasources="postings.rdf" ref="urn:weblog:data">
```

In addition to the datasources attribute, there's also a ref attribute that points to the
start of data access within the document. This is matched to an rdf:about value,
which you'll see later when we get to the datafile.

The next XML added to the document defines the columns and provides a titlebar
for each:

```
<treecols>
  <treecol id="category" label="Category" primary="true" flex="1"/>
  <treecol id="title" label="Title" flex="2"/>
</treecols>
```

Following the columns, the template element and the rule element are added,
because at this point, all of the treeview structure is connected to the data in some
way. This simple case needs only one rule because there is no processing splitting the
data across different columns or some other specialized processing.

Following the template and rule is the treeitem element, containing an attribute, uri,
which tells the processor to repeat this element for every resource within the file:

```
<treeitem uri="rdf:*">
```

The "resource" referenced is the resource identified with a URI. It is defined using a
standard rdf:Description element within the RDF/XML.

Finally, the rest of the treeview elements are added; for every left-side treecell, the
data defined as category is displayed. For every right treecell, the data defined as
title is displayed, as shown next.

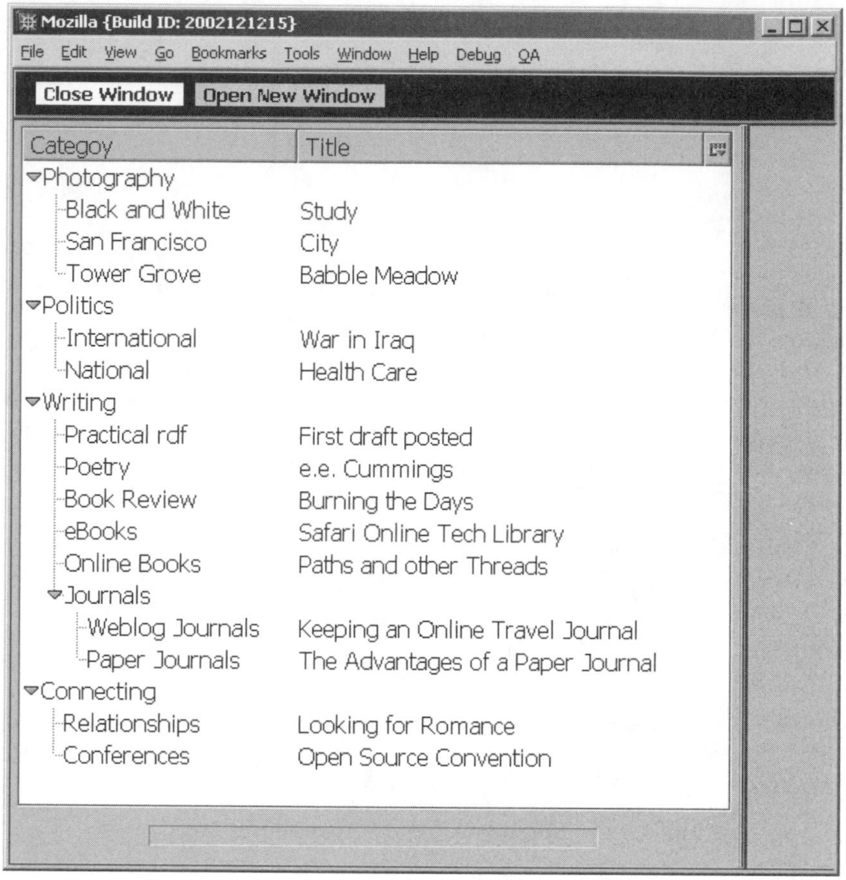

Figure 14-2. XUL application under development that contains a treeview widget populated by an external RDF/XML file, through a template

```
<treerow>
    <treecell label="rdf:http://weblog.burningbird.net/postings#category"/>
    <treecell label="rdf:http://weblog.burningbird.net/postings#title"/>
</treerow>
```

Since the application isn't using any advanced template processing, the entire `treeview` isn't very large (see Example 14-1, which contains a complete XUL application containing the `treeview` just described).

Example 14-1. XUL application containing treeview with data controlled
through a template

```
<?xml version="1.0"?>
<?xml-stylesheet href="chrome://global/skin" type="text/css"?>

<window xmlns:html="http://www.w3.org/1999/xhtml"
  xmlns="http://www.mozilla.org/keymaster/gatekeeper/there.is.only.xul"
```

```
  align="vertical">

<tree flex="1" width="500"
      datasources="postings.rdf" ref="urn:weblog:data">

  <treecols>
    <treecol id="category" label="Category" primary="true" flex="1"/>
    <treecol id="title" label="Title" flex="2"/>
  </treecols>

  <template>
    <rule>
      <treechildren>
        <treeitem uri="rdf:*">
          <treerow>
            <treecell label="rdf:http://weblog.burningbird.net/postings#category"/>
            <treecell label="rdf:http://weblog.burningbird.net/postings#title"/>
          </treerow>
        </treeitem>
      </treechildren>
    </rule>

  </template>
</tree>
</window>
```

If you were to open this page in a browser that supports XUL, such as Mozilla, you'd see only an empty `treeview` control because you also need the RDF/XML document, `postings.rdf`.

The RDF/XML used for XUL templates isn't anything odd or unusual, and no special namespaces are needed other than those you create for your own data. The structure of the data is to some extent determined by the outcome of the display, but the RDF/XML is, itself, nothing more than valid RDF/XML (with a caveat, as you'll see later).

For this use, the categories and their associated titles become list items within a container, a Seq to be exact. Each category is given a different container, and each title a different list item. This provides the structure of the TOC. To add the data, each resource is defined in a separate block, with properties matching the cell values contained within the resource. Though it's a bit large for the book, the entire RDF/XML document for the example is duplicated in Example 14-2 as it's important to see the mapping between the RDF/XML document, the template, and the `treeview`.

Example 14-2. RDF/XML document used to provide data in template

```
<?xml version="1.0"?>

<rdf:RDF xmlns:rdf="http://www.w3.org/1999/02/22-rdf-syntax-ns#"
```

Example 14-2. RDF/XML document used to provide data in template (continued)

```
        xmlns:bbd="http://weblog.burningbird.net/postings#">


    <rdf:Description rdf:about="urn:weblog:photos">
      <bbd:category>Photography</bbd:category>
    </rdf:Description>

        <rdf:Description rdf:about="urn:weblog:photos:bwstudy">
          <bbd:category>Black and White</bbd:category>
          <bbd:title>Study</bbd:title>
        </rdf:Description>

        <rdf:Description rdf:about="urn:weblog:photos:sanfran" >
          <bbd:category>San Francisco</bbd:category>
          <bbd:title>City</bbd:title>
        </rdf:Description>

        <rdf:Description rdf:about="urn:weblog:photos:tower">
          <bbd:category>Tower Grove</bbd:category>
          <bbd:title>Babble Meadow</bbd:title>
        </rdf:Description>

    <rdf:Description rdf:about="urn:weblog:politics">
      <bbd:category>Politics</bbd:category>
    </rdf:Description>

        <rdf:Description rdf:about="urn:weblog:politics:international">
          <bbd:category>International</bbd:category>
          <bbd:title>War in Iraq</bbd:title>
        </rdf:Description>

        <rdf:Description rdf:about="urn:weblog:politics:national">
          <bbd:category>National</bbd:category>
          <bbd:title>Health Care</bbd:title>
        </rdf:Description>

    <rdf:Description rdf:about="urn:weblog:writing">
      <bbd:category>Writing</bbd:category>
    </rdf:Description>

        <rdf:Description rdf:about="urn:weblog:writing:rdfbook">
          <bbd:category>Practical rdf</bbd:category>
          <bbd:title>First draft posted</bbd:title>
        </rdf:Description>

        <rdf:Description rdf:about="urn:weblog:writing:poetry">
          <bbd:category>Poetry</bbd:category>
          <bbd:title>e.e. Cummings</bbd:title>
        </rdf:Description>

        <rdf:Description rdf:about="urn:weblog:writing:review">
          <bbd:category>Book Review</bbd:category>
```

```
            <bbd:title>Burning the Days</bbd:title>
        </rdf:Description>

        <rdf:Description rdf:about="urn:weblog:writing:ebook">
          <bbd:category>eBooks</bbd:category>
          <bbd:title>Safari Online Tech Library</bbd:title>
        </rdf:Description>

        <rdf:Description rdf:about="urn:weblog:writing:online">
          <bbd:category>Online Books</bbd:category>
          <bbd:title>Paths and other Threads</bbd:title>
        </rdf:Description>

        <rdf:Description rdf:about="urn:weblog:writing:journal">
          <bbd:category>Journals</bbd:category>
        </rdf:Description>

        <rdf:Description rdf:about="urn:weblog:writing:journal:weblog">
          <bbd:category>Weblog Journals</bbd:category>
          <bbd:title>Keeping an Online Travel Journal</bbd:title>
        </rdf:Description>
        <rdf:Description rdf:about="urn:weblog:writing:journal:paper">
          <bbd:category>Paper Journals</bbd:category>
          <bbd:title>The Advantages of a Paper Journal</bbd:title>
        </rdf:Description>

  <rdf:Description rdf:about="urn:weblog:connecting">
    <bbd:category>Connecting</bbd:category>
  </rdf:Description>

        <rdf:Description rdf:about="urn:weblog:connecting:relationships">
          <bbd:category>Relationships</bbd:category>
          <bbd:title>Looking for Romance</bbd:title>
        </rdf:Description>

        <rdf:Description rdf:about="urn:weblog:connecting:conferences">
          <bbd:category>Conferences</bbd:category>
          <bbd:title>Open Source Convention</bbd:title>
        </rdf:Description>

  <rdf:Seq rdf:about="urn:weblog:data">
    <rdf:li>
        <rdf:Seq rdf:about="urn:weblog:photos">
          <rdf:li rdf:resource="urn:weblog:photos:bwstudy"/>
          <rdf:li rdf:resource="urn:weblog:photos:sanfran"/>
          <rdf:li rdf:resource="urn:weblog:photos:tower"/>
        </rdf:Seq>
    </rdf:li>
    <rdf:li>
        <rdf:Seq rdf:about="urn:weblog:politics">
          <rdf:li rdf:resource="urn:weblog:politics:international"/>
          <rdf:li rdf:resource="urn:weblog:politics:national"/>
```

```
          </rdf:Seq>
      </rdf:li>
      <rdf:li>
          <rdf:Seq rdf:about="urn:weblog:writing">
            <rdf:li rdf:resource="urn:weblog:writing:rdfbook"/>
            <rdf:li rdf:resource="urn:weblog:writing:poetry"/>
            <rdf:li rdf:resource="urn:weblog:writing:review"/>
            <rdf:li rdf:resource="urn:weblog:writing:ebook"/>
            <rdf:li rdf:resource="urn:weblog:writing:online"/>
            <rdf:li>
              <rdf:Seq rdf:about="urn:weblog:writing:journal">
                  <rdf:li rdf:resource="urn:weblog:writing:journal:weblog"/>
                  <rdf:li rdf:resource="urn:weblog:writing:journal:paper"/>
              </rdf:Seq>
            </rdf:li>
          </rdf:Seq>
      </rdf:li>
      <rdf:li>
          <rdf:Seq rdf:about="urn:weblog:connecting">
            <rdf:li rdf:resource="urn:weblog:connecting:relationships"/>
            <rdf:li rdf:resource="urn:weblog:connecting:conferences"/>
          </rdf:Seq>
      </rdf:li>
    </rdf:Seq>

</rdf:RDF>
```

Note that the top-level rdf:Seq is given a URI of urn:weblog:data, matching the starting position given in the template. Each major category is given its own sequence and its own resource. Each title item is listed as an rdf:li and defined as a separate resource with both category and title.

When the data is processed, the rule attached in the template basically states that all category values are placed in the left column, and all titles in the right. Since the major categories don't have titles, the treecells for these values are blank. However, clicking on the drop-down indicator next to the categories displays both the minor category (subcategory) and titles for each row.

Earlier I mentioned there was a caveat about the validity of the RDF/XML used in the example. The RDF/XML document shown in Example 14-2 validates with the RDF Validator, but not all RDF/XML documents used in providing data for templates in Mozilla do. For instance, I separated out each rdf:Seq element, something that's not necessary with XUL but is necessary to maintain the RDF/XML striping (arc-node-arc-node). In addition, many of the XUL RDF/XML documents also don't qualify the about or resource attributes, which is discouraged in the RDF specifications. This doesn't generate an error, but does generate warnings. However, when you create your own RDF/XML documents, you can use the qualified versions without impacting on the XUL processing.

The Mozilla group wasn't the only organization to use RDF/XML to facilitate building a user interface. The Haystack project at MIT, *http://haystack.lcs.mit.edu/*, uses RDF as the primary data modeling framework.

Creative Commons License

The Creative Commons (CC) is an organization formed in 2002 to facilitate the movement of artists' work to the public domain. One of the outputs from the organization is the Creative Commons licenses: licenses that can be attached to a work of art such as a writing, a graphic, or a song, that provides information about how that material can be used and reused by others.

The Creative Commons web site is at *http://creativecommons.org*.

The CC licenses don't replace copyright and fair use laws; they primarily signal an artist's interest in licensing certain aspects of his copyright to the public, such as the right to copy a work, to derive new works from an original creation, and so on. The license is associated with the art in whatever manner is most expeditious, but if the art is digitized on the Web, the license is usually included with the art as RDF/XML.

The RDF/XML for use can be generated at the CC web site when you pick what particular license you want to apply. For instance, the following RDF/XML is generated when you pick a license that requires attribution and doesn't allow derivative works and/or commercial use:

```
<rdf:RDF xmlns="http://web.resource.org/cc/"
    xmlns:dc="http://purl.org/dc/elements/1.1/"
    xmlns:rdf="http://www.w3.org/1999/02/22-rdf-syntax-ns#">
<Work rdf:about="">
<license rdf:resource="http://creativecommons.org/licenses/by-nd-nc/1.0" />
</Work>

<License rdf:about="http://creativecommons.org/licenses/by-nd-nc/1.0">
   <requires rdf:resource="http://web.resource.org/cc/Attribution" />
   <permits rdf:resource="http://web.resource.org/cc/Reproduction" />
   <permits rdf:resource="http://web.resource.org/cc/Distribution" />
   <prohibits rdf:resource="http://web.resource.org/cc/CommercialUse" />
   <requires rdf:resource="http://web.resource.org/cc/Notice" />
</License>

</rdf:RDF>
```

Normally this RDF/XML is included as part of a larger HTML block, and the RDF is enclosed in HTML comments to allow the page to validate as XHTML. Unfortunately, since HTML comments are also XML comments, this precludes accessing the

RDF/XML directly from the page for most parsers, which will ignore the data much as the HTML browsers do.

The CC RDF Schema makes use of several Dublin Core elements, such as dc:title, dc:description, dc:subject and so on. You can see the model breakdown at *http:// creativecommons.org/learn/technology/metadata/implement#learn* and the schema itself at *http://creativecommons.org/learn/technology/metadata/schema.rdf*. The schema includes definitions for the CC elements, though it uses the dc:description and dc:title elements for this rather than the RDFS equivalents of rdfs:comment and rdfs:label. The namespace for the Creative Commons schema is http://web. resource.org/cc/, and the prefix usually used is cc.

Though CC makes use of Dublin Core elements, the data contained within these elements does differ from other popular uses of Dublin Core. A case in point is dc: creator. For the most part, dc:creator usually contains a string literal representing the name of the person who created the work. However, the CC folks, following from an earlier overly involved discussion in the RDF Interest Group surrounding the concept that "strings don't create anything," provided a bit more detail—in this case, that a dc:creator is an "agent," with a dc:title equivalent to the agent's name. In the following RDF/XML, the dc:creator field is boldfaced to demonstrate the structure of the data used by CC:

```
<rdf:RDF xmlns="http://web.resource.org/cc/"
    xmlns:dc="http://purl.org/dc/elements/1.1/"
    xmlns:rdf="http://www.w3.org/1999/02/22-rdf-syntax-ns#">
<Work rdf:about="http://rdf.burningbird.net">
   <dc:title>Practical RDF</dc:title>
   <dc:date>2003-2-1</dc:date>
   <dc:description>Sample CC license for book</dc:description>
   <dc:creator><Agent>
      <dc:title>Shelley Powers</dc:title>
   </Agent></dc:creator>
   <dc:rights><Agent>
      <dc:title>O'Reilly</dc:title>
   </Agent></dc:rights>
   <dc:type rdf:resource="http://purl.org/dc/dcmitype/Text" />
<license rdf:resource="http://creativecommons.org/licenses/by-nd-nc/1.0" />
</Work>

<License rdf:about="http://creativecommons.org/licenses/by-nd-nc/1.0">
   <requires rdf:resource="http://web.resource.org/cc/Attribution" />
   <permits rdf:resource="http://web.resource.org/cc/Reproduction" />
   <permits rdf:resource="http://web.resource.org/cc/Distribution" />
   <prohibits rdf:resource="http://web.resource.org/cc/CommercialUse" />
   <requires rdf:resource="http://web.resource.org/cc/Notice" />
</License>

</rdf:RDF>
```

The data type for `dc:creator` is PCDATA, which means that the CC innovation wouldn't validate using the DC DTD. However, there's no requirement that RDF/XML validate, only that it be well formed. Still, if you're processing this field for a string representing a name, and you get this structure instead, you're going to have some interesting processing challenges. All of this demonstrates that, though RDF helps in the process of defining a metamodel for data, it doesn't necessarily close all the doors leading to confusion.

MIT's DSpace System Documentation

DSpace is a repository and multitier application being developed by MIT and HP Labs to track the intellectual output at MIT. It's based in Java and implemented as a J2EE application residing on Unix and using PostgreSQL as a database. The application has been carefully documented, including detailed installation instructions, as well as excellent overall architecture and usage documentation.

 DSpace is a Source Forge project, with a home page at *http://www.dspace.org/*. Download the source at *http://sourceforge.net/projects/dspace/* or at the HP Labs download page (at *http://www.hpl.hp.com/research/downloads/*). View systems documentation at *http://dspace.org/technology/system-docs/index.html*. DSpace is open source, available under a BSD license.

DSpace works by allowing to the establishment of major organization divisions, which the project calls communities. Within the communities, intellectual output is further categorized into collections. Each unique output item gets a Dublin Core record attached to it and is then combined with any external material such as images into a bundle. This bundle is then formatted as a *bitstream*, and the format for the bitstream is attached to it. With this infrastructure in place, each output is a complete package including the metadata information associated with it, through the addition of the Dublin Core record.

DSpace users can submit a document or other material for inclusion with the system, and its inclusion can be reviewed and accepted or rejected. If accepted, the material can be uploaded; information about the material is then available for search and browsing. In addition, when the material is loaded, it's assigned a handle based on the CNRI Handle System for direct access to the material.

 More information on CNRI can be found at *http://www.handle.net/*.

The type of material that can be accommodated within DSpace includes documents in all forms, books, multimedia, computer applications, data sets, and so on. In addition to getting access to the material through search, browsing, or directly through the handle, users can also subscribe to a specific collection within a DSpace community and be notified by email when a new item has been added.

FOAF: Friend-of-a-Friend

For use of RDF to become widespread, its growth must occur in two directions: through use in sophisticated commercial applications such as those detailed in the next chapter, and through small, friendly, easy-to-use, and open source applications such as FOAF—Friend-of-a-Friend.

 You can find out more about FOAF at the its main web site at *http:// rdfweb.org/foaf/*. In addition, an FOAF Wiki is at *http://rdfweb.org/ rweb/wiki/wiki.pl?FoafVocab*. The RDF Schema for FOAF is at *http:// xmlns.com/foaf/0.1/*. A mailing list for interested persons can be found at *http://rdfweb.org/pipermail/rdfweb-dev/*.

FOAF is a way of providing affiliation and other social information about yourself; it's also a way of describing a network of friends and others we know for one reason or another, in such a way that automated processes such as web bots can find this information and incorporate it with other FOAF files. The data is combined in a social network literally based on one predicate: knows.

Consider the scenario: I know Dorothea and she knows Mark and he knows Ben and Ben knows Sam and Sam knows... and so on. If the old adage about there being only six degrees of separation between any two people in the world is true, it should take only six levels of knows to connect Dorothea to Mark to Ben and so on. Then, once the network is established, it's very easy to verify who a person knows and in what context, and you have what could become a web of knowledge, if not exactly a web of trust.

The FOAF namespace is `http://xmlns.com/foaf/0.1/`, and the classes are `Organization`, `Project`, `Person`, and `Document`. There is no special meaning attached to each of these classes, they're meant to be taken at face value. In other words, a document is a document, not a special type of document. Though the other classes are available, most FOAF files are based on `Person`, and that's what's most used.

There are several FOAF properties, many of which are rarely used, a few of which are even a joke (`dnaChecksum` comes instantly to mind). However, almost every FOAF files uses the following properties:

mbox
　　An Internet email address in a valid URI format

surname
　　Person's surname

---

nick
> Person's nickname

firstname
> First name of person

givenname
> Given name of person

homepage
> Person's home page URL

projectHomepage
> URL of a project home page

title
> Person's title or honorific

phone
> Person's phone

publications
> Link to person's publications

knows
> A person the person knows

There are other properties, but if you examine several FOAF files for people you'll find that the ones just listed are the most commonly used. In fact, the best way to understand how to create an FOAF file for yourself is to look at the FOAF files for people you know. Another way is to create the beginnings of a FOAF file using the FOAF-A-Matic.

The FOAF-A-Matic

I derived the name for my Query-O-Matic tools described in Chapter 10 in some part from the FOAF-A-Matic name. However, unlike my tools, which query existing RDF/XML, the FOAF-A-Matic is used to generate the RDF/XML for a specific FOAF file.

 Access the original FOAF-A-Matic at *http://www.ldodds.com/foaf/foaf-a-matic.html*. Work is underway for a new version of the FOAF-A-Matic at the following web site: *http://www.ldodds.com/wordtin/Wiki.jsp?page=FOAFaMaticMark2*.

The FOAF-A-Matic is a web form with several fields used to record information such as name, home page, email, workplace information, and so on. In addition, the form also allows you to specify people that you know, including their name and a page to see more about them. In the example, I added two people: Simon St.Laurent, the editor of this book, and Dorothea Salo, one of the tech editors. When the fields are filled in, clicking the FOAF Me! button generates the RDF/XML, as shown in Example 14-3. You can then copy this, save it to a file, and modify the values—changing or adding new properties and more friends, whatever.

Example 14-3. FOAF RDF/XML file generated by FOAF-A-Matic

```
<rdf:RDF
      xmlns:rdf="http://www.w3.org/1999/02/22-rdf-syntax-ns#"
      xmlns:rdfs="http://www.w3.org/2000/01/rdf-schema#"
      xmlns:foaf="http://xmlns.com/foaf/0.1/">
<foaf:Person>
<foaf:name>Shelley Powers</foaf:name>
<foaf:title>Ms</foaf:title>
<foaf:firstName>Shelley</foaf:firstName>
<foaf:surname>Powers</foaf:surname>
<foaf:nick>Burningbird</foaf:nick>
<foaf:mbox_sha1sum>cd2b130288f7c417b7321fb51d240d570c520720</foaf:mbox_sha1sum>
<foaf:homepage rdf:resource="http://weblog.burningbird.net"/>
<foaf:workplaceHomepage rdf:resource="http://burningbird.net"/>
<foaf:workInfoHomepage rdf:resource="http://burningbird.net/about.htm"/>
<foaf:schoolHomepage rdf:resource="http://www.cwu.edu/"/>
<foaf:knows>
  <foaf:Person>
    <foaf:name>Simon St.Laurent</foaf:name>
    <foaf:mbox_sha1sum>65d7213063e1836b1581de81793bfcb9ad596974</foaf:mbox_sha1sum>
    <rdfs:seeAlso rdf:resource="http://www.simonstl.com/"/>
  </foaf:Person>
</foaf:knows>
<foaf:knows>
  <foaf:Person>
    <foaf:name>Dorothea Salo</foaf:name>
    <foaf:mbox_sha1sum>69d0c538f12014872164be6a3c16930f577388a8</foaf:mbox_sha1sum>
    <rdfs:seeAlso rdf:resource="http://www.yarinareth.net/caveatlector/"/>
  </foaf:Person></foaf:knows>
</foaf:Person>
</rdf:RDF>
```

Notice in the example that the property mbox_sha1sum is used instead of mbox. That's because one of the options used to generate the file was the ability to encode the email address so that it can't easily be scraped on the Web by email *spambots*—annoying little critters.

Notice also in the example that rdfs:seeAlso is used to map to a person's URL of interest. FOAF is first and foremost RDF/XML, which means the data it describes can be combined with other related, valid RDF/XML.

Once the FOAF file is to your liking, you can link to it from your home page using the link tag, as so:

```
<link rel="meta" type="application/rdf+xml" href="my-foaf-file.xrdf" />
```

This enables FOAF autodiscovery, or automatic discovery of your FOAF file by web bots and other friendly critters. Speaking of friendly critters, what else can you do with your FOAF file?

FOAF Technologies

Any technology that can work with RDF/XML can work with FOAF data. You can query FOAF files to find out who knows whom, to build a page containing links to your friends' pages, and so on. However, in addition to using traditional RDF/XML technologies with the FOAF data, there are also some FOAF-specialized technologies.

Edd Dumbill, the editor of XML.com, created what is known as the FOAFBot. This automated process sits quietly in the background monitoring an IRC (Internet Relay Chat) channel until such time as a member of the channel poses a question to it. For instance, at the FOAFBot web site a recorded question and answer exchange between an IRC member and the FOAFBot is:

```
<edd> foafbot, edd's name
<foafbot> edd's name is 'Edd Dumbill', according to Dan Brickley,
    Anon35, Niel Bornstein, Jo Walsh, Dave Beckett, Edd Dumbill,
    Matt Biddulph, Paul Ford
```

FOAFBot has access to a knowledge base consisting of data that's been gleaned from FOAF files on the Internet. You can read more about FOAFBot and download the Python source code at *http://usefulinc.com/foaf/foafbot*. (Note the source code is built on Dave Beckett's Redland framework, described in Chapter 11.)

In the FOAFBot page that opens, there's also a link to an article about how to digitally sign your FOAF file.

Another use of FOAF data is the codepiction project, which uses the foaf:depiction property to search for images in which two or more people are depicted together in the same photo. You can read more about the codepiction project at *http://rdfweb.org/2002/01/photo/index.html* and see a working prototype at *http://swordfish.rdfweb.org/discovery/2001/08/codepict/*.

Finally, there's been effort to extend the concept of FOAF to a corporate environment, including defining a new vocabulary more in line with corporate connectivity than personal connectivity. You can check out the work on this project, called FOAFCorp, at *http://rdfweb.org/foaf/corp/intro.html*.

## CHAPTER 15

A World of Uses: Commercial Uses of RDF/XML

While so much of RDF's early focus has been on the Semantic Web, it's important to note that there are companies that are utilizing RDF and focusing their products on immediate real-world uses. The mark of a technology entering maturity is not the number of technologies it's implemented in, but the number of viable applications that use it. It wasn't until XML started getting wider use within the business community that it become less of a technology for the lab and more of a technology for the office. This same principle holds true for RDF.

Just as happened with XML, and even HTML, it isn't until people see a technology being used for "practical" applications that business starts to become more comfortable in its use. Without business acceptance, developers are hesitant to work with a technology that may not have a payback in terms of job potential. Without mainstream developers supporting the use of, and finding uses for, RDF/XML, its acceptance is going to be limited. Luckily, though, I found several commercial uses of RDF and RDF/XML, in applications ranging from intelligence-community use to more efficient site navigation to alternative database structures and personal information management.

This chapter takes a look at some of the planned and existing commercial applications I found. This includes a personal information manager currently in design (OSAF's Chandler), an Application Server (Intellidimension's RDF Gateway), and Adobe's use of RDF/XML in existing products. In addition, we'll also look at Siderean Software's Seamark server for site navigation, and Plugged In Software's Tucana Knowledge Store for sophisticated searches.

The chapter is by no means an exhaustive summary of the existing potential and commercial uses of RDF; it is, I hope, a comprehensive view of the different uses of RDF within the business community.

Chandler: RDF Within an Open Source PIM

Chandler is a product resulting from an unusual project, managed through the Open Source Applications Foundation (OSAF), founded by Mitch Kapor. If that name doesn't ring any bells, Mitch founded Lotus Development Corporation and created Lotus 1-2-3.

 As of this writing, Chandler is in the design stage, a process that's quite open. For more information, access the OSAF main web page at *http://osafoundation.org*. A Wiki has been set up to handle external contributions to the design at *http://wiki.osafoundation.org/bin/view/ Main/WikiHome*.

Chandler is a personal information management (PIM) application, being designed in the open, based on open source technologies and specifications including RDF and RDF/XML.

OSA incorporates RDF into its architecture in two places. The first is an import/ export mechanism allowing import and export of data from Chandler into RDF/ XML. The hope is that this functionality allows Chandler to incorporate data from other sources more easily; data sources such as FOAF, described in Chapter 14, would be a natural candidate for information in a PIM.

In addition, according to the technology overview of the product, Chandler's own data model will support RDF Schema semantics, which means that the data conforms to all of the semantics defined by the RDF specification, including the very basic concept of triple. According to the Chandler Architecture document, OSAF decided on RDF:

> ...because of its ability to describe data in a very flexible format and exchange semantic information between applications in a standard format without loss. Because RDF is a World Wide Web Consortium standard, we hope to gain benefit from the existing tools, validators and applications that have been developed or will be developed.

The group is also focusing on a Python object-based data store based on ZODB, the Zope database (at *http://www.zope.org/Products/StandaloneZODB*). Rather than the more traditional approach of storing RDF in the form of triples, the Chandler development team is pursuing a possible mapping between RDF and the object classes supported in ZODB. There originally was an interest in a mapping between Zope and RDF (at *http://www.zope.org/Resources/Mozilla/Projects/RDFSupport/*), but there hasn't been any activity on this for several months. Whether Chandler will rekindle activity in a mapping between Zope, ZODB, and RDF should become more apparent as progress on Chandler continues.

At this time, Chandler is in the planning/design/early implementation stages. To follow the progress of this product, you can subscribe to or view the archives of the

OSA mailing lists at *http://osafoundation.org/mailing_lists.htm*, in addition to accessing the main web site and the Wiki.

RDF Gateway, a Commercial RDF Database

RDF Gateway is a database and integrated web server, utilizing RDF, and built from the ground up rather than on top of either an existing web server (such as Apache) or database (such as SQL Server or MySQL). At this time, it works only within the Windows environment, specifically Windows NT 4.0, 2000, or XP. The installation is extremely easy; I was able to download, install, and run the application in less than five minutes.

 Download an evaluation version of RDF Gateway at *http://www.intellidimension.com*. This chapter was written with the beta version of the product, but Version 1.0 released as this went into production.

RDF Gateway is an application server providing web page template support similar to ASP or JSP. This includes data storage, support for a scriptlike data query language, and web services. Aside from the use of RDF, all aspects of the tool are proprietary, though many are based on current open source efforts, including the RDF parser associated with Redland (discussed in Chapter 11).

Once installed, an RDF Gateway icon is added to the system tray. Right-clicking on this opens a menu that can be used to start or stop the server or to open a properties window with information about the Gateway, such as port, database location, and so on. The properties page is informational only—unless there's a problem with the server, these settings shouldn't need to be changed.

The Gateway can be managed through an online interface, where you can do things such as add or remove users from access to the repository, as shown in Figure 15-1.

You can also view the data tables used for the RDF Gateway repository or add COM objects, web services, packages, and so on. These externally created extensions to the Gateway can then be accessed through the scripting language supported by the product: RDFQL, an ECMAScript-based scripting language. RDFQL is used within RDF Server Pages (RSP) similarly to how Java is used in JSP and VBScript in ASP. As do these embedded scripting page approaches, RDFQL supports several built-in and global objects to facilitate application development. Among the objects supported with the released version of RDF Gateway are:

DataSource
> Provides access to RDF statements stored in an external file or within the database

Request
> Contains HTTP request information, including environment variables

---

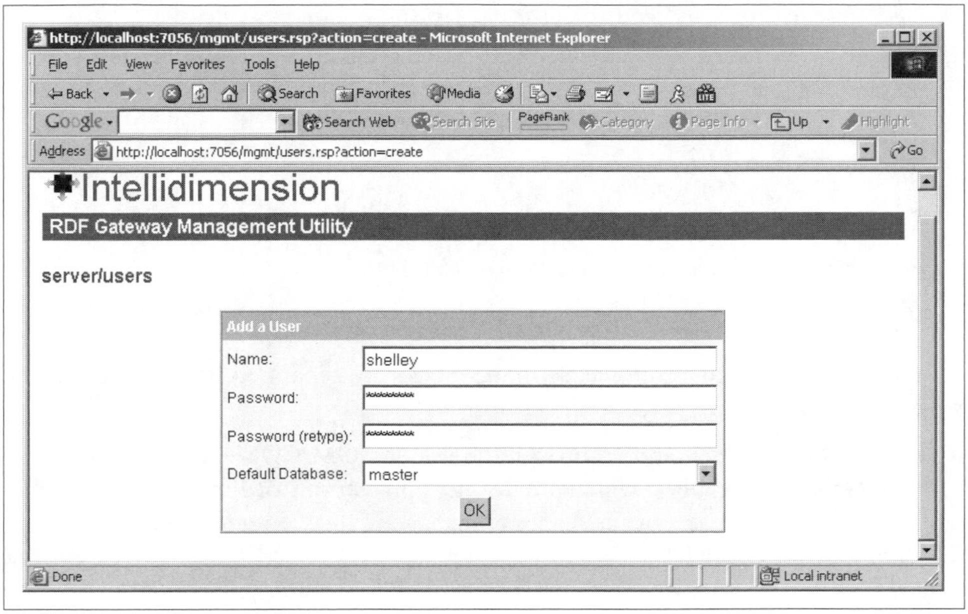

Figure 15-1. Adding a new user for RDF Gateway

Response
> To return response

Security
> Access to RDF Gateway security features

Server
> Access to server features

Session
> Created for every session and used primarily for setting session variables

RDFNode
> To access a specific piece of information from an RDF data source

Package
> Access to an RDF Gateway package

There are other objects such as strings, enumerators, and so on, but this listing gives you an idea of the built-in capability associated with RDFQL. Example 15-1 is a simple RSP that does nothing more than read an external RDF/XML page into a DataSource object and then use that object's formatting capability to print the RDF/XML out to the page.

Example 15-1. Reading in and writing out remote RDF/XML document

```
<%
// Create an in-memory data source
// connect to remote RDF/XML document using the Inet data service
```

Example 15-1. Reading in and writing out remote RDF/XML document (continued)

```
var monsters = new DataSource("inet?url=http://burningbird.net/articles/monsters1.
rdf&parsetype=rdf");

//set the content type
Response.ContentType = "text/xml";

//use the Format command on the datasource to generate an rdf+xml representation of the
//contents of the datasource
Response.Write(monsters.Format('application/rdf+xml'));

%>
```

As you can see from the example, scripting blocks are separated from the rest of the page with angle bracket/percent sign enclosures.

RDF Gateway can be extended through the use of COM/COM+ objects, as well as through Gateway packages, which are distinct applications or libraries of functions, which can be used in any of the Gateway-managed pages. In addition, the underlying data repository for RDF Gateway can be accessed directly through JDBC from within Java applications and through ADO if you're programming Windows-based applications. RDFCLI, a Win32 library, also provides the fastest and most direct access to the RDF Gateway services.

At first glance RDF Gateway appears similar to IIS/COM+ and other application/web servers of similar make, until you take a closer glance at the data queries. This is where the product's RDF roots shine through.

I pulled an example of how data manipulation can work with RDF Gateway from the help files included with the application. Example 15-2 shows how to create and insert RDF statements into an in-memory data source and then how to print select predicate values out.

Example 15-2. Creating and then querying RDF data within memory datastore

```
foaf = new DataSource();

INSERT
    {[http://www.w3.org/1999/02/22-rdf-syntax-ns#type]
     [mailto:drepchick@intellidimension.com]
     [http://xmlns.com/foaf/0.1/Person]}

    {[http://xmlns.com/foaf/0.1/firstName]
     [mailto:drepchick@intellidimension.com]
     "Derrish"}

    {[http://xmlns.com/foaf/0.1/knows]
     [mailto:drepchick@intellidimension.com]
     [mailto:gchappell@intellidimension.com]}

    {[http://www.w3.org/1999/02/22-rdf-syntax-ns#type]
```

```
    [mailto:gchappell@intellidimension.com]
    [http://xmlns.com/foaf/0.1/Person]}

    {[http://xmlns.com/foaf/0.1/firstName]
    [mailto:gchappell@intellidimension.com]
    "Geoff"}

    {[http://xmlns.com/foaf/0.1/knows]
    [mailto:gchappell@intellidimension.com]
    [mailto:drepchick@intellidimension.com]}

    INTO #foaf;

var ary = foaf.getObjects();

for (var i = 0; i < ary.length; i++)
{
    dumpPerson(ary[i]);
}

function dumpPerson(node)
{
    var s = node["http://xmlns.com/foaf/0.1/firstName"];

    var ary = node["http://xmlns.com/foaf/0.1/knows"];

    if (ary != null)
    {
        s += " -> ";

        for (var i = 0; i < ary.length; i++)
        {
            if (i > 0)
                s += ", ";

            s += ary[i]["http://xmlns.com/foaf/0.1/firstName"];
        }
    }

    Response.write(s);
}
```

After exposure to RDQL in Chapter 10, the insert statements based on an RDF tri-ple in the first part of the code should be relatively familiar. Once the data's added to the store, the second part of the code example accesses the firstName property for both the FOAF resource, as well as all the resources that map to the knows predicate, resulting in an output of:

```
Derrish -> Geoff
Geoff -> Derrish
```

RDF Gateway also provides the ability to query against multiple datastores, merging the results as appropriate. For instance, you can access data from three different data sources with a query such as the following:

```
select ?p ?s ?o using #ds1, #ds2, #ds3 where {?p ?s ?o};
```

RDF Gateway also includes strong inferential support through two types of rules: statement and function. These allow incorporation of process logic within the semantics of the more traditional query. Again, using examples from the help file for the Gateway product, a statement rule would be like the following:

```
INFER {[acme:size] ?product_id "big"} FROM
{[itd:size] ?product_id "large"} OR {[itd:size] ?product_id "x-large"};
```

That's a lot of strange syntax, but what this statement is really saying is that there is a rule, {[acme:size] ?product_id "big"}, that is true if the body, {[itd:size] ?product_id "large"} OR {[itd:size] ?product_id "x-large"}, evaluates to true, and which can then be used within an RDFQL query as follows:

```
SELECT ?acme_size FROM inventory WHERE {[acme:size] ?product_id ?acme_size};
```

The use of an inferential rule allows you to map one type of schema on to another and to then use these within the queries.

How rules work becomes even more apparent when one looks at a function rule, such as the following:

```
INFER GetLeadTime(?product_id, ?lead_time) FROM
    {[itd:assembly_time] ?product_id ?assembly_time} AND
    SWITCH
    (
    case {[itd:component] ?product_id ?component_id}:
        GetLeadTime(?component_id, ?lead_time_comp)
            AND ?lead_time = ADD(?lead_time_comp,
?assembly_time)
    default:
        ?lead_time = ?assembly_time
    )
```

Using this function rule within a query, such as the following, returns the lead time for large products. However, within the rule itself, the actual lead time is accumulated from summing all lead times for the individual components that make up the part:

```
SELECT ?lead_time USING inventory WHERE
    {[itd:size] ?product_id "large"} AND  GetLeadTime(?product_id, ?lead_time);
```

Learning to work with the inferential engine of RDF Gateway isn't trivial, but the potential of encapsulating complex logic into a form that can be used and reused within queries has considerable appeal. To enable this encapsulation, RDF Gateway provides support for a *rulebase*, a set of RDFQL rules that can be included within a query. Redefining the function statement into a rulebase would be as follows:

```
rulebase app_rules
{
    // ITD size to Acme size mapping rule
```

```
        INFER {[acme:size] ?product_id "big"} FROM
        {[itd:size] ?product_id 'large'} OR {[itd:size] ?product_id "x-large"};

        // Lead time function rule

        INFER GetLeadTime(?product_id, ?lead_time) FROM
        {[itd:assembly_time] ?product_id ?assembly_time} AND
        SWITCH
        {
        case {[itd:component] ?product_id ?component_id}:
            getLeadTime(?component_id, ?lead_time) AND ?lead_time = ADD(?lead_time,
    ?assembly_time)
        default:
            ?lead_time = ?assembly_time
        };
    };
```

The rulebase would then be used in a query in the following manner:

```
SELECT ?product_id USING inventory RULEBASE NONE WHERE {[itd:size] ?product_id
"big"};
```

It is this inferential engine support, in addition to the RDF/XML base, that makes
RDF Gateway unique among application servers.

Siderean Software's Seamark

Siderean Software's Seamark is a sophisticated application providing resources for
intelligent site querying and navigation. The company makes use of a faceted metadata search and classification scheme for describing page characteristics. It is
intended for larger, commercial applications and web sites, providing the infrastructure necessary for this type of search capability.

Siderean Software's web site is at *http://siderean.com*. I was given
access to a beta version of the software for the Windows environment
at the time of this writing.

By *faceted metadata*, Siderean is talking about defined properties or characteristics of
objects. Seamark allows searching on variations of this type of data. Once the
Seamark repository is installed, it's quite simple to load data into it from external
RDF/XML files. The data in these files is then combined with existing data in the
Seamark database. There is no specialized Seamark RDF Schema, which means the
RDF/XML can be from any vocabulary.

Aside from the repository, Seamark's second main component is what Siderean calls
search models. Once these models are defined, they can then be incorporated into the
navigation and search functionality of the applications based on Seamark. The query
language used to define the search models is based on XRBR, XML Retrieval by
Reformulation format, a query language proprietary to Siderean. Once a search is
defined, Seamark can generate a customizable ASP or a JSP page that incorporates

the search and to which you can add custom code as needed. Additionally, you can access the Seamark services through the Seamark API, a SOAP-based protocol.

The user interface for Seamark is quite simple, consisting of a main model/RDF document page, with peripheral pages to manage the application data. Once the application is installed, the first steps to take after starting the application are to create a model and then load one or more RDF/XML documents. Figure 15-2 shows the page form used to identify an internal RDF/XML document. Among the parameters specified is whether to load the document on a timed schedule, or manually, in addition to the URL of the file and the base URL used within the document. The page also provides space for an XSL stylesheet to transform non-RDF XML to RDF/XML.

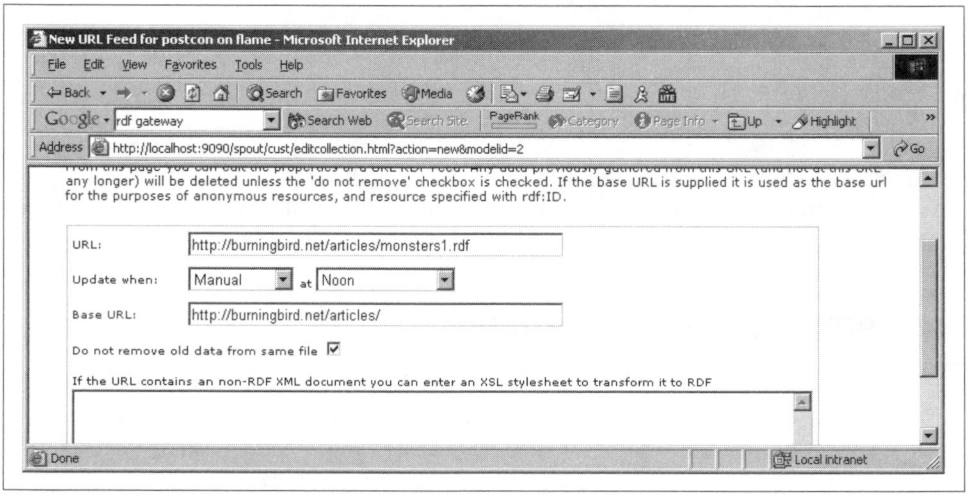

Figure 15-2. Adding a URL for an external RDF/XML data source

Once the external feed is defined, the data can then be loaded manually or allowed to load according to the schedule you defined.

After data is loaded into the Seamark repository, you can then create the search queries to access it. In the query page, Seamark lists out the RDFS classes within the document; you can pick among these and have the tool create the query for you or manually create the query.

For instance, the example RDF/XML used throughout the book, *http://burningbird. net/articles/monsters1.rdf*, has three separate classes:

pstcn:Resource
    Main object and any related resources

pstcn:Movement
    Resource movements

rdf:Seq
    The RDF sequence used to coordinate resource history

For my first query, I selected the Resource object, and had Seamark generate the query, as shown in Figure 15-3.

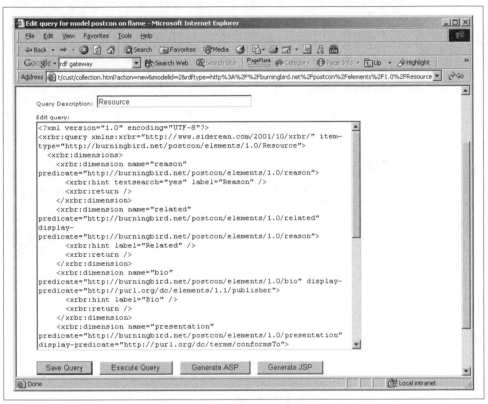

Figure 15-3. An automatically generated query in Seamark.

As you can see from the figure, XRBR isn't a trivial query language, though a little practice helps you work through the verbosity of the query. Once the initial XRBR is generated, you can customize the query, save it, execute it, or generate ASP or JSP to manage the query—or any combination of these options. Executing the query returns XRBR-formatted data, consisting of data and characteristics, or *facets* for all the Resource classes in the document. At this point, you can again customize the query or generate an ASP or JSP page.

When you add new RDF/XML documents to the repository, this new data is incorporated into the system, and running the query again queries the new data as well as the old. Figure 15-4 shows the page for the model with two loaded RDF/XML documents and one query defined.

Seamark comes with a default application called *bookdemo* that can be used as a prototype as well as a training tool. In addition, the application is easily installed and configured and comes with considerable documentation, most in PDF format. What

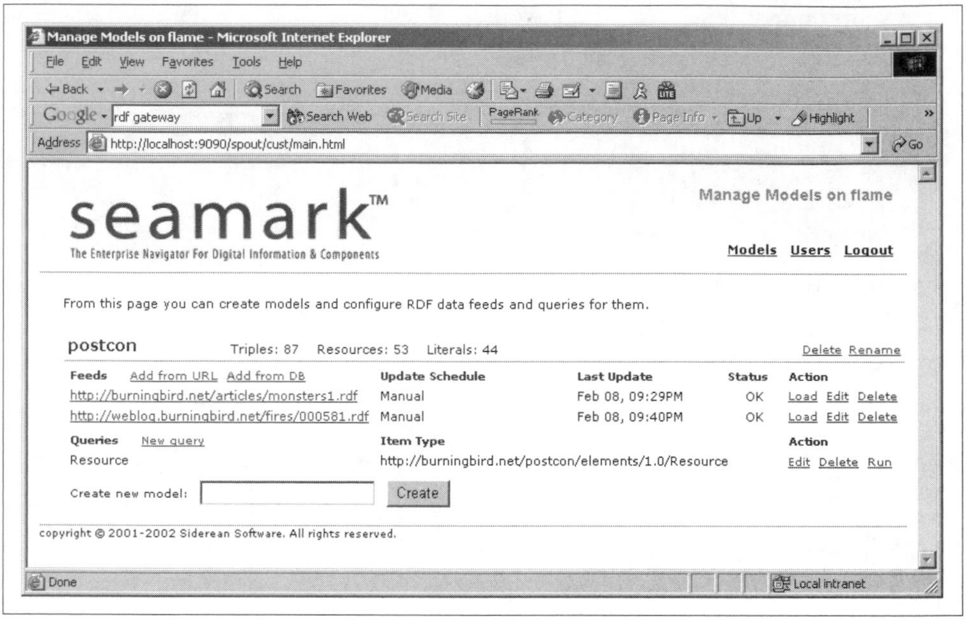

Figure 15-4. PostCon Seamark model with two data sources and one query

I was most impressed with, though, was how quickly and easily it integrated my RDF/XML data from the PostCon application into a sophisticated query engine with little or no effort. Few things prove the usefulness of a well-defined metadata structure faster than commercial viability.

Plugged In Software's Tucana Knowledge Store

Plugged In Software's Tucana Knowledge Store (TKS) enables storage and retrieval of data that's designed to efficiently scale to larger datastores. The scalability is assured because distributed data sources are an inherent part of the architecture, as is shown in the diagram in Figure 15-5.

> You can download an evaluation copy of Tucana Knowledge Store at *http://www.pisoftware.com/index.html*. In addition, if you intend to use the application for academic purposes, you can download and use an academic copy of the application for free.

In situations with large amounts of potentially complex data, this distributed data repository may be the only effective approach to finding specific types of data. TKS has found a home in the defense industry because of the nature of its architecture and is being used within the intelligence as well as defense communities.

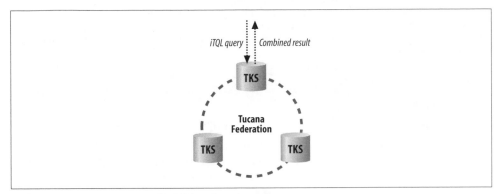

Figure 15-5. Demonstration of TKS distributed nature

TKS pairs the large-scale data storage and querying with a surprisingly simple interface. For instance, the query language support (iTQL) functionality can be accessed at the command line by typing in the following command:

```
java -jar itql-1.0.jar
```

This command opens an iTQL shell session. Once in, just type in the commands necessary. I found TKS to be as intuitively easy to use as it was to install. I followed the tutorial included with TKS, except using my example RDF/XML document, *http://burningbird.net/articles/monsters1.rdf*, as the data source. First, I created a model within TKS to hold the data:

```
iTQL> create <rmi://localhost/server1#postcon>;
Successfully created model rmi://localhost/server1#postcon
```

Next, I loaded the data from the external document:

```
iTQL> load <http://burningbird.net/articles/monsters1.rdf> into <rmi://localhost/
server1#postcon>;
Successfully loaded 58 statements from http://burningbird.net/articles/monsters1.rdf
into rmi://localhost/server1#postcon
```

After the data was loaded, I queried the two "columns" in the data—the predicate and the object—for the main resource, `http://burningbird.net/articles/monsters1.htm`:

```
iTQL> select $obj $pred from <rmi://localhost/server1#postcon> where <pstcn:release>
$pred $obj;
0 columns: (0 rows)
iTQL> select $obj $pred from <rmi://localhost/server1#postcon> where <http://
burningbird.net/articles/monsters1.htm> $pred $obj;
2 columns: obj pred (8 rows)
        obj=http://burningbird.net/articles/monsters2.htm        pred=http://burn
ingbird.net/postcon/elements/1.0/related
        obj=http://burningbird.net/articles/monsters3.htm        pred=http://burn
ingbird.net/postcon/elements/1.0/related
        obj=http://burningbird.net/articles/monsters4.htm        pred=http://burn
ingbird.net/postcon/elements/1.0/related
        obj=http://burningbird.net/postcon/elements/1.0/Resource        pred=htt
p://www.w3.org/1999/02/22-rdf-syntax-ns#type
```

```
        obj=rmi://flame/server1#node123 pred=http://burningbird.net/postcon/elem
ents/1.0/bio
        obj=rmi://flame/server1#node134 pred=http://burningbird.net/postcon/elem
ents/1.0/relevancy
        obj=rmi://flame/server1#node147 pred=http://burningbird.net/postcon/elem
ents/1.0/presentation
        obj=rmi://flame/server1#node164 pred=http://burningbird.net/postcon/elem
ents/1.0/history
```

The blank nodes are identified with TKS's own method of generating bnode identifiers, in this case a concatenation of a local server name and a specific node identifier. As you can see from this example, the TKS query language iTQL is very similar to what we've seen with RDQL and other RDF/XML-based query languages.

In addition to the command-line shell, there's also a web-based version that might be easier to use, especially when you're new. However, the basic functionality is the same.

The power of TKS is accessing the services that the TKS server provides from within your own applications. For this, TKS comes with custom JSP tags for interoperating with the TKS server. In addition, you can access the services through COM objects, within a Windows environment, through SOAP, through a specialized JavaBean, and through two drivers: a JDBC driver and a native TKS driver. This makes the query capability of TKS available in all popular development environments, as shown in Figure 15-6.

Bottom line: the power of TKS is just that—power. By combining a simple and intuitive interface with an architecture that's built from the ground up for large-scale data queries, the application is meant to get you up and running, quickly.

RDF and Adobe: XMP

Rather than integrate RDF into the architecture of a tool from the ground up, as occurred with the previous applications discussed in this chapter, other companies are incorporating RDF and RDF/XML into their existing applications. Adobe, a major player in the publications and graphics business, is one such company. Its RDF/XML strategy is known as XMP—eXtensible Metadata Platform. According to the Adobe XMP web site, other major players have agreed to support the XMP framework, including companies such as Microsoft.

XMP focuses on providing a metadata label that can be embedded directly into applications, files, and databases, including binary data, using what Adobe calls XMP packets—XML fragments that can be embedded regardless of recipient format. Regardless of where the material is moved or located, the data contained in the embedded material moves with it and can be accessed by external tools using the XMP Toolkit. Adobe has added support for XMP to Photoshop 7.0, Acrobat 5.0,

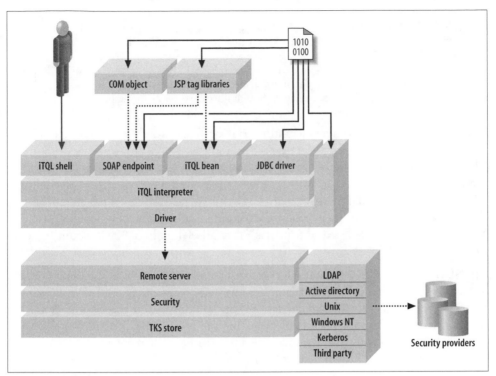

Figure 15-6. Client/Server architecture supported by TKS

FrameMaker 7.0, GoLive 6.0, InCopy 2.0, InDesign 2.0, Illustrator 10, and Live-Motion 2.0.

The information included within the embedded labels can be from any schema as long as it's recorded in valid RDF/XML. The XMP source code is freely available for download, use, and modification under an open source license.

 Read more about Adobe XMP at *http://www.adobe.com/products/xmp/*. Download the SDK at *http://partners.adobe.com/asn/developer/xmp/ main.html*.

Unlike so much of the RDF/XML technology, which emphasizes Java or Python, the XMP Toolkit provides only support for C++. Specifically, the toolkit works with Microsoft's Visual C++ in Windows (or compatible compiler) and Metrowerks CodeWarrior C++ for the Mac.

Within the SDK is a subdirectory of C++ code that allows a person to read and write XMP metadata. Included in the SDK is a good set of documentation that provides samples and instructions on embedding XMP metadata into TIFF, HTML, JPEG, PNG, PDF, SVG/XML, Illustrator (*.ai*), Photoshop (*.psd*), and Postscript and EPS formats.

The SDK is a bit out of date in regard to recent activities with RDF and RDF/XML. For instance, when discussing embedded RDF/XML into HTML documents, it references a W3C note that was favorable to the idea of embedding of RDF/XML into HTML. However, as you read in Chapter 3, recent decisions discourage the embedding of metadata into (X)HTML documents, though it isn't expressly forbidden.

The SDK contains some documentation, but be forewarned, it assumes significant experience with the different data types, as well as experience working with C++. The document of most interest is the Metadata Framework PDF file, specifically the section discussing how XMP works with RDF, as well as the section on extending XMP with external RDF/XML Schemas. This involves nothing more than defining data in valid RDF and using a namespace for data not from the core schemas used by XMP. The section titled "XMP Schemas" lists all elements of XMP's built-in schemas.

The SDK also includes C++ and the necessary support files for the Metadata Library, as well as some other utilities and samples. I dusted off my rarely used Visual C++ 6.0 to access the project for the Metadata Toolkit, Windows, and was able to build the library without any problems just by accessing the project file, *XAPToolkit.dsw*. The other C++ applications also compiled cleanly as long as I remembered to add the paths for the included header files and libraries.

One of the samples included with the SDK was XAPDumper, an application that scans for embedded RDF/XML within an application or file and then prints it out. I compiled it and ran it against the *SDKOverview.pdf* document. An excerpt of the embedded data found in this file is:

```
<rdf:Description rdf:about=''
 xmlns:pdf='http://ns.adobe.com/pdf/1.3/'>
 <pdf:Producer>Acrobat Distiller 5.0.5 for Macintosh</pdf:Producer>
 <!—pdf:CreationDate is aliased—>
 <!—pdf:ModDate is aliased—>
 <!—pdf:Creator is aliased—>
 <!—pdf:Author is aliased—>
 <!—pdf:Title is aliased—>
</rdf:Description>
```

Embedding RDF/XML isn't much different than attaching a bar code to physical objects. Both RDF and bar codes uniquely identify important information about the object in case it becomes separated from an initial package. In addition, within a publications environment, if all of the files are marked with this RDF/XML-embedded information, automated processes could access this information and use it to determine how to connect the different files together, such as embedding a JPEG file into an HTML page and so on.

I can see the advantage of embedded RDF/XML for any source that's loaded to the Web. Eventually, web bots could access and use this information to provide more intelligent information about the resources that they touch. Instead of a few key-words and a title as well as document type, these bots could provide an entire history of a document or picture, as well as every particular about it.

Other applications can also build in support for working with XMP. For instance, RDF Gateway, mentioned earlier, has the capability of reading in Adobe XMP. An example of how this application would access data from an Adobe PDF would be:

```
var monsters = new
DataSource("inet?url=http://burningbird.net/articles/monsters3.pdf&parse
type=xmp");
```

An important consideration with these embedded techniques is that there is no adverse impact on the file, nothing that impacts on the visibility of a JPEG or a PNG graphic or prevents an HTML file from loading into a browser. In fact, if you've read any PDF files from Adobe and other sites that use the newer Adobe products, you've probably been working with XMP documents containing embedded RDF/XML and didn't even know it.

What's It All Mean?

In my opinion, Adobe's use of RDF/XML demonstrates how RDF/XML will be integrated in other applications and uses in the future—quietly, behind the scenes. Unlike XML with its public exposure, huge fanfare, and claims of human and machine compatibility and interoperability, RDF was never meant to be anything more than a behind-the-scenes metadata model and an associated serialization format. RDF records statements so that they can be discovered mechanically—nothing more, nothing less. However, this simple act creates a great many uses of RDF/XML because of the careful analysis and precision that went into building the specification upon which RDF resides and which RDF/XML transcribes.

RDF assures us that any data stored in RDF/XML format in one application can be incorporated with data stored in RDF/XML format in another application, and moving the data from one to the other occurs without loss of information or integrity. While sharing and transmitting, merging and coalescing the data, we can attach meaning to objects stored on the Web—meaning that can be accessed and understood by applications and automated agents and APIs such as those covered in this book.

As the use of RDF grows, the dissemination of RDF/XML data on the Web increases and the processing of this data is incorporated into existing applications, the days when I'll search for information about the giant squid and receive information on how to cook giant squid steaks will fade into the past. I will be able to input parameters specific to my search about the giant squid into the computer and have it return exactly what I'm looking for, because the computer and I will have learned to understand each other.

This belief in the future of RDF and RDF/XML was somewhat borne out when I did a final search for information on the giant squid and its relation to the legends and to that other legendary creature, Nessie the Loch Ness Monster, as I was finishing this book. When I input the terms *giant squid legends Nessie* in Google, terms from my subject lists associated with the article that's been used for most of the examples in this book, the PostCon RDF/XML file for my giant squid article was the first item Google returned.

It's a start.

Index

Symbols

(pound sign), indicating relative URI, 44

Numbers

3-tuple representation of RDF triples, 18
4RDF, Python-based RDF API, 191

A

A Relational Model of Data for Large Shared
        Data Banks, 86
absolute URI, 22
addProperty method, Jena, 152
Adobe XMP (see XMP)
aggregators, RSS, 11, 268–274, 278–280
Alt (alternative) container, 60, 64, 65, 89
AmphetaDesk aggregator, 269–270
anonymous nodes (see blank nodes)
Apache, PHP support with, 183
APIs
    Drive, for C#, 215–218
    Informa RSS Library, for Java, 278
    Jena, for Java (see Jena)
    PerlRDF (see PerlRDF)
    RDF API for PHP, 183–187
    RDFLib, for Python, 187–191
    RDFStore, for Perl, 182
    Wilbur, for LISP, 218
    (see also frameworks; software)
applications based on RDF
    Chandler, 303
    Creative Commons Licenses, 295–297
    FOAF (Friend-of-a-Friend), 298–301
    MIT DSpace, 297

Mozilla, 11, 286–294
RDF Gateway, 304–309, 317
Seamark, 193, 309–312
TKS (Tucana Knowledge Store), 193,
        312–314
XMP (eXtensible Metadata
        Platform), 314–317
    (see also software)
arcs, in RDF graph, 20
ARP2 (Another RDF/XML Parser, second
        generation), 136–138
    (see also Jena)
autodiscovery
    of FOAF file, 299–300
    of RSS file, 268

B

Bag container, 58, 64, 65, 89
base document, resolving relative URIs
        with, 44
Beckett, Dave (Expressing Simple Dublin
        Core in RDF/XML), 122
Berkeley Database
    persisting RDF data to, with
        PerlRDF, 174
    Redland using, 222
Berners-Lee, Tim
    describing uses of Semantic Web, 2
    views on the term context, 16
blank nodes, 20, 41–43
    identifiers generated for, 42
    merging, 26
    none, indicating grounded graph, 26
BlankNode class, RDF API for PHP, 183

We'd like to hear your suggestions for improving our indexes. Send email to *index@oreilly.com*.

bnodes (see blank nodes)
books
    about Mozilla, 288
    about RSS, 254
    (see also specifications and documents)
Boswell, David (Creating Applications with
        Mozilla), 288
Brickley, Dan
    creator of RubyRDF, 218
    editor, RDF Schema specification, 2
    Expressing Simple Dublin Core in
        RDF/XML, 122
    RDF: Understanding the Striped
        RDF/XML Syntax, 35
BrownSauce, RDF/XML browser, 132–135
browser (BrownSauce), 132–135
business model (see ontology)

C

C#, API for (see Drive)
C, API for (see Redland)
CC licenses (see Creative Commons Licenses)
Chandler, 303
channel element, RSS, 257
circles, in RDF graph, 20
classes
    Drive, 216
    Jena, 150, 154–157
    OWL, 244–247
    PHP XML, 203–210
    RDF API for PHP, 183
    RDF Schema, 87–90, 118
    Redland, 222
CLOS, API for (see Wilbur)
CNRI Handle System, 297
Codd, E. F. (A Relational Model of Data for
        Large Shared Data Banks), 86
codepiction project, FOAF used by, 301
collections, 65
    compared to containers, 114
    history of, 57
Collins, Pete (Creating Applications with
        Mozilla), 288
complement classes, OWL, 246
constraints, RDF Schema, 95
containers, 57–65
    Alt (alternative), 60, 64, 65
    alternative to, 61
    Bag, 58, 64, 65
    compared to collections, 114
    creating with Jena, 161–164
    current specifications for, 64–65

distributive referents of, 61
history of, 57
initial specifications for, 58–61
PostCon example using, 114–116
referents (items) of, 61
semantics of, 66
Seq (sequence), 59, 63, 64, 65
typed node specification revisions
        for, 62–64
Content module, RSS, 265
Content Syndication with XML and
        RSS, 254
context
    meaning of, within RDF, 16
    searching Internet based on, 15
core modules, RSS, 264–267
Creating Applications with Mozilla, 288
Creative Commons Licenses, 295–297
CSS, RDF compared to, 7

D

DAML (DARPA Agent Markup
        Language), 8, 229
daml:Class element, compared to
        rdfs:Class, 230
DAMLModelImpl class, Jena, 150
DAML+OIL, 8
    compared to OWL, 234
    compared to RDFS, 230
    converting to OWL, 231
    history of, 229
    Jena support for, 151
    specifications for, 231
DARPA Agent Markup Language (see
        DAML)
data handshaking, 9
data types, 53
    built-in, XML Schema, 54
    of literal nodes, 20
    of literal predicates, 53
database (see relational database)
DataSource object, RDF Gateway, 304
DB_File object, PerlRDF, 174
DC (see Dublin Core Metadata Initiative)
DC-dot generator, 129
description element, RSS, 257
directed graph (see RDF graph)
disjoint classes, OWL, 247
distributive referents, 61
Document Type Definition (see DTD)
documents (see specifications and
        documents)

IsaViz, RDF/XML editor, 142–146
item element, RSS, 262
item element, RSS Content module, 266
items element, RSS, 258–261
items element, RSS Content module, 266
iTQL query language, TKS, 313

J

Java
  APIs for (see Jena; Redland)
  browser based on (see BrownSauce,
      RDF/XML browser)
  databases based on (see Inkling database)
  editors based on (see IsaViz; RDF Editor
      in Java)
  ontology editors based on (see Protégé
      ontology editor; SMORE), 248
  parser based on (see VRP)
JDBC connection, using with Jena, 169
Jena, 149–151
  ARP included with, 149
  classes, 150, 154–157
  classes of, used by IsaViz, 142
  containers, creating, 161–164
  DBConnection problem with, 169
  encapsulating vocabulary in wrapper
      class, 153–157
  modeling RDF and creating
      RDF/XML, 151–164
  nested resources, 157–159
  outputting data in alternate
      formats, 164–166
  persisting data to relational
      database, 168–171
  querying with API, 164–168
  querying with RDQL, 150
  RDQL support, 198–203
  striped syntax, 157–159
  system requirements for, 149
  typed nodes, 159–161
  version used in this book, 149
  (see also ARP2)

K

Kapor, Mitch (founder of OSAF), 303
King, Brian (Creating Applications with
    Mozilla), 288
Krech, Daniel (creator of RDFLib), 188

L

language for RDF/XML, 53
Lassila, Ora
  co-editor of RDF M&S specification, 218
  editor of RDF specification, 2
link element, RSS, 257
LISP, API for (see Wilbur)
listObjects method, Jena, 165
listObjectsOfProperty method, Jena, 166
listStatements method, Jena, 166
listSubjects method, Jena, 166
Literal class, RDF API for PHP, 183
literals, 36, 53
  listing in resource element, 50
  multiple (see containers)
  nodes, 20
  PerlRDF module for, 175
  RDF API for PHP class, 183
  RDF Schema classes for, 87, 89
  RDFLib object for, 188
  typed, 53, 263

M

McBride, Brian (creator of Jena), 149
media companies, RSS used by, 253
Meerkat aggregator, 271–274
Melnik, Sergey (creator of Stanford Java
    API), 182
merging lemma, 27
merging RDF graphs, 25
metadata, 84–86
  faceted, in Seamark, 309
  RDF purpose for, 2
  RDF Schema and, 86
  reification used for, 81
  (see also Dublin Core Metadata Initiative;
      XMP)
Miller, Eric (Expressing Simple Dublin Core
    in RDF/XML), 122
MIME type, for RDF/XML document, 54
MIT DSpace, 297
Model class, Jena, 150
Model class, RDF API for PHP, 183
ModelCom class, Jena, 150
ModelFactory class, Jena, 150
ModelMem class, Jena, 150
ModelRDB class, Jena, 150
modules, RSS, 263–268
Mono C# compiler, 215

owl:onProperty element, 243
owl:Ontology element, 236
owl:Restriction element, 243
owl:someValuesFrom element, 243
owl:SymmetricProperty element, 241
owl:TransitiveProperty element, 241
owl:unionOf element, 245
owl:versionInfo element, 236

P

Package object, RDF Gateway, 305
parsers
    ARP2, 136–138
    PerlRDF as, 179–181
    uses of, 135
    VRP, 138–142
partial URI, 22
PDES (Product Data Exchange
    Specification), 9
PeopleSoft, OWL compared to, 10
Perl
    RDFStore API for, 182
    Redland classes for, 222
    W3C Perl library, 173
    web site for, 172
    XML::RSS module for, 281
PerlRDF, 173–182
    building RDF model, 175–179
    in-memory data storage, 174
    parsing RDF/XML documents, 179–181
    persistence to relational
        database, 174–175
    querying RDF data, 181–182
    rdf:about element, replacing, 176
    updates to, 173
    web site for, 173
persistence to relational database
    Jena used for, 168–171
    PerlRDF used for, 174–175
    PostGreSQL used for, 174, 194
    rdfDB used for, 193
    RDQL in PHP used for, 207
    RDQL_DB in PHP used for, 203
    Redland used for, 222
PHP
    RDF API for, 183–187
    web site for, 172, 203
    XML classes for RDF, 203–210
Plugged In Software, Tucana Knowledge
    Store (see TKS)
PNG graphics file, output by IsaViz, 146

POSC, 9
PostCon example
    containers in, 114–116
    defining business and scope for, 101
    defining business domain
        elements, 103–105
    Dublin Core elements used in, 124–129
    Dublin Core qualifiers used in, 123
    Dublin Core title element in, 122
    Java-based implementation of, 157
    prototyping vocabulary for, 106–117
    repeating predicates in, 110–114
PostGreSQL database, 174, 194
pound sign (#), indicating relative URI, 44
predicates, 17, 36–38
    formatting convention for, 36
    multiple, enclosing in one resource
        block, 49
    multiple, listing as resource attributes, 50
    reification and, 72
    repeating, 110–114
PrintWriter class, Jena, 152
Product Data Exchange Specification (see
    PDES)
properties
    OWL, 240–244
    RDF triple, 17
    RDFS, 90–96, 118, 119
Property class, Jena, 152
property value, RDF triple, 17
Protégé ontology editor, 248–252
protocol, specifying in URI, 22
Python
    RDFLib, 187–191
    Redfoot Hypercode using, 225
    Redland classes for, 222
    web site for, 172

Q

QNames, 39–41
Query class, Jena, 198, 199
query languages
    iTQL, used by TKS, 313
    rdfDB QL, 193
    RDQL and RDQL_DB, for PHP, 203–210
    RDQL, for Jena, 150, 198–203
    Sesame, 210–214
    SquishQL, 194–197
    Versa, 191
    web site about, 192
    XRBR, used by Seamark, 309–312
    (see also querying)

RDF vocabulary (*continued*)
  encapsulating in Jena, 153–157
  example of (see PostCon example)
  formalizing with RDFS, 118–120
  mixing with DC elements, 124–129
  namespace URI for, 106
  prototyping, 106–117
  repeating predicates in, 110–114
  (see also RDFS)
RDF Vocabulary Description Language 1.0:
      RDF Schema, 83
RDF Vocabulary Description Language
      specification, 4
rdf:about property, 32, 256
  (see also URI)
rdf:aboutEach property, 61, 64
rdf:aboutEachPrefix property, 61, 64
rdf:Alt element (see Alt container)
rdf:Bag element (see Bag container)
rdf:bagID property, 77
  (see also URI)
RDF::Core modules, PerlRDF
  building RDF model, 175–179
  parsing RDF/XML documents, 179–181
  persistence to relational
      database, 174–175
  querying RDF data, 181–182
rdf:datatype property, 53, 89
rdfDB, 193
rdfDB QL, 193
rdf:Description element, 32
  compared to reification statement, 72
  used in RDF Schema, 88
RDFEdge class, Drive, 216
rdf:first property, 91
RDFGraph class, Drive, 216
rdf:ID property, 44, 74
  (see also URI)
rdf:li element, 59, 62, 64
RDFLib, 187–191
RDFLib.Bnode object, RDFLib, 188
RDFLib.Literal object, RDFLib, 188
RDFLib.Namespace object, RDFLib, 188
RDFLib.URIRef object, RDFLib, 188
rdf:List element, 89
rdf:_n element, 59, 62, 64
RDFNode class, Drive, 216
RDFNode object, RDF Gateway, 305
rdf:nodeID property, 42
rdf:object property, 70, 91, 95
RdfParser class, RDF API for PHP, 183

rdf:parseType property, 36–38
  Collection setting, 65
  Literal setting, 36, 53
  Resource setting, 37, 109
  using with RSS, 263
rdf:predicate property, 70, 91, 95
rdf:Property element, 89, 90, 238
rdf:RDF element, 31
rdf:resource property, 33, 44, 50, 70
  (see also URI)
rdf:rest property, 91
RDF/RSS (see RSS)
RDFS (RDF Schema), 83, 87–95
  alternatives to, 97–99
  browser for (see BrownSauce, RDF/XML
      browser)
  checking with VRP, 140
  classes, 87–90, 118
  compared to DAML+OIL, 230
  compared to OWL, 247
  compared to relational database
      schema, 86
  constraints, 95
  declaration for, 87
  formalizing vocabulary with, 118–120
  properties, 90–96, 118
  relationship to OWL, 235
  for RSS, 256
  specification for, 2
  (see also RDF vocabulary)
rdfs:Class element, 87, 88, 230
rdfs:comment property, 88, 91, 93, 135
rdfs:Container element, 87, 88
rdfs:ContainerMembershipProperty
      element, 87
rdfs:Datatype element, 87, 88
rdfs:domain property, 91, 95, 238
rdf:Seq element (see Seq container)
RdfSerializer class, RDF API for PHP, 183
rdfs:isDefinedBy property, 91, 93
rdfs:label property, 91, 93, 135
rdfs:Literal element, 87
rdfs:member property, 91, 93
rdfs:range property, 91, 96, 238
rdfs:Resource element, 87
rdfs:seeAlso property, 91, 92
rdfs:subClassOf property, 91, 232, 243
rdfs:subPropertyOf property, 91
rdf:Statement element, 89
RDFStore, Perl-based RDF API, 182
rdf:subClassOf property, 91
rdf:subject property, 70, 91, 95

About the Author

Shelley Powers is an independent contractor, currently living in St. Louis, who specializes in technology architecture and software development. She's authored several computer books, including *Developing ASP Components*, *Unix Power Tools*, Third Edition, and *Essential Blogging*. In addition, Shelley has also written several articles related primarily to web technology, many for O'Reilly.

Colophon

Our look is the result of reader comments, our own experimentation, and feedback from distribution channels. Distinctive covers complement our distinctive approach to technical topics, breathing personality and life into potentially dry subjects.

The animal on the cover of *Practical RDF* is a secretary bird. It is a bird of prey and is related to the hawk. It is so named because the crest of feathers located at the back of its head are thought to resemble quill pens, which were carried by male secretaries in the 19th century. It stands between 3 and 4 feet tall, and has mostly gray feathers, except for its wing tips and legs, which are black, and its face, which has orange and yellow markings.

Although it can fly quite well, the secretary bird tends to spend most of its time on the ground. It lives off a diet of snakes, insects, and any small animal that might be easily swallowed. The bird usually kills its prey by beating it with its feet, using its long wings to protect itself from counterattacks. These birds tend to choose one mate for life, and also remain loyal to their nest site. Instead of leaving, they add to the nest each year; nests can grow up to eight feet long. The secretary bird lays two to three eggs at a time, of which the incubation is about 45 days. The baby birds leave home at around eight weeks.

Mary Brady was the production editor and proofreader for *Practical RDF*. Norma Emory was the copyeditor. Claire Cloutier and Sarah Sherman provided quality control. Jamie Peppard, Derek Di Matteo, and Judy Hoer provided production support. Angela Howard wrote the index.

Ellie Volckhausen designed the cover of this book, based on a series design by Edie Freedman. The cover image is a 19th-century engraving from the Dover Pictorial Archive. Emma Colby produced the cover layout with QuarkXPress 4.1 using Adobe's ITC Garamond font. David Futato designed the interior layout. This book was converted by Andrew Savikas with a format conversion tool created by Erik Ray, Jason McIntosh, Neil Walls, and Mike Sierra that uses Perl and XML technologies. The text font is Linotype Birka; the heading font is Adobe Myriad Condensed; and the code font is LucasFont's TheSans Mono Condensed. The illustrations that appear in the book were produced by Robert Romano and Jessamyn Read using Macromedia FreeHand 9 and Adobe Photoshop 6. The tip and warning icons were drawn by Christopher Bing. This colophon was written by Mary Brady.

Other Titles Available from O'Reilly

XML

SAX2

By David Brownell
1st Edition January 2002
240 pages, ISBN 0-596-00237-8

This concise book gives you information you need to effectively use the Simple API for XML (SAX2), the dominant API for efficient XML processing with Java. With SAX2, developers have access to information in XML documents as they are read without imposing major memory constraints or a large code footprint. SAX2 gives you the detail and examples required to use SAX2 to its full potential.

SVG Essentials

By J. David Eisenberg
1st Edition, February 2002
368 pages, ISBN 0-596-00223-8

SVG Essentials shows developers how to take advantage of SVG's open text-based format. Although SVG is much more approachable than the binary or PostScript files that have dominated graphics formats so far, developers need a roadmap to get started creating and processing SVG files. This book provides an introduction and reference to the foundations developers need to use SVG, and demonstrates techniques for generating SVG from other XML formats.

Programming Jabber

By DJ Adams
1st Edition January 2002
480 pages, ISBN 0-596-00202-5

This book offers programmers a chance to learn and understand the Jabber technology and protocol from an implementer's point of view. Every detail of every part of the Jabber client protocol is introduced, explained, discussed, and covered in the form of recipes, mini-projects or simple and extended examples in Perl, Python, and Java. *Programming Jabber* provides a walk-through of the foundation elements that are common to any messaging solution, including a detailed overview of the Jabber server architecture.

Web Services Essentials

By Ethan Cerami
1st Edition February 2002
304 pages, ISBN 0-596-00224-6

This concise book gives programmers both a concrete introduction and handy reference to XML web services. It explains the foundations of this new breed of distributed services, demonstrates quick ways to create services with open-source Java tools, and explores four key emerging technologies: XML-RPC, SOAP, UDDI, and WSDL. If you want to break through the Web Services hype and find useful information on these evolving technologies, look no further.

Content Syndication with RSS

By Ben Hammersley
1st Edition March 2003
216 pages, ISBN 0-596-00383-8

Written for web developers who want to offer XML-based feeds of their content, as well as developers who want to use the content that other people are syndicating, this book explores and explains metadata interpretation, different forms of content syndication, and the increasing use of web services in this field. If you're interested in producing your own RSS feed, this step-by-step guide to implementation is the book you'll want in hand.

Programming Web Services with SOAP

By James Snell, Doug Tidwell &
Pavel Kulchenko
1st Edition December 2001
264 pages, ISBN 0-596-00095-2

In typical O'Reilly fashion this book moves beyond the theoretical and explains how to build and implement SOAP web services. The book begins with a solid introduction to SOAP, detailing its history and structure, followed by an introduction to the three major types of SOAP applications: SOAP-RPC, SOAP-Messaging, and SOAP-Intermediaries. Each SOAP application is illustrated with an in-depth implementation.

O'REILLY®

To order: *800-998-9938* • *order@oreilly.com* • *www.oreilly.com*
Online editions of most O'Reilly titles are available by subscription at *safari.oreilly.com*
Also available at most retail and online bookstores.

How to stay in touch with O'Reilly

1.   **Visit our award-winning web site**

http://www.oreilly.com/

★ "Top 100 Sites on the Web"—PC Magazine
★ CIO Magazine's Web Business 50 Awards

Our web site contains a library of comprehensive product information (including book excerpts and tables of contents), downloadable software, background articles, interviews with technology leaders, links to relevant sites, book cover art, and more. File us in your bookmarks or favorites!

2.   **Join our email mailing lists**

Sign up to get email announcements of new books and conferences, special offers, and O'Reilly Network technology newsletters at:

http://elists.oreilly.com

It's easy to customize your free elists subscription so you'll get exactly the O'Reilly news you want.

3.   **Get examples from our books**

To find example files for a book, go to:

http://www.oreilly.com/catalog

select the book, and follow the "Examples" link.

4.   **Work with us**

Check out our web site for current employment opportunities:

http://jobs.oreilly.com/

5.   **Register your book**

Register your book at:

http://register.oreilly.com

6.   **Contact us**

O'Reilly & Associates, Inc.
1005 Gravenstein Hwy North
Sebastopol, CA 95472 USA
TEL: 707-827-7000 or 800-998-9938
        (6am to 5pm PST)
FAX: 707-829-0104

order@oreilly.com
For answers to problems regarding your order or our products. To place a book order online visit:

http://www.oreilly.com/order_new/

catalog@oreilly.com
To request a copy of our latest catalog.

booktech@oreilly.com
For book content technical questions or corrections.

corporate@oreilly.com
For educational, library, government, and corporate sales.

proposals@oreilly.com
To submit new book proposals to our editors and product managers.

international@oreilly.com
For information about our international distributors or translation queries. For a list of our distributors outside of North America check out:

http://international.oreilly.com/distributors.html

adoption@oreilly.com
For information about academic use of O'Reilly books, visit:

http://academic.oreilly.com

O'REILLY®

To order: *800-998-9938* • *order@oreilly.com* • *www.oreilly.com*
Online editions of most O'Reilly titles are available by subscription at *safari.oreilly.com*
Also available at most retail and online bookstores.